Paradise from behind the Iron Curtain

Literature and Translation

Literature and Translation is a series for books that address literary translation and for books of literary translation. Its emphasis is on diversity of genre, culture, period and approach. The series uses an open access publishing model to disseminate widely developments in the theory and practice of translation, as well as translations into English of literature from around the world.

Series editor: Timothy Mathews is Emeritus Professor of French and Comparative Criticism, UCL

Paradise from behind the Iron Curtain

Reading, translating and staging Milton in Communist Hungary

Miklós Péti

First published in 2022 by
UCL Press
University College London
Gower Street
London WC1E 6BT

Available to download free: www.uclpress.co.uk

Text © Author 2022
Images © Copyright holders named in captions, 2022

The author has asserted his rights under the Copyright, Designs and Patents Act 1988 to be identified as the author of this work.

A CIP catalogue record for this book is available from The British Library.

This book contains third-party copyright material that is not covered by the book's Creative Commons licence. Details of the copyright ownership and permitted use of third-party material is given in the image (or extract) credit lines. If you would like to reuse any third-party material not covered by book's Creative Commons licence, you will need to obtain permission directly from the copyright owner.

This book is published under a Creative Commons Attribution Non-commercial Non-derivative 4.0 International licence (CC BY-NC 4.0), https://creativecommons.org/licenses/by-nc/4.0/. This licence allows you to share, copy, distribute and transmit the work for personal and non-commercial use providing author and publisher attribution is clearly stated. If you wish to use the work commercially, use extracts or undertake translation you must seek permission from the author. Attribution should include the following information:

Péti, M 2022. *Paradise from behind the Iron Curtain: Reading, translating and staging Milton in Communist Hungary*. London: UCL Press. https://doi.org/10.14324/111.9781787358539

Further details about Creative Commons licences are available at http://creativecommons.org/licenses/

ISBN: 978-1-78735-855-3 (Hbk.)
ISBN: 978-1-78735-854-6 (Pbk.)
ISBN: 978-1-78735-853-9 (PDF)
ISBN: 978-1-78735-856-0 (epub)
ISBN: 978-1-78735-857-7 (mobi)
DOI: https://doi.org/10.14324/111.9781787358539

Contents

List of figures vi
Acknowledgements viii
A note on texts x

Introduction 1

1 Forms of attention and neglect: Milton's epics in print
   and on stage – and in oblivion 19

2 Samson: an unlikely hero of socialism 65

3 A tale of two scholars: Milton's prose in communist Hungary 90

4 'I rebel quietly': revolution and gender in Hungarian
   translations of Milton's shorter poems 121

Epilogue 144

Appendix 150
Bibliography 273
Index 282

List of figures

1.1 György Szlovák's caricature of the 1970 performance of *Paradise Lost*, published in the 14 July 1970 issue of the daily *Magyar Nemzet*. The original caption reads: 'Az aktualizált Paradicsom angyalokkal, hippikkel és a bürokratával' (Paradise made topical with angels, hippies, and a bureaucrat). © HUNGART 2022. 53

1.2 Scene from the 7 July 1970 performance of *Paradise Lost* directed by Károly Kazimir; Vera Venczel as Eve, András Kozák as Adam and Cecília Esztergályos (lying down) as Raphael. Photograph by Imre Benkő. © MTI Fotó/Benkő Imre. 54

1.3 Scene from the 7 July 1970 performance of *Paradise Lost*. The upper part of the stage represents Heaven with God sitting and the Son standing behind him; below, Adam and Eve are standing with the fallen angels sitting before them. Photograph by Imre Benkő. © MTI Fotó/Benkő Imre. 56

1.4 Scene from the 7 July 1970 performance of *Paradise Lost*. The Son judging the first human couple. Vera Venczel as Eve (on her knees bowing down), András Kozák as Adam (kneeling) and Péter Vallai as the Son (behind them). Photograph by Imre Benkő. © MTI Fotó/Benkő Imre. 57

1.5 Scene from the 7 July 1970 performance of *Paradise Lost*. Vera Venczel as Eve, András Kozák as Adam. Photograph by Imre Benkő. © MTI Fotó/Benkő Imre. 58

1.6 Scene from the 7 July 1970 performance of *Paradise Lost*. Satan and his crew. Tibor Bitskey (in the centre) as Satan, to his left Péter Simon as Belial, to his right Ildikó Hámori as Sin, to her right Gábor Csikós as Moloch. Photograph by Imre Benkő. © MTI Fotó/Benkő Imre. 59

1.7 Scene from the 5 October 1970 performance of
Paradise Lost. Samu Balázs as God, Péter Vallai as the
Son and Mária Gór Nagy (to their right) as Michael.
Photograph by Imre Benkő. © MTI Fotó/Benkő Imre. 60
2.1 'Samson Agonistes', *The Comrade* 1.9 (June 1902): 196. 69

Acknowledgements

The foundations of this book were laid more than 10 years ago when I was working – together with Tibor Fabiny, the leader of our project, and Gábor Ittzés – on the critical edition of István Jánosy's translation of *Paradise Lost* (OTKA project no. 101928). That was also when I started working on an article on Milton's Hungarian translations for the volume *Milton in Translation* edited by Angelica Duran, Islam Issa and Jonathan Olson (Oxford University Press, 2017). The regular discussions with the Hungarian project members, and the guidance I received from the editors, greatly helped sharpen the focus of my research. So did the various conferences and symposia – the 2015 RSA in Berlin, the 11th International Milton Symposium in Exeter (2015), the 2017 Conference on John Milton at the University of Alabama in Birmingham, and the online 'Work-in-Progress' seminar at Eötvös Loránd University in December 2020 – where I could introduce to fellow Miltonists some of the chapters in their preliminary form.

I am grateful for permission to adapt material from previously published articles. Most of Chapter 4 was originally published in the essay '"I am not 'masculine' I am weak": Ágnes Nemes Nagy's translation of sonnet 23', published in *Women (Re)writing Milton*, edited by Mandy Green and Sharihan Al-Akhras (London: Routledge, 2021). Some paragraphs in the Introduction and most of Chapter 2 were originally published in the essay 'Samson: an unlikely hero of socialism' in *Locating Milton*, edited by David Ainsworth and Thomas Festa (Clemson, SC: Clemson University Press, 2021). The last section of Chapter 1 is adapted from my article '*Paradise Lost* on the Hungarian stage in 1970', *Milton Quarterly* 52.3 (2018), which also contains the bilingual script reprinted in the Appendix. I am grateful to the Európa Publishing House and the Manuscript Collection of the Petőfi Literary Museum for granting permission to consult their archives. Much of the research was carried out in the collections of the National Széchényi Library and the Library and Information Centre of the Hungarian Academy of Sciences.

I thank all the wonderful scholars and friends who patiently helped me at various stages of this project and during the preparation of the final version of the manuscript: David Ainsworth, Sharihan Al-Akhras, Ádám Berta, Ágnes Bonácz, Péter Dávidházi, Karen Edwards, Annamária Fábián, Győző Ferencz, Mimi Fenton, Thomas Festa, Judit Friedrich, Bálint Gárdos, Mandy Green, Edward Jones, Géza and Kata Kállay, Deni Kasa, András Kiséry, Larisa Kocic-Zámbó, Zsolt Komáromy, György Kurucz, Csilla Markója, Ádám Nádasdy, Ágnes Péter, Márton Péti, Joanna Picciotto, Natália Pikli and Veronika Ruttkay. Needless to say, all errors that remain are my own.

I dedicate this book to my love, Rita Dózsai, who (like every Hungarian schoolchild in the 1980s) was a fellow 'young pioneer'.

A note on texts

All references to Milton's original texts (poetry and prose) are to the following editions: *Paradise Lost*, edited by Barbara K. Lewalski (Oxford: Blackwell, 2007); *Complete Shorter Poems*, edited by Stella P. Revard (Chicester: Wiley-Blackwell, 2009); *Prose: Major Writings on Liberty, Politics, Religion and Education*, edited by David Loewenstein (Chichester: Wiley-Blackwell, 2013). References to specific passages in *Paradise Lost* and *Paradise Regained* are given in parentheses in the following format: the abbreviation *PL* or *PR* followed by book and line number(s), thus: 'Nothing will please the difficult and nice' (*PR* 4.157).

Unless otherwise indicated, all Hungarian texts that are quoted are translated by the author. Whenever Hungarian texts are quoted in the main body of the text, the English translation (in quotation marks) is followed by the original in italics in parentheses. In block quotations the original Hungarian comes first in italics followed by the English translation in parentheses.

Internal reader's reports commissioned by publishing houses were not intended for publication and constitute confidential material: therefore I disclose their authors' names only if the reports are in public collections (e.g. the Petőfi Literary Museum), or the author has granted permission to do so.

In transcribing Hungarian archival material (e.g. readers' reports, unpublished documents, etc.) I have retained the idiosyncratic orthography and punctuation of the original documents. Obvious typos were silently corrected.

Introduction

> *Valaki arra kér, hogy írjak kizárólag magyar dolgokról, amíg a háború tart. Ezt írja: 'Tudom, hogy Milton jóval nagyobb, mint Czuczor. De a magyar lét ma azt kívánja, hogy csak a Czuczorokról beszéljünk, s hallgassunk a Miltonokról.'*[1]
>
> (Somebody asks me to write exclusively of Hungarian things while the war lasts. This is what he writes: 'I know that Milton is far greater than Czuczor. But Hungarian existence today requires that we talk only about the Czuczors, and keep silent about the Miltons.')

This is how László Cs. Szabó, a leading Hungarian intellectual of the mid-twentieth century,[2] starts his article 'Milton or Czuczor'. Cs. Szabó refused the request to write only of 'Hungarian things', but the suggestion that he should give preference to the works of Gergely Czuczor, a Hungarian lexicographer and minor poet of the nineteenth century, to those of Milton and 'the Miltons', i.e. the great authors of English and European literature, gave him pause. He admits to being puzzled by the choice his correspondent poses between the national and the European tradition, since, as he argues, 'the great educators, liberators, absolvers and martyrs were all great importers' (*A nagy nevelők, felszabadítók, feloldozók és vértanúk mind nagy importálók voltak*), and 'our great intellects were all great translators; polishing the mirror of Hungarian-ness with the silvering of world literature' (*Nagy szellemeink mind nagy fordítók is; a világirodalom foncsorával fényesítették a magyarság tükrét*).[3] In other words, according to Cs. Szabó, there is no meaningful choice between Milton and Czuczor. Both are part of Hungarian and the wider European culture: ignoring the former in favour of the latter would only be counterproductive since it would imply an unnecessary sense of inferiority. 'Let us keep on talking about Milton and Vörösmarty [an important nineteenth-century Hungarian poet], and when it is necessary, about Czuczor' (*Beszéljünk csak változatlanul Miltonról és Vörösmartyról, s amikor kell, Czuczorról!*), he concludes, countering the narrow-minded nationalist cultural agenda of his correspondent with a wide-reaching, enlightened European, yet patriotic programme.

Cs. Szabó wrote this essay in 1944, the darkest and most disastrous year of the twentieth century for Hungary and Hungarians.[4] With hindsight it is impossible not to notice a certain naïveté in these remarks. Witnessing the unfolding tragedy of fascism and Nazism, several leading European (among them Hungarian) intellectuals became disillusioned about the redeeming potential of such a broadly conceived model of 'European culture'. Thomas Mann is one of the most famous examples: up to the 1930s his professed views about Germany and German culture were, *mutatis mutandis*, similar to, and largely compatible with, Cs. Szabó's ideas, but, as Hitler consolidated his power, and especially with the advent of World War II, he became a highly vocal critic of traditional conceptions of 'German-ness'.[5] Cs. Szabó, although an anti-fascist himself, apparently did not (or did not want to) go so far. His contention that 'To know about European things, to know about them *constantly*, means knowing our own things' (*Európai dolgokról tudni, s azokról folyton tudni annyi, mint a magunk dolgát ismerni*)[6] reflects a belief not only in the integrity and immanent value of European humanistic culture. Significantly, it also implies that this culture serves as an antidote to the brutal present, and is an essential token of Hungarians' own identity, regardless of any temporary or permanent political and military conflicts. If this assessment sounded overly optimistic in 1944, it is strikingly more so if we take a longer view of twentieth-century Hungarian history. Little did Cs. Szabó know that within a few years of writing his essay, Hungary (together with a handful of other countries in Eastern and Central Europe), still reeling from the horrors of World War II, would plunge into another totalitarian rabbit hole, that of 'actually existing socialism', forcing him into exile, and a great many of his intellectual peers into silence.[7] Nor would he have dreamt that under this new system the humanistic idea of the European tradition he was propagating would again come under sustained attack, this time not from nationalism, but from a new, nominally 'Marxist-Leninist' and internationalist cultural policy.

To put it simply, for about four decades after World War II, Hungarian cultural policy was less concerned with the dynamic between the native (the Hungarian) and the foreign than with the question of the political currency of any work by any author. The native and the foreign were both interpreted from the perspective of political 'progression' – with interestingly varied results. As this period is far from homogeneous, such interpretations were of course not always proposed with the same intensity, nor was it always easy to find a pretext under which a poem, a drama or a novel written in the past could be brought ideologically up to date. However, it could be generally stated that the cultural policies of communist Hungary (and all countries of the Eastern bloc) advocated a radical reshaping of the received canons, a rewriting of the tradition that laid much emphasis on, and sometimes even construed reasons for, *how* rather than *why* the work of a given author *should* matter (whether or not he or she is a national treasure or a foreign classic). This is of course similar to how any dictatorial system would try to appropriate the cultural sphere, but the speciality of the Hungarian communist approach was the (at least nominal) shedding of a nationalistic/chauvinistic agenda (such as that of the Nazis in the Third Reich) for an internationalist perspective.[8] In this system, at least officially, the critical difference between the works of Milton and Czuczor derived not from their provenance primarily, but from the extent to which they could be serviceable to the prevailing political agenda.

This book documents how during the four decades of Hungarian state socialism such cultural policies influenced the reception of the works of John Milton – the foreign author Cs. Szabó singled out as the emblematic figure of European culture. As a major author who actively participated in the English Civil War (or the English Revolution), Milton was of course an intriguing figure throughout the era, which was heavily invested in the idea of social revolution. At the same time, the fact that Milton was a deeply religious Christian writer proved to be a strong complicating factor: quite predictably, it was a mild embarrassment for hardline ideologues of communism, a cautionary feature for moderates, and a liberating subtext for dissidents. The inextricable interweaving of revolution and religion in Milton's oeuvre was, consequently, tackled in a variety of ways, ranging from the enthusiastic but tenuous application of communist propaganda through the superficial endorsement of current ideological strains or tendentiously selective readings, to instances of passive resistance.[9] This book will provide a representative selection of these responses, focusing on the work of some of the most eminent Hungarian translators, critics and scholars (as well as a theatre director) of the post-war period. Some of the critical and creative interpretations documented and commented on in the chapters below will inevitably reveal more about the mechanisms of communist cultural policy than about Milton. But as we shall see, some of them contain insights that provide alternative perspectives to received (Western) traditions of Milton criticism. Although at worst Milton through the Iron Curtain looks like a dummy of sorts, whose words were selected and ventriloquised in less than authentic ways, at best his works provided the opportunity for historical (self-)reflection in ways that Cs. Szabó had imagined for them.

The scope of the book

Milton's works have been read, translated, interpreted and appropriated in Hungary since the late seventeenth century.[10] In the chapters below I deal with a small yet significant segment of this long reception history as I introduce the most important and most characteristic Hungarian interpretations of Milton's works from the period between 1948 and 1989 (the years of the communist takeover and the change of system, respectively). The criticism, translation and adaptation of Milton's works in these four decades comprised almost all the genres of the Miltonic corpus, but the different periods and parts of Milton's oeuvre received varying degrees of attention – not always corresponding to the canon that has consolidated in the Anglo-American critical tradition. Therefore, instead of the chronological order in which Milton's works came into existence, I will proceed according to the peculiar logic of reception characteristic of communist Hungary.

Chapter 1 deals with the widely divergent reception of Milton's two epics in post-war Hungarian culture. Whereas *Paradise Regained* was practically forgotten and even actively suppressed during the four decades of state socialism, *Paradise Lost* went through several important reinterpretations, including two landmark translations and a unique stage adaptation. Roughly corresponding to the changes in communist cultural policy, the two translations (done 20 years apart by Lőrinc Szabó and István Jánosy, respectively) register two very different approaches to the topicality of Milton's epic. The stage production (the script of which, together with a parallel English translation, is reproduced in the Appendix) is significant for several reasons: it can justly claim to be the first full-scale professional staging of *Paradise Lost* since John Dryden's *The State of Innocence and Fall of Man* (1674), but it also represents an intriguing 'recomposition-in-performance' of the epic which brings Milton's 'great Argument' (*PL* 1.24) up to date, critically reflecting both on Milton's original theodicy and its possible interpretations in communist Hungary. Due to the lack of surviving footage, I try to describe this production as much as possible through reviews, interviews and a set of archival photographs.

In Chapter 2 my focus is on communist and socialist interpretations of Milton's classically inspired tragedy, *Samson Agonistes*. In this chapter I introduce a distinct tradition of interpreting Milton's Samson as a proto-Marxist or socialist hero in British and American intellectual life, and also show how a similar school of interpretation flourished beyond the Iron Curtain. Before World War II Milton's tragedy had not been translated into Hungarian and was heavily criticised in the spirit of Thomas Babington Macaulay as 'the least successful effort of Milton's genius'.[11] In the post-war period, by contrast, two different translations of *Samson Agonistes* were published in the span of two decades, both of them surrounded by critical texts that emphasised the 'revolutionary' nature of Milton's tragedy. It is true that these overtly and rather simplistically politicised approaches exhibit an understanding of the drama's political potential long before the great resurgence of critical interest in *Samson* in recent decades, but, as we shall see, for all the beating of the revolutionary drums, the overall picture of the reception of Milton's tragedy is more about the tacit and mutually inconvenient compromises between artists, cultural policymakers and the audience that were characteristic of the late decades of state socialism.

Chapter 3 provides a survey of how Milton's prose works were used and interpreted in the four decades of state socialism. The post-war reception of Milton's prose was closely bound up with the work of two scholars, Tibor Lutter and Miklós Szenczi, who became the fountainheads of all things Miltonic in the period under discussion. The ways in which Lutter and Szenczi handled Milton's prose works are not only emblematic of the broader trends of Milton's reception in communist Hungary, but, on another level, they also provide a running commentary, as it were, on these two scholars' careers (which sometimes involved very un-Miltonic compromises). As we shall see in this chapter, the wider context of the post-war translation and interpretation of Milton's pamphlets in Hungary puts to a severe test the 'authentically puritan opposition between the hollowness of habitual compliance with external forms . . . and the integrity of inner commitment', which, according to N. H. Keeble, characterises Milton's writings.[12]

In Chapter 4 I turn to Hungarian interpretations of Milton's lyric poetry, which present curious anomalies both in the Hungarian and in the larger international contexts of reception. On the one hand, we can witness the prevalence of a 'bourgeois' translator's work: Árpád Tóth's 1921 renderings of 'Lycidas' and a handful of sonnets and other minor poems, albeit not exceptionally faithful to Milton's original, had been considered an unsurpassable feat throughout the post-war period, which resulted in their canonisation in university curricula as specimens of the English 'Baroque'.

On the other hand, the translation of Sonnet 23 ('Methought I saw my late espoused Saint'), one of Milton's most personal poems, by a woman poet, Ágnes Nemes Nagy, challenged not only the mainstream communist ideological positions in relation to Milton's work, but also the predominantly patriarchal Hungarian contexts of reception. In this chapter, therefore, we shall witness how one of the most subversive modern interpretations (even by international standards) of a Milton sonnet emerged in a cultural context that professed to be ideologically radical yet remained remarkably conservative from both an aesthetic and a gender perspective.

As becomes clear from these short summaries, in this book I concentrate primarily on translations as well as criticism (or scholarship) directly dealing with parts or the whole of Milton's oeuvre. Besides published documents (books, newspaper and journal articles) I occasionally turn to archival material, such as correspondence, interviews or internal reader's reports for publishing houses. The scope of the discussion is largely determined by the subject of the book. For several reasons – for example, the difficulties readers have to face (Milton famously sought 'fit audience . . . though few', *PL* 9.31), or the fact that both Milton and his works require extraordinary attention to their actual historical and political contexts – Milton's Hungarian 'cult' has never reached the same proportions as Shakespeare's.[13] That is of course not to say that Milton has not made a lasting impact on Hungarian culture in general, or that he has not entered the broader cultural memory of Hungary: it is enough to think of the formative Milton debate of the late eighteenth century revolving around questions of literary translation, or the nineteenth-century works of the painter Mihály Munkácsy or the writer Mór Jókai – all of which have been documented for the English reading public.[14] However, in the period under discussion Milton's influence was predominantly confined to translation and criticism, and instead of monumental visions (like Munkácsy's painting), only a few lyric pieces seemed to revive the poet's memory for the wider public. As we shall shortly see, these poems are interesting, if not very high-quality modern attempts to appropriate Milton's historical role, but the chapters below will intend to demonstrate that Milton's own words and ideas, and how they might be wielded in Hungarian, were a far greater concern in the post-war period.

Critical contexts

But why is it important that this account of a narrow and (in international terms) rather marginal segment of Milton's international reception should be written? What can it add to reception studies in general or

Milton studies in particular if we get to know how Milton's different works were interpreted in a relatively small and relatively unknown country from the Eastern bloc? Are there more compelling reasons to focus on Hungarian interpretations than the obvious one, that is, the nationality of the writer of these lines? Let me proceed by positioning the subject of my research within a broader context, that of Milton's reception as a 'radical', and, occasionally, a left-leaning revolutionary.

Wherever his works have been read, Milton never seems to have been seen as less than a 'contemporary', whether as an inspiring, venerable predecessor or a dangerous precedent. Moreover, as has been freshly shown by Nigel Smith, the conception of Milton as a 'radical' and the focus on 'a Milton with partisan political and religious views, an actor in the public sphere as opposed to someone who was primarily poet of the nation' have been central features of Milton's critical and historical reception in the English-speaking world.[15] Left-leaning political and critical traditions also appropriated Milton and his works, although, as Don Wolfe warned almost 60 years ago (when he compared Milton to the Digger Gerrard Winstanley): 'No pacifist, and no internationalist, Milton was far indeed from being a socialist.'[16] As we shall see in Chapter 2, *Samson Agonistes* in particular has frequently elicited the admiration of thinkers sympathetic to the ideas of communism or socialism, but Milton as a revolutionary figure has also been a strong inspiration to the left since the nineteenth century. Indeed, we find significant references to Milton in the works of both Marx and Engels. 'Let us never forget Milton, the first defender of Regicide,' warned Engels in 1847 in *The Northern Star*, asserting the priority of English revolutionary ideas over French ones.[17] Marx, on the other hand, in a draft of *The Civil War in France*, highlighted Milton's stalwart perseverance as a model against 'The whole sham of State mysteries and State pretensions' which

> was done away [with] by a Commune, mostly consisting of simple working men . . . doing their work publicly, simply, under the most difficult and complicated circumstances, and doing it, as Milton did his *Paradise Lost*, for a few pounds, acting in bright daylight, with no pretensions to infallibility, not hiding themselves behind circumlocution offices, not ashamed to confess blunders by correcting them.[18]

For Marx Milton seems to be a workmanlike figure who labours tirelessly ('publicly', and one might suspect, in a community) to revise and edit his work. What is more, in illustrating the difference between productive and unproductive work, Marx again singles out Milton as someone whose work, at least at the time of the composition of *Paradise Lost*, did not further the 'capitalist production process':

> Milton, for example, WHO DID *Paradise Lost*, was an unproductive worker. In contrast to this, the writer who delivers hackwork for his publisher is a productive worker. Milton produced *Paradise Lost* in the way that a silkworm produces silk, as the expression of his own nature. Later on he sold the product for £5 and to that extent became a dealer in a commodity.[19]

Fascinatingly, Marx here seems to bracket divine inspiration (a defining feature of Milton's self-fashioning in *Paradise Lost*) entirely to replace it with a kind of 'immanent inspiration' (in which Milton expresses his own nature rather than divine dictates). Thus, for Marx, Milton is an exemplary historical figure not only because of his public political role, but also as a writer, a quasi-secularised artist, labouring against an oppressive regime – in short, someone who is liberated (or strives to be liberated) from the 'two masters' of religion and state.[20]

Variations on these ideas can also be found in the Marxist literary criticism and historiography of the first half of the twentieth century, especially in Britain. As early as 1937 Christopher Caudwell considered Milton as 'England's first openly revolutionary poet' in his Marxist literary history *Illusion and Reality*.[21] However, the most remarkable leftist interpretation of Milton is in the early works of Christopher Hill and his circle both before and after World War II. In 1940 Hill edited a slim volume entitled *The English Revolution 1640*. One of the contributors was Edgell Rickword, whose 'Milton: The revolutionary intellectual' makes no qualms about the topicality of Milton's thought: 'The fog of Mediævalism which he swept aside is not unfamiliar to us to-day . . . he fought to free us from the tyranny of the parish priest as well as of arbitrary and irresponsible executive power.'[22] In 1946 the Marxist philosopher George Thomson published *Marxism and Poetry*, in which Milton, although a bourgeois poet, is enrolled among the poets who are 'conscious revolutionaries' and, together with Shelley and William Morris, as a predecessor of those modern poets who 'surmounted the barrier between poetry and the people and restored the broken harmony between poetry and life'.[23] A couple of years later, in the spring 1949 issue of the *Modern Quarterly* (later the *Marxist Quarterly*) the anonymous headnote (written presumably by the issue's editor Christopher Hill) makes it clear that the intellectual heritage of the revolution is more current than ever: 'The visions of freedom and of peace, seen in their different ways by Winstanley and by Milton, approach their realisation as wider and wider forces enter the struggle for a new and classless social order.'[24]

Not all left-leaning intellectuals were pleased with Hill's views in the 1940s. C. L. R. James (writing under the pseudonym G. F. Eckstein) labels Hill and his circle 'Stalinists', and states that 'today it is quite clear that the Milton of *Paradise Lost* and *Samson Agonistes* represented the *end* of an age' (the forward momentum being the Puritan preachers and propagandists).[25] Pauline Kogan, writing in 1969 in the periodical *Literature and Ideology*, would probably have agreed with the latter point: 'As a bourgeois poet Milton's greatest ambition was to make the bourgeois world outlook legitimate.'[26] However, she also states that Milton's poetry 'belongs to the great heritage of revolutionary literature of the world and hence it is a great source of inspiration to the working and oppressed people fighting U.S imperialism now.'[27] In the long run, Hill's work became more nuanced and less orthodox – already in the 1949 reissue of *The English Revolution 1640* he talks about the 'crudities and oversimplifications' of his own original article[28] – but Milton's radicalism and his revolutionary role remained one of his major themes. This made him a conventional and convenient reference point for a number of Hungarian critics during the years of communism, who cited works from the various phases of Hill's career in accordance with the prevalent ideologies.

The situation in the United States was different. Although, as Sharon Achinstein has shown,[29] and as I shall briefly discuss in Chapter 2, there were attempts to appropriate Milton by communist sympathisers in the period of the Red Scare, these represented only a segment of a wider-reaching concern with Milton among progressives. It was again Achinstein who documented how in the post-war American debates about intellectual and academic freedom Milton's name was frequently invoked, lending 'colour and authority to contemporary arguments'.[30] The controversies ranged from the broad public sphere to the narrower field of academia, but the significance of Milton in the Cold War period is aptly reflected in the work of Don Wolfe, whose commentary in the first volume of the Yale edition of Milton's prose works 'maintained for American Miltonists an interested and engaged, presentist paradigm'.[31]

These uses of Milton, the historical figure and his work, among British and American intellectuals are well known and have become part of Milton's critical heritage. But what happened in the other half of Europe, cut off by the Iron Curtain? In this book I try to answer this question by taking the special but representative example of Hungary, a small country variously categorised as Western, Central or Eastern European. For much of the past 300 years, Milton's Hungarian reception followed trends from the West, although with some delay and necessary changes effected by the different socio-cultural context.[32] To cite only one, albeit emblematic example: the eminent Hungarian writer, critic and man of letters Antal Szerb turned to Milton in his reflections on fascist Europe at the same time when in Britain G. Wilson Knight proposed that Milton should be central to the British Empire's fight against the threat of Nazism.[33] However, when Szerb was 'contemplating the degeneracy of Europe into barbarism', he evoked the professed self-sufficiency of Milton's Satan ('What matter where, if I be still the same', *PL* 1.256) rather than the wrath of the Son in Book 6 of *Paradise Lost* (whose 'power-impregnated righteousness' Knight held up as a model).[34] Szerb and Knight focused on different parts, even different aspects of *Paradise Lost*, but there is no doubt that – although citizens of countries on opposing sides of the conflict – they were on the same page.

Starting in 1948, the four decades of state socialism brought an end to such parallel, if somewhat asynchronous strains of reception. To put it in minimal terms, words *about* Milton and words *by* Milton were probably never at greater odds in Hungarian culture than in the 40 years after World War II. The Hungarian Milton criticism and scholarship of the period attempted a conscious departure from Western ('bourgeois') traditions, coaxing Milton and his works towards maximum 'radicalism' – according to their own interpretation of the word 'radical'.[35] For critics of the age, Milton was indeed 'the poet of revolution' – not quite in the nuanced, historically informed way Nicholas McDowell's book of that title shows him to be,[36] but more in accordance with 'Marxist-Leninist' cultural doctrines dictated by party ideologues – their interpretations propped up by references to British Marxist critics such as Christopher Hill, but largely conforming to the topical requirements of communist cultural policy.[37] 'Revolution' was of course an especially loaded word in the period: the official communist ideology branded opposition movements (among them the uprising of 1956, today designated as a revolution) counter-revolutionary: thus, the emphasis on the 'revolutionary' nature of Milton's works could be used in a number of ways, from placing the poet and his works in the service of cultural propaganda to making him (and his works) look acceptable for the ideologically 'enlightened' reading public.

Criticism, however, is just one aspect of the various channels of reception, and the period under discussion also saw the emergence of interpretations which were by their nature much less categorically ideological. The published translations and adaptations of Milton's works, sometimes done with the active help of, and even by, the aforementioned critics, tell a different story than the critical commentaries. In and around these works, too, we can witness attempts to accommodate topical ideological considerations, most conspicuously in their paratexts (prefaces, postscripts, commentaries), or the way they were selectively rendered, and even suppressed. But when it comes to the actual texts, Milton's words and their translators often resist the interpretations forced on them. Although these translations did not cancel out those who stepped up to speak for Milton, they allowed the Miltonic text to speak for itself – and by extension for a range of voices not recognised by the official ideology.

It is here that we could touch briefly upon the four poems that constitute the post-war Hungarian 'Milton cult', since in their own way they demonstrate the complexity of responses to Milton and his works under communism. György Faludy (in the English-speaking world often referred to as George Faludy), a writer and translator who was persecuted by the communist regime and therefore emigrated in 1956, wrote a three-stanza invective against Milton (entitled 'John Milton') from exile in which he criticises Milton's role as part of an oppressive regime (as Cromwell's chief propagandist), and conceives of the poet as essentially a treacherous intellectual and a despicable regicide. The poem starts with the statement that 'His poems read now as Miltonic parody' and ends with the blunt proposition 'Myself, I would have hung him high as Haman'.[38] Another poet and translator (and once Faludy's friend), József Fodor, made peace with the communist regime after 1956; his 1958 volume of poetry contains two pieces in which he uses Milton's historical persona for poetic self-presentation and self-justification. The shorter poem is entitled 'Milton's complaint against his selfish and defeatist comrades-in-arms' ('Milton panasza önző és kishitű harcostársai ellen'); it bears an epitaph from Milton's poem 'On the new forcers of conscience', and chides those who 'run together with the Party, and stop in the fight, when it [i.e. the Party] has reached its goal' (*Együtt-futója a Pártnak: s megállva a harcban, ha az célba ért*).[39] The same haughty and pessimistic tone characterises Fodor's poem 'Milton', a 115-stanza-long internal monologue written in 1949. In a later recollection Fodor claims this piece is 'witness to [the poet's] emotions during evil times' (*a költő . . . rossz idők alatti . . . érzései tanúbizonyságát*) prompted by the injustices of dictatorship.[40] In the poem 'Milton' muses (often in abstruse terms) about his career and historical role, and reflects on the degeneration of his times where 'rough Hypocrisy is running wild, celebrating' (*A durva álság tombol, ünnepel*).⁴¹ Alluding to *Paradise Lost*, Fodor's Milton contends that 'Everybody carries within himself his heaven, or his rotten soul, ready for all bad' (*Mindenki magában / hordja mennyét, vagy minden rosszra kész / Rongy lelkét*), reflecting once again on the inseparable chasm between himself and the compromisers.⁴² If Faludy's poem is rather crude and undiscerning in its abuse of Milton, Fodor's pieces are self-important, bombastic and often bathetic. In contrast to both, Győző Csorba, a largely apolitical lyric poet, translator and journal editor, focused, in Milton's manner, on the personal plight of the old poet. His 'The old Milton' ('Az öreg Milton') is a short but powerful dramatic monologue evoking the main motifs of *Paradise Lost* (the Fall, Eden, exile, redemption) to reflect on the hopeless situation of the poet: 'I who once moved with certainty in the realms of Heaven and Hell, and from Turkestan to Rome, and Mexico, am now merely stumbling between bed and table' (*Menny és Pokol / térségein ki biztosan mozogtam, / s Turkesztántól Rómáig, Mexikóig: / ma ágy és asztal közt is csak botorgok*).⁴³ By far the most enjoyable of the post-war Milton poems, Csorba's piece is a rethinking of Milton's own fears of the debilitating effects of ageing (cf. for example *PL* 9.44–5), but can also be read as an allegory of the social and personal predicaments of intellectuals through the long, decaying years of communism.

These brief flashes of Milton-related Hungarian poems from the post-war period show in miniature the more general point that I have tried to sketch above. While in America 'Milton became a powerful historical point of reference in the shaping of postwar liberalism',⁴⁴ in Hungary a quiet but prolonged cultural cold war was fought around Milton and the Miltonic oeuvre. Cultural conflict was of course an integral part of Milton's own life and works, and has thoroughly saturated Milton's critical heritage,⁴⁵ but in the chapters below we will encounter a mode of reception where, ironically, such tensions emerged within a system that was actively promoting and working towards the suppression of dissent. To greater or lesser extents this was of course characteristic of other countries of the former Eastern bloc,⁴⁶ but the Hungarian situation is remarkable for the breadth and intensity of reception. Spanning four decades, the history of Hungarian communism ranged through various phases from totalitarian dictatorship to the convenient but ultimately untenable compromises of 'goulash communism', with each phase producing its own special cultural policy (to which I will return), and its own special version of Milton in the form of translations, adaptations and critical works. Although many of these interpretations will strike (sometimes amuse) twenty-first-century readers as superficial, simplified or outright disingenuous, some of them are landmark achievements that justly deserve the attention of the international scholarly community. Given the fact that Hungarian culture is based on a Finno-Ugric language with relatively few speakers (and one that is generally thought to be rather difficult to master), one of my purposes in this book is to bring these achievements to the attention of the English-speaking world. That is why, whenever necessary and justifiable, I quote generously from the various texts under discussion, providing both the Hungarian original and its close English translation (in the case of translations, this means providing a word-by-word paraphrase). To cast my net as widely as possible, in the Appendix I have included the script of the 1970 stage version of *Paradise Lost* which I 'translated back' into Milton's English.

Historical contexts

The impact of Soviet-style cultural policies on various forms of literature has been widely and diversely documented. Among classic English authors, Shakespeare has received special attention in this respect: several collections, monographs and articles have been published about the Bard's reception under communist regimes.[47] While Shakespeare was often designated as the 'Great Realist' in communist countries,[48] Milton could certainly be labelled the 'Great Revolutionary'; curiously, however, reflection on such appropriations of his works and historical figure is not nearly as extensive. Although there is one recent dissertation about the Russian reception of Milton with a substantial chapter on the communist period, and in the important recent volume *Milton in Translation* a number of chapters are devoted to Milton's reception in post-war Estonia, Czechoslovakia, Yugoslavia and Hungary, there is no large-scale study available on how Milton's oeuvre was read in the former Eastern bloc.[49] If not to fill in a blank page, this book at least attempts to sharpen a grainy image in the history of Milton's European reception, one that shows what was going on beyond the Iron Curtain. Before, however, we embark upon exploring the various ways in which Milton and his works were used in state socialism, a brief introduction is needed to the fundamental context of my project, the changing shape of Hungarian cultural policy from 1948 to 1989. In the following chapters I often elaborate on how communist policymakers intervened in the creation, publication and reception of literature; my aim here is to provide a simplified summary of some of the most important concepts and names, linking them to the major political and cultural characteristics of the period under discussion. Many readers will not need this summary. It is designed simply to make it easier to map Milton's reception onto Hungary's political and cultural history from 1945 to 1989.

The four decades of state socialism are far from homogeneous. As György Péteri has pointed out, the period was characterised by 'alternating periods of increased isolation, regimentation, and terror, and periods of "Thaw", increased openness, emulation, and the softening of Iron into Nylon',[50] and these fluctuations were complemented by parallel changes in cultural policy.[51] The whole system of literature, including writers, institutions (publishing houses, literature departments, libraries, etc.) and readers, was controlled and manipulated according to the prevailing official ideology. At the beginning of the communist era, in the years of Mátyás Rákosi's dictatorship (1948–56), the aim was to reach Lenin's ideal of total control over cultural life, where 'cultural organizations (all forms of intellectual, scientific, and artistic practice) were subsidiary to educational and political organizations, and all forms of cultural production were to be fully supervised by the party'.[52] In practice this meant radical centralisation and suppression of all possible dissent. Publishing houses were nationalised, censorship was introduced, and many writers were persecuted or silenced (with translation remaining as their only creative outlet and source of income). The chief 'cultural commissar' of the period between 1948 and 1953 was József Révai, a zealous pro-Soviet man of letters who promoted the dubious aesthetics of 'socialist realism', and criticised heavily (and menacingly) those who failed to achieve it. Access to foreign literature was largely confined to the works of Soviet or communist writers who were published by the Új Magyar Könyvkiadó (New Hungarian Publishing House), which in 1957 became the famous Európa Kiadó (Európa Publishing House), the most important forum for world literature in translation even after the change of system.

In tandem with Khrushchev's 'thaw', from 1953 Rákosi's position weakened somewhat, and a brief period of détente set in: in the cultural sphere the ideological rigour softened, and writers who were previously forced into silence could publish their works again. A new world literature periodical entitled *Nagyvilág* was started, with the first issue (published in 1956) introduced by the Marxist philosopher György Lukács (who had been largely cold-shouldered by the elite during the previous years), emphasising that the Twentieth Congress of the Communist Party of the Soviet Union 'put an end to the dogmatic control of literature' (*véget vetett az irodalom dogmatikus irányításának*) and that 'writers and readers are no longer regarded as children needing guardianship, but as adults who feel their responsibility consciously' (*az írókat és olvasókat nem tekintik többé gyámságra szoruló gyerekeknek, hanem felnőtt, felelősségüket tudatosan érző embereknek*).⁵³ These thoughts might call to mind the recurring motif of childhood vs. maturity in Milton's *Areopagitica*, especially the point that in 'the dyeting and repasting of our minds . . . every mature man might have to exercise his owne leading capacity',⁵⁴ but Lukács's loosely parallel argument might well be coincidental. There are very few references to Milton's works in Lukács's writings, and none of them commendatory: in *Goethe and His Age*, for example, he characteristically labels *Paradise Lost* 'the great unsuccessful attempt to depict, with classical plasticity, the necessarily idealistic existence and destiny of the citizen'.⁵⁵ His library (now in the Lukács Archive of the Hungarian Academy of Sciences) holds only a handful of items by or on Milton.⁵⁶ From the perspective of this book, it is rather ironic that Lukács, one of the wellsprings of Western Marxism (who was, moreover, well known internationally throughout the period under discussion) seems to have been rather unenthusiastic about Milton.

The 'liberalism' of the mid-1950s was relative and short-lived, as demonstrated by the events of late 1956. The revolution, starting on 23 October 1956, was quickly quelled, János Kádár took power and enacted retributions which did not spare the cultural sphere. Some writers (among them one of Milton's translators, as we shall see in Chapter 2) chose to emigrate, and many among those who remained were persecuted, imprisoned or silenced again for long periods of time. In the long run, however, Kádár opted for compromise: a long period of 'consolidation' began in the 1960s and 1970s, when relative economic prosperity was accompanied by a less rigorous ideological course. The relationship between artists and the state was also re-established on the basis of a new set of compromises. The chief figure of the Kádár era in the cultural sphere was György Aczél, whose policy of 'three Ts', referring to the three Hungarian words signifying *tiltott* ('forbidden'), *tűrt* ('tolerated') and *támogatott* ('supported') works, came to dominate the 1960s and 1970s.⁵⁷ Divisions between these three categories were fuzzy and far from impermeable: artists could find themselves within different categories at different times, and it could also happen that only part of their output was considered acceptable by the authorities. A much wider range of world literature was published in translation than during Rákosi's dictatorship,⁵⁸ but some works (mostly those that were openly critical of the system) were still considered to be dangerously seditious (these were circulated in unauthorised publications). As István Bart (a prominent late twentieth-century writer, translator and publisher) has pointed out, although there was no written 'translation policy' in the period, translators and publishers had to construe what was acceptable from scattered references in Party decrees.[59] With the slow agony of the communist system in the 1980s, conformity to communist or 'socialist' values became largely nominal, and although the state strove to maintain control over all walks of life (not least by maintaining a vast network of agents recruited from among ordinary citizens), a thriving and semi-public countercultural sphere (linked in many ways to the fledging 'democratic opposition')[60] came into existence. As we shall see in Chapter 2, it was in this final phase of tacit compromises – which earned the name 'goulash communism' and during which Hungary was often regarded as the 'happiest of barracks' among the countries of the Eastern bloc – that Milton was published for the last time in Hungary before the new millennium.

These are, then, the broad historical, ideological and cultural contexts that formed the background to Milton's reception in Hungary in the post-war period. Some of the artists introduced below openly professed allegiance to the system, while others were vocal or silent critics of the achievements of 'actually existing socialism'. It will be clear from the following chapters, however, that none of them could particularly flourish under the general atmosphere of confinement and restrictedness characteristic of this period. The ways in which they read, translated or performed Milton's works are, therefore, also a testimony to their own frustrations, inhibitions and coping mechanisms, which might occasionally make present-day readers feel 'profoundly uneasy' – just as similar stories certainly did for Stephen Greenblatt five years after the demise of communism.[61] Such other-than-literary aspects of Milton's Hungarian career may well be tangential to my argument, but as they surface in the discussion, they will, I hope, be instrumental in 'closing up truth to truth'.[62]

Notes

1. Cs. Szabó 2005, 174.
2. Cs. Szabó belongs to the second generation of the *Nyugat* periodical (published from 1908 to 1941). He left Hungary after the war and settled in London, where he worked for the Hungarian programme of the BBC and became one of the intellectual leaders of the Hungarian emigration.
3. Cs. Szabó 2005, 175. Indeed, Czuczor himself was deeply interested in English literature.
4. In 1944 Hungary became a battlefield: from the west German and from the east Soviet troops invaded the country. Regent Miklós Horthy resigned, and the fascist Arrow Cross Party formed a new government, starting an appalling wave of terror against Hungarian Jews.
5. See Koopman 1982. *Doctor Faustus*, Mann's most critical fictional work of modern German politics and culture, dates from the period between 1943 and 1947.
6. Cs. Szabó 2005, 176, emphasis in the original.
7. In this book, I will use the terms 'communism' and 'state socialism' interchangeably to refer to the Soviet-influenced political systems of the Eastern bloc prevalent in the second half of the twentieth century.
8. For a discussion of Hungarian internationalism, see Mark and Apor 2015.

9. On the different attitudes to, and forms of, resistance before and after 1956, see Mark 2005.
10. For a detailed overview of the earlier reception history of Milton's oeuvre, see Péti 2017.
11. Macaulay 1825, 314.
12. Keeble 2016, 129.
13. On the cultic element in Shakespeare's Romantic and Hungarian reception, see Dávidházi 1998b, 8–9 and *passim*.
14. See Tarnai 1965, Kovács 2012, Péter 2011 and Péter 2012.
15. Smith 2021, 199.
16. Wolfe 1963, 32. Parts of the next few passages are adopted from Péti 2021b.
17. Engels 1847, 398.
18. Marx 2000, 601. See also Marx and Engels 1993, 448, where it is claimed that the composition of *Paradise Lost* did not further the 'capitalist production process'.
19. Marx and Engels 1993, 448.
20. For the idea of modern individuals becoming 'slaves with two masters', see Mohamed 2011, 83–4.
21. Caudwell 1937, 84. See also Chapter 2.
22. Rickword 1949, 131.
23. Thomson 1946, 65–6.
24. Hill 1949, 7–8. See also Visick 1949.
25. James 1949, 254.
26. Kogan 1969, 39. A similar, but theoretically more nuanced argument is present in Kendrick 1986.
27. Kogan 1969, 22.
28. Hill 1949, 6.
29. Achinstein 2010.
30. Achinstein 2008, 806.
31. Achinstein 2008, 830.
32. See Péti 2017, Tarnai 1965 and several references in the chapters below.
33. Knight 1942.
34. See Péter 2012, 165–7 and Knight 1942, 162.
35. Cf. Milton's earliest critics who, according to Joseph Wittreich, tried to 'coax *Paradise Lost* back into orthodoxy'. Wittreich 2011, 267.
36. See McDowell 2020.
37. The earliest signs of a new direction toward Milton are detectable as early as 1948 with the publication of the three essays of *The English Revolution 1640* (edited by Christopher Hill, together with the original, openly Marxist Preface from 1940) in the translation of Ádám Réz in the 'Science and Progress' (*Tudomány és haladás*) series of the Szikra (i.e. 'Spark') Publishing House.
38. Faludy 1985, 114.
39. Fodor 1963, 438.
40. Fodor 1975, 170–1.
41. Fodor 1963, 702.
42. Fodor 1963, 704.
43. Csorba 1978, 424.
44. Achinstein 2008, 808.
45. Lewalski 2010, 23–5.
46. See the 'Central and East European Translations' section of the volume *Milton in Translation* (Duran, Issa and Olson 2017).
47. See, e.g., Shurbanov and Sokolova 2001, Makaryk and Price 2006, Schandl 2008, Kostihová 2010, Thomas 2014, Sheen and Karremann 2016, Davies 2018, etc.
48. Makaryk and Price 2006, frontmatter.
49. See Uzakova 2014, and Duran, Issa and Olson 2017.
50. Péteri 2006, 10.
51. For a more detailed English discussion of the literature of the period, see Czigány 1984, 441–84.
52. Yurchak 2005, 12.
53. Lukács 1956, 5.
54. Milton 2013, 192.
55. Lukács 1968, 155.

56. German translations and criticism: *Das verlorene Paradies* (Stuttgart: Spemann, 1883); *Milton's poetische Werke*, vol. 6; Alfred Stern, *Milton und seine Zeit* (Leipzig: Duncker und Humblot, 1877–9). The library also holds Wallace's edition of Milton's prose, Hilaire Belloc's *Milton* (London: Cassell, 1935), a Hungarian and a German translation of Christopher Hill's 1940 volume on the English Revolution, and Denis Saurat's *Milton et le matérialisme chrétien en Angleterre*. There are no underlinings, marked passages or marginalia in any of these volumes.
57. László Kontler (1999, 445) translates the 'three Ts' as the 'three Ps' (promote, permit, prohibit). See also Czigányik 2011.
58. Indeed, Ferenc Takács (2002, 78) claims this was 'the greatest and most productive era of literary translation' in Hungarian history. This was to a large extent due to the fact that many writers – among them some of Milton's translators (as we shall see in later chapters) – were allowed only this form of publication.
59. Bart 2002, 14–15.
60. On the 'democratic opposition' in English, see Csizmadia 2015.
61. Cf. Greenblatt et al. 1995, 7.
62. Milton 2013, 205–6.

1
Forms of attention and neglect: Milton's epics in print and on stage – and in oblivion

'I shudder to think of Milton, the magnificent': Milton and the translator's drudgery

On 23 February 1949 Lőrinc Szabó, the foremost Hungarian poet-translator of the mid-twentieth century, wrote two letters: one to his wife, Klára Mikes, the other to his long-time lover, Erzsébet Korzáti. Predictably, the subject, the tone and the mood of the letters are very different, but both end on the same note. 'I shudder to think of Milton, the magnificent, whom I should really start now' (*Borzadva gondolok Miltonra, a nagyszerűre, akit most már komolyan el kell kezdeni*),[1] writes Szabó to his wife. 'Milton is waiting for me. (And who knows what unknown evils . . .!)' (*vár Milton. [S ki tudja, milyen ismeretlen rossz . . .!]*)[2] he intimates to his lover. The 'Milton' who looms large in the backgrounds of both letters is Szabó's translation of *Paradise Lost* which, except for the first two books, never came to be. As we shall see, Szabó's anxiety is as much fuelled by personal artistic concerns as the workings of communist cultural policy: the way his translation was commissioned and then dropped by the Franklin Publishing House is emblematic of Milton's Hungarian reception under the communist dictatorship of the 1950s. 'Milton, the magnificent' presented a daunting task to Szabó on both the private and the public level.

Szabó's misgivings about translating *Paradise Lost* are anything but surprising. Milton's epic has been associated with difficulty for centuries, practically since its publication. Although the epic narrator claims to be 'inspire[d] / Easie' (*PL* 9.23–4), the difficulties besetting the creation, the subject, the style and the reception of the poem are proverbial. Andrew Marvell was the first to spot these: in his commendatory poem prefixed to the 1674 edition ('On Mr Milton's *Paradise Lost*') he 'misdoubt[ed]' the poet's 'intent', then 'fear[ed]' the 'success' (i.e. the outcome), but also felt 'Jealous' of the 'less skilful hand[s]' who might 'pretend a share' in Milton's 'Labours'.[3] Samuel Johnson's verdict might also be cited here: the eighteenth-century critic gives credit where credit is due by pointing out that Milton's 'purpose was the most useful and the most arduous' and that 'he was born for whatever is arduous', but also asserts that the 'perusal [of *Paradise Lost*] is a duty rather than a pleasure. We read Milton for instruction, retire harassed and overburdened, and look elsewhere for recreation.'[4]

Attention to the sublime difficulties of the subject and style of *Paradise Lost*, as well as the burden these impose on readers, has also been characteristic of Milton's Hungarian reception: the epic's eighteenth-century translator, Sándor Bessenyei, warns readers to be attentive, since Milton 'rarely goes on the regular, trodden ways of the human mind and of imagination, but is almost always at the highest or the lowest extremes' (*ritkánn megyen az Emberi elmének vagy képzelődésnek rendes tört-úttyán, hanem többnyire mindenkor a' leg-felsőbb vagy a' leg-alsóbb végekenn jár*).[5] Much later, in 1930, in the preface to the republished late nineteenth-century version by Gusztáv Jánosi, László Ravasz, a bishop of the Hungarian Reformed (Calvinist) Church, writes that 'Milton undertook a special, I could almost say impossible task' (*Milton sajátságos, szinte azt mondhatnám lehetetlen feladatra vállalkozott*) and that *Paradise Lost* is 'the most serious, most solemn and most sublime poem in the world' (*a legkomolyabb, a legünnepélyesebb és a legmagasztosabb költemény a világon*); therefore, 'Milton's work cannot be measured with any other standard than itself' (*Milton művét nem szabad más mintával mérni, csak önmagával*).[6] Such views persisted to the period under discussion: Szabó was not the only modern Hungarian translator who felt oppressed by the prospect of having to turn *Paradise Lost* into Hungarian. István Jánosy, whose complete translation was published in 1969, confessed to an initial reluctance to the project on similar grounds:

> I must admit that when I was commissioned by the Európa Publishing House to make a new, complete translation of *Paradise Lost* I embarked on it with considerable reluctance. I expected to be imprisoned in the work for years and saw myself sequestered from contemporary life for a long, long time. My prejudice against Paradise was moreover strengthened by T. S. Eliot's very critical attitude towards it. After this great detour would I ever be able to find my way back to my own era again?[7]

The range of difficulties that translating *Paradise Lost* presented for these poets went beyond the unpleasantness of drudgery, or the personal anxieties underpinning both Szabó's premonitions and Jánosy's reminiscences (does the translator have the time, the energy and the means to finish this great project?). Both Szabó and Jánosy hint at the complex dilemma every Hungarian translator of Milton's works must face. Will the Hungarian reading public be interested in the new translation? Can such a work enter into meaningful communication with contemporary Hungarian literature and culture? Does Milton matter at all? Over the centuries of Hungarian Milton reception there have been a number of different direct and indirect answers to these questions, but perhaps none more significant and certainly none more widely resounding than those in relation to *Paradise Lost* in the post-war period until the 1989 change of system. In this chapter, therefore, I will present a survey of the ways Hungarian critics and translators engaged with Milton's great epic in the period between 1948 and 1989. Importantly, while in those four decades *Paradise Lost* became a forum for cultural innovation, Milton's brief epic, *Paradise Regained*, seems to have been lost, and, in certain cases, systematically obscured, for the Hungarian canon. This discrepancy in the responses to Milton's different epic works is not accidental; one could go so far as to claim that *Paradise Lost* could only run its spectacular course in communist Hungary at the expense of the suppression of *Paradise Regained*. This will become all the more apparent if we first take a brief look at Milton's earlier reception in Hungary, in which attempts to contrast the two works were different, and not nearly as absolute.

The 'prompted Song else mute': *Paradise Regained* lost in Hungary

When a complete Hungarian translation of *Paradise Lost* first appeared at the end of the eighteenth century, it was together with the first Hungarian version of *Paradise Regained*: Sándor Bessenyei translated Milton's epics from Nicolas-François Dupré de Saint-Maur's French *Paradis perdu* and *Paradis reconquis*.[8] The work was published in two volumes in 1796 in Kassa (now Kosice, Slovakia); the second volume contained a commendatory poem 'On Milton's *Paradise Lost*' ('A' Milton' Elvesztett Paraditsomáról') attributed to the foremost poet of the day, Mihály Csokonai Vitéz.[9] Csokonai considered the relationship of the two poems as complementary: he evoked the iconography of the birth of Venus from the sea to illustrate how *Paradise Lost* created the essential context for

Paradise Regained, and resorted to wit to tackle the critical commonplace (rife since Milton's time)[10] about the brief epic's inferiority:

> Maradgyon hát ama Tudós komor Kritikájával,
> A' ki Miltont óltsárollya ezzel a' hibájával:
> Hogy a'mit az el vesztettbenn nyert fenn járó múzsája,
> Azt a' viszsza nyertbenn mind el-veszté lassú hárfája.
> Úgy van! ezt maga Milton is éppen nem tagadhattya,
> Mert a' Pokol az el-vesztett Paraditsom magzattya.
> Igaz hogy ebből ki-esvén az ember poklot nyere,
> Ebben készül a' sok tsudák' 's a' kénkövek' Tengere.
> A' viszsza nyert Paraditsom, mely el-törlője lett e'
> Gyötrelmeknek, a' mit nyerett egészszen el-vesztette.[11]

(Let that scholar be left alone with his grim criticism / who blames Milton for the fault / that what his lofty Muse won in *Paradise Lost* / his slow harp lost in *Paradise Regained*. / That is right! *Milton* himself would not deny it, / since the offspring of *Paradise Lost* is Hell. / It is true that man having been exiled from this [i.e. Paradise] won Hell, / in which many wonders and the sea of brimstone are wrought. / Paradise regained, which annihilated these / miseries, lost completely what [man] had won.)

Csokonai's argument (presented in a rather involved way) turns on a pun: in Hungarian different forms of the same verb (*nyer*, i.e. 'win') are used for the ideas of 'winning' and 'regaining'. The Hell (damnation) that mankind 'won' by losing Paradise is lost by the 'winning back' of Eden. The complementary relationship of the two epics proposed by Csokonai resonated well with many early readers of Milton in Hungary. Bessenyei's twin translations went on to become a popular religious book in the nineteenth century. Read mainly among rural Protestant communities, and published together several times, the two epics were clearly considered to be one organic unit.[12]

But *Paradise Regained* was also read and referenced by the intelligentsia of the nineteenth century: for Imre Madách, the author of *The Tragedy of Man* (*Az ember tragédiája*; a nineteenth-century Hungarian drama generally believed to be inspired by *Paradise Lost* and Goethe's *Faust*), it was the only work by Milton in his library (albeit in German translation),[13] while the ethnographer and poet János Kriza resorted to Csokonai's idea of 'regaining by losing' in his elegiac distich on Milton: 'Great Poet! Your eyes were put out by flame sword of the cherubim: / since you ventured to regain lost Eden' (*Nagy költő! szemeid kerubim lángtőre kioltá: / Mert a veszett édent visszaszerezni meréd*).[14] Pál Harsányi, a minor writer and editor, uses Milton's language to celebrate 'the wilderness becoming Eden' (*a' vadon lett édenné*) in the 'Paradise regained' (*visszanyert paradicsom*), the fine garden of the country seat and park of Archduke Joseph Habsburg (Palatine of Hungary).[15] Discussions of the brief epic were an integral part of critical appraisals of Milton's work. Thus, Károly Szász, one of the foremost translators and critics of the second half of the nineteenth century, devoted a whole chapter to *Paradise Regained* in his two-volume *Great Epics of World Literature* (*A világirodalom nagy époszai*). Szász considers the brief epic as the 'satellite moon' to *Paradise Lost*, whose superiority he repeatedly asserts. According to Szász, *Paradise Regained* is 'more of a moral-didactic poem than an epic' (*Erkölcsi irányú tanköltemény inkább, mint éposz*), which 'fails to convince and leaves us cold' (*meg sem győz, hidegen is hagy*),[16] but it is not without its merits as it has all the virtues of Milton's poetry: noble sentiments, powerful images and enchanting diction.[17] A couple of years later Gusztáv Jánosi, in the preface to his blank verse translation of *Paradise Lost*, also talks about *Paradise Regained* as 'a truly beautiful didactic poem, but not an epic' (*igen szép tanköltemény, de nem eposz*), and regards its hero as 'the ideal of Puritan virtue' (*a puritan erény ideálja*).[18] Finally, at the end of the century, Ede Reményi in an article entitled 'Leírások Milton eposzaiban' ('Descriptions in Milton's epics') talks about the two epics as 'an epic cycle' (*epikus cyklus*), and in another article about Milton's Christ and Satan again adopts what we could term a 'holistic' approach tracing the development of characters *across* both epics.[19]

Essentially the same attitude characterises the critics of the first half of the twentieth century: *Paradise Lost* and *Paradise Regained* are often discussed together, but the independent merits of the brief epic are also highlighted in their writings. Arthur Yolland considers the later work the inferior of the two, but also points out its characteristically Miltonic merits ('brilliant descriptions and vast imagination'), and, importantly, and quite uniquely among twentieth century critics, links it to eighteenth-century sensibilities: 'The regeneration of mankind is not achieved through images, but resolute, manly efforts, just as in the eighteenth-century works of Addison and Steele' (*Az emberek regenerálása nem képekben, hanem határozott, férfias törekvésekben rejlik, mint amelyek a XVIII. században Steele és Addison munkáiban jutottak érvényre*).[20] István B. Pap in his 'Commemoration of Milton' ('Emlékezés Miltonról') explains the relative plainness of the brief epic's style with its sublimity, while Géza Voinovich defines it as the separate, albeit less admirable 'finishing piece' (*befejező darab*) of *Paradise Lost*.²¹ Lajos Lengyel, in his survey of the 'fundamental problem of philosophy' in Madách's *The Tragedy of Man*, claims that in Madách's work 'the epic of *Paradise Lost* and *Paradise Regained* is repeated' (*Az elveszett és visszanyert paradicsom' eposza ismétlődik meg*). According to Lengyel, the Adam of Madách's tragedy 'regains lost Eden on the level of ideals' (*Ádám az eszmében visszanyerte az elvesztett édent*) – in contrast to the tragic or (even tragicomical) character of Lucifer, who remains a 'representative of materialist-positivist rationalism' (*materialista-pozitivista racionalizmus képviselője*).²²

In the wider intellectual discourse about literature, we see the same balanced approach: the 'profound reflections' of both epics are recommended as especially apt to 'raise religious sentiments' in a pedagogical lexicon published in 1936, while at another end of the ideological spectrum, in a debate about literature and politics on the pages of the social-democratic periodical *Szocializmus*, László Ascher and Soma Braun agree that both *Paradise Lost* and *Paradise Regained* are essentially political works.²³ At least a superficial knowledge about Milton's brief epic seems to be ubiquitous in the period. The sculptor József Damkó used its title in his sculpture representing the postlapsarian Adam and Eve with their first child.²⁴ But 'paradise regained' as a stock phrase with strong Miltonic resonances also crops up in widely different contexts during the inter-war years. It is used to characterise Sir Alfred Mond's ideas of 'social justice' (in implicit criticism of Marxism), and is deployed as an emblematic expression of the wishful fantasy about the recovery of lost Hungarian territories,²⁵ but, through the serialised translation of Robert Blatchford's 1907 novel *The Sorcery Shop*, it also appears in a socialist utopia.²⁶

Such comprehensive approaches in which Milton's epics were considered together all but disappeared in the post-war period. So did almost all independent discussions of *Paradise Regained*: apart from a very few reflections it virtually ceased to exist for Hungarian audiences. But even in the rare cases when *Paradise Regained* is evoked, its importance is often played down, and its possible connections to *Paradise Lost* are seldom mentioned. In an article commemorating the three hundred and fiftieth anniversary of Milton's birth (and the three hundredth of Oliver Cromwell's death), for example, Jesus is not named, but simply referred to as 'one of the figures of *Paradise Regained*' (*A Visszanyert Paradicsom egyik alakja*) whose confession about his intention 'to learn and know, and thence to do / What might be publick good; . . . to promote all truth, / All righteous things' (PR 1.203–6) is labelled simply as Milton's 'self-confession' (*önvallomás*).²⁷

In the same year in another commemoration we can witness the use of the same vague language about *Paradise Regained*, which is said to be 'singing the work of personal, internal redemption' (*az egyéni, benső megváltás művét éneklő*), alongside characteristically lavish praise heaped upon *Samson Agonistes*. From the conclusion of the latter article it can be gleaned why the brief epic was neglected in the 1950s: the author argues for dispensing with the distinction between the Milton 'the revolutionary intellectual and the poet'. Referring to the decision of the World Peace Council to commemorate Milton's birth, the article concludes: 'Those trusting in a better future for mankind will love Milton, the ardent progressive . . . they will understand in his poetry the words of the great artist worried about the fate of humankind' (*Az emberiség jobb jövőjében bízók szeretik a haladás eszméiért hevülő Miltont . . . poézisében megértik az emberiség sorsán aggódó . . . nagy művész szavát*).[28] In all probability, the 'paradoxically militant quietism' (Thomas Corns's phrase)[29] of Milton's Jesus did not go well with the combative rhetoric of communist Cold War aesthetics, but Jesus' aversion towards the 'people' must also have struck a discordant note. Thus, an article about the images of Jesus changing through the ages (published in the leftist periodical *Világosság*) singles out (among other examples) Milton's 'Christ who 'appears as a superior intellectual . . . [and] looks down upon the people who are, according to him, a confused rabble' (*magasabb rendű, intellektuális személyként jelenik meg, aki lenézi a népet, mint zavaros tömeget*).[30]

Unsurprisingly, the only relatively extended discussions of *Paradise Regained* in the era can be found in the work of the two leading Miltonists of the age, Tibor Lutter and Miklós Szenczi.[31] The brief epic seems to have been something of an embarrassment for both critics (despite their essential differences in method and beliefs), and both try to distance it as much as possible from *Paradise Lost*. Lutter deploys a 'consistently Marxist' theoretical and interpretive framework when he claims that the British Marxist critic Christopher Caudwell was essentially wrong in positing *Paradise Regained* as a 'defeatist' work which resorts to postponing the final victory of the revolution. *Paradise Regained*, according to Lutter, is neither the finishing piece, nor the completion of *Paradise Lost*, although it is informed – as are, in Lutter's view, all Milton's late masterpieces – by the 'great cause' (*nagy ügy*) of 'redemption on earth' (*földi megváltás*). Bending *Paradise Regained* more than any other Miltonic work to his agenda, Lutter concludes that the purpose of the brief epic, only understood if one gets through to the 'topical significance of biblical phraseology' (*a bibliai frazeológia időszerű jelentőségét*), is to establish 'firm obedience to the cause [of the revolution]' (*szilárd engedelmesség az ügy iránt*) as a chief moral principle.[32]

Writing in the late 1960s, Szenczi – whose criticism usually offers fresh and balanced correctives to Lutter's readings – does not, in this case, offer much better perspectives. Trained as a classicist, Szenczi is clearly perplexed at Jesus' denunciation of Satan's tendentious interpretation of classical culture. In his 1969 essay 'Milton Agonistes' he points out that 'Milton here passes judgment over his own humanist learning' (*Milton itt saját humanista műveltsége felett mond ítéletet*), and calls the hero of the brief epic a character with 'almost obscurantist features' (*szinte obskurantista vonásokkal*).[33] Szenczi's use of the word 'obscurantist' is especially striking, since it had long been one of the favourite derogatory terms in communist propaganda, often used together with 'reactionary', 'anti-democratic' or 'antiquated'. No wonder that a couple of years later, in his history of early English literature, he diplomatically leaves this qualification out, asserting in a brief paragraph that *Paradise Regained* is 'the most ascetic child of Milton's muse' (*Milton múzsájának legaszketikusabb gyermeke*) in which the author 'represents new aspects of his changing thoughts and sentiments with new poetic devices' (*változó gondolat- és érzelemvilágának új oldalait ábrázolja, új költői eszközökkel*).[34] We do not get to learn these new thoughts and sentiments, much less the novel poetic devices: for once in Szenczi's critical oeuvre insight is not accompanied by precision.

It seems, then, that *Paradise Regained* was not merely neglected, but actively pushed to the background in the four decades between 1948 and 1989. Separating the brief epic from Milton's other works and obscuring it as much as possible was politically justifiable on thematic and even poetic grounds (i.e. that it represents a New Testament episode without much relevance to the revolution, and is traditionally considered to be inferior to Milton's other epic), but it also served the agenda of foregrounding *Paradise Lost* and *Samson Agonistes* as the masterpieces in which Milton's revolutionary thought reached its artistic zenith.

Nowhere is this more explicitly formulated that in György Jánosházy's 'Afterword' to his translation of *Samson Agonistes* (first published in 1977).[35] Jánosházy, who considers *Samson Agonistes* Milton's 'other masterpiece', states with some regret that 'this time [i.e. at the time Milton was writing *Paradise Regained*] the theologian got the upper hand over the poet' (*Ezúttal a teológus kerekedett fölébe a költőnek*), and remarks disparagingly that the debate between Jesus and Satan is 'drowned in the scholastic spirit of the debates at the English universities of the time' (*az egykorú angol egyetemek skolasztikus szellemében felépített vitába fúl*). According to Jánosházy, while in *Paradise Lost* 'we readily forgive the dryness [of theology] in exchange for the artistic beauties of the poem' ([a teológia] szárazságát szívesen megbocsátjuk a költemény művészi szépségei kedvéért), it is only in *Samson Agonistes* that the poet sheds this 'ballast of his final creative period' (*Utolsó alkotó korszakának . . . nehezéke*).[36] Beset by such assumptions, *Paradise Regained* was bound to fade out of view.

'Majestic though in ruin': Lőrinc Szabó's incomplete *Paradise Lost*[37]

The brief epic, thus, came to be collateral damage in the post-war effort to make Milton if not exactly a 'contemporary', then at least an author palatable to communist tastes. Consequently, *Paradise Lost* became the main forum for 'domesticating' Milton: the great epic's revolutionary character was an overarching theme of Milton's reception in the literary criticism of the four decades of communism. Ironically, the translations of *Paradise Lost* available in this period did not always live up to such critical expectations; as a result, they were sometimes used selectively by critics, but also became sites of indirect resistance to the officially prevailing ideology. We can witness the interaction of these disparate forces in the 1970 stage production of *Paradise Lost*, arguably the most important Hungarian contribution to the international reception history of Milton's epic. In the rest of this chapter, I will highlight the most important stages, in the critical heritage as well as in translation, of the complex process leading to this ground-breaking production.

Let us start with the views of Tibor Lutter, the chief Milton critic of the 1950s according to whom even Milton's most radical prose works waned in comparison with the revolutionary potential of *Paradise Lost*.[38] Throughout his critical work Lutter strove to present Milton as the 'poet of the English bourgeois revolution', and *Paradise Lost* as a 'progressive, pioneering' work, but he could only achieve this by making big compromises. In the chapter 'The meaning of *Paradise Lost*' ('A *Paradicsom Elvesztése* értelme') in his 1956 monograph entitled *John Milton, the Poet of the English Bourgeois Revolution* (*John Milton, az angol polgári forradalom költője*), Lutter tendentiously strips away certain aspects of Milton's epic in order to emphasise its topicality. His basic contention is that Milton created *Paradise Lost* on 'the fundamental principle of redemption on earth' (*a földi megváltás alapeszméje*), and thus, far from indulging in a tragic vision of history, the epic does not take the salubrious, progressive ideas of the revolution for a lost cause.[39] In driving his message home Lutter lambasts both what he terms the 'bourgeois' schools of criticism and 'Satanist' Marxist critics such as Christopher Caudwell; nevertheless, in his account of Milton's artistry in *Paradise Lost* (plot construction, imagery, versification and so on) he heavily relies on a solid muster of nineteenth- and early twentieth-century critics (Masson, Tillyard, C. S. Lewis and some German critics), none of whom might be considered especially progressive by any standard. This theoretical and critical inconsistency is accompanied by his selective reading of the epic plot: stating that the 'first half' of the epic can only be understood from the 'topical' perspective of the 'second half' (i.e. what happens on Earth), he confines his quotations and commentary almost exclusively to Books 11 and 12. As a result, *Paradise Lost* emerges in Lutter's interpretation as Milton's reflections on the class struggle of the seventeenth century, where the 'disgraced feudal order' (*levitézlett feudális rend*) represented by the 'counter-revolutionary' forces of Satan was in conflict with Parliament and the republic.[40] Lest the topical application of these tenets be missed, Lutter characteristically and repeatedly equates 'Puritan' with 'progressive', stressing that the Christian aspects of Milton's work are a mere 'religious mantle'. The fact that Milton's insights are presented in poetry, a notoriously polyvalent medium, comes in handy for Lutter, since it allows him to 'discover' the 'true meaning', and 'rectify previous misconceptions', of *Paradise Lost* relatively easily, with appeal to the correct 'Marxist' doctrinal standards of interpretation.

The lack of a fresh translation or an up-to-date (or perhaps ideologically 'updated') complete Hungarian version of *Paradise Lost* in the 1950s might have contributed to Lutter's highly selective reading. The text he quotes sparingly is Gusztáv Jánosi's translation, which was first published in 1890 and remained the standard version for the first half of the twentieth century (it was republished in 1904, then in a revised edition in 1916 and 1930). Jánosi's translation remained popular for such a long time with good reason: it is a highly accurate blank-verse rendition which uses relatively simple and brisk Hungarian and faithfully reproduces the poetic qualities of the original (the high-flown rhetoric, the extended similes, repetitions, etc.). For late twentieth- and twenty-first-century readers it might seem somewhat mannered, yet, importantly, it is not only the first complete verse translation, but also the basis and inspiration for later modern versions of *Paradise Lost*. Indeed, both post-war translators of *Paradise Lost* must have used Jánosi's version as a crib for their own work – as witnessed by their frequent borrowings from it.[41]

For all its virtues, Jánosi's version must have presented major problems to such a post-war critic as Lutter who wanted to bring Milton's epic in conformity with prevailing ideologies. For one, Jánosi was a

Catholic priest, and in the period before World War II his translation was often hailed as a trans-denominational intellectual feat. What is more, the editions available all contained prefaces which had a rather different take on the progressive and topical aspects of the work. This is certainly true of Jánosi's original preface, which states that the real hero of the epic is Satan, a 'captivating', 'human', 'truly heroic', 'dramatic' (*megragadó ... emberi ... igazán hősi ... drámai*) figure, but also points out keen-sightedly that 'we [readers] are pleased to be deceived' (*szívesen hagyjuk magunkat megcsalatni*) by him.[42] But the same is true of the essay by Calvinist bishop László Ravasz, which replaced Jánosi's preface in the 1930 edition and which celebrated *Paradise Lost* as 'the epic of Protestantism' (*a protestantizmus eposza*) and placed Milton beside Dante at the peak of European literature.[43] These critical contexts clearly went against all that Lutter was trying to represent in Milton, and he consequently used as little of Jánosi's translation in his monograph as possible. Indeed, in the anthologies he edited and co-edited during the 1950s Lutter refrained from quoting Jánosi altogether, choosing excerpts from the first post-war translation of *Paradise Lost*, Lőrinc Szabó's incomplete version, instead.[44]

Lőrinc Szabó belonged to the second generation of the *Nyugat*, the leading literary periodical of the first half of the twentieth century (published from 1908 to 1941). He was a prolific translator of lyric poetry from across the centuries, who provided excellent versions of classic texts (his translations are still enjoyable today). Szabó describes the process of translation as the enthusiastic 'joy of appropriation deriving from the recomposing of the poem, which is about the same as the joy of creation' (*birtokbavétel öröme, amit a vers újraköltése nyújt, s amely körülbelül azonos a teremtés örömével*), stating at the same time that 'nobody can translate above his/her original poetic rank' (*nem fordíthat senki a maga eredeti költői rangján felül*).[45] As the critic Lóránt Kabdebó points out, the close integration of Szabó's original work with his output as a literary translator bears out these propositions: throughout his career the choice of poems to be translated and his poetics of translation changed in tandem with the evolution of his poetry.[46]

The personal and professional contexts for Szabó's translation of *Paradise Lost* are therefore worth a closer look. As we saw at the beginning of this chapter, the task to provide a new Hungarian version of Milton's epic sparked some uneasy feelings in the poet. This ambivalence towards Milton, however, seems to have derived from more than just a sense of being overburdened. In the post-war years Szabó's political views and his activity before and during World War II came to be considered highly controversial (and have been so ever since): although he was known for saving several of his contemporaries from anti-Semitic persecution, in his published journalism he often flirted with anti-Semitism and the far right. In 1939 he published two reports in the Hungarian press about Hitler's speech in the Kroll Opera House (28 April 1939) which record his fascination with Hitler's oratorical skills (he expressly refrains from comment on the speech's content, though).[47] What is more, in 1938 he reworked his 1928 poem 'Leader' ('Vezér' – the Hungarian word is readily associated with dictators, and is one of the possible renderings of the German word 'Führer'), in which he originally presented a dramatic monologue using a generic persona of a dictator. Szabó's revision of this poem is rather tendentious: as Zoltán Kulcsár-Szabó points out, he 'found means to dissolve the ambivalences of the Leader's self-presentation, (self-)legitimation and "truth"' (*Eszközöket talált arra, hogy a vezér önmegjelenítésének, (ön) legitimációjának és „igazságának" ambivalenciáit feloldja*), and 'did not or did not want to understand his own poem' (*nem értette vagy nem akarta érteni saját versét*).[48] Because of these performances immediately after the war Szabó was subjected to two 'procedures of justification' (*igazolási eljárás*), one by the Free Association of Artists (Művészek Szabad Szervezete – the predecessor of the Hungarian Writers' Association), and the other by the National Association of Hungarian Journalists (Magyar Újságírók Országos Szövetsége).[49]

Instead of settling his account, these procedures have cast a long shadow over Szabó's life and work. As Károly Horányi points out even if Szabó was eventually 'justified', his trial has been continuing in the critical reception ever since.[50] Indeed, as a consequence of his compromised political position for some years after the war Szabó could not publish his original poetry, and his main source of income during this period of forced silence was the translation of the classics of European literature (Goethe, Pushkin, Burns, Heine, Hugo).[51] It was only in 1947 that he published *Cricket Song* (*Tücsökzene*), a volume in which he collected the autobiographically inspired lyric poetry he wrote after the war in a composition that reaches almost epic proportions.[52] According to Gáspár Miklós Tamás, Szabó's poetry is one of the greatest expressions in world literature of 'burning sensual shame – and the bitter defiance and "meta-ethical" egoism that derives from it', and *Cricket Song* in particular is 'a religious narrative of the highest order'.[53] Importantly, Szabó's translation of *Paradise Lost* also dates from the same years, and several of the poems in *Cricket Song* make explicit references to Milton's epic. In the poem 'Eternal change' ('Örök változás') the self is represented as 'Unapproachable as the light / Of that Blind One' (*Megközelíthetetlen, mint a fény, / ama Vaké*),⁵⁴ and in the vision of 'Something happened' ('Valami történt'), where reflection on a pivotal change in personal life is offset by images of larval metamorphosis, the last line echoes the hymn to Holy Light in the invocation to Book 3 of *Paradise Lost* (which Szabó had translated by then):

> *valami történt, valami,*
> *ami mást hozott: a láp férgei*
> *elhagyták küszöbüket, a vizet* . . .
> *Üdvözlégy, Fény, testvérem, Örök-Egy!*⁵⁵

(Something happened, something, / which brought something different: the worms of the fen / have left their threshold, the water . . . / Hail, Light, my brother, Eternally One!)

It seems, then, that Szabó's misgivings about the daunting task of the translation rested on a complicated interplay of both personal and political factors. Milton's poetry was clearly a strong inspiring force for Szabó, and his lifelong fascination with monumental, Satan-like dictator figures must have inevitably drawn him to *Paradise Lost*. At the same time, he might have felt a special kinship with the blind poet who completed his epic after the Restoration in a similarly difficult public and personal position, 'fall'n on evil dayes . . . and evil tongues' (*PL* 7.25–6). In an 1956 radio interview (recorded days after the quelling of the revolution, and thus never aired), he expresses his wish 'never to take a commission to translate again' (*Szeretnék többé soha nem vállalni fordítást*), but after the interviewer presses him, confesses that 'if I lived long enough, I would like to finish one more thing: Milton's *Paradise Lost*' (*ha nagyon hosszú lenne az életem, egyvalamit még szívesen befejeznék, Milton Elveszett Paradicsomát*).⁵⁶ Although the wish to undertake the translation of the entire epic had accompanied him through the 1950s (we find it expressed in a typescript of his CV in 1952),⁵⁷ he did not live to finish the project. It is, however, quite fascinating to reflect that he did complete the first two books of *Paradise Lost*, since (as we shall soon see) Milton's dominant focus on the figure of the fallen Satan in these parts of the epic allowed Szabó to confront and reconsider once more the changes that took place in and around him between the pre-war and the post-war periods.

Of course, the fortunes of Szabó's translation did not entirely depend on the translator's personal circumstances and choices. In the late 1940s, when Szabó was embarking on the translation, the rapidly changing political atmosphere (the establishment of the 'dictatorship of the proletariat') was less and less welcoming towards the project, while after 1956, when he was financially relatively secure (having received government recognition with the Kossuth Prize), his health was already failing. Szabó's uncertainty becomes clear from the correspondence with his wife where the question of 'the Milton' (i.e. the translation) regularly comes up with varying degrees of hope and despair (mostly the latter). On 15 July 1949, for example, he writes 'I have no strength for the Milton. Its fate is uncertain anyway' (*A Miltonhoz nincs erőm. Hiszen amúgy is bizonytalan még mindig a sorsa*) and a week later, on 22 July, he complains that 'The Milton is sinking . . .' (*A Milton viszont úgy süllyed . . .*). Yet another week later it becomes clear that his uncertainty is partly the result of the publishing house's indecision:

> *A Milton kissé lóg az 1950. szeptember 1-i terminussal is. Ami pénzt kapok; azt* nem *a Miltonra kapom tehát: arra Z. A. most nem* mer *adni. Ez a Milton-ügy nagyon kényes viselkedést igényel: se lemondani, se egészen vállalni nem akarom.*[58]

> (The Milton is suspended a little bit even with the 1 September 1950 deadline. The money I receive is *not* for the Milton; A. Z. does not *dare* give money for that now. This Milton matter requires very careful behaviour: I don't want to pull out, but I am not wholly committed either.)

The A. Z. mentioned was Anna Zádor, one of Hungary's great art historians of the twentieth century, but at the time of Szabó's letter also the acting director of the renowned Franklin Publishing House, which was about to be nationalised.[59] To complicate Szabó's relationship to the 'Milton' even more, we should remember that Zádor was a Jewish intellectual whose family perished in the Holocaust, while she herself was rescued at the last moment from a forced labour unit. The fact that she was cooperating with Szabó (who, as we have seen, was accused of Nazi sympathies) on the new version of *Paradise Lost* might explain some part of Szabó's unease about the translation, but it certainly shows the complexity of the cultural landscape in the years following World War II. As becomes clear from a letter sent by Klára Mikes, Szabó's wife, to the poet, Zádor was hoping to publish *Paradise Lost*, but in the summer of 1949 she was 'unable to predict that far ahead whether the Milton would be needed then' (*nem tudhatja ilyen messzire, hogy akkor kell-e majd Milton*), i.e. in the autumn of 1950, barely a year from the time of writing. Szabó's wife comments: 'This is straight talk and one can understand why she rushes the publication of this book' (*Ez egészen világos beszéd s érteni lehet, hogy miért sürgeti a kiadását ennek a könyvnek*).⁶⁰ For twenty-first-century readers Zádor's hesitation and Mikes's letter sound more like coded language, and one can easily guess at the exact reasons why 'the Milton' was such a sensitive case. In the fledgling days of communist dictatorship the freshly nationalised and centrally controlled publishing houses had to reorient their production towards more 'topical' writers of world literature (which meant mostly Soviet writers).⁶¹ Although no party guidelines or suggestions seem to have survived from the period, it is safe to say that Milton would not have been among the promoted authors. If they wished to publish such material, publishers had to move cautiously and swiftly, hoping that their proposed volumes would slip past the censors. This makes Zádor's hesitation and the extremely tight deadline understandable, although the speed required for finishing *Paradise Lost* (a little more than a year) would have made it, if not totally impossible, then at least extremely difficult for even the most professional of translators (like Szabó) to complete the task.⁶²

'The Milton' thus remained incomplete, but Szabó published most of the excerpts he completed in the two-volume collection of his literary translations, *Our Eternal Friends* (*Örök barátaink*). Books 1 and 2 of the epic were published at the end of volumes 1 and 2 respectively, while the 'Hymn to light' (*PL* 3.1–55), 'Evening in Eden: Eve to Adam' (*PL* 4.641–56), and 'Adam and Eve's morning prayer' (*PL* 5.153–208) were inserted in volume 2.⁶³ In the appended biographical note Szabó states that 'Milton is the genius of calm, sublime, classical style, the succinct expression of sentiment and thought, and melodious diction, although sometimes he can be dry and rhetorical' (*Milton zseniális mestere a nyugodt, fenséges, klasszikus stílusnak, az érzés és gondolat tömör kifejezésének, a verszenének; néha mindamellett száraz és szónokias*) and we might expect that, with the exception perhaps of the last two objections, his translations would represent these qualities.⁶⁴ Indeed, in the published excerpts Szabó masterfully modulates the voices of Milton's poetry from the solemnly sublime to the intensely passionate (as the situation represented requires), and his version is especially successful in its attempt to reproduce, at least partly, some of the effects of the original. The translator's narrative skills are amply shown in his rendering of Satan's journey from hell:

> So eagerly the fiend
> Ore bog or steep, through strait, rough, dense, or rare,
> With head, hands, wings, or feet pursues his way,
> And swims or sinks, or wades, or creeps, or flyes (*PL* 2.947–50)

> *Úgy megy, csak megy a Gonosz*
> *tavon, bércen, hágón, sziken s bozótban,*
> *fejest vagy kézen, szárnyon vagy a talpán:*
> *úszik, merűl, csúsz, gázol vagy repűl.*[65]

(So goes, on goes the Evil One / through lake, hill, strait, marsh and shrub, / head-on or on hands, on wings or on his feet / he swims, sinks, creeps, wades, or flies.)

The repetition of the simple verb *megy* (goes), the substitution of *Gonosz* (Evil One) for 'the fiend', and the magnificent effect of the catalogue of words describing Satan's movement through pairs of internal rhymes (*úszik–csúsz, merűl–repűl*) lend immediacy and speed to the passage, as a result of which Milton's distant glimpse of Satan's toil becomes in the Hungarian version an imminently threatening, horrifying vision of the unobstructed progress of evil. A similarly spectacular effect is achieved, again through internal rhymes, when at the end of Book 2 Satan manages to leave Chaos behind:

> *Satan* with less toil, and now with ease
> Wafts on the calmer wave by dubious light
> And like a weather-beaten Vessel holds
> Gladly the Port, though Shrouds and Tackle torn
> Or in the emptier waste, resembling Air,
> Weighs his spread wings, at leasure to behold
> Farr off th'Empyreal Heav'n, extended wide
> In circuit, undetermind square or round (*PL* 2.1041–8)

> *Sátán, nyugodva már, majd könnyedén*
> *száll a derengő, csöndesült habon,*
> *ahogy viharcert hajó, boldogan*
> *fut **révbe**, bár kötél, vitorla **tépve**;*
> *vagy az üresebb és **légszerű térben***
> *lebeg tárt szárnyon, ked**vére** vigyázván*
> *távolról a Fény-Ég négyszögletes, vagy*
> *tán gömbalakú, roppant birodalmát*[66]

(Satan, calm now, then easily / flies on the dawning, quiet waves / like a tempest-beaten ship happily / runs to port, although its ropes and sail are torn; / or in the emptier and more air-like space / hovers on extended wings, watching at will / from afar the Light Sky's square, or / perhaps spherical, immense empire.)

As Satan's predicament in Chaos gradually abates and his situation becomes more hopeful, the diction becomes smoother and the repetition of the *é–e* sounds positively rocks readers into idyllic complacency, while it also anticipates Satan's destination: **Éden**.

Szabó's version is, however, not interesting merely as a poetic tour de force, but also as a series of reflections on how and why Milton might have mattered for the translator – and, by extension, his audience – at the end of the 1940s. We find this in his translation of the invocation to Book 1:

> Of Mans First Disobedience, and the Fruit
> Of that Forbidden Tree, whose mortal tast
> Brought Death into the World, and all our woe . . .
> That to the highth of this great Argument
> I may assert Eternal Providence,
> And justifie the wayes of God to men. (*PL* 1.1–3, 24–6)

> *Az Ember törvényszegését, az elsőt,*
> *s a tiltott Fa gyümölcsét, mely halállal*
> *mérgezte létünk, s kínt szült ...*
> *hogy tárgyam magasán védhessem az*
> *Örök Gondviselést és igazoljam*
> *emberek előtt Isten útjait.*[67]

(Of Man's break of law, the first, / and the fruit of the forbidden Tree, which with death / poisoned our existence and gave birth to misery . . . I may defend / Eternal Providence and justify / before men the ways of God.)

The translation is remarkable for how it foregrounds certain aspects of Milton's original. Rendering disobedience by *törvényszegés* (break of law), Szabó highlights a legal framework which will also influence the expressions *véd* (defend, for Milton's 'assert', see *OED* 2) and *igazol* (justify) – themselves emphatically placed at the end of lines. A legalistic interpretation of the original sin is of course part of Milton's theodicy: as Alison Chapman points out, the poet 'invites his readers to judge the ways of God not only according to reason and conscience, but also according to widespread ideas about legal justice',[68] but the terminology employed by Szabó seems to tip the balance in favour of the world of human law and human courts. As Zoltán Kulcsár-Szabó points out, the appearance of legal vocabulary and judicial themes in the Hungarian literature of the first part of the twentieth century is part of a general, late modern trend,[69] but the word *igazol* (justify) in Milton's invocation must have been especially loaded for Szabó, who was subjected to two 'procedures of justification' in 1945. Szabó's choice of allotting equal significance to the audience and the object of this justification (by reversing the syntactical order: 'before men the ways of God') also suggests acute sensitivity to the human dimension in the cosmic drama of redemption. This impression is strengthened by Szabó's substitution of the metaphor of poisoning for the original's reference to the 'mortal tast' of the fruit, and the fact that his is the only Hungarian version that brings out the motif of birth implicit in the original's 'Brought . . . into the World'. The metaphor of poisoning seems to echo the phrasing of the earliest surviving Hungarian prose text, the late twelfth-century *Funeral Sermon and Prayer* (*Halotti beszéd és könyörgés*), a well-known cultural landmark for most Hungarian speakers which also opens with the evocation of the Creation and the Fall. Szabó's version thus evokes the very experience of death and mourning rather than the abstract notion or the allegorical figure present at this point in Milton's epic.[70] Additionally, in Szabó's version it is 'our existence' that is 'with death poisoned': his focus is again clearly on the human drama of the Fall, and the consequences seem more fatal. Such highly idiosyncratic but powerful renditions of the keywords of Milton's invocation must have resonated well with the audience still reeling from, and gradually reckoning with, the enormity of the tragedy of World War II.

Szabó thus engages his audience with directness and intensity, and his text is informed by an acute awareness of how Milton's poetry might be used to reflect on both modern humanity's general and his own personal predicament. Based on his published work we can say that his genius was predominantly lyrical, which explains his selection of intimate paradisal scenes (which are standard anthology pieces in English-language publishing) for translation, but also lends special potency to several instances of poetic self-fashioning in the invocations. When, for example, Milton complains about his blindness and how he is 'Cut off' from 'the chearful wayes of men' (*PL* 3.46–7), Szabó translates *a nép vidám útjai / tilosak* ('the cheerful ways of the people / are forbidden'),[71] aggravating the pathos of Milton's description of visual deprivation with the implication of a legal interdiction. The personal implications of the situation depicted become even more pronounced if we consider that the expression Szabó uses (*a nép vidám útjai* – 'the cheerful ways of the people') evokes both an idealised, rustic image of ethnic community promoted by the so-called *népi* movement that Szabó sympathised with[72] and the discourse preferred and propagated by communist ideologues, thereby reflecting elegiacally on Szabó's exclusion from major segments of the post-war literary scene.

The most splendid reflection of Szabó's lyric energies is, however, in the figure and speeches of Satan. The fallen angel's stalwart and defiant, yet deeply angst-ridden character was a special inspiration for Szabó: in one of his diary entries he talks about the need to 'bow down before the sinner, the future sinner, frightened and shocked, regretfully and in terror' (Leborulni a bűnös, a leendő bűnös előtt, *rémülten és megrendülve, sajnálkozva és rettegve*), and he singles out 'Satan in Milton!!' (*Miltonban a Sátán!!*) as an example of the 'pure' (*tiszta*) thought and sentiment of 'the great Sinners, the great enthusiasts, the great fallen ones' (*A nagy bűnösök, nagy rajongók, nagy el- bukottak!*).[73] As we have seen above, Szabó's infatuation with powerful dictator figures informed the pieces (the revised poem 'Vezér' and his two reports on Hitler's speech) which proved to be the most objectionable to post-war cultural policymakers and which therefore incurred the 'procedures of justification', but it is clear from the title of one of his early volumes of poetry (*A Sátán műremekei – The Masterpieces of Satan*, 1926) as well as his posthumously published poem 'Under siege' ('Ostromzár alatt') that he found Milton's Satan especially captivating.

> *Mondják, sárkányok futnak rajtad át*
> *s nem is tudsz róluk, kígyók, sugarak,*
> *kik egekből egekbe ugranak,*
> *mindenségjáró villámkatonák,*
> *rémálmoknál rémítőbb fénycsodák,*
> *s hogy, bár nincsenek rá érzékeid,*
> *benned kicsiben ugyanaz folyik,*
> *ugyanaz a háború: a Világ*
> *óriás-törpe véletlene vagy,*
> *s azt, amin kívűl nincs számodra hely,*
> *Föld-hazádat tűz s csillagközi fagy*
> *folyton úgy ostromolja, szörny erő,*
> *ahogy a regék hajnala előtt*
> *rohamozta, s Miltonban, Lucifer.*[74]

(They say dragons are running through you, / and you don't even know about them, serpents, rays, / which leap from sky to sky, / world-soldiers traversing the universe, / light-wonders more terrible than nightmares, / and that, although you cannot perceive it, / the same takes place in you in miniature, / the same war: of the

World / you are a gigantic-dwarfish accident / and that outside of which there is no place for you / your Earth-home, is by fire and interstellar frost / besieged constantly, monstrous force, as before the dawn of fables / it was stormed, and, in Milton, by Lucifer.)

The putative parallels between turbulent cosmic phenomena and the struggles of the self in this poem achieve mythic dimensions through a range of Miltonic allusions, from the less direct 'dragons', 'serpents' and 'light wonders' to the explicit evocation of Milton's Lucifer. Importantly, however, the poem does not stay on the level of meditating the correspondence of macro- and microcosm. Szabó's description of the 'Earth-home' (*Föld-hazád*) as 'that outside of which there is no place for you' (*az, amin kívűl nincs számodra hely*) evokes verbatim the poem entitled 'Appeal' ('Szózat') by the nineteenth-century Romantic poet Mihály Vörösmarty, which, as Lóránt Czigány points out 'became a sort of second national anthem for Hungarians on account of its basic premiss: its irresistible message demanded unconditional and unflinching loyalty from each member of the then emerging nation.'[75] The description of the 'gigantic-dwarfish' self at once accommodating and embattled by Satanic forces thus also invites reflections on modern Hungarian-ness in general as well as the role of Hungarian artists in particular – with the inevitable implication that the apostrophised general 'you' in the poem is in fact the medium for Szabó's poetic self-presentation. Considering this example, it is no wonder that Szabó's lifelong involvement with the figure of Satan results, in his translation of *Paradise Lost*, in a memorable portrait of Milton's fallen angel monumental in ambition and fired by lyric acumen:

> The mind is its own place, and in it self
> Can make a Heav'n of Hell, a Hell of Heav'n.
> What matter where, if I be still the same,
> And what I should be, all but less then he
> Whom Thunder hath made greater? (*PL* 1.254–8)

> *Saját világa a szív, önmagában*
> *Eget Pokollá tehet, s Poklot Éggé,*
> *mit számít, hogy: hol, ha én én vagyok,*
> *s mit, hogy mi, ha nem kisebb Nála, kit*
> *mennyköve megnövelt?*[76]

(The heart is its own world, in itself / can make a Hell of Heaven, and a Heaven of Hell, / what does it count where [I am] if I am myself, / and [what does it count] what [I am], if not smaller than Him whom / Thunder has magnified.)

Interpreting Satan's 'mind' as *szív* (heart), changing the English 'place' for *világ* (world), and swapping the original narrative order of locations ('Hell of Heaven' first instead of 'Heav'n of Hell'), Szabó creates a microcosm of despair, a very private experience of Hell, but at the same time illustrates Satan's superior, sacrilegious pride with the emphatic self-identification 'I am myself' (recalling the biblical assertion of the Godhead). In the rapid colloquial thrust of monosyllabic words the fallen archangel's self-justification shows him vulnerable, yet immensely powerful, as a result of which the passage gives readers a vivid impression of what Milton terms (in describing Beelzebub) 'Majestic though in ruin' (*PL* 2.305) and Szabó *fenség, bár csupa rom* ('sublimity/majesty, although entirely in ruins').

Of course one cannot help but read into this compelling representation of Satan Szabó's strong interest in, and attention to, dictator figures and their impact on their audiences. Indeed, if we compare his translation of the dissolution of the infernal council in Book 2 with his account of Hitler's 1939 speech, the parallels in the two descriptions are astonishing:

> at once with him they rose;
> Thir rising all at once was as the sound
> Of Thunder heard remote. Towards him they bend
> With awful reverence prone; and as a God
> Extoll him equal to the highest in Heav'n:
> Nor fail'd they to express how much they prais'd,
> That for the general safety he despis'd
> His own (*PL* 2.475–82)

> *Mind fölkelt, együtt vele,*
> *s együttes keltük mint valami messze*
> *mennydörgés, zúgott. Feléje hajolnak*
> *ijedt hódolatban, s Isten gyanánt*
> *ünneplik, egyszint a Menny Fő-Urával.*[77]

(They all rose, together with him, / and their rising together like some remote / thunder roared. They lean toward him / in frightened reverence, and as God / they celebrate him, on the same level as the Chief Lord of Heaven)

Csak a zárójelenetben nő hozzá méltóvá a hallgatóság, a birodalom képviselő-testülete, amikor a két himnusz mennydörgésében igazán félelmes, elszánt és amellett meghitt egységbe olvad egyén és nép, vezér és vezetett. A földszint egyenruhában csillogó képviselőserege, a háttér katonaméltóságai, a diplomaták karzata és a két erkély közönsége akaratlanul felállt, amikor szólásra hívta az elnöklő Göring.[78]

(It is only in the final scene [of the ceremony in the Reichstag before Hitler's speech] that the audience, the representative body of the empire, rises to his [Hitler's] worth, when in the thunder of the two anthems, the individual and the people, the leader and the led, merge into a truly frightful, resolute and yet intimate unity. The glittering army of MPs in uniform on the ground floor, the military dignitaries in the background, the diplomatic corps and the audience on the two balconies involuntarily rose to their feet when the presiding Goering called on him to speak.)

Mesmerised by Hitler's oratorical skills, Szabó describes him as 'An artist wrestling with fate when he is speaking' (*Művész, aki a sorssal birkózik, amikor beszél*).[79] The same is largely true of his representation of Satan, except that here Szabó is also keenly aware of the fallen angel's hubris:

> High on a Throne of Royal State, which far
> Outshon the wealth of Ormus and of Ind,
> Or where the gorgeous East with richest hand
> Showrs on her Kings Barbaric Pearl and Gold,
> Satan exalted sat, by merit rais'd
> To that bad eminence; and from despair
> Thus high uplifted beyond hope, aspires
> Beyond thus high, insatiate to pursue
> Vain Warr with Heav'n, and by success untaught
> His proud imaginations thus displaid. (PL 2. 1–10)

> *Királyi trónján fent, mely messze túl-*
> *ragyogta kincses Ormuzt s Indiát*
> *s hol csak esőz dús gyöngyöt s aranyat*
> *vad uraira a Pazar Kelet,*
> *büszkén ült Sátán: érdem vitte ily*
> *gonosz fenségbe; kétségbeesésből*
> *reményen túltörve s túlon is*

*túlvágyik, hiu harcát telhetetlen
folytatni a Mennyel; s mert [nem] okúlt,
így fejtette ki gőgös terveit.*[80]

(High on his royal throne which far out- / shone Ormuz and India full of treasures, / and where rich pearls and gold are raining / on its wild Lords from the luxurious East, / Satan sat proudly: merit brought him to such / evil majesty; from despair / breaking through hope, and even beyond / what is beyond aspiring, his vain struggle insatiable / to continue with Heaven, and since he did [not] learn, / this is how he laid out his haughty plans.)

If Milton is censorious of the figure of Satan masquerading in royal pomp, Szabó's description makes the rebel angel outright repulsive. Instead of the exotic 'Barbaric' kings, in Szabó's version Satan is compared to the 'wild Lords' (*vad urai*) of the East, a stereotypical commonplace of lawless tyrants, and the only thing his 'merit' (*érdem*) achieves is 'evil majesty' (*gonosz fenség*) – which, in turn, casts doubt on his merit. The (self-)destructive excess in his personality is brilliantly illustrated by Szabó's repetition of the word *túl* (an adverb or verbal prefix with the meanings 'overly', 'excessively', 'beyond', 'past'), but by rendering 'proud imaginations' as 'haughty plans' (*gőgös tervei*) the translator also intimates a sense of Satan's aggressive, calculating nature. Although Szabó never got as far as Book 5 in his translation, in such passages we are reminded of Abdiel's diagnosis of Satan's irreversible corruption: 'I see thy Fall / Determind' (*PL* 5.878–9).

Szabó's engagement with the figure of Satan, however, reached beyond a (conscious or unconscious) reckoning with his own pre-war predilections and the resulting perceptive reading of the fallen angel's individual tragedy. He was also attentive to the political contexts in which Satan's character was functioning both within the text and its historical reception. For example, when he translates 'Better to reign in Hell, then serve in Heav'n' (*PL* 1.263) as *jobb itt a trón, mint a rabság a Mennyben* ('the throne is better here than captivity in Heaven'),[81] he evokes the language of nineteenth-century Hungarian nationalism and the struggle against Habsburg domination. Similarly, Szabó uses the slightly archaic word *pártütő* ('rebel' or 'insurgent', a favourite expression of nineteenth-century poets) several times for Satan and his 'rebellious rout' (*PL* 1.747). His view of rebellion is, however, far from being simply nostalgic: when the fallen angels indulge in 'partial', i.e. polyphonic and/or biased song (*PL* 2.552), Szabó's version reads

> Thir Song was partial, but the harmony
> (What could it less when Spirits immortal sing?)
> Suspended Hell, and took with ravishment
> The thronging audience. (*PL* 2.552–5)

> *Daluk pártos volt, de a szelíd összhang*
> *(s örök szellem dala mi volna más?)*
> *enyhítette a Poklot s elbüvölte*
> *hallgatói tömegét.*[82]

> (Their song was partisan, but the gentle harmony / (what else would be the song of an eternal spirit?) / alleviated Hell, and charmed the masses of their audience.)

The 'charmed audience' once again recalls Szabó's interest in mesmerised masses, but significantly, here it is a 'partisan' (*pártos*) song that enthrals them. As Szabó was well aware, an important change in the meaning of the word *pártos* was taking place at the time he was translating Milton's epic: in nineteenth- and early twentieth-century poetry it was used to denote strongly biased or even rebellious persons or ideas, but after World War II it started to acquire the additional significance of somebody complying with the official party line. Around the 'year of change' (1948) the word was already used favourably in communist cultural propaganda. As one editorial of the daily *Magyar Nemzet* puts it in 1949:

> *Pártatlan irodalom nem volt, nincs és nem is lehet. A haladó írók minden időben a pártos írók közé tartoztak. Pártos volt Homérosz, pártos volt Dante, pártos volt Shakespeare, pártos volt Molière, pártos volt Goethe, pártos volt Petőfi, pártos volt Ady és pártos volt József Attila is. Mi a nép érdekeit szolgáló, pártos irodalmat akarunk.*[83]

> (There has never been and there can never be impartial literature. Progressive writers were partisan writers at all times. Homer was partisan, Dante was partisan, Shakespeare was partisan, Molière was partisan. Goethe was partisan, Petőfi was partisan, Ady was partisan, and Attila József was partisan. We want partisan literature serving the interest of the people.)

Although Szabó's text evokes the original meaning of the expression *pártos*, his translation is also a bold (self-)critical reflection on artists enticed by propaganda with blind partisan zeal – and in this respect it is probably a moot point whether he meant the pre-war or the post-war version of totalitarianism. Instead of 'suspending', i.e. deferring Hell, one possible meaning of the Miltonic original, in Szabó's version the song of the fallen angels merely 'alleviates' its pains, 'enchanting' rather than transporting the hearers. For all his admiration for the great rebel, Satan, it seems that Szabó at this point in his life was rather uneasy about how the idea of rebellion could be hijacked and misrepresented in the world of artists. Perhaps this is also why in the letter to his lover quoted at the beginning of this chapter he mentioned Milton together with 'unknown evils': the translation inevitably became a record of, and a critical reflection on, his – and by extension many other artists' – artistic and political, public and private vicissitudes before and after World War II.

We could go on enumerating the various virtues of Szabó's translation, but even from these short excerpts it becomes clear that he created one of the most original interpretations of Milton's epic in the twentieth century. Both as a poet and a translator Szabó was eminently qualified for translating *Paradise Lost*, and as we have seen above, his constant struggle with his own demons, his problematic position and the general political situation after World War II in many ways promoted rather than hindered his project. This remained true to the end of his life: after the 1956 revolution he turned for the first time to a kind of public, political lyric, which would probably have strengthened his spiritual kinship with the author of *Paradise Lost*.[84] But he died in 1957, while in the late 1940s it was the rapidly changing tide of cultural and editorial policy and to a considerable extent his own compromised position that made it impossible for him to progress with the work. Adapting Alexander Pope's verdict about John Dryden as a translator, we may only say that it is a 'great Loss to the Poetical World' that Szabó 'did not live to translate' *Paradise Lost* in its entirety.[85]

'In Milton's prison': István Jánosy's translation of *Paradise Lost*

Having come to maturity among the great poets of the early twentieth century (most of whom died before 1945), Szabó was one of the survivors of the pre-war past and his seniority guaranteed him a certain degree of artistic autonomy, even if his position was politically precarious. As we have seen above, his translation of *Paradise Lost* is as much informed by his reckoning with the pre-war world (and his own role as an artist in it) as by the 'new world' of communist dictatorship. In the late 1940s and 1950s he obviously had to maintain close contact with the new cultural elite, but he remained, as far as we can judge, unaffected by the prevalent

'Marxist' tendencies in literature and literary criticism. Roughly at the time of Szabó's death these critical tendencies were also laid to rest, or at least neutralised. The zealous, mechanical, openly biased 'Marxist-Leninist' (in effect, rather Stalinist) approach of Tibor Lutter and his ilk quickly went out of fashion after 1956. The 'partisan' spirit did not completely disappear – even as late as 1967 we find a piece of criticism lambasting the New Critics for 'deliberately rejecting the ravishing power of Milton's revolutionary vision' (*elzárkózott Milton forradalmi látomásának magával ragadó ereje elől*)[86] – but the general atmosphere of the 'consolidation era' became gradually more tolerant, if somewhat belatedly, towards certain modern ideas in Western scholarship. Marxist critics, especially Christopher Hill, were still among the favourites, but students and professors of English studies had more access to foreign books and could occasionally travel to the West. As we will see in Chapter 3, this era was dominated by the basically benign influence of Miklós Szenczi, who, in spite of the many compromises he was willing, or forced, to make during his career due to political reasons, managed to preserve his own scholarly integrity as well as to mediate, and even contribute to, some of the international trends in Milton scholarship.

From the restarting of his career in 1956, Szenczi strove to promote Milton and his work among both Hungarian scholars and the wider reading public,[87] but in 1971 he also contributed a long English-language article to a collection of essays (entitled *Studies in English and American Philology*) published by the English Department of Eötvös Loránt University (ELTE). According to the editors of this volume (Szenczi among them), the 'contents [of this collection] seem to have a certain unity, owing to the fact that most of the contributors approach the problems under discussion with a claim to Marxist interpretation',[88] but, as the cautious phrasing suggests, in many cases this is merely a conformity on the surface. Szenczi's article is a case in point: depending on the reader's background, the title of his essay ('Milton's dialectic in *Paradise Lost*') can be interpreted in different ways. For an international audience, Szenczi's choice of the word 'dialectic' would probably suggest a strong focus on philosophy from perhaps Kantian, Hegelian or Marxist perspectives. For readers from the Eastern bloc the term rang a different bell as it clearly evoked the 'materialist dialectic' of Marxist-Leninist thought, a central tenet of the indoctrinating programmes which were present in education from secondary school upwards.

The article delivers on both accounts, although with different intensity: Szenczi engages in a philosophical discussion of what he calls the paradoxes of *Paradise Lost* (aspects of the plot, Milton's attitude to his subject, and the ups and downs of historical reception), and positions them in a balanced, up-to-date critical context, but he also peppers his argument with harmless commonplace references to Marx and Engels.[89] It is true that in the conclusion of his article, he insists that Milton does matter in contemporary Hungarian 'socialist' society, but his emphasis is clearly on Milton's achievement rather than the revolutionary aspects of his work or of his modern critics:

> It is a tribute to Milton's genius, an evidence of the universal appeal of *Paradise Lost*, that the full text of a seventeenth-century religious epic and the dramatic version of a Biblical story could find such favour, to be felt to be an adequate statement of the human situation in a country engaged in the reconstruction of society on socialist lines and professing a secular, scientific outlook.[90]

The 'full text' and the 'dramatic version' of Milton's epic Szenczi refers to are the 1969 translation of *Paradise Lost* by István Jánosy, and its theatrical adaptation which was staged in 1970. In both of these Szenczi was a major contributor: he provided the essential philological background to the translator's work, compiled a concise critical commentary and an important biographical essay ('Milton Agonistes') to the translation, and he also worked with the translator and director Károly Kazimir on the theatrical script. In the following reflections on Jánosy's translation and the performance directed by Kazimir, therefore, we should bear in mind that some aspects of these productions might well be attributed to Szenczi's influence.

István Jánosy (not a relative of the nineteenth-century translator Gusztáv Jánosi) was close to the intellectual circle of the *Újhold* literary periodical (published from 1946 to 1948), which carried on the progressive heritage of the *Nyugat*.[91] Besides being a poet, Jánosy was a prolific translator, which was a forced career path – not only for him, but also for many authors of his generation. From the 1950s well into the 1980s the state exerted strong control over the publishing industry, and the printing of 'tolerated' (let alone 'banned') writers was often disallowed or deferred.[92] Simultaneously with these restrictions, some of these writers were commissioned by state- (i.e. party-)controlled publishing houses to translate classic works, as we have already seen in the case of Lőrinc Szabó; indeed, for several of them translation was the only means of artistic expression. These restrictions resulted in something of a small-scale 'golden age' for literary translation: what was a curse for many outstanding authors (who had access only to this form of publication) proved a blessing to the Hungarian readers who were treated to high-quality translations (but were deprived of the translators' original works). Jánosy's translation of *Paradise Lost* was in several ways the product of, but also a possible corrective to, these trends in socialist cultural policy. Educated as a Lutheran theologian and preacher, Jánosy certainly could not be accused of over-faithfulness to the party line. He must have felt the strange ambivalence resulting from the socialist state's control over his work as he records his struggle with the translation in several essays, one of which bears the title 'In Milton's prison' – suggesting that the commission to translate was more of 'an offer he couldn't refuse' than a heartfelt choice. In an English-language article (published in the *New Hungarian Quarterly*) adapting much of 'In Milton's prison' Jánosy catalogued his dislike of some aspects of Milton's epic: he found, for instance, the whole task anachronistic – albeit through the anachronistic lens of T. S. Eliot's criticism of Milton – and he considered the strictness of God in Book 3 or the Son's martial victory in Book 6 'outright repellent'.[93] At the same time, he claims that Milton is 'one of the most modern poets who throws prophetic light . . . on the most serious questions of our century':

> The questions raised by the armaments race, the atomic war, the population explosion, the frightening gulf between poor and rich nations, the possibilities of genetic manipulation, the dislocation of ecological balance, the pollution of the environment, the apparently irremediable ills of urban life, the spread of drugs and many other disturbing issues are reflected in the Miltonian symbolism of the Tree of Knowledge.[94]

Thus, for Jánosy, Milton matters because – in spite of his anachronistic project and quaint theology – his interpretation of the ancient biblical story is a prophetic myth about the permanent sense of crisis besetting modernity. According to the translator, the language used for the narrative representation of this symbolic myth is an essential part of the reading experience:

> When I began to translate the work, I found the majestic, murmuring monotone of the lines slowly exerting a tranquilising effect, and I became conscious of writing line after line with increasing attachment, even with passion. Why? Because the mysterious music emanating from this sublime yet austere poetry penetrated the depths of my heart and quickened my innermost nature like Beethoven's five last string quartets. *Es muss sein* [it must be].[95]

The special poetic language adopted by Jánosy is one of the aspects of his translation where the translator's ambivalence towards the project proves ultimately productive. Jánosy's idiom reflects the remoteness, but also the astonishing topicality of *Paradise Lost*: he sprinkles the contemporary Hungarian text with archaic words, or expressions from the Protestant Bible (the 'Károlyi' Bible of 1590), uses pleasantly irregular blank verse, often alludes to the versions of his predecessors (Jánosi and Szabó), and is keen to reproduce some effects of the original (puns, enjambments, etc.). As far as the aural effect of the translation is concerned, the result is spectacular: not only does the diction manage to reflect something of the 'Babylonish dialect' of the original (a phrase Samuel Johnson adopted from Samuel Butler to describe Milton's poetic language), but it also puts readers on alert, thus contributing to the effect described by Stanley Fish in *Surprised by Sin*: they become aware of what is at stake in the plot as well as of their own performance. For an example let us take a look at part of the invocation of the first book:

> Of Mans First Disobedience, and the Fruit
> Of that Forbidden Tree, whose mortal tast
> Brought Death into the World, and all our woe . . .
> That to the highth of this great Argument
> I may assert Eternal Providence,
> And justifie the wayes of God to men. (*PL* 1.1–3, 24–6)

> *Az ember legelső bűnét, s a tiltott*
> *fa gyümölcséből-kóstolást, amely*
> *halált hozott a földre, kínt reánk . . .*
> *hirdessem az örök Gondviselést,*
> *s embernek igazoljam Isten útját.*[96]

> (Of man's very first sin, and from the forbidden / tree fruit-tasting that / brought death to this earth and misery on us . . . I may preach/ proclaim Divine / Providence and justify the way of God to man.)

Jánosy mixes real archaisms (*reánk*), archaic-sounding expressions and compounds (*Isten útját, gyümölcséből-kóstolást*) and simple words current in modern Hungarian. He translates 'disobedience' as *bűn* (sin), and uses the verb *hirdet* for 'assert' which, as Péter Dávidházi has pointed out, carries the double meaning of 'announcing' and 'preaching'.[97] The choice of words is not accidental: in Jánosy's version the narrator soaring 'Above th'*Aonian* Mount' and ambitiously pursuing 'Things unattempted yet in Prose or Rhime' (*PL* 1.15–16) also sounds like a preacher delivering a sermon from the pulpit, an effect reinforced by Jánosy's bold use of the singular *embernek* ('to man') for Milton's 'men' in the last line. Thus, while Szabó's version of the invocation engages readers with its brisk and intense modernity reflecting on the legal aspects of justification, Jánosy's text surprises us with the mixing of the epic and the predicatory sublime.

The theologically oriented interpretation of the prayer-like invocations is just one possible use of Jánosy's special fusion of the archaic and the modern for a special effect. Far from being a rigid medium, Jánosy's idiom functions like a kind of epic *Kunstsprache* (artificial speech) that can be modulated according to the requirements of plot or character. Translating the climactic lines from Satan's Niphates soliloquy, for example, Jánosy writes:

> So farwel Hope, and with Hope farwel Fear,
> Farwel Remorse: all Good to me is lost;
> Evil be thou my Good (*PL* 4.108–10)

> *Isten hozzád, remény és rettegés,*
> *szív-furdalás! Minden jó veszve nékem!*
> *Rossz, légy te üdvöm!*[98]

> (God be with you, hope and terror, / heart-pangs! All good is lost for me! / Evil, be my salvation!)

Jánosy here also lends a distinctly archaic (and therefore slightly heroic) tinge to the text by adapting the translation of the line 'Farwel Remorse: all Good to me is lost' from his nineteenth-century predecessor, Gusztáv Jánosi.[99] However, he brings this into contrast with the rough modernity of *rettegés* (terror), and also adds dark irony to the passage by translating 'Farwell' with the traditional form of goodbye ('God be with you') and by substituting *üdv* (salvation) for 'Good'. In this mixing of registers and contexts we get a distinct glimpse of Satan's desperate, indignant and ultimately confused attempt to retain his heroic pose, but also a clear suggestion about the perversity of his enterprise.

The translations's linguistic ingenuity is complemented by Jánosy's attention to the system of motifs and cross-references within Milton's epic, sometimes even at the expense of slightly departing from the original, as in the description of Abdiel's taking leave of the rebel angels in the concluding lines to Book 5:

> From amidst them forth he passd,
> Long way through hostile scorn, which he susteind
> Superior, nor of violence fear'd aught;

And with retorted scorn his back he turn'd
On those proud Towrs to swift destruction doom'd. (*PL* 5.903–7)

Közöttük elvonult,
Bár rázúdult az ellen gúnya, mit
Fölénnyel tűrt, s harctól se rettegett.
Gúnnyal felelve hátat fordított
A vészre ítélt, hetvenkedő Toronynak.[100]

(He passed among them, / although the scorn of the adversary was poured on him which / he bore with superiority, nor was terrified of combat. / Replying with scorn he turned his back / on the doomed, swaggering Tower.)

The scorn 'pouring on' Abdiel clearly evokes – for Adam as well as the reader – the 'Hoarce murmur' of Satan's evil crew, likened by the narrator to 'the sound of waters deep' (*PL* 5.872–3) some 30 lines before. In extending this motif from simile to narrative Jánosy, perhaps unconsciously, reinforces the prelapsarian immediacy that characterises the communication of Adam and Raphael in the embedded narratives of Books 5–7.[101] What is more, while in the passage quoted above Milton's 'proud Towrs' refers to the 'Palace of great *Lucifer*' (*PL* 5.760), Jánosy's 'swaggering Tower' is apparently also Satan who, as readers might remember, in Book 1 'Stood like a Towr' (*PL* 1.591). This bold, and perhaps not un-Miltonic, transformation of the original leaves readers at the end of Book 5 with an image of Satan ridiculous rather than heroic in his towering rigidity.

It seems, then, that Jánosy opted for a more historicised, and perhaps also more comprehensive and balanced, albeit certainly less edgy version of *Paradise Lost*. His version is informed not so much by conflicting energies (as Szabó's certainly is), but rather by a tendency to reconcile received and modern interpretations. His Satan, for example, is less of a splendid rebel when he says *Inkább Pokolban úr, mint szolga Égben* ('rather a Lord in Hell than a servant in Heaven'; compare Szabó's version above), but the loss of pathos is compensated by intercultural depth. Jánosy's phrasing duly reproduces the classical (Odyssean) allusion implicit in the original,[102] but by translating the Miltonic verb 'reign' with the noun *úr* (lord) he also evokes, perhaps ironically, the Old Testament, and in the contrast of *úr* (lord) and *szolga* (servant) the communist vocabulary of the class struggle.

Another example offers itself in Jánosy's translation of the 'factious opposition' of postlapsarian history (*PL* 11.664) as *pártvillongás*, a slightly archaic word denoting the conflict between political parties, but one which in the Kádár era was sometimes used to refer to internal struggles within the Communist Party (cf. the collocation *belső pártvillongás*, internal strife in a party). In these examples Jánosy is treading cautiously: his choice of words can be interpreted as attempts to historicise the text and remove it from the possibility of immediate applicability, but the same phrases also seem to preserve faint echoes of contemporary political discourse. Such compromises between various interpretive possibilities are also apparent in the way he adopts his predecessors' work. In the description of the fallen angels' pastime in Hell, for example, he harks back to Szabó's version:

> Thir Song was partial, but the harmony
> (What could it less when Spirits immortal sing?)
> Suspended Hell, and took with ravishment
> The thronging audience. (PL 2.552–5)

> ... *daluk bár pártos, összecseng,*
> *(össze, hisz halhatatlanok dala),*
> *s elzsongatja a Poklot, bűvöli*
> *sok hallgatóit.*[103]

> (Their song, although partisan, harmonises / (it does, since it is the song of immortals), and entrances Hell, enchants / its many listeners).

While Szabó emphasised the currency of the word *pártos* (partisan) by bringing it into focus at the beginning of the line, in Jánosy's version the word loses much of its strength in a concessive clause. In Szabó's version (quoted above) the song is primarily partisan, but its gentle harmony (*szelíd összhang*) alleviates (*enyhítette*) the misery of Hell and enchant (*bűvöl*) listeners. By contrast, in Jánosy it is the harmony that is emphasised: it enchants (*bűvöli*) listeners notwithstanding the fact the song is partisan. Importantly, Jánosy trades Szabó's clinical *enyhít* (alleviate) for *elzsongat* (entrance), which suggests a reduction in pain, but also the loss of consciousness (almost like a drug-induced delirium). The difference is tiny, but it tells a lot about the two translators' divergent perspectives on the creative process. Szabó is concerned about the (political) role of the artist, while Jánosy reflects critically on the effect of art (which might well be politically charged) on the audience. By muffling the direct personal and political stakes of his text, Jánosy, on the one hand, presents a compromise befitting the 'consolidation' era (and reminiscent of how Szenczi's critical work 'consolidated' Milton criticism after 1956),[104] but he also seems gently to call out his audience for being naively transported by art.

Jánosy's translation received general applause, with several reviewers emphasising its faithfulness to the original, and the way it makes available Milton's work and thought to the Hungarian audience in an accessible, modern version. Writing in the prestigious journal of world literature *Nagyvilág*, Antal Wéber cites Szenczi's essay 'Milton Agonistes' (which, as mentioned before, served as an afterword to Jánosy's translation) and emphatically proposed that instead of forming 'an easy-to-solve parable' (*megfejthető parabola*), the 'personal and historical implications' (*a személyhez és korhoz kötött mozzanatot*) of Milton's epic manifest themselves in the poet's 'monumental vision' (*a látomás monumentális voltában*), which comprises an ethics based on biblical and classical values as well as 'the nostalgies for greatness, dignity and happy harmony' (*a nagyság, a méltóság, és a boldog harmónia iránti nosztalgiákban*).[105]

Similarly, in a review published in the leading literary weekly *Élet és irodalom* Miklós Hernádi, after stating that 'everybody has to struggle with Milton in their own individual way' (*Miltonnal … mindenkinek meg kell vívnia a maga harcát*), suggested that the modern reader is astonished by the mere '*possibility* and the *realisation*' (lehetősége *és* megvalósulása) of Milton's work, and complimented the translator on 'the precise and discerning rendering of … *great forms*' (a *nagy formák* … pontos, értő visszaadása).[106] One cannot help but notice the fascination with Milton's great subject and grand style in these reviews: it seems that by the early 1970s, the 'progressive sublime' of the 1950s, in which the chief artistic merit of Milton's epic was its revolutionary potential, gave way to more traditional, and historically certainly more informed evaluations. However, these enthusiastic strains about the monumentality of Jánosy's translation also hint indirectly at what was felt to be missing from the physically and politically cramped, half-open world of the 1960s and 1970s. For Hungarian readers Jánosy's intuitions about the global topicality and symbolic significance of *Paradise Lost* seem to have rung true, and his work provided a glimpse through the Iron Curtain onto a larger world.

'Angels, hippies, and a bureaucrat': *Paradise Lost* on the Hungarian stage in 1970[107]

Jánosy's translation has had a splendid career: it was republished in 1978 and 1989, and to this day it has remained the standard Hungarian version of *Paradise Lost*.[108] For twenty-first-century readers its language might already seem dated and mannered, but, especially around the time of its publication, it was considered a long-awaited modern version of a little-known classic work. Its cultural importance is attested to by the fact that the neo-avant-garde director Károly Kazimir decided to adapt it for the stage in 1970. Kazimir's chief achievement is that with this landmark production he managed to make *Paradise Lost* available to a much larger audience than the 'fit . . . though few' (*PL* 7.31) whom Milton originally designated for his readership, but this production should also be noted for amplifying some of the critical tendencies in Jánosy's translation.

In 1959 Kazimir founded a summer venue known as the Theatre in the Round (Körszínház), and systematically started to direct experimental dramatised versions of the great epics of world literature. In the 1960s *Paradise Lost* was preceded on the stage by performances of Dante's *Divine Comedy* (1968) and the *Kalevala* (1969), and in the early 1970s it was followed by adaptations of the *Ramayana* (1971) and *Gilgamesh* (1975). In the composition of this repertoire we can see an attempt to reinterpret Milton's poem: the line-up of different epics means that the director's concern must have been more on presenting contrasting cosmic visions than on exploiting the 'revolutionary' energies of *Paradise Lost*. From the perspective of Milton studies, Kazimir's production is especially important, since it represents probably the first modern professional theatrical adaptation of Milton's work, which, as far as we know, evolved quite independently from Dryden's failed 1674 attempt (*The State of Innocence and Fall of Man*) and also preceded Hugh Richmond's 1988 staging of *Paradise Lost*.[109]

In the absence of any film footage of these performances, it is of course difficult to imagine the original atmosphere of the production. All the documents that remain point to an exceptional, experimental performance which very consciously aimed to create a dialogue between past and present, and between the West and communist Hungary. We can get at least a glimpse of what *Paradise Lost* on the Hungarian stage might have looked and sounded like if we turn to photographs, reviews and interviews about the production. The most extended trace of Kazimir's *Paradise Lost* is, however, the script (reproduced in the Appendix), which was prepared by Jánosy himself with the active help of Miklós Szenczi and the director and which provides the outlines of Kazimir's special interpretation of Milton's epic.

The typescript of the play comprises 89 pages. The play is divided into two parts and the cast features 19 characters: in addition to Milton's main actors (God, the Son, Satan, Adam, Eve, etc.), anonymous angels and devils are also featured. The text of the play is based on Jánosy's

Figure 1.1 György Szlovák's caricature of the 1970 performance of *Paradise Lost*, published in the 14 July 1970 issue of the daily *Magyar Nemzet*. The original caption reads: 'Az aktualizált Paradicsom angyalokkal, hippikkel és a bürokratával' (Paradise made topical with angels, hippies, and a bureaucrat). © HUNGART 2022.

translation with only minor alterations (about which more below), and the plot closely follows *Paradise Lost*. The only significant addition to the Miltonic material can be found towards the end (*EP* 2.1138–97),[110] where the Hungarian version includes some material from Imre Madách's *Tragedy of Man*, a nineteenth-century Hungarian drama (influenced to a large extent by Milton) whose status in Hungarian culture is somewhat similar to the position of *Paradise Lost* in the canon of English literature.[111] Inspired by the last two books of *Paradise Lost*, Madách's drama presents an extended vision of mankind's future, and the handful of new characters (i.e. Slave, St Peter, Patriarch, Skeleton, the Emperor Rudolph, Whore, Condemned Man, Quack Doctor, Musician, Elder, Plato, Eskimo – they do not appear in the *dramatis personae* of the script) make their brief appearances to provide a culturally accessible version of the history that the archangel Michael narrates in Milton's epic. Words and motifs from Madách's *Tragedy of Man* carry a strong cultural currency among Hungarians, and the astonishing effect of fusing the unfamiliar new Milton translation and the over-familiar Madách text must have been guaranteed – some reviewers at least found this aspect of the performance the most objectionable.[112]

Jánosy and Kazimir had to rework the original epic narrative in different, often unexpected ways. They either cut the descriptive parts and used them as stage directions (which do not appear in the typescript: we know them only from Jánosy's account of the production[113]),

Figure 1.2 Scene from the 7 July 1970 performance of *Paradise Lost* directed by Károly Kazimir; Vera Venczel as Eve, András Kozák as Adam and Cecília Esztergályos (lying down) as Raphael. Photograph by Imre Benkő. © MTI Fotó/Benkő Imre.

or included them in the characters' speeches. Satan's irritated soliloquy on the state of bliss in Paradise is, for instance, complemented by Adam and Eve's description of themselves (*EP* 1.488–553) – quite correctly, since in the epic we receive this information through Satan's narrative focus (cf. *PL* 4.285–6). It should also be noted that in this excerpt (and elsewhere) the translator and the director switch tenses to emphasise the present time of the performance.

Further, while in another famous late twentieth-century production of Milton's epic, Hugh Richmond's 1980s staging, the narrator (the blind Milton) was represented on stage,[114] in the Hungarian performance parts of the epic's invocations were distributed among the characters. The very beginning of the play is a cento of the invocations of Books 1 and 3, with Adam, Eve, Satan, Beelzebub, Belial, Moloch, Michael and Raphael each reciting one or two lines (1.1–72). As a metatheatrical device, this certainly helped to introduce the cast, but Jánosy and Kazimir also added some poignant touches of irony, as in Beelzebub's question to the Holy

Light: 'May I express thee unblam'd?' (*PL* 3.3; *EP* 1.42), and in Satan's reply 'Thee I re-visit now with bolder wing, / With other notes then to th'Orphean Lyre' (*PL* 3.13, 17; *EP* 1.47–8).

The cento-like arrangement of the original text remains characteristic of the entire play. This editorial technique creates interesting temporal and thematic correspondences between several strands of the plot. The intersections of different plotlines can highlight those aspects of the epic's original structure which usually become apparent only after several readings of the work. One such remarkable instance is the scene in which the council in Heaven in Book 3 is brought into relief by Satan's Niphates soliloquy in Book 4 (*EP* 1.456–89). In these lines Fall and redemption – which in Milton's original narrative are necessarily presented as temporally distinct events – are merged on a single time plane, a kind of eternal present emphasised by Satan's dogged questioning.

In the whole production there seems to have been a shift of emphasis from Milton's dynamic theodicy to the tragic consequences of the first human pair's actions against the background of the nuances of infernal and heavenly politics. Book 7 (the Creation) is entirely cut, which certainly accelerates the action, but also allows a sharper parallel between Satan's revolt and Adam's disobedience. Moreover, the witty rendition of the beginning of the infernal council ironically reflects on the use and misuse of power in both Heaven and Hell (*EP* 1.100–56). After Satan has called the fallen angels together using words from Book 6 ('O now in danger tri'd, now known in Armes', etc.; *PL* 6.418–24) and Book 1 ('Hail, horrours, hail', etc.; *PL* 1.250–63), the council proceeds in the order that we have in *Paradise Lost*, albeit according to a simplified structure. Interestingly, however, in the script the archangel Michael and two angels are also witnessing the scene; in fact, their 'asides' suggest they are on a spying mission.

> ANGEL 1: A secret conclave? (*PL* 1.795; *EP* 1.154)
>
> ANGEL 2: In close recess? (*PL* 1.795; *EP* 1.155)
>
> ANGEL 1: Let's go and report it! (*EP* 1.156)

The single un-Miltonic line in this excerpt ('Let's go and report it!') sets the whole scene into a new relief. While the zeal of the angel creates an essentially comic effect, it is also a chilly reminder that the communist government employed huge networks of agents from its own citizenry to spy on and report 'illegal' political activities. Moreover, the angel's use of the plural in proposing to report the 'secret conclave' points to how

Figure 1.3 Scene from the 7 July 1970 performance of *Paradise Lost*. The upper part of the stage represents Heaven with God sitting and the Son standing behind him; below, Adam and Eve are standing with the fallen angels sitting before them. Photograph by Imre Benkő. © MTI Fotó/Benkő Imre.

such systems encourage comradeship and complicity – not much differently from Satan's seemingly democratic system in Hell. Indeed, with this arrangement of the scene Jánosy and Kazimir seem to pass criticism on both Satan's and God's operations, against which the first human couple stand helplessly exposed.

Political aspects of the production were also quite apparent in the scenery. Satan and his crew were represented as hippies, and the music accompanying their scenes and movements was rock and roll. The 'counterculture' of the Summer of Love and the late 1960s was viewed with great suspicion by communist policymakers: hippies were declared to be victims complicit in the drug-fuelled decadence of rotting capitalism. At the same time, large swathes of Hungarian youth were keen to adapt and emulate progressive trends from the West (at least what they had access to). This ambivalence towards current popular culture was certainly reflected in the production. As Kazimir said in an interview:

Figure 1.4 Scene from the 7 July 1970 performance of *Paradise Lost*. The Son judging the first human couple. Vera Venczel as Eve (on her knees bowing down), András Kozák as Adam (kneeling) and Péter Vallai as the Son (behind them). Photograph by Imre Benkő. © MTI Fotó/ Benkő Imre.

> Satan . . . as I see him is neither disreputable nor Lucifer-like [i.e. like the character of Lucifer in Madách's *Tragedy of Man*]. He could just as well be the leader of some hippie gang at the flowery, mud-bespattered, merry-making Woodstock hippie festival, corrupted by the rottenness of the consumer society, yet hungering and thirsting after righteousness.[115]

Jánosy is of the same opinion:

> [Kazimir] was quick to see that eating the apple is very like taking LSD: an ecstatic 'trip' is followed by desperate depression and mutual accusation. They have abruptly changed into modern hippies; they make love in a narcotic ecstasy and afterwards turn on each other in an excess of revulsion.[116]

However, neither the director nor the translator seem to have been convinced of the absolute benevolence of heavenly powers: God wore the three-piece suits of bureaucrats complete with bowler hat and umbrella,

Figure 1.5 Scene from the 7 July 1970 performance of *Paradise Lost*. Vera Venczel as Eve, András Kozák as Adam. Photograph by Imre Benkő. © MTI Fotó/Benkő Imre.

his rigid posture on the throne all the more strengthened by excerpts from Bach accompanying his appearances and the group of uniformed angels surrounding him (the Son included). Indeed, the whole performance was – as one of the critics put it – a 'provocation in style'

Figure 1.6 Scene from the 7 July 1970 performance of *Paradise Lost*. Satan and his crew. Tibor Bitskey (in the centre) as Satan, to his left Péter Simon as Belial, to his right Ildikó Hámori as Sin, to her right Gábor Csikós as Moloch. Photograph by Imre Benkő. © MTI Fotó/ Benkő Imre.

(*stílusprovokáció*),[117] and the political implications of this eclectic staging were probably not lost on the contemporary audience. As another reviewer mused:

> Which is more modern, more profoundly twentieth-century? The character of Satan who by way of compensation for his earlier hymns of praise becomes a member of 'the opposition'? Or is it Raphael who almost becomes envious of man's fate of buying happiness through suffering?[118]

It seems, then, that for the Hungarian audience in 1970 Milton's 'play' struck a particularly modern note, one which keenly reflected the loneliness and weakness of humans as individuals and small communities against larger, inhuman systems of power which – on the level of propaganda – profess sympathy towards humanity, but are in fact overwhelmingly destructive in their operation. In this respect, the performance achieved the director's and the translator's aim that 'the irresistible

Figure 1.7 Scene from the 5 October 1970 performance of *Paradise Lost*. Samu Balázs as God, Péter Vallai as the Son and Mária Gór Nagy (to their right) as Michael. Photograph by Imre Benkő. © MTI Fotó/ Benkő Imre.

wealth, allurement and beauty of Milton's world should be brought to life again by all available means old and new, whether by ancient ceremony or modern montage'.[119]

The play was on stage for just one season, but, as the enthusiastic tone and number of reviews testify, the production proved a great success.[120] Word about the adaptation reached Miltonists in the West, too, albeit with some delay. In a 1972 issue of *Milton Quarterly* the Hungarian-born Paul E. Vesenyi published a short description of one of the opening nights (10 July 1970). Vesenyi is fully aware that staging Milton's epic is 'a rather delicate affair in regard to the ruling regime's allergy to biblical stories', but also that 'Mr Kazimir decided to adapt it not only to the stage but, in a certain way, also to time'.[121] Consequently, Vesenyi dwells at length on the modernising features of the play (partly enumerated above) to conclude that 'in this bold interpretation of *Paradise Lost*, Milton did not get lost'.[122] Intriguingly, Vesenyi, an émigré academic and writer, and Zsuzsanna Nemes G., a contemporary Hungarian critic, both single out the appearance of barbed wire at the end of the performance (in the exile scene) as one of the most remarkable modern features of the staging. However, while for Vesenyi the stage prop is a 'modern and accurate' symbol of 'twentieth-century... horrors and lost Edens' especially meaningful for 'the traveller who has just crossed the border between Vienna and Budapest', for Nemes G. – writing in the Marxist-leaning periodical *Kritika* – it evokes 'fascism and the inquisition', and proves that 'in the progress of our lives one of the most significant motifs is that of fighting against narrow-minded laws and lawful narrow-mindedness' (*életünk alakulásában a korlátolt törvények és a törvényes korlátoltság elleni harc motívuma az egyike a legjentősebbeknek*).[123]

Both critics are characteristically cautious and ambiguous: Vesenyi suggests that the reference to the Iron Curtain leaves no doubt about 'the director's intentions', but he does not specify what these are; Nemes G., on the other hand, claims that it is 'posterity – children' (*az utókor – a gyerekek*) who will put an end to 'narrow-mindedness', without going into details about what this means precisely. Nevertheless, it is clear that Vesenyi meant his remarks as a half-covert criticism of the communist regime, while Nemes G.'s observations sound more like indirect support for the Eastern bloc. It testifies to the power of Kazimir's special 'recomposition in performance' (to borrow a term from classical studies) of Milton's epic that in its critical reception it prompted a range of appreciative responses on such a wide political spectrum. While on the other side of the Iron Curtain, in American intellectual life Milton 'became a powerful historical point of reference in the shaping of postwar liberalism',[124] Kazimir's 1970 production of *Paradise Lost* performed a 'consolidation' fostered by, but also critical of, Kádár's 'consolidation era' by providing a forum for 'much arguing, much writing, [and] many opinions'.[125]

Notes

1. Szabó 1993, 85.
2. Szabó 2000, 402.
3. Milton 2007, 8.
4. Johnson 2009, 100, 114, 108.
5. Milton 1796, vol. 1, sig. a3r.
6. Milton 1930, xviii, xx, xxi. Cf. Károly (Carl) Kerényi, who in 1920 adapts the difficulty trope to the readerly pleasures and critical appreciation of *Paradise Lost*: 'For those who started to listen to it [Milton's epic song], how difficult it is to leave off, for those who have started to praise it, how difficult to fall silent' (*Aki hallgatni kezdte, olyan nehéz annak megválnia tőle, s aki dicsérni kezdte, elhallgatnia*). Kerényi 1984, 15.
7. Jánosy 1970, 216.
8. For more about this work, see Péti 2017.
9. See Szilágyi 1979.
10. Cf. how Milton 'could not hear with patience' when *Paradise Regained* was unfavourably compared with *Paradise Lost*. Darbishire 1932, 76.

11. Milton 1796, vol. 2, sig. A5ᵛ.
12. Szigeti 1970.
13. Lukácsy 1983, 1763.
14. Kriza 1893, 123. I would like to thank Veronika Ruttkay for this reference.
15. Harsányi 1837, 2.
16. In this Szász seems to echo Hippolyte Taine, whose history of English literature was enormously popular in Hungary and according to whom *Paradise Regained* is a 'cold and noble epopoea' (*hideg és nemes epopoea*): see Taine 1882, 2:456.
17. Szász 1882, 2:656.
18. Milton 1890, 17.
19. Reményi 1895, 223; Reményi 1898.
20. Yolland 1912, 513. See Péti 2021a on how *Paradise Regained* looks forward to the eighteenth century.
21. B. Pap 1909, 119; Voinovich 1926, 82.
22. Lengyel 1942, 157.
23. Olgyay 1936, 85; Ascher and Braun 1934, 52–3.
24. Divald 1900, 622.
25. Nagy 1927, 2; Császár 1937, 626.
26. Blatchford 1925.
27. Veress 1958. Veress's article was published in *Utunk*, a periodical of ethnic Hungarians in Romania, known and referenced in Hungary (see e.g. the 'Bibliography' section of the world literature quarterly *Helikon* 5.3–4 (1959)).
28. Anon. 1958. For the elevation of Samson as a Socialist hero, see Chapter 2.
29. Corns 2016, 518.
30. 'D. P.' 1971, 746.
31. On the relationship and different critical approaches of these scholars, see Chapter 3.
32. Lutter 1956a, 191, 198. In his 1951 course synopsis (on which see Chapter 3) Lutter devotes a single short paragraph to *Paradise Regained*, agreeing 'with Johnson in considering it a much less valuable poem'. Lutter 1951, 68.
33. Szenczi 1989, 196.
34. Szenczi, Szobotka and Katona 1972, 214.
35. On this translation, see Chapter 2.
36. Milton 1977, 79–80.
37. Some paragraphs from the following two subchapters are adapted from Péti 2017.
38. On Lutter's career and the reception of Milton's prose in detail, see Chapter 3.
39. Lutter 1956a, 174.
40. Lutter 1956a, 165, 170.
41. On Jánosi's influence, see Péti 2017, 333–4.
42. Milton 1890, 14–5.
43. Milton 1930, xxii. On Ravasz's preface in detail, see Péter 2012.
44. See Lutter 1960a, 103–8; Sőtér 1962, 205–13.
45. Szabó 2002, 1:6.
46. Szabó 2002, 2:939–41.
47. The articles are '135 minutes of world history in the Kroll Opera' ('135 világtörténelmi perc a Kroll Operában'), and 'Hitler, the orator ('Hitler, a szónok'), originally published in *Magyarország* and *Pesti Napló*, respectively, on 29 April 1939. Szabó 2003a, 476–7, 478–80.
48. Kulcsár-Szabó 2012, 467.
49. Kulcsár-Szabó 2012, 445.
50. Horányi 2010.
51. See Szabó 2002, 2:927.
52. Kabdedbó 1992, 221.
53. Tamás 1991.
54. Szabó 2003b, 2:179–80.
55. Szabó 2003b, 2:210.
56. Szabó 2008, 608.
57. Szabó 2008, 598.
58. Szabó 1993, 115, emphasis in the original.
59. On Zádor's significant role in twentieth century Hungarian intellectual life, see Markója 2008.
60. Szabó 1993, 568.

61. This changed in 1953: see the Introduction.
62. Zádor supervised the publication of the four-volume complete works of Shakespeare which was published in 1948, and was later heavily criticised by Lutter for its 'bourgeois' commentary (Lutter 1949).
63. Szabó 2002, 2:10, 134, 839.
64. Szabó 2002, 2:997.
65. Szabó 2002, 2:918.
66. Szabó 2002, 2:920–1. Emphases mine.
67. Szabó 2002, 1:695–6.
68. Chapman 2017, 6.
69. Kulcsár-Szabó 2010, 353.
70. Cf the sentence in the *Funeral Sermon and Prayer*: 'And the juice of that fruit was so bitter that it stuck in his [Adam's] throat' (*Eſ oz gimilſnek vvl keſeruv uola vize. hug turchucat mige zocoztia vola*).
71. Szabó 2002 2:11–12.
72. On the pre-war Hungarian *népi* (populist) movement as 'ethico-aesthetic and political project(s) . . . in the broader context of civic cultivation', see Taylor 2021, *passim*. On the twentieth-century 'populist' (*népi*) writers, see Czigány 1984, 381–98.
73. Szabó 2008, 397, emphases in the original.
74. Szabó 2003b, 2:303–4.
75. Czigány 1984, 128–9.
76. Szabó 2002, 1:702–3.
77. Szabó 2002, 2:905.
78. Szabó 2003a, 478–9.
79. Szabó 2003a, 480.
80. Szabó 2002, 2:891–2. An obvious misprint makes the emendation in line 9 necessary: without the *nem* (no/not) the line does not scan as an iambic pentameter, and means just the opposite of what we have in Milton, i.e. that Satan was 'by success taught'.
81. Szabó 2002, 1:703.
82. Szabó 2002, 2:907.
83. Sós 1949, 2.
84. See Pomogáts 2000.
85. Pope 1969, 598.
86. Hernádi 1967, 98
87. See Chapter 3 for a discussion of Szenczi's career.
88. Kéry and Szenczi 1971, 4.
89. Szenczi 1971, 70, 71.
90. Szenczi 1971, 88.
91. Ágnes Nemes Nagy, Milton's only woman translator in Hungary, and the main figure in Chapter 4, was also part of this circle.
92. On the system of the '3 Ts' or '3 Ps' (promoted, permitted or prohibited authors and works), see the Introduction.
93. Jánosy 1970, 219.
94. Jánosy 1970, 219.
95. Jánosy 1970, 217.
96. Milton 1969, 13.
97. Dávidházi 1998a, 93.
98. Milton 1969, 93.
99. Milton 1904, 132.
100. Milton 1969, 148.
101. On this, see Péti 2014, especially 285–8.
102. Cf. *Odyssey* 11.488–91 and Porter 1993, 90–1.
103. Milton 1969, 49.
104. See Chapter 3.
105. Wéber 1970, 1726.
106. Hernádi 1970, emphases in the original.
107. Much of this subchapter is adapted from Péti 2018.
108. A new translation by Viktor Horváth has been underway for some time now, but at the time of the publication of this book (2022), it is still some years away from being completed.

109. See Richmond 1988.
110. Henceforth I refer to this script with parenthetical references containing *EP* (an abbreviation of *Elveszett Paradicsom* [*Paradise Lost*]) followed by act and line numbers.
111. On Madách and Milton see Horváth 1995 and Liebert 2008.
112. See e.g. Kürti 1970; Molnár Gál 1970; Ungvári 1970; Vesenyi 1972.
113. See Jánosy 1970.
114. See Richmond 1988.
115. Jánosy 1970, 220.
116. Jánosy 1970, 218. It is interesting to note that a year after the stage production of *Paradise Lost* a major Hungarian writer, Tibor Déry, published a novel entitled *An Imagined Report on an American Pop Festival* (*Képzelt riport egy amerikai popfesztiválról*), which addressed the American pop- and countercultural scene quite directly.
117. Ungvári 1970.
118. Abody 1970, 12.
119. Jánosy 1970, 221.
120. See Abody 1970, Almási 1970 and Molnár Gál 1970.
121. Vesenyi 1972, 16.
122. Vesenyi 1972, 17.
123. Nemes G. 1970, 61.
124. Achinstein 2008, 808.
125. Milton 2013, 207.

2
Samson: an unlikely hero of socialism

'Milton . . . like a communist': leftist appropriations of Milton's Samson in the Anglo-American West

In 1949, at the height of the Red Scare, William Carlos Williams published a slim book of poetry entitled *The Pink Church*. The volume's first poem 'Choral: The pink church' ends with an adaptation of Schiller's 'Ode to joy' and a curious reference to Milton's *Samson Agonistes*:[1]

> Joy! Joy!
> —out of Elysium!
>
> —chanted loud as a chorus from the Agonistes—
> Milton, the unrhymer,
> singing among
> the rest . . .
>
> like a Communist.[2]

The allusion to Milton is relevant on several levels. Williams, like Milton, was a 'prosodic rebel',[3] who started out as a rhymer, but as a mature artist proposed to 'seek . . . a new measure or a new way of measuring that will be commensurate with the social, economic world in which we are living as contrasted with the past'.[4] Further, the specific reference to *Samson Agonistes* seems to hint at possible parallels between the poetic work of Williams, the medical doctor, and the medicinal effects of tragedy as described by Milton in the preface to his drama.[5] Finally, Milton joins the chorus of joyful celebration, like a 'Communist' (note the capital C, differentiating him from ordinary 'commies'), and thus becomes an important model for Williams, the self-confessed 'Pink', who 'was not a communist . . . but a sympathizer with the communist *ideal* of egalitarianism'.[6] As Milton A. Cohen points out:

> Milton's political daring in supporting and working for the revolutionary Cromwell parallels what Williams sees as his aesthetic daring in writing blank verse . . . 'Communist', then, has the positive connotations of rebel and innovator.[7]

Written in a decade when Milton's name was often cautiously invoked in defence of intellectual and academic freedom and in protest against McCarthyism,[8] Williams's poem seems to be a radical, if ironic, attempt to claim Milton for the left. It is uncertain whether Williams is thinking about a particular 'chorus from the Agonistes', but the celebration of God-sent deliverance after the departure of Harapha in Milton's drama certainly comes close to the 'Elysian joys' described in Williams's 'Choral':

> Oh how comely it is and how reviving
> To the Spirits of just men long opprest!
> When God into the hands of thir deliverer
> Puts invincible might
> To quell the mighty of the Earth, th'oppressour,
> The brute and boist'rous force of violent men
> Hardy and industrious to support
> Tyrannic power, but raging to pursue
> The righteous and all such as honour Truth. (lines 1268–76)

Williams thus appropriates Milton as a model for his own political and poetic radicalism.[9] The fact that he invokes *Samson Agonistes* is not particularly striking: Milton's tragedy has been involved in politics practically since it was first published. As several critics have demonstrated, in *Samson* Milton participated in the late seventeenth-century discourse about toleration and dissent,[10] and Blair Worden reminds us of the long critical tradition promoting the view that 'Samson's predicament corresponds to Milton's experience of the Restoration, and to the struggle of the blind poet to come to terms with the defeat of the Puritan cause.'[11] Neither is it surprising that Williams enrols Milton in the annals of progressive politics: as Sharon Achinstein has pointed out, Milton is 'a figure who crops up in radical writing during numerous politically inflammatory moments – the American Revolution; the French Revolution; the Russian Revolution'.[12] Indeed, as Achinstein demonstrates in another important article, 'fractures within the Left' in post-war North America were also reflected in different attitudes to Milton, 'a shared object of cultural capital'.[13] For Don Wolfe, editor of the first volume of Milton's prose works in the Yale edition, for example, Williams's casting of Milton as singing 'among the rest . . . like a Communist' would have been quite a stretch. According to Wolfe, Milton was undoubtedly radical and (in Christopher Hill's words) 'open to the left',[14] but he was 'no pacifist, and no internationalist' and 'far indeed from being a socialist'.[15]

Wolfe also contended that in his youth Milton might have cherished ideas about dispensing 'Natures full blessings . . . In unsuperfluous eeven proportion' (*Comus*, lines 772–3), but in his maturity he was for various reasons 'unwilling . . . to disturb the fundamental practices of economic order'.[16] Thus, even within the Anglo-American left there was a wide spectrum of opinion on Milton, resulting in different appropriations of his texts. Needless to say, as with all appropriations, these were also selective and tendentious in their own way, especially when checked against Milton's own words. It is enough to take a look at Milton's complex 'attitude to the people', which, as Paul Hammond has demonstrated, 'changes according to political circumstances and the polemical needs of the moment', and is often in conflict with his image as a radical.[17] The words of the Jesus of *Paradise Regained*, for example, could easily be interpreted either as the scornful verdict of an elitist, conservative reactionary or as the expression of distrust by a fundamentalist communist detesting the ideologically uneducated, retrograde populace:

> And what the people but a herd confus'd,
> A miscellaneous rabble, who extol
> Things vulgar, & well weigh'd, scarce worth the praise,
> They praise and they admire they know not what;
> And know not whom, but as one leads the other (*PR* 3.49–53)

To this we might add that the Messenger's last sentence in *Samson Agonistes* ('The vulgar only scap'd who stood without', line 1659), occasionally interpreted as a sign of Milton's humane perspective, is also deeply ambiguous: it seems to deprive the 'people' (characterised by Samson as 'Impetuous, insolent, unquenchable', line 1422) of any agency in the significant event.

What is important from our point of view is that (as the quotation above by Williams suggests) for some Western thinkers and artists Milton, and emphatically *Samson Agonistes*, might have played an integral part in the long march of the proletariat towards sovereignty. Indeed, Williams's 'Choral' is not even an exception: as I shall shortly show, Milton's tragedy has often been invoked in Anglo-American Marxist and socialist writings from the early twentieth century to the present. Interestingly, these strands of Milton's modern reception have been largely ignored by Miltonists – with the important exception of Christopher Hill, one of the Western critics whose works were cited and appreciated behind the Iron Curtain throughout the decades of state socialism. Readers who have made it thus far in this book will therefore hardly find it surprising that – partly influenced by Hill's works – Hungarian critics of the communist era also introduced their own special interpretation of Milton's tragedy, whose main character, Samson, became in their handling a proto-socialist hero, one who acts 'for the people'. Through the example of the Hungarian versions of *Samson Agonistes* in this chapter I will document how Milton's tragedy and the figure of Samson were used under state socialism. Although one could argue that the overtly politicised views of Samson I am about to introduce exhibit a keen understanding of the drama's political potential, long before the great resurgence of critical interest in *Samson* in the past decades, the consideration of the different translations of Milton's tragedy together with their criticism and publication history might ultimately tell us more about the workings of communist cultural policies than about Milton's drama.

First, however, let us see how Milton's Samson has fared among leftist writers in the Anglo-American world. As we saw in the Introduction, both Marx and Engels referred to Milton as a prominent historical forerunner, a secular revolutionary who in his own limited ways was acting against an oppressive regime. Later socialist and communist writers and intellectuals went further than a mere honourable mention, and, curiously, it is often Milton's tragedy that they invoked in their attempt to find a venerable historical precedent for their own strivings. The first piece of evidence for such an interpretive context is in one of the first issues of the American periodical *The Comrade: An illustrated socialist monthly*, where Milton's Samson is evoked in a modern emblem. A caricature – entitled 'Samson Agonistes' and placed between two printer's ornaments featuring lightning bolts – shows the blindfolded figure of Samson between the columns of the temple, with a halo over his head inscribed 'Labor', and six lines from Longfellow's poem 'The warning' below the image (see Figure 2.1).

Longfellow's poem was originally written as an anti-slavery piece, and it is clearly part of an important, but hitherto largely unexplored nineteenth-century set of Miltonic references in anti-slavery writings.[18] In *The Comrade*, however, the poem's resounding Miltonic echoes (invoking the language and motifs of *Areopagitica*, *Paradise Lost* and *Samson Agonistes*) are used to further the cause of the proletariat. Text

"There is a poor blind Samson in this land,
Shorn of his strength, and bound in bonds of steel;
Who may, in some grim revel, raise his hand
And smite the pillars of our commonweal;
Till the vast temple of our liberties,
A shapeless mass of wreck and ruin lies."—*Longfellow.*

Figure 2.1 'Samson Agonistes', *The Comrade* 1.9 (June 1902): 196.

and image together issue a prophetic warning, in distinctly Miltonic terms, about the impending rise of the oppressed. Some three decades later this view of Samson was promoted by the Marxist literary critic Christopher Caudwell, according to whom Milton after the 'defeatist' *Paradise Regained* 'recovers his courage' in *Samson Agonistes* and 'hopes for the day when he can pull the temple down on the luxury of his wanton oppressors and wipe out the Philistine court'.[19]

This interpretation of Samson is, however, only one side of the coin. A couple of years after his debut in *The Comrade*, Milton's Samson reappeared, albeit in very different light, on the pages of the *Daily People* (before 1900 and after 1914 published weekly as *The People*), the New York-based newspaper of the Socialist Labor Party of America. Daniel DeLeon, one of the party's leaders and the paper's most prominent journalist, refers to the biblical figure of Samson several times. He contrasts the emblematic figure of the 'Blind Samson' (e.g. 'the old style of unionism ... [which] acts merely as an ally of large capitalism') with the 'Seeing Samson' (e.g. 'the new style of unionism') who 'clears the path for the Social Revolution'.[20] Consequently, when he invokes Milton's Samson in the title of one of his articles, it is essentially with a satiric purpose, to pass ironic criticism on the Russian tsar 'performing, however unwittingly, a Samsonian task – the task of tearing down the pillars of sanctimony that uphold the superstructure of "Vested Rights"'.[21] Two years later DeLeon uses the same allusion to lambast Teddy Roosevelt: 'As a Samson Agonistes Roosevelt clutches the pillars of the Capitalist Temple, gives them another shake, and makes assurance doubly sure that the iniquitous structure must collapse.'[22] DeLeon emphasises the revolutionary potential of the biblical Samson figure, but he associates Milton's hero with defeat, misdirected action and unintended consequences. A similar sentiment might have fuelled the editor of the American Marxist periodical the *New International*, who used the subtitle 'Stalin Agonistes' in his editorial to illustrate 'the cost of Stalinism', which became all the more apparent after the Munich Agreement.[23]

It seems, then, that allusion to *Samson Agonistes* was a commonplace in Western leftist discourse in the first half of the twentieth century, although critical assessments of the tragic figure of Samson were clearly not unanimous. In the post-war era allusions to Milton's tragedy continued to crop up in English Marxist or socialist writings, but, importantly, the evaluation of Samson's character became less ambiguous. Roughly at the same time that Williams's *Pink Church* was published, Mary Visick discussed Milton as a revolutionary figure in the spring 1949 issue of the *Modern Quarterly* (edited by Christopher Hill). Visick states that Milton 'moved from a religious to a political revolutionary position, and from the Right to the Left wing of the revolutionary parties; and in his course his mind comes close to the thought of the Levellers'. Characteristically, Visick references the Chorus of *Samson Agonistes* (including the lines quoted above: 'O how comely it is') to illustrate that 'Paradise within' was 'still possible as a dynamic ideal because the concept of virtue was still virile and did not preclude action in the political world.' Thus, 'Samson's way is through patience to action "to quell the mighty of the Earth"'.[24]

We find similar views in the December 1958 issue of the British magazine *Labour Monthly*, in a two-page article that was published to commemorate the three hundred and fiftieth anniversary of Milton's birth. The anonymous author quotes the sonnet to Cromwell besides *Samson Agonistes* to illustrate that Milton 'well knew the need of dictatorship to defend liberty against both malignants and monarchists and against "new foes"'.[25] The tribute also quotes the choric song quoted above ('O how comely it is') with the comment: '[Milton] in that same towering drama *Samson Agonistes* could utter the roar of revolutionary defiance that has been echoed in our own day as the Bastilles of imperialism totter and fall.'[26] Some critics wished for a wider focus: in a review of the commemorative effort in the *Labour Monthly* Brian Pearce deplores that the article does not mention *Areopagitica*, which 'Communists and socialists have made good use of . . . on numerous occasions', and proceeds with a call to the Marxist critic Arnold Kettle, to give to his students as 'an educative exercise . . . to "compare and contrast" Milton's book [his defences of the English people] and Trotsky's [*In Defence of*

Terrorism] as polemical defences of revolutionary governments against their detractors'.[27] Regardless of whether such 'educative exercises' have actually been performed, from our perspective it is important to see that Milton, and especially his tragedy, were once again regarded and read as supporting the cause of the 'damned of the Earth' – i.e. the proletariat, as the socialist anthem the *Internationale* calls them.

Most of these documents are political journalism or propaganda pieces, and, with one or two exceptions (the articles by Caudwell and Visick), they do not fall within the categories of literary criticism or scholarship. To be sure, there was one outstanding critic and historian, Christopher Hill whose work, as Elizabeth Sauer has pointed out, was characterised by an 'inclination to cast Milton as a forerunner of Marx'.[28] Hill indeed cherished very similar ideas to the ones quoted above: according to him, *Samson Agonistes* is a 'call of hope to the defeated'. This interpretation of Milton's tragedy remains important for Hill throughout his long career, since it shows that Milton 'put his hope in the efforts of regenerate individuals – rather like Narodnaya Volya in similar discouraging circumstances in the eighteen-seventies and -eighties'.[29] In Milton studies Hill is generally credited with renewing critical interest in *Samson Agonistes*, but on the basis of the views collected above, it is clear that in a wider context of Anglo-American socialist thought his work is just one example of exploring the revolutionary potential of Milton's tragedy. Indeed, such attempts have persisted to the recent past: in a 2002 issue of the *Socialist Review* Paul Foot argues for collective and organised action of workers by quoting Samson's words from Milton's tragedy:

> In his last great poem, *Samson Agonistes*, John Milton, who played an active part in the English Revolution of the 1640s, asked:
>
> > 'But what more oft in nations grown corrupt,
> > And by their vices brought to servitude
> > Than to love bondage more than liberty –
> > Bondage in ease, than strenuous liberty?'
>
> In the triumph of Royalist counter-revolution Milton saw the dangers of political passivity, of ideological sloth. The reactionaries took advantage of that passivity and sloth to restore their tyranny. The alternative to bondage in passivity was strenuous liberty. In plain terms, this meant that if you want to change the world for the better you have to do something about it. And, as the Levellers proved in the English Revolution, you are much more likely to do something effective if you act in concert with others.[30]

Foot's move to the Levellers in his last sentence puts Milton in a radical company again, and thus rejuvenates the age-old topos of Samson as a proto-socialist hero. A hundred years after the publication of the Samson Agonistes caricature in *The Comrade*, Milton's Samson still inspires some the Western world's proletariat.

'The great Prodigal, Samson': Milton's tragedy in pre-war Hungary

Let us now switch to Hungary, where the cultural policies instituted by the different communist regimes had a serious impact on Milton's reception. The reinterpretation of the revolutionary character of Milton and his writings according to 'Marxist-Leninist' tenets resulted in a radical sifting of Milton's works. Some pieces (such as *Paradise Lost* and the revolutionary sonnets) were promoted; others (such as the prose pamphlets or *Paradise Regained*) were selectively read or pushed to the background; and some (such as *Comus*, or the Latin poems) remained more or less forgotten. The most astonishing change, however, took place in the reception of *Samson Agonistes*, which emerged from near-complete oblivion to become the flagship piece of the Miltonic oeuvre. Samson, who was a potential hero for a few Western socialists, came to be profiled in the post-war period as the Miltonic hero with great potential for the wider audiences of state socialism. As we shall see below, this development in Milton's Hungarian reception has resulted in a fascinating, yet characteristically tendentious reinterpretation of the structure of the Miltonic oeuvre, which still stands as an emblematic instance of the workings of communist cultural policies.

The theme of heroic suicide involving the destruction of an oppressive enemy is present in Hungarian national lore,[31] and allusions to Samson the biblical hero abound in Hungarian literature and criticism since the late sixteenth century, mostly emphasising the hero's strength or his propensity to fall for Delilah.[32] References to Milton's *Samson*, however, are generally sparse in the pre-war period both in critical discussions and the wider cultural discourse. The first time the Hungarian reading public heard about Milton's tragedy was in an 1860 translation of Macaulay's essay 'Milton', in which the drama is pronounced to be 'the least successful effort of the genius of Milton'.[33]

Possibly influenced by this verdict, those late nineteenth- and early twentieth-century Hungarian writers and critics who did write about

Milton's tragedy were not too enthusiastic either. Gusztáv Jánosi, the nineteenth-century translator of *Paradise Lost*, mentions *Samson* in the preface to his translation as a 'cold, dark, sublime tragedy' (*hideg, sötét és magasztos tragédia*) which represents the 'hero of vengeance' (*bosszú hősét*) and Milton's 'real hatred of his enemies' (*igazi gyűlölettel gyűlölte ellenségeit*).[34] Arthur Yolland, professor at the English Department in Budapest, points out in 1912 that in his late masterpieces Milton is 'bewailing his promising past and himself' (*siratja a sokat igért multját, önmagát*) and that 'the symbolism of *Samson Agonistes* is moving, but depressing' (*Samson Agonistes symbolizmusa megható, de szomorító*).[35] A couple of decades later, László Ravasz, a Calvinist bishop and a prominent Protestant intellectual, in his 1930 preface to a new edition of Jánosi's translation of *Paradise Lost* conceives of the drama as Milton's attempt to represent his own fate 'in the figure of the great Prodigal of the Old Testament, Samson' (*Sámson, az ótestamentomi nagy Tékozló alakjában*) who, with the final gathering of his strength, destroys 'his tyrant, the laughing rabble, as well as his own shattered life' (*kényurát, a nevető csőcseléket és saját összetört életét*).[36] Also in the 1930s, Mihály Babits, the leading West-leaning classicist-modernist poet and critic of the first part of the twentieth century, in his *History of European Literature* (1934–6) claims that 'the blind Milton dreamt of himself in the figure of the blind Samson . . . This was his last work. A bitter farewell to art and to life' (*A vak Sámsonban a vak Milton önmagát álmodta . . . ez volt az utolsó műve. Keserű búcsuzás a művészettől és az élettől is*).[37] In like manner, Antal Szerb, another leading man of letters of the inter-war period, points out in his *History of World Literature* (1941) that in *Samson*

> *Milton még egyszer összefoglalja benne, amit mondania adatott: a legyőzött lázadók törhetetlen dacát, megvetését az emberi gyöngeség megtestesítői, a nők iránt, rajongását az antik szépségekért, és hozzáfűzi az elmúlás bánatát.*[38]

> (Milton once more summarises what was his share to say: the unconquerable pride of the vanquished, his contempt of women who are the representatives of human frailty, his enthusiasm towards ancient beauty, together with his melancholy over passing away.)

Although Szerb sounds very much like his contemporaries, his view is quite remarkable for its reflection on the sexism of the Delilah episode, especially if we contrast it to that of Lőrinc Szabó, another leading artist and intellectual, and the first post-war translator of *Paradise*

*Lost.*³⁹ Szabó, in his brief comment on *Samson* in a biographical note to his collection of shorter literary translations *Our Eternal Friends* (*Örök barátaink*, 1941), reinterprets the motif revenge in a characteristically patriarchal manner: 'the blind hero takes revenge on his enemies and his base wife' (*a megvakult hős bosszút áll ellenfelein és hitvány feleségén*).⁴⁰

Not translated before World War II, *Samson* thus emerged in prewar criticism as a largely autobiographical piece, a bitter, dark tragedy, much to be appreciated for its classical perfection, but more of an afterthought or an appendix to the great masterpieces, *Paradise Lost* and *Paradise Regained*.

But what a difference a world war and the subsequent communist takeover can make! After 1948 the Hungarian reception of Milton's tragedy took an unprecedented turn. This of course happened in tandem with the general reappraisal of Milton's work in accordance with the 'Marxist-Leninist' tenets of communist cultural policy, but while all other segments of the Miltonic oeuvre had a long reception history (involving translation as well as critical reflections) reaching back at least to the nineteenth century, Milton's tragedy was, as we have just seen, passed over in a few words, but more frequently ignored before World War II. After 1948, however, *Samson Agonistes* suddenly became Milton's second most important work, favoured by translators and critics alike. In the short space of two decades two translations of the drama were published in several editions, two radio plays were produced, and a handful of weighty critical reflections emerged which hailed the tragedy as Milton's crowning achievement. Indeed, based on the attention *Samson* received in the communist era, it seems that of all Milton's works this text and its hero were the easiest to incorporate into the revolutionary aesthetic of the communist era – whether it was the hardline dictatorship of the early days or the softer versions of state socialism in later decades.⁴¹

'Spiriting emotions': Tihamér Dybas's *Sámson*

The first translation of *Samson*, by Tihamér Dybas, was published in 1955, a period of slight 'thaw' but still some of the darkest days of Rákosi's Stalinist dictatorship. The editorial policy of the publisher – Új Magyar Könyvkiadó (New Hungarian Publishing House), which in later decades became (under the name Európa) Hungary's foremost publisher of world literature – was undergoing a significant change around this time.

Between 1949 and 1954, they had focused predominantly on Russian and Soviet literature (publishing works by, for example, Veniamin Kaverin and Vera Inber), but from the mid-1950s onwards they started to widen their scope of publications to include Western classics (such as works by Charles Dickens, Anatole France, Thomas Mann and Louis Aragon). The publication of the first Hungarian translation of Milton's tragedy – entitled *Sámson* and illustrated with engravings by Gustave Doré – was clearly part of this trend. Dybas, who graduated in English in Budapest, was at this point in his twenties, and already a prolific translator of not only English but also neo-Latin and Russian poets. He was working on the translation for some years: prior to the publication of the volume he published parts of the tragedy in literary periodicals. Dybas, like many of his contemporaries, chose to emigrate after the quelling of the 1956 revolution. He ended up in Scotland, took the name Ian MacLeod, and continued to work as a translator, from Hungarian to English (his translation of Imre Madách's *Tragedy of Man* was published in 1993).

The political context of Dybas's *Sámson* left its hallmark on the volume: the preface (written by the translator) starts with the inevitability of revolution in seventeenth-century England:

> *A csöndes elégedetlenség lassanként ideológiai-vallási és politikai ellenállássá acélozódott, az uralkodó az önkényuralom fegyveréhez nyúlt – az ellenállás hatalmas folyammá növekedett . . . Öles léptekkel haladt az idő a forradalom felé, amely, ha időlegesen is, elsöpörte a királyság intézményét és közel másfél évszázaddal a francia forradalom előtt, szinte annak igéretéül, megnyitotta a polgári forradalmak korszakát.*[42]

> (Quiet discontent slowly hardened into ideological-religious and political resistance; the monarch used the weapon of tyranny – resistance grew into a mighty river . . . Time marched with giant steps towards revolution which, if only temporarily, swept away the institution of monarchy and nearly 150 years before the French Revolution [indeed, as if its promise] opened the era of bourgeois revolutions.)

The somewhat agitated rhetoric later gives way to more restrained, professional discussion of Milton's life and work, but at the conclusion of his essay Dybas returns to the revolutionary potential of *Samson*, pointing out Milton's 'painful, but incontestable optimism' (*fájdalmasan ható, de kétségbevonhatatlan optimizmussal*), 'his belief in the final victory of the just cause' (*hitét az igaz ügy végső győzelmében*), as well as his hope that the Samson-like 'deceived, humiliated, blind giant of the revolution' (*a forradalom megcsalt, megalázott, világtalan óriását*) will be 'inspired to make one final effort' (*még egy erőfeszítésre lelkesíti*). According to Dybas, this constitutes the 'eternal teaching' of Milton's drama (*És ez a Sámson örök tanítása*),[43] and it is difficult not to hear echoes of the slogans of contemporary communist propaganda, from the rising of the oppressed to the optimistic insistence on the 'final victory'. Indeed, we can trace the attempt to present an 'up-to-date' Samson not only in the paratexts of Dybas's translation but also, occasionally, in the translator's choice of words to render the original. A fine example is in one of Samson's speeches (quoted above by Paul Foot) in which the hero exonerates himself from blame and puts the responsibility 'On *Israel's* Governours, and Heads of Tribes':

> But what more oft in Nations grown corrupt,
> And by thir vices brought to servitude,
> Then to love Bondage more then Liberty,
> Bondage with ease then strenuous liberty (lines 268–71)

> *De bűneiktől szolgaságra vitt*
> *És romlott nemzeteknek, ó, mi gyakran*
> *A rabság kedvesebb, nem a szabadság,*
> *Kényelmes rabság, nem szorgos szabadság.*[44]

> (But for nations brought to servitude by their sins / and grown corrupt, oh, how often / bondage is preferable, not liberty, / comfortable bondage, not industrious liberty.)

As the quasi-oxymoronic expressions 'Bondage with ease' and 'strenuous liberty' show, Samson's speech is riddled with contradictions. Šárka Kühnová observes that the adjective 'strenuous' creates 'uncomfortable tensions', since it is 'suggestive not only of energetic, bold action but of taxing effort'.[45] Indeed, the speech, like the whole of Milton's tragedy, 'invites several different modes of contemporary application',[46] ranging from self-justification to prophetic admonishment to resignation. Dybas's translation, in contrast, treads with special care as it neutralises the ambiguity the original's 'strenuous liberty' with the use of the adjective *szorgos* (industrious, diligent) while possibly evoking the production-centred collectivist discourse of the 'dictatorship of the proletariat' in the 1950s. The original's opposition of 'Bondage with ease' and 'strenuous liberty' would readily have reminded Hungarian readers of the language of nineteenth-century nationalism and the historical struggles for national independence and sovereignty. In Dybas's translation, however, 'industrious' liberty (presented in a forceful alliterative expression) is pitted against *kényelmes* (comfortable, easy-going, indolent) bondage, which, while it echoes the Puritan opposition between idleness and industry, is also reminiscent of the conventional contrast made in communist propaganda between the industrious workers of peoples' democracies and the rotting, torpid world of capitalism wallowing in luxuries. Dybas's choice of words clearly struck a resonant chord with contemporary critics: a short review of the 1970 radio play made of his translation singled out the terms *kényelmes rabság* and *szorgos szabadság* in its synopsis of the fundamental problems Milton addressed in *Samson*.[47]

Such careful, 'topical' solutions and critical strains notwithstanding (some of which, especially in the preface, the translator was probably required to incorporate into his essay), Dybas cannot be accused of presenting a politically conformist version of Milton's tragedy. Certain aspects of his version are actually rather reactionary: it is a metrically correct version, reproducing Milton's tragedy in the same number of lines; the diction often echoes the archaic words of the Hungarian Protestant Bible; and he opens his brief afterword about the difficulties of translating Milton's language on a decidedly aestheticist note: 'Beauty justifies its existence by satisfying the desire and need for beauty within us' (*A szép a bennünk levő szépségvágy és szépségigény betöltésével igazolja, hogy valóban szép*), and closes it on a note of patriotic pride in 'enriching' (*gazdagabbá tettem*) Hungarian readers and the 'country' (*hazámat*). Furthermore, when it comes to a key moment in Milton's drama, Samson's famous 'rousing motions' (line 1382), Dybas uses a rich Hungarian phrase, *lelkesítő indulatok* (literally 'spiriting emotions'), leaving ample room for both religious and secular interpretations. Similarly, in the exchange between Samson and 'his Wife', Dybas's version amplifies the original with touches of pathos, adding depth to Delilah's character. When Delilah remonstrates to Samson that she was not bribed, but

> the Magistrates
> And Princes of my countrey came in person,
> Sollicited, commanded, threatn'd, urg'd,
> Adjur'd by all the bonds of civil Duty
> And of Religion (lines 850–4)

Dybas renders it thus:

> *főemberek,*
> *És hercegek jöttek személyesen:*
> *Kérleltek, parancsoltak, fenyegettek,*
> *Eskettek minden honpolgári és*
> *Vallási kötelékre.*[48]

(Mighty people / and princes came in person: / they asked, commanded, threatened / and forced me to swear on every civil and / religious bond.)

In the Hungarian the chiastic structure of the original line – where 'Sollicited' is balanced by 'urg'd' – is exchanged for a three-part structure progressing towards maximum psychological pressure with 'threatening', and complemented in the next line with the introduction of 'forced oaths'. No wonder that when Milton's Delilah confesses that the 'grounded maxim ... that to the public good / Private respects must yield; with grave authority / Took full possession of me and prevail'd' (lines 865, 867–9), then in Dybas's version she feels completely vanquished, and admits that the same maxim 'defeated me with enormous weight and overwhelmed me completely' (*hatalmas súllyal / Legyőzött s teljesen lenyűgözött*).[49] Samson's enthralment, humiliation and subsequent tragic fate are bound up with his status of being 'Select, and Sacred, Glorious' (line 343), but the vulnerability and helplessness of Dybas's Delilah uncannily resembles the quotidian suffering of ordinary individuals under totalitarian regimes.

Dybas's text received a mixed response in the contemporary press. László Kardos, one of the period's doyens of literary translation, praised the translator's technical skills even before the work was published.[50] One of the prominent Shakespeare scholars of the post-war era, László Kéry, on the other hand, while convinced of the significance of Samson's 'last, greatest heroic act which elevates him to the rank of a liberator' (*utolsó, legnagyobb hőstette, amely a felszabadító rangjára emeli* – the term 'liberator', *felszabadító*, was officially adopted in communist Hungary for the occupying Soviet army), is less enthusiastic about the translation: according to him, Dybas's verse cannot always soar as high as Milton's original would require.[51] Most critics, however, did not bother with the minutiae of prosodic or stylistic issues, but were keen to explore the 'message' of Milton's drama to the present. Thus, János Viktor writes in the daily *Magyar Nemzet*:

Akármennyit hallottunk is Miltonnak az angol forradalomban játszott szerepéről, meglepő, hogy árad az aktuális mondanivaló az ő új fogalmazásában a régi-régi históriából. Nyilvánvaló, számára közügy volt a költészet, politikai eszköz.[52]

(However much we have heard about Milton's role in the English revolution, it is surprising *how profusely his topical message flows from the newly formulated age-old story*. It is obvious that for him poetry was a public affair, a political *tool*.)

Viktor's words are echoed by Tibor Lutter, the chief Miltonist of the day.[53] For Lutter *Samson* is a highly topical, prophetic, revolutionary piece wrapped in biblical symbolism and with more emphasis on the final victory than on temporary failure: 'For Milton the reality of the redemption-ideal depicted in the revolutionary objectives is evident, the temporary failure only delays the final victory' (*A forradalmi célikitűzésekben megrajzolt megváltás-eszme realitása Milton számára kézenfekvő, az átmeneti bukás a végső győzelmet csupán időben tolja el*).[54] Hence, '*Samson Agonistes* is a tragedy; its final denouement, however, sounds the note of triumphant and hopeful joy' ([A] Sámson Agonistes *tragédia ugyan, de végső kibontakozása mégis diadalmas derűlátás*).[55] Lutter does quote from Dybas's fresh translation in his monograph, but not exclusively: in the discussion of Samson's great monologue (lines 66–109), he prefers the brisker rendering of another young translator, István Eörsi.[56]

Lutter's use of an alternative translation one year after the publication of Dybas's version suggests that what seemed a relatively smooth reception of Dybas's *Samson* in the 'official' press might have a more turbulent backstory. Indeed, if we take a look at a reader's report prepared in 1954 or 1955 for the Új Magyar Könyvkiadó (New Hungarian Publishing House) by one of the leading poets and translators of the day, then a more complicated situation emerges. In this document, written to evaluate Dybas's book proposal (and obviously not intended for publication), we find a mixture of pre-war interpretations (about the bitterness of *Samson*) and post-war critical reflexes (about the drama's revolutionary character). The reader starts out by appraising Milton's drama, and pointing out that although *Samson* is 'consistent with Milton's revolutionary thought' (*következetesen illeszkedik Milton forradalmi gondolkodásába*), we 'do not find the faith and trustful strength of *Paradise Lost* in it; it contains more bitterness and loneliness often turning into misanthropy' (*nem találjuk meg* Az elvesztett paradicsom *hitét és bízó erejét, több benne a keserűség és sokszor embermegvetésig fokozódó magányosság érzése*).

For the author of this report Satan's 'individual revolutionary character' (*individualista forradalmisága*) in *Paradise Lost* seems 'more forceful and human' (*erőteljesebb és emberibb*) than Samson's. He is also unsure about the translator's creative powers, and goes to great lengths to illustrate the low points of the rendering. Altogether it is a question for the reader whether the translation should be published: he is afraid that the audience would simply think it is a religious drama; 'not even a clever and popular introduction (although I need not point out how doubtful it is whether we can get such an introduction) would help much' (*egy még oly okos és népszerű bevezetés [bár mondanom sem kell, milyen kétséges, hogy ilyenre szert tudnánk-e tenni] sem segítene sokat*).[57]

Although the reader finally did not recommend the translation for publication, hinting at some personal animosity between himself and the translator, and remarking that 'Dybas managed to attract significant attention with his translation' (*Dybas eléggé nagy feltünést tudott tudott kelteni fordítsa iránt*), he insists other experts (such as the above-cited Lutter and Kéry) should also look at the work.[58] Whether these experts were consulted or not, Dybas eventually managed to publish his translation, together with a 'clever and popular' introduction, as we have seen above. Due to his decision to leave Hungary in 1956, however, the later reception of Dybas's translation was beset by both aesthetic and political considerations. In a 1958 internal reader's report to the Európa Publishing House another prominent literary translator of the second part of the twentieth century muses what publication would be most fitting to celebrate the anniversary of Milton's birth, and summarises in one succinct sentence the contemporaneous problems with Dybas's work: 'If we didn't have any objections to the person of the defector translator, we cannot talk about congeniality in relation to his translation' (*Ha a disszidált fordító személye ellen nem is volna kifogásunk, munkájáról szólván nem emlegethetünk congenialitást*).[59] But in 1958, merely two years after the 1956 revolution, and still during the period of retaliation, it is certain that serious objections were raised against the person of the 'defector translator' on all levels of the official publishing and literary sphere, and thus it is not a surprise that no excerpts from Dybas's *Sámson* made it into the anniversary volume.[60]

In spite of such concerns about the translator and his translation, Dybas's 1955 *Sámson* was occasionally used: it was quoted in a 1958 article commemorating Milton, and Miklós Szenczi sampled it extensively in his comprehensive history of English literature.[61] Even before it was published, the Hungarian Radio produced a radio play of Dybas's text on 16 November 1954, featuring some of the most popular actors in Hungary at the time.[62] In 1970 another radio play was produced, again with a stellar cast; it was aired twice: on 23 October 1970, and on 11 May 1978.[63] As the advertisement for the latter production pointed out, 'The biblical theme is only a pretext – the drama is an open testimony about the revolution. Samson unites in one figure the poet and his fellow fighters, the leaders of the revolution. This is why the work is more than just a mere "classic" for us' (*A bibliai téma csak ürügy – a dráma nyílt vallomás a forradalomról. Sámson a költőt és harcostársait, a forradalom vezetőit sűríti egy alakba. Ezért is több számunkra e mű puszta 'klasszikusnál'*).[64] Even after the 1989 change of system, Dybas's work was used, most notably by Ágnes Heller, who in her philosophical survey of the various historical adaptations of the Samson story calls the exchange between Samson and Delilah 'one of the saddest, although not the most tragic dialogue of modern literature' (*a modern irodalom egyik legszomorúbb, bár nem legtragikusabb, párbeszéde*) and claims that 'Milton reads Samson's story as the chronicle of hopeless love' (*Milton úgy olvassa Sámson történetét, mint a szerelem reménytelensége krónikáját*).[65] Importantly, Heller singles out Dybas's translation of the above-quoted lines by Delilah to support her point that the conflict unfolding between the former lovers is not tainted by misogyny (as, she claims, the chorus following the exchange certainly is).

'A captive people's dreams': György Jánosházy's *A küzdő Sámson*

Another translation of Milton's tragedy, entitled *Samson Agonistes* or *The Struggling Samson* (*A küzdő Sámson*) and prepared by György Jánosházy, was published in 1975 by the Bucharest-based Romanian Kriterion Publishing House (whose portfolio was multilingual).[66] Jánosházy was a Transylvania-based ethnic Hungarian poet who translated widely from European literature. The text was originally intended for a reading public consisting mostly of ethnic Hungarian readers in Romania (primarily in Transylvania) who probably did not have access to (or did not even know about) Dybas's *Sámson*, whose print run was limited to a mere 3000 copies. Linguistically, this rendering is more radical: Jánosházy remains faithful to the original and presents a metrically impeccable rendition, but he also recreates Milton's drama in an easily readable, modern Hungarian text. Compared to Dybas's version, Jánosházy's translation is often understated: we certainly find this in his rendering of Delilah's protest (discussed above) where he translates Delilah's phrase '[the grounded maxim] Took full possession of me and prevail'd' simply as 'won over me' (*győzött rajtam*).[67] Another example offers itself in Jánosházy's translations of 'strenuous liberty' as *dolgos szabadság* ('hard-working liberty'), which, just like Dybas's version, cancels out much of the original's ambiguity, but, unlike Dybas, does so without adding possible propagandistic overtones to the expression. While such solutions certainly facilitate the reception of Milton's tragedy, the text sometimes becomes too light to carry the weight of the original. Thus, 'rousing motions' are translated by Jánosházy as *pezsdülés* ('sparkling', or perhaps 'seething'), a much weaker expression which, however suggestive it is of some psychosomatic phenomenon, bypasses the problem of divine inspiration. Both the virtues and the vices of Jánosházy's approach can be demonstrated on the following excerpt from Samson's famous lament, especially if we compare it with Dybas's version:

> O dark, dark, dark, amid the blaze of noon,
> Irrecoverably dark, total Eclipse
> Without all hope of day!
> O first-created Beam, and thou great Word,
> Let there be light, and light was over all;
> Why am I thus bereav'd thy prime decree? (lines 80–5)

> *Ó, éj, éj, éj a déli napverőn!*
> *Gyógyíthatatlan napfogyatkozás,*
> *Hol fényre nincs remény.*
> *Ó, első fénysugár s te ős ige,*
> *'Legyen világosság!' – s világosság lőn –*
> *Tőlem mért vontad meg végzésedet?* (Dybas) [68]

(O night, night, night in the noon sunbeat! / Incurable eclipse / where there is no hope of light. / O you first ray of light and you ancient word, / 'Let there be light' – and light there was – / why did you bereave me of your decree?)

> *Ó éj, éj, éj a déli ragyogásban*
> *Megbonthatatlan éj, teljes sötétség*
> *Hajnal reménye nélkül!*
> *Elsőnek teremtett sugár, s te nagy ige:*
> *'Legyen világosság, és lett a fény,'*
> *Őstörvényedből mért vagyok kizárva?* (Jánosházy)[69]

(O night, night, night in the noon splendour / Unbreakable night, total darkness / without hope of dawn! / First-created Beam and you, great Word: / 'Let there be light, and there was light' / Why am I excluded from your ancient law?)

Dybas is clearly more adventurous with the use of the nonce word *napverő* ('sunbeat'), the catachrestic yet vigorous expression of *Gyógyíthatatlan napfogyatkozás* ('incurable eclipse') and the rendering of the line 'Let there be light, and light was over all', where the repetition of *világosság* for 'light', and the use of the archaic verb *lőn*, clearly evoke the language of the Hungarian Protestant Bible. Jánosházy, by contrast, stays close to the original by faithfully reproducing its syntactical structure, and his text is easily digestible for an average reader. It is striking, however, that he uses the expression *teljes sötétség* ('total darkness') for 'total eclipse' (significant in a Miltonic context, cf. *PL* 1.597), and in rendering the biblical paraphrase of 'Let there be light, and light was over all' he uses two different Hungarian expressions (*világosság* and *fény*) for 'light', only one of which (*világosság*) evokes archaic biblical phrasing. Overall, it can be said that Jánosházy trades the original's poetic and allusive richness for clarity and intelligibility; on the other hand, his attempt to faithfully interpret the content and the dramatic structure of his source as well as his avoidance of archaisms make for an easily readable text.

Jánosházy's translation thus presented an up-to-date, marketable version of Milton's tragedy for audiences in the 1970s. Curiously, however, his 'Afterword' (*Utószó*) to the translation seems to hark back to an earlier era. Here Jánosházy strikes a critical note familiar from the 1950s: he lays great emphasis on the drama's revolutionary nature and Samson's 'Promethean' qualities, although he states that Milton 'could not yet see in Prometheus the "patron saint of the proletariat" like the modern Marxist historian, Thomson' (*még nem láthatta Prométheuszban 'a proletariátus védőszentjét', mint Thomson a modern marxista történelemtudós*).[70] In the 'Afterword' Jánosházy identifies *Samson Agonistes* as 'the other masterpiece by Milton' (*Milton másik remeke*) which 'has been overshadowed by *Paradise Lost*' (*így szorította mindmáig háttérbe Az Elveszett Paradicsom*) and which is more 'human' (*emberibb*) and expresses the poet's intention 'more clearly, more evidently' (*világosabban, egyértelműbben*) than the great epic.[71] The tragedy is a great step forward for Milton, since 'the service of God is here practically the service of the people' (*Isten szolgálata itt gyakorlatilag: népszolgálat*). Samson is thus a symbol, 'the embodiment of a captive people's dreams and desires' (*egy láncon tartott nép álmainak és vágyainak megtestesülése*), and his 'victory ... anticipates the historic triumph of the people' (*győzelme a ... nép történelmi diadalát vetíti előre*).[72]

It may seem strange that the paratext of a translation published in a period of mild state socialism (the mid-1970s) should present an interpretation of Milton's drama with such explicit 'Marxist-Leninist' overtones – as if nothing happened in two decades, or the spirit of Tibor Lutter has risen from the dead. One could even argue that the Marxist strains are much more integrated in Jánosházy's afterword than in Dybas's preface (where they seem to be obligatory add-ons). One possible way to explain the amplification of the ideological content is concerned with the circumstances of publication: Jánosházy's translation was published at the heyday of Nicolae Ceaușescu's communist regime in Romania (which, by the 1970s, followed a less 'liberal' course than its Hungarian counterparts), and the need to produce it probably required strong justification in the critical apparatus.

Jánosházy's afterword might well have been the product of (self-)censorship, but for Hungarian publishers working in the 1970s (who quickly noticed the new version) the ideological buttressing of Milton's drama seems to have been of little importance in the process of selecting works for publication. Szabolcs Várady, in a reader's report prepared for the Európa Publishing House (for a volume of Milton's selected works) appreciates the 'great poetry' (*hatalmas költészet*) of Milton's drama requiring 'immense linguistic energy and exceptional congeniality' (*roppant nyelvi erőt és kivételes beleérzőképességet követel*) from a translator, and praises Jánosházy's version for being 'correct, and at times beautiful work' (*korrekt, sokhelyütt szép munka*).[73] In a second report another reader writes, perhaps with some irony: 'In the characteristically thorough and insightful afterword *written with some natural bias* Jánosházy draws a convincing picture of Milton's career' (*Jánosházy a rá annyira jellemző gondossággal és hozzáértéssel és egy kis természetes elfogultsággal megírt utószavában meggyőző pályaképet rajzol Miltonról*).[74] Tellingly, when Európa finally published its landmark Milton volume in 1978 (containing most of the minor poems, *Paradise Lost* and *Samson*), it reprinted Jánosházy's translation with the translator's notes to the text, but without the afterword. In the long run, Jánosházy's version became the standard text of Milton's tragedy; it was also reprinted, together with Jánosy's *Paradise Lost*, in 1987.

Paradise Lost . . . to Which Is Added Samson Agonistes – and the last days of communism

The fact that the Európa Publishing House got rid of Jánosházy's 'Afterword' but kept and (re-)published his translation testifies to the general trend observed throughout this book: by the late 1960s and the

1970s Milton's works did not have to be wrapped in explicitly didactic 'Marxist-Leninist' ideas to be publishable. This, of course, did not mean that the revolutionary potential of Milton's works was no longer explored by critics, nor did it diminish the status of *Samson Agonistes* as Milton's 'other masterpiece'. When, for example, in 1968, seven years after it was published, Mihály Szegedy-Maszák reviewed *Milton's God* he picked Empson's chapter on Samson as

> *különösen meggyőző [mivel] megérteti az olvasóval, hogy Milton itt magához közelebb eső témát választott, közvetlen utalás nélkül a keresztény túlvilágra, miközben az erkölcsi összetettség kérdését még tovább űzte.*

> (especially convincing [since] they make the reader understand that Milton chose a topic closer to himself without direct reference to the Christian otherworld, pursuing questions of moral complexity even further.)

Samson thus becomes 'yet another step in the development of an immense intellect' (*még további fok egy hatalmas szellem fejlődésében*).[75] A year later, in 1969, a new translation of *Paradise Lost* by István Jánosy was published, with Miklós Szenczi's essay on Milton's life and work entitled 'Milton Agonistes' as afterword (up to 1987 this milestone essay was republished at the end of every major volume of Milton's poetry in Hungary).[76] Szenczi's reading of *Samson* in this essay is a far cry from the tendentious 'Marxist-Leninist' interpretations sampled above: he is alert to the moral nuances of Milton's tragedy as well as the contradictions hidden in the word 'agonistes', and, significantly, he does not imply that the tragedy represents the climax of Milton's career. Still, the title of his essay with its apparent strangeness helped to keep Milton's tragedy in the focus of attention, and to secure *Samson*'s place as the 'other masterpiece' for Hungarian readers.

The widespread endorsement of the work of Christopher Hill among Hungarian academics in the period under discussion also contributed to the promotion of Milton's tragedy. Thus, in 1975, Hill's essay 'Milton the radical' (originally published in the *Times Literary Supplement* and presenting *Samson* as Milton's most radical work) was translated into Hungarian by Ferenc Takács for the 'materialist' periodical *Világosság*. In his introductory note to the translation, Takács criticises the 'Marxists of the 30s' (such as Christopher Caudwell or Edgell Rickword) for their 'undifferentiated notion of progress', and promotes Hill's more nuanced interpretation of Milton's radicalism.[77] Intriguingly, Hill – like Szenczi eight years before him – adopted the title 'Milton Agonistes' for one of the subchapters of his conclusion of *Milton and the English Revolution*, reinforcing the parallel between the hero of Milton's tragedy and the Milton 'the radical' himself.[78] For Hungarian critics this (certainly accidental) parallel between the work of Szenczi and Hill must have provided some reassurance about the validity of their efforts.

Samson Agonistes thus became the second most important and most widely published of Milton's works for Hungarian readers in the period under discussion. This was also the Miltonic work that, through the original publication of Jánosházy's translation by the Bucharest-based Kriterion Publishing House, reached the widest range of Hungarian readers (Hungarians in Hungary as well as ethnic Hungarians in Romania). What is more, its reputation seems to have lingered well beyond the change of system in 1989. Ágnes Heller, writing in 2007, half a decade after the post 9/11 renewal of the *Samson* debate, repeats as self-evident the idea that *Samson* is Milton's 'crowning achievement' (*életének megkoronázása*), quite ignoring contemporary readings of the text.[79] But nowhere is this peculiarity of the Hungarian reception more apparent than in the last volume of Milton's poetry published before the collapse of communism. In 1987 *Paradise Lost* was published together with *Samson Agonistes*, and this hybrid volume, which could well bear the title *Paradise Lost to Which Is Added Samson Agonistes* has served as the definitive collection of Milton's late masterpieces for much of the past three decades.[80]

This treatment of Milton's tragedy and its hero is not remotely similar to the post-war developments in English and American criticism and scholarship. As is well known, the resurgence of critical interest in *Samson Agonistes*, heralded by Christopher Hill in *Milton and the English Revolution* and initiated by Joseph Wittreich's seminal *Interpreting Samson Agonistes*, has led to a memorable debate in international Milton studies between what are usually called the redemptionist (or traditionalist) and the revisionist schools of interpretation, justifying and problematising Samson's actions, respectively.[81] The Western critical tradition thus continued to explore the possible conflicts and tensions within Milton's tragedy and its hero, investigating the ways in which 'this drama invites readers to recognize the frailty and fallenness of all leaders and peoples'.[82] By contrast, the alternative and somewhat obscure tradition of *Samson* criticism we have surveyed in this chapter – practised in some socialist circles in the West, but much more rife among literary critics in communist Hungary – remained one-sided: it developed its own 'redemptionist' or 'traditional' school (without a 'revisionist' side) justifying in Samson's vengeful act not the ways of God, but mostly the cause of the revolution and 'the people'. Partly inspired and strongly influenced by some of those Western critics (most notably William Empson and Christopher Hill) – who reflected critically on what John P. Rumrich calls the 'invented Milton' of modern Milton criticism[83] – Hungarians used *Samson* to invent their own Milton. The tragedy became the revolutionary masterpiece, its chief character the exemplary hero acting for the people. The individual critical positions are naturally varied and nuanced, but one of the implied premises in all cited sources seems to be that in *Samson Agonistes* Milton commendably managed to get rid of his religious ballast.

This line of interpretation might well be paralleled by Milton's career in other Eastern European countries: most recently Oydin Uzakova has shown how in 1964 the Soviet critic R. M. Samarin celebrated Milton's 'revolutionary classicism' in *Samson*, and how he played down the importance of *Paradise Regained* to find 'revolutionary parallels' between *Paradise Lost* and *Samson*.[84] But whereas in Milton's Russian reception, we can also observe a pre-communist and a post-communist tradition of translating and interpreting *Samson Agonistes*,[85] in Hungary the reception of Milton's tragedy remains within the paradigm sketched above, since the pre-war phase of the reception is, as we have seen, confined to a few stereotypical remarks. At the end of the day, we are left with a dilemma. On the one hand, the consistent emergence of *Samson Agonistes* as the 'other masterpiece' both in translation and criticism is an interesting and unique phenomenon that might warrant further critical attention. On the other hand, the professedly selective reading of Western critical trends and the constant balancing of *Paradise Lost* with *Samson* (quite literally in the 1987 volume which contains only these two works) is uncannily reminiscent of the special practice of 'goulash communism',[86] the tacit and compromised introduction of Western (capitalist) values while preserving the rickety facade of 'Marxist-Leninist' ideology. Applying both the negative and the positive senses of the proverb, might we risk observing that Hungarian Miltonists, by shaping Milton's tragedy as 'the other masterpiece' and Samson as a proto-socialist hero, might just have wanted – in a rather un-Miltonic manner – to have their cake and eat it too?

Notes

1. This chapter is adapted from my article 'Samson: An unlikely hero of socialism': see Péti 2021b.
2. Williams 2001, 180.
3. Wesling 1980, 48.

4. Brown, Finch and Kumin 2005, 168.
5. See Milton 2009, 461.
6. Cohen 2010, 216, emphasis in the original.
7. Cohen 2010, 215.
8. See Achinstein 2008 and Achinstein 2010.
9. On Williams's indebtedness to Milton in his other poems, see Duran 2014.
10. See, e.g. Achinstein 1996; Keeble 1987, 188–9 and *passim*.
11. Worden 1995, 111.
12. Achinstein 2010, 47.
13. Achinstein 2008, 806.
14. Hill 1977, 470.
15. Wolfe 1963, 32. For Wolfe's pragmatist, presentist position in detail, see Achinstein 2008.
16. Wolfe 1963, 323.
17. Hammond 2014, 249.
18. Present e.g. in the works of John Brown and Frederick Douglass; see Blight 2018, 309.
19. Caudwell 1937, 84; see also MacDonald 2005, 30–1.
20. DeLeon 1903, 3.
21. DeLeon 1906, 1.
22. DeLeon 1908, 1.
23. Anon. 1938, 325.
24. Visick 1949, 189–90.
25. Anon. 1958b, 551.
26. Anon. 1958b, 553.
27. Pearce 1958, 332.
28. Sauer 2001, 159. For post-Cold War scholarship of Milton informed by Marxism, see Kendrick 1986, Jameson 1986 or Bartolovich 2012.
29. Hill 1977, 441, 446.
30. Foot 2002, 16–17.
31. Titusz Dugovics is reputed to have pulled a Turk to his death from the wall at the siege of Nándorfehérvár (Belgrade) in 1456. See e.g. Alexander von Wagner's painting *Titusz Dugovics Sacrifices Himself* (1859) in the collection of the Hungarian National Gallery, Budapest.
32. The earliest Hungarian adaptation of the Samson story is in a romance written by Péter Kákonyi (1579). Samson's strength serves to illustrate the hero's prowess in János Arany's nineteenth-century epic *Toldi* (3.5), while another nineteenth-century poet, Mihály Tompa, wrote an ode to Samson warning him of the enchanting embrace of Delilah and the cunning Philistines. Several elements of the Samson story are represented on medieval stone reliefs in the crypt of Pécs Cathedral.
33. Macaulay 1825, 314. The Hungarian translation is by Mihály Könyves Tóth (Könyves Tóth 1860, 505).
34. Milton 1890, 17.
35. Yolland 1912, 507.
36. Milton 1930, viii–ix.
37. Babits 1934, 267–8.
38. Szerb 1957, 1:367.
39. On Szabó's translation of *Paradise Lost*, see Chapter 1.
40. Szabó 2002, 2:997. On the patriarchal element in Milton's Hungarian reception see Chapter 4.
41. In 1954 a popular novel entitled *Sámson* was published by Sándor Rideg. Its hero, a Hungarian peasant youth, resembles the biblical Samson in his strength, but during his prewar adventures, he also gets into contact with the underground communist movement and becomes persecuted by the 'counter-revolutionary' police.
42. Milton 1955, 5–6.
43. Milton 1955, 14.
44. Milton 1955, 35.
45. Kühnová 2007, 345.
46. Hammond 2014, 239–41.
47. Anon. 1970.
48. Milton 1955, 58–9.
49. Milton 1955, 59.
50. Kardos 1954, 117.

51. Kéry 1956, 1039–40.
52. Viktor 1955, 5, emphases in the original.
53. On Lutter's work, see Chapter 3.
54. Lutter 1956a, 212.
55. Lutter 1956a, 200.
56. To my knowledge, Eörsi translated only these lines from Milton's drama.
57. Anon. 1954/5, 2–3.
58. Anon. 1954/5, 11.
59. Anon. 1958c, 1.
60. For a more detailed discussion of this 1958 volume as well as the reader's report, see Chapter 4.
61. Veress 1958, 2; Szenczi, Szobotka and Katona, 1972, 215–16.
62. Anon. 1954, 4. The event was advertised as a 'special literary event'. Samson was played by Ferenc Bessenyei; Delilah was Lőrinc Szabó's daughter, Klára Gáborjáni (on Lőrinc Szabó's translations, see Chapter 1).
63. Samson was played by Gábor Mádi-Szabó, and Delilah by Hédi Váradi.
64. Anon. 2021.
65. Heller 2007, 168.
66. Neubauer 2004, 59.
67. Milton 1977, 37.
68. Milton 1955, 27.
69. Milton 1977, 13.
70. Milton 1977, 86.
71. Milton 1977, 73–4. We should also remember how in the process he lambasts *Paradise Regained* in the same 'Afterword'; see Chapter 1.
72. Milton 1977, 83, 85.
73. Várady 1975, 1–2. I thank Szabolcs Várady for the permission to quote from his report.
74. Anon. 1975, 1, emphasis mine.
75. Szegedy-Maszák 1968, 161. A similarly teleological but naturally much more nuanced view of the position of *Samson Agonistes* in Milton's oeuvre, which takes account of religion's role in the tragedy, is in Radzinowicz 1978.
76. On Szenczi's essay, and Jánosy's translation, see Chapters 1 and 3.
77. Takács 1975, 406–8.
78. Neither Szenczi nor Hill are original in their use of the phrase 'Milton Agonistes': as far as I can ascertain, Edward Harold Visiak's 1923 book was the first to use the phrase, which suggests a strong parallel between Milton's Samson and Milton himself.
79. Heller 2007, 156.
80. The situation has slowly but surely changed in the past few years. In early 2019 a new prose translation of *Paradise Regained* was published, and a new translation of *Paradise Lost* is underway.
81. See Gregerson 2014 for a short description of these schools and the challenge of the status quo in recent criticism.
82. Lewalski 2010, 43.
83. Rumrich 1996, 2–4.
84. Uzakova 2014, 121.
85. On Milton's Russian reception in general, see also Boss 1991.
86. See Kovrig 1986.

3
A tale of two scholars: Milton's prose in communist Hungary

Great expectations

During the short democratic spell between 1945 and 1947 the literary historian István Gál[1] published a proposal to improve English coursebooks for Hungarian students in secondary schools. He concluded on an optimistic note, suggesting that teaching English could gain historic momentum in the coming years:

> A magyar újságírás, a magyar szónoklat, a magyar történetírás, de maga a magyar széppróza is megérett a megújhodásra, a fölfrissülésre. A magyar prózára régebben a latin, a francia, az olasz, sőt a spanyol irodalom is jótékony hatással volt. A századforduló, helyesebben egy évszázad óta a francia hatás élvez egyeduralmat. Kossuthot és Babitsot kivéve, az angol próza Magyarországon, a lírával ellentétben, még alig hatott. E téren valóban évszázadok mulasztásait kell behoznunk. Majesztétikus, terjengős, nehézkes prózastílusunknak legalább a XVII. századi angol próza hajlékonyságát, kifejezőkészségét, érzékletességét kell utolérnie. [...] Az angol valóságérzék, az angol reális stílus, az angol költői szárnyalás rajongóinak és híveinek új seregét a középiskolai angol nevelésnek kell kinevelnie.[2]

(Hungarian journalism, rhetoric, historiography and Hungarian fictional prose itself is ripe now for renewal and refreshment. In the old days Latin, French, Italian and even Spanish literature had exerted a beneficial influence on Hungarian prose. Since the turn of the century, or, more precisely, for the last hundred years, the French influence has been exclusive. With the exception of Kossuth and Babits, and quite unlike English poetry, English prose has not had any influence in Hungary. In this respect we are indeed centuries behind. Our pompous, long-winded, heavy prose style must achieve the flexibility, expressiveness and vividness of seventeenth-century English prose at the least . . . A new host of devotees of the English sense of reality, of the English realistic style, and of English poetic flights must be raised in the English education of secondary schools.)

We can only speculate what seventeenth-century English writers Gál had in mind as exemplars of 'flexibility, expressiveness and vividness', but Milton's prose works must have been among them. Earlier in the article Gál praises an eighth-grade secondary school textbook for illustrating English–Hungarian relations with an excerpt from Milton. The textbook in question features Cromwell's letter of May 1655 addressed to the Transylvanian prince György Rákóczi (Transylvania at that point was ruled by Hungarians) which garners support for the Protestant cause and sympathy for the massacred Waldensians (this was probably the first document written by Milton to be read by Hungarians).[3] Later Gál commends Gábor Halász's 1942 anthology *The Treasure-House of English Literature* (*Az angol irodalom kincsesháza*) where, among other specimens of English prose (by Evelyn, Pepys, Bunyan or Defoe), an excerpt from *Areopagitica* (containing the reference to the 'grave and frugal *Transilvanian*',[4] of which more below) is published in Hungarian translation. According to Gál's optimistic assessment, Milton's prose was to matter more in Hungarian culture than ever before.

It took less than two years for such enthusiasm to be chilled by the communist takeover of 1948 and the switching of Hungary to Cold War mode. During the four decades of communism English as an academic subject was viewed by the establishment with varying degrees of suspicion; at the extreme, during Rákosi's dictatorship, students and professors of English were even considered 'agents of imperialism'.[5] In such a cultural milieu Gál's wishes for a new generation of anglophile enthusiasts educated on English masters of prose could never come true. In Milton's case this meant that his openly political and religious prose, and especially the strong parrhesiastic thrust of *Areopagitica* – in which it is proposed that the 'free and bold speech' of a 'citizen offering sincere criticism' be listened to 'without censure'[6] – was hardly to be tolerated. Not surprisingly, among all Milton's works published in Hungary, it was the prose works that had the poorest post-war reception in terms of volume. No prose piece by Milton, not even the short *Of Education*, was translated or published in its entirety during the four decades of state socialism. Even in an international context, Milton's prose works have of course never been as popular as his poetry, but it is quite telling that in Hungary in the years 1948 to 1989 *Paradise Lost, Samson* and the minor poems were republished several times, but only one rather thin volume featured the prose writings. This 1975 volume – edited by Miklós Szenczi, the foremost Milton scholar of the day, and entitled *Milton, the Mirror of the English Revolution* (*Milton, az angol forradalom tükre*) – provided a representative, albeit highly selective cross-section of Milton's English and Latin pamphlets, correspondence and other prose writings.[7] It has, however, remained largely unnoticed in modern Hungarian culture.

Despite this apparent lack of interest, the reception of Milton's prose in communist Hungary provides an important interface to uncover the ambivalent attitudes towards Milton's oeuvre and cultural status in the four decades of state socialism. As a public pamphleteer and orator whose political thinking was inseparable from his deep religious convictions, Milton clearly presented a problem, and the achievements of his 'left hand' (a phrase he uses for his prose works in the *Reason of Church Government*[8]) had to be heavily curated before they were made public. To make matters more complicated, communist cultural policymakers, who were often snobbish and elitist,[9] were keen to marshal classical precedents in service of the new 'revolutionary' ideas, and Milton's prose works, with their insistence on confronting questions of liberty, freedom of conscience or popular sovereignty head on, could – at least in theory – have been ideal vehicles for such purposes. Dealing with Milton's prose, then, was to be a delicate task, and it is no wonder that only the two most prominent Hungarian Milton scholars of the post-war period, Tibor Lutter and Miklós Szenczi, ventured into the field. As frequent references and quotations in all chapters of this book demonstrate, both Lutter and Szenczi were chief actors in Milton's post-war Hungarian reception. This chapter will, however, offer an extensive and comprehensive consideration of their work on Milton, highlighting characteristic differences in their professional contexts and respective careers. By the end of the discussion it will become clear that the ambivalence towards Milton the man and his work in the Party's official cultural policy was intriguingly paralleled in the different, and differently emblematic, courses these two scholars took (and were forced to take) through their lives. First, however, let us briefly survey the Hungarian career of Milton's prose works before 1945.

'The black sin of regicide' vs 'captivating ideas': Milton's prose in pre-war Hungary

Milton took pride in his political achievement – the 'noble task, / Of which all Europe talks from side to side'[10] – which, until the beginning of the eighteenth century, accounted for most of his fame both in Britain and abroad.[11] Just like in Western Europe, in late seventeenth-century Hungary it was not *Paradise Lost* but Milton's prose writings, and especially the regicide tracts, that found an early audience – some even in Milton's lifetime. The Teleki-Bolyai Library in Marosvásárhely (now Târgu-Mureş, Romania) holds a 1652 copy of *Defensio pro Populo Anglicano* (bound in the same volume with Salmasius' *Defensio Regia pro Carolo I*) which belonged to István Csengeri, preacher and later professor of the Calvinist College of Nagyenyed (today Aiud, Romania), who probably bought the volume during his journey to London. Milton's *Defensio* was considered near-illicit material, and Csengeri's copy of the pamphlet is unique in Central and Eastern Europe in that its possessor can be identified – even decades later it was customary to leave only one's initials on such dangerous writing.[12] From extant copies in libraries and private collections it can be inferred that in the eighteenth century the regicide tracts were read and studied mostly by intellectuals connected with the Protestant colleges,[13] but knowledge about Milton's political writings was probably widespread among Hungarian readers. This is suggested, for example, by the journalist Sándor Szacsvay's proverbial reference to Milton 'who could defend the bad cause of the English in the execution of Charles I very well' (*a' ki az Anglusok roszsz ügyét I.ső Károly el-vesztésében igen jól tutta védelmezni*) in the twenty-second issue of the *Magyar Kurír* (Hungarian courier) in 1792.[14] By the 1790s Milton's Hungarian reception was already dominated by discussions (and translations) of *Paradise Lost*,[15] but Szacsvay's quip indicates that his political work also contributed significantly to his reputation.

This dual image of Milton as a poet and a politician remained prevalent in the early nineteenth century. The several different forms and forums of striving for national independence and culture (the culturally vibrant period of Hungary between 1825 and 1848 is called the 'Reform Era'), however, provided a variety of critical attitudes ranging from outright rejection to enthusiastic endorsement of his political works. The first detailed discussion of his oeuvre, an essay which was published in three parts in *Honművész* (*The Patriotic*

Artist), a periodical catering primarily for women readers, provides an ambiguous assessment. The author (indicated only by the initials 'N. A.') seems to commend Milton and pity Charles I at the same time as observing that Milton, 'enraptured by the fire of his nation, wrote much about the freedom of the Church and overmuch against his hapless prince' (*Nemzete tüzétől elragadtatva igen sokat irt az egyház szabadságáról, és szerfölött is sokat szerencsétlen fejedelme ellen*) and, alluding to the sonnet quoted above, concludes that 'due to the determination shining in these works [the regicide tracts] all the world was talking about him' (*E' munkájiban tü[n]döklő elszántságáért az egész világ róla beszélt*).[16] By contrast, the editor of the periodical *Religio*, the Catholic priest János Danielik, who in the first stage of his career was fiercely loyal to the Habsburgs, included Milton's regicide tracts among the examples of 'such teaching and such principles' (*illy tanitás, és illy elvek*) as are characterised by 'angry passions, selfishness, party spirit, revenge and disobedience' (*dühös szenvedélyeknek, önzésnek, pártszellemnek, bosszunak, engedetlenségnek*).[17]

The second part of the nineteenth century brought a significant change in Hungarian conceptions of Milton as a historical figure,[18] and also as a writer of political prose. This was the time when Hungarian intellectuals discovered Thomas Babington Macaulay's writings, among them his famous essay (translated several times during the nineteenth century) in which Milton is celebrated not only as 'the glory of English literature' but also as 'the champion and the martyr of English liberty'.[19] This transition towards a new image of Milton the politician is well captured in the first scholarly dissertation on Milton, Lázár Petrochevich Horváth's inaugural address to the Hungarian Academy of Sciences, which voices the old concerns about 'the black sin of regicide' (*a királygyilkosság' fekete bűne*), but at the same time promotes 'the captivating ideas' (*megragadó gondolati*) of *Areopagitica*, whose 'robust language makes us recognise the poet of *Paradise Lost*' (*Ezen erőteljes nyelvről ismerni rá a Vesztett Paradicsom' költőjére*).[20] Similarly, Gusztáv Jánosi, a Catholic priest and the translator of *Paradise Lost*, in the preface to his translation, mentions *Areopagitica* as Milton's 'masterpiece' (*remek művét*) but reserves some sarcasm for the other political tracts in which Milton 'believed the illusions he created' (*beleéli magát . . . maga szerezte illusióiba*), and chiefly for the *Defensio*, which 'became the prayer book of Puritans' (*a puritánok imádságos könyve lőn*).[21]

Although the *Defensio* was occasionally still recognised as 'the most notable work [Milton] wrote in prose' (*Legjelesebb műve, melyet folyóbeszédben írt)*,[22] from the time of the 1848–9 revolution and war of independence writers' and critics' attention shifted to *Areopagitica*. The chief political concern of the period chimed well with Milton's 1644 pamphlet: the first of the Twelve Points (a list of demands by the revolutionary youth of 1848) demanded the freedom of the press and the abolition of censorship (*Kívánjuk a' sajtó szabadságát, censura eltörlését*), and Mihály Táncsics, one of the emblematic figures of the revolution, had published a pamphlet in 1844 entitled *A Prisoner's Views on the Freedom of the Press* (*Sajtószabadságról nézetei egy rabnak*).[23] Thus, we find the ethnographer Henrik Wlislocki publishing a brief but enthusiastic appreciation of *Areopagitica* in the periodical of the Hungarian Academy of Sciences (*Egyetemes Philologiai Közlöny*) in 1884, the year when prosecutors of the Budapest court could still mount an eventually unsuccessful libel suit against two Workers' Party activists for reading out a Marxist manifesto in public.[24]

Macaulay's view of Milton remained a major influence on Hungarian literature and culture in the first part of the twentieth century (and even into the post-war period),[25] and *Areopagitica* in particular was celebrated as Milton's definitive achievement in prose. There are, of course, curious exceptions: Arthur Yolland, an Englishman by birth and the founder of the first university department of English studies in Hungary, published an article on Milton in 1912 where almost all of Milton's political prose works are rather severely treated: *Areopagitica* is only passingly mentioned, *Eikonoklastes* is a 'scurrilous attack' (*förmedvény*) and the *Defensio* is described as a 'ramshackle apology' (*roskadozó apológia*) characterised by 'political immaturity [and] grammatical hair-splitting' (*politikai éretlenség, grammatikai szőrszálhasogatás*).[26] A more characteristic assessment of Milton's prose is provided by Géza Voinovoich who, in his history of English literature, states that Milton 'has no greater work than *Areopagitica* (1644), which is the most fiery apology of the freedom of the press' (*nincs hatalmasabb munkája az Areopagiticánál (1644), mely a legtüzesebb védirat a sajtószabadság mellett*), and considers Milton a forerunner of Rousseau's idea of popular sovereignty in the regicide tracts.[27]

Finally, this period also serves up an interesting example of Hungarian intellectuals exploring and using the less familiar, intolerant side of Milton: in his discussion of *Areopagitica* the conservative agrarian politician István Bernát evoked Milton's ideal, 'the successful prevalence of Christian spirit through liberty' (*a keresztény léleknek a szabadság révén való érvényesülése*) in *Areopagitica*, to establish what he deemed to be necessary preconditions for the freedom of the press.[28]

Milton, the 'poet of the English bourgeois revolution'

Thus, by the beginning of the twentieth century we find a good number of references to *Areopagitica*, even though the first long excerpt from this pamphlet was translated and published only during World War II in Gábor Halász's *The Treasure-House of English Literature* (*Az angol irodalom kincseskháza*, 1942).[29] Halász selected a number of texts from the various phases of Milton's career ('Il penseroso', Sonnet 19, Satan's speech from Book 1 of *Paradise Lost*), concluding with a long paragraph from *Areopagitica* in Miklós Szentkuthy's rendering.[30] In the paragraph in question Milton draws an explicit contrast between the famously 'quick, ingenious, and piercing spirit' of the English and the forces (the 'obdurate Clergy') that make them 'the latest and backwardest Schollers' in the present. What is at stake, Milton proposes in the same passage, is the recognition and understanding of God's will, the 'reforming of Reformation it self', although Milton's fellow-countrymen 'mark not the method of his counsels, and are unworthy' – as is apparent in the 'fantastic terrors [i.e. fears] of sect and schism'.

In the headnote to Milton's texts, Gábor Halász emphasises the religious character of Milton's pamphlet when he points out that 'In his magnificent prose invective against censorship [Milton] defended the freedom of conscience' (*a lelkiismereti szabadságot védte nagyszerű prózai vádiratában a cenzúra ellen*).[31] The Miltonic passage in Halász's anthology, however, also opens alternative avenues of interpretation: it contains Milton's well-known formulation 'Where there is much desire to learn, there of necessity will be much arguing, much writing, many opinions; for opinion in good men is but knowledge in the making,' but for Hungarian readers it must also have been remarkable for its reference to Transylvanian sojourners to England: 'Nor is it for nothing that the grave and frugal *Transilvanian* sends out yearly from as farre as the mountanous borders of *Russia*, and beyond the *Hercynian* wildernes, not their youth, but their stay'd men, to learn our language, and our *theologic arts*.' In 1942, merely two years after the Second Vienna Award in which Hungary re-annexed the northern part of Transylvania, this reference (as well as Milton's ardently nationalist rhetoric) must have resonated with a number of Hungarian readers.[32]

Coming to the era that is the focus of our discussion, it is important to state that although 1948 brought drastic changes in Hungarian cultural policy, in the case of Milton's works this did not entail a radical programme of commissioning new translations. As we shall see in Chapter 4, Árpád

Tóth's translations of the minor poems (published in the 1920s) were frequently reprinted under communism, and even Gusztáv Jánosi's late nineteenth-century translation of *Paradise Lost* was widely referenced in the criticism of the post-war period (although its translator and its pre-war reception were certainly suspicious for their conspicuously religious tendencies).[33]

In a similar vein, an edited version of the same excerpt from *Areopagitica* was also reprinted in 1960 in an anthology of English literature edited by Tibor Lutter (one of the chief figures in this chapter), published 'exclusively for school students' (*Csak iskolai tanulók részére*). In his headnote to the Milton section of the anthology Lutter focuses on the revolutionary character of Milton's life and oeuvre: echoing Friedrich Engels, he makes it clear that even in Milton's late poetry 'the symbolic significance of the biblical subject applies to the English revolution, since this revolution was fought in the mantle of religious slogans' (*a bibliai tárgy jelképes értelme az angol forradalomra vonatkozik, hiszen ezt a forradalmat még vallási jelszavak köntösében vívták*).[34] The excerpts from Milton's texts are selected accordingly: *Areopagitica* is placed at the front, followed by the sonnet to Cromwell and the dialogue of Satan and Beelzebub from Book 1 of *Paradise Lost* (1.50–224). The only point where the revolutionary ardour seems to abate somewhat is in the piece concluding the selection, Eve's famous and much-anthologised love poem to Adam (*PL* 4.641–56).

If the excerpt from *Areopagitica* in Halász's anthology was brief, Lutter managed to make it even more succinct. The reference to Transylvania and the extolling of English national virtues were cut from the beginning, understandably, since in the post-war years any discussion of Transylvania (a part of Romania since the Versailles Peace Treaty, then partly re-annexed by Hungary in 1940, then in turn re-annexed by Romania in 1945) was extremely sensitive and carefully avoided whenever possible. As a result of Lutter's editing, the text not only loses its nationalistic tone and frame of reference (in service of a more 'internationalist' interpretation), but also starts on a millenarian note not altogether alien from the Stalinist rhetoric of the 1950s: 'Now once again by all concurrence of signs and by the generall instinct of holy and devout men . . . God is decreeing to begin some new and great period in his Church, ev'n to the reforming of Reformation it self.'

It is also interesting to observe how one of the less felicitous turns of phrase in Szentkuthy's translation serves Lutter's revolutionary agenda. In the original Milton complains that 'Under these fantastic terrors of sect and schism, we wrong the earnest and zealous thirst after knowledge and understanding which God hath stirr'd up in this city.' Szentkuthy translates Milton's 'fantastic terrors' as *fantasztikus rémuralma* ('fantastic terrorism'). The translation is based on an obvious error: Milton's mentioning of 'terrors' has nothing to do with terrorism, but is a clear reference to what David Loewenstein calls the 'fear-mongering, anti-tolerationist Presbyterian discourse which was aggressively promoting an increasingly divisive religious worldview'.[35] What is more, the adjective *fantasztikus* in Hungarian is primarily used to refer to something shocking or astonishing, as opposed to the English 'fantastic' which means, in the original context, 'imaginary' or 'unreal'.[36] By leaving the phrase *fantasztikus rémuralma* ('fantastic terrorism') uncorrected in this reprinting of Szentkuthy's translation, Lutter presented a distinctly anti-sectarian text to Hungarian readers – quite the opposite of what Milton had originally set down. Given that Lutter was certainly aware of the correct interpretation of Milton's text (and knew Szentkuthy as a friend),[37] and that 'sectarianism' has since the *Communist Manifesto* been one of the anathemas of Marxist thinking, it seems highly unlikely that leaving the mistranslation uncorrected was mere editorial oversight.

Lutter's edition of this anthology is practically his last independent professional achievement (he died in 1960), and the way he presents Milton's works, and *Areopagitica* in particular, certainly reflects some of his long-standing convictions about Milton and his significance in English literary history. Although much of what he published has now been relegated to oblivion, or eclipsed by the achievements of some of his contemporaries (most notably the other chief figure of this chapter, Miklós Szenczi), Lutter has cast a long shadow on the modern Hungarian reception of Milton – to the present day, his 1956 monograph *John Milton, the Poet of the English Bourgeois Revolution* (*John Milton, az angol polgári forradalom költője*) remains the only extended discussion of Milton's oeuvre in Hungarian. His reputation as one-time director (and according to many, the nemesis) of the Eötvös József Collegium has been consistently low since the 1960s, yet even in 1991 Lutter was referred to as 'Milton's . . . monographer, the well-trained scholar of English studies' (*Milton ... monográfusa, a jólképzett anglista*) in an article otherwise highly critical of his activities.[38] In order to get a fuller understanding of this difficult legacy, therefore, it is necessary to go beyond the isolated case of the 1960 anthology, and take a closer look at Lutter's career, with special focus on his works on Milton.

Born in 1910 in a Catholic family, Lutter graduated in English, French and Hungarian from Pázmány Péter University, Budapest in

1933. He received his doctorate in 1936, then became a *Privatdozent* for the English enlightenment in 1948, and obtained his CSc (Candidate of Sciences, the equivalent of a PhD) in literature in 1955.[39] By this time he was one of the authorities on English literature in Hungary: he published on a wide variety of authors from Chaucer to Joyce, supplied a number of prefaces and commentaries to Shakespeare's plays, translated some English and American works into Hungarian (such as Stella Gibbons's *Here Be Dragons*, and Washington Irving's *Sketch Book*), and contributed reader's reports to publishing houses.[40] Throughout his career Lutter strove for some comprehensive, yet up-to-date vision of English literature (and history),[41] and his efforts seem to culminate in what he terms his 'Marxist-Leninist' interpretation of Milton's oeuvre. His main focus seems to have been on a number of classic authors – quite in conformity with his own recommendations in one of his reader's reports for a publishing house: 'Our progressive literary policy follows the right path if it breaks once-for-all with the temptation of bestsellers, and commissions the translation only of outstanding works from the moderns, or classics' (*haladó irodalompolitikánk akkor jár helyes úton, ha egyszer-s-mindenkorra szakít a bestseller-kísértéstől; a modernek közül csak kimagaslóan nagyot, vagy klasszikust fordítani*).[42]

Lutter's most important works on Milton are dated, intriguingly, to the years of hardline communist dictatorship (1948–56). During these eight years Lutter contributed an article to a volume reassessing the classics of world literature, taught at least one university course on Milton and seventeenth-century English literature (a typed synopsis of which is in the holdings of the National Széchényi Library), completed and defended a CSc dissertation on 'Milton, the Poet of the English Bourgeois Revolution', and published the revised text of this in a monograph in 1956. It is in these documents – the monograph, the lecture notes and the several shorter essays published during this period – that we can witness the development of Lutter's strategies to adapt Milton's life and work to the aesthetic tenets of communism.

One of the earliest reflections of Lutter's views on Milton, and one in which he is at his most radical, is a lengthy study he published in 1952 in *World Literature Yearbook* (*Világirodalmi évkönyv*), a publication of the Közoktatásügyi Kiadóvállalat (Public Education Publishing House) run by the Ministry of Public Education. The objective of the *Yearbook* was, according to its editor, László Kardos, to provide a survey of recent Hungarian research 'mainly on Soviet and classical Russian literature, the literature of the People's Democracies, and the progressive aspects of Western literatures' (*főleg a szovjet és klasszikus orosz irodalomnak, a népi demokráciák irodalmának és a nyugati irodalmak haladó mozzanatainak*). The articles in the volume were supposed to demonstrate that modern Hungarian research 'has essentially disentangled itself from the embrace of positivism and Geistesgeschichte' (*lényegileg kibontakozott a pozitivizmus és a szellemtörténet öleléséből*), and the editor had high hopes that the volume would be a 'weapon . . . in the worldwide fight for peace' (*fegyver . . . a békéért folyó világharcban*).[43]

Lutter's study goes a long way to fulfil these requirements, as it sets out to 'elucidate . . . the meaning of *Paradise Lost*, and its connection to the seventeenth-century English revolution' (*megvilágítsa . . . A Paradicsom Elvesztése . . . értelmét, s viszonyát a 17. századi angol forradalomhoz*).[44] Right at the beginning of his study Lutter proposes that

> *itt az ideje annak, hogy a Milton-kérdésben – miként a világirodalom más nagy kérdéseiben is – a marxista-leninista tudomány fegyvereivel s az élenjáró szovjet tudomány módszereinek útmutatása alapján leleplezzük a burzsoá áltudomány mesterkedéseit s a világirodalom oly kimagasló alakját, mint Miltont, helyesen értelmezve, méltó helyre állítsuk.*[45]

(It is time that in the Milton question – as in other great questions of world literature – we expose the machinations of bourgeois pseudo-science with the weapons of Marxist-Leninist scholarship and on the basis of the guidelines provided by the methods of Soviet science, the most advanced of all, and restore this great figure of world literature, Milton, to the place he deserves, by interpreting [his works] correctly.)

Lutter's 'Marxist-Leninist' reappraisal of Milton's work is thorough indeed: the 'bourgeois revolution' is interpreted as class struggle fought 'in a religious mantle' in which Milton takes an active part throughout his whole career. There is, therefore, heavy emphasis on the 'fact' that Milton considered poetry a 'public cause' (*közügy*) from his earliest years and that he was 'consistently gravitating *to the left*' (*következetesen balra tolódott el*).[46] Lutter also takes great pains to lambast the 'bourgeois' tradition of criticism which tries to replace 'the poet of the English revolution' (*az angol forradalom költője*), an 'unrelenting fighter of the progressive ideas of *his age*' (*a maga kora haladó eszméinek meg nem alkuvó harcosa*), with an image of Milton conforming 'to the *present* taste of the bourgeoisie' (*a burzsoázia mostani szájaíze szerint való*).[47] Long-standing critical debates are categorically decided, the symbolic significance of religious themes is once and for all decoded, and, to make sure that the message is driven home, topical keywords such as 'counter-revolution' (*ellenforradalom*) or 'politics' (*politika*) are italicised throughout. Lutter's combative and didactic tone is firmly in keeping with the rest of the articles in the volume, each of which tries to present its subject – whether it be the latest trends in Romanian poetry, Dante or Anatole France – in the most 'progressive' way possible.

Considering the general objective and attitude of the whole volume, one would expect the author to make much of Milton's pamphlets. Interestingly, however, Lutter's article has relatively little to say about the prose works: *Areopagitica* and the *Defences* are briefly mentioned as examples of Milton's progressive left-leaning tendencies, but not much ink is spilt on crucial questions, such as Milton's anticlericalism, or the idea of (Christian) liberty. Lutter is not only selective, but also highly tendentious in his readings, even to the point of inventing new contexts for Milton's politics. When *Areopagitica* is briefly quoted, for example, it is to demonstrate the pervasive presence of 'Puritan republicanism' in Milton's thinking: the strong millenarism in the passage about 'the reforming of the Reformation itself' (discussed above) is, he says, nothing but a thinly disguised 'mantle' (*köntös*) hiding the 'extremely opposed class interests' (*a legellentétesebb osztályérdekek*) between the Presbyterians and the Levellers fighting for 'the genuine causes of the people' (igazi népi érdekekért). Disregarding pervasive evidence to the contrary in Milton's works and the critical tradition, Lutter goes on to link Milton's republicanism to the Levellers, turning him into a kind of posh Winstanley.[48]

Although the professed aim of Lutter's article is to open a new page in Milton criticism, the overall impression to the modern reader is that of a thinly veiled political manifesto skimming the surface of some aspects of Milton's works. This impression is vindicated when we take a look at another document from the same period, Lutter's English-language 'synopsis to a fourteen weeks' course' at Eötvös Loránd University (formerly Pázmány Péter University, from where Lutter graduated and where he became professor of English). The course (probably taught in 1951 and/or 1952) starts with 'A survey of Marx's and Engels's interpretation of the Civil Wars', in which Lutter provides a number of excerpts (ranging from the *Communist Manifesto* to Christopher Hill's 1948 essay 'The English Civil War interpreted by Marx and Engels'), contrasting these with the views of such 'bourgeois historians' who 'are trying hard to deny the class content and economic reasons of the Civil Wars'.[49] It is only by week five that Lutter starts to move on to Milton:

> Our aim is first of all to show how the class struggles of the age reflected themselves in the mind of John Milton, the greatest literary genius of the period, and to prove that his poetry was intimately connected with that revolutionary radicalism in which the most progressive aims of his age found expression. Such an approach of Milton's poetry necessarily involves revaluation in many points and its success depends on how firmly we are determined to destroy and expose the bourgeois falsifications of Milton's work, especially those of the imperialist epoch. (27)

As an introduction to the direct discussion of Milton, Lutter vilifies not only the 'imperialist decadence' of modern Western traditions of criticism (positivism, the history of ideas and what he calls the 'metaphysical school') but also the canon revisions they propose, such as the rediscovery of the metaphysical poets at the beginning of the twentieth century (34–5). At the same time he declares 'Puritan' poetry to exhibit 'the noblest and most progressive aims of the period', stressing that he uses the term 'Puritan' not 'in the narrow religious sense', but rather 'to denote more: a moral and political attitude' (35). One might thus expect a radical reconsideration of Milton's prose works, but – just like in the 1952 *Yearbook* – the revolutionary potential of Milton's prose seems to leave Lutter strangely cold. He does walk the course's students through most of the major prose works, but his concise summaries seem to be informed largely by Masson's great nineteenth-century biography, and his conclusions about the erudition displayed in Milton's pamphlets and the importance of the Miltonic prose style for later centuries would not pass for more than mere 'bourgeois' platitudes by his own standards. Again, just like in the *Yearbook*, in this course synopsis it is *Paradise Lost* that represents for Lutter Milton's true revolutionary ideas; this seems to be the bedrock of the critical programme Lutter carried through in his later publications during the decade, albeit with decreasing political zest.

The partisan zeal of Lutter's work from the beginning of the 1950s makes it seem absurd today as literary criticism, but it cannot really be considered successful propaganda either. The level of exaggeration in the political overtones of some of Lutter's arguments makes them appear more like vows of political allegiance, and one may in fact wonder about the author's actual level of commitment to what he professes. It is not that we would be tempted to read irony into Lutter's tenets, but rather that the sense of drudgery is obvious in the belaboured application of Stalinist doctrine – as it is, for that matter, in all the other pieces in the *World Literature Yearbook*. Indeed, as the decade progressed and, after Stalin's death in 1953, a relative thaw set in across much of the Eastern bloc, Lutter's work lost some of its combative edge in service of an ideologically still unshakeable, yet more nuanced and comprehensive (and therefore arguably more 'professional'), approach. This is apparent in his cautiously critical reconsideration of Christopher Caudwell's critical legacy, as well as in his proposition that the literary critic's political 'commitment' should not preclude an essentially inclusive approach.[50] To provide another example, in an article published in 1955 about 'Contemporary bourgeois trends in English literary history' ('A polgári angol irodalomtörténetírás mai útjai') Lutter promotes the cause of 'progressive' literary historians (such as George Thomson, Christopher Hill or Jack Lindsay) against their 'bourgeois' counterparts (such as T. S. Eliot, Douglas Bush or E. M. W. Tillyard), yet devotes much of the article to a serious consideration of the latter group's results, and even suggests there is much to learn from their methods.[51] That Lutter's tendency to relent while preserving the facade of relentlessness was not merely a theoretical and/or rhetorical ploy is further exemplified in his report on a Cambridge conference (published in the first issue of the world literature periodical *Nagyvilág*) where Lutter again commends the 'sober, quiet, scholarly realism' (*józan, csendes, tudományos realizmus*) of old-school ('bourgeois') British scholars like E. M. W. Tillyard against the 'nervous impatience' (*ideges türelmetlenség*) of the New Critics.[52]

Lutter's *magnum opus*, his monograph *John Milton, the Poet of the English Bourgeois Revolution* (*John Milton, az angol polgári forradalom költője*), published in 1956, registers the same tension between the need to provide a comprehensive treatment of Milton and his age and to re-evaluate Milton's oeuvre in 'Marxist-Leninist' terms. The book grew out of Lutter's CSc dissertation, and the minutes of the viva (published in 1955) explicitly highlight the author's attempt to tread the narrow line between a politically determined approach and a 'complete' treatment of both Milton's work and its critical heritage. Lutter's opponents criticise him simultaneously for a historically and ideologically narrow approach and for being Marxist only nominally. Torn between conflicting requirements in his reply, Lutter resorts to a 'certain picture' (*bizonyos kép*) he has formed of Milton through long years of study, one that is based on 'experiencing the personality and the works of Milton in the most complete way'

(*Milton egyéniségének és alkotásainak minél teljesebb átélésére*) and which he, consequently, would not like to discard.[53] This idea of a 'complete' picture also informs his monograph, in which Lutter sets out to

> *mély marxista meggyőződésem szilárd talajáról kíséreltem meg Milton egyéniségének és költészetének azokat a vonásait megrajzolni, amelyek puritán forradalmisága etikumát igazolják, s ennek az etikai igazságnak költői hitelét támasztják alá*[54]
>
> (draw, on the solid grounding of my deep Marxist convictions, those features of Milton's personality and poetry which justify his Puritan revolutionary ethics, and support the authentic poetic representation of this ethical truth.)

The picture Lutter aims to draw of Milton is self-confessedly complete in its partiality: he traces the development of Milton's radical and revolutionary ideas from the poet's earliest pieces to *Paradise Lost* and *Samson Agonistes*, concentrating for the most part on 'authentic poetic representation', i.e. Milton's English and Latin poems.

Counter-intuitively in this critical programme, but in line with Lutter's previously published work, Milton's prose works are again given a rather meagre treatment: most of them are diligently listed and summarised, but seem to be important only insofar as they represent progressive stages in Milton's radicalisation culminating in *Paradise Lost* and *Samson Agonistes*. When he does interpret actual passages, Lutter plays down the significance of Milton's religious views, consigning them to the 'religious mantle', or reading them selectively. In his discussion of *Areopagitica*, for example, he asserts that 'Milton breaks with the largely ecclesiastical phraseology, the biblical style and structure of the pamphlets of his age' (*Milton szakít a kor röpiratirodalmának nagyrészt egyházias frazeológiájával, bibliai fordulatokat követő stílusával, szerkesztési modorával*) and returns to ancient rhetorical tradition.[55] Lutter projects the idea of freedom of the press as one of the 'personal freedoms', and suggests that it informs even Milton's ecclesiastical pamphlets. It is characteristic how he curtails and interprets a sentence from *The Reason of Church Government* in which Milton uses the expression 'liberty of free speech':

> For me I have determin'd to lay up as the best treasure, and solace of a good old age, if God voutsafe it me, the honest liberty of free speech from my youth, where I shall think it available in so dear a concernment as the Churches good.[56]

Lutter translates, or rather, paraphrases this sentence in the following way:

> *Ami engem illet, ifjúkoromtól fogva arra kérem az Istent, adjon nekem tisztes öregkort, amelyben becsületes szólásszabadság legyen osztályrészem.*[57]
>
> (As for me, from my youth I have asked God to give me honourable old age, in which I should have honest freedom of speech as my lot.)

In the original, Milton wishes for the divinely inspired, unreserved and straightforward speech of his youth to remain with him throughout his life. Importantly, as Kevin Dunn points out, Milton is here 'co-opting the prophetic tradition of the Old Testament into his stance as youthful proponent of the gospel',[58] that is, the chief context of this personal wish is the Church and its reformation. Lutter's version, on the other hand, by misdirecting the interpretation of the expression 'the honest liberty of free speech from my youth' and leaving out the reference to the church, reads as a direct political statement focused on the freedom of expression.

Another example of Lutter bending Milton's prose to his own governing assumptions about Milton's career can be found in the treatment of *The Tenure of Kings and Magistrates*, in Lutter's formulation the epitome of 'the constitutional principles of Puritan democracy' (*a puritán demokrácia alkotmányos eszméi*), which provides the 'ideological foundations' (*eszmei alapjai*) of *Paradise Lost*.[59] Accordingly, while Milton talks about how 'the power of Kings and Magistrates' is 'only derivative . . . [and] transferr'd and committed to them in trust from the People, to the Common good of them all',[60] in Lutter's rendering power becomes transferred 'as a sign of trust . . . for the good of the whole people' (*a bizalom jeleképpen . . . az egész nép javára*), making the transaction merely symbolic and 'the people' (a heavily charged expression and concept in communist ideology) the exclusive beneficiaries of the 'bond of covenant' (Milton's phrase) that, in the original, is presented as mutually beneficial.[61] As Warren Chernaik reminds us, for all its republican tendencies, the *Tenure* 'is never wholly secular': in the passages surrounding the quoted sentence Milton relies heavily on scriptural evidence for his argument.[62] In Lutter's reading this aspect of the pamphlet vanishes, and we cannot say that he reserves this interpretive sleight of hand only to Milton's revolutionary prose: Puritan republicanism also becomes the *leitmotif* in his cursory summary of *De Doctrina Christiana* (arguably the least likely of Milton's prose works to be interpreted as a repository of early modern republican thought).

Milton's prose works, thus, clearly presented a serious dilemma to Lutter. On the one hand they had to be reckoned with, both as necessary stages in Milton's radicalisation (his progressive leaning 'to the left') and as the theoretical foundations of Milton's republican thought. On the other hand, the embarrassingly pervasive presence and importance of religious concerns – inextricable from both the subjects Milton chose to write on and the style he employed – had to be minimised, if not eliminated altogether. It is also important to remember that in Lutter's teleological perspective of Milton's oeuvre, according to which all creative forces unite to culminate in the poetry of *Paradise Lost* and *Samson Agonistes*, prose works could not take a central role; that is also the reason why the chapter 'Milton in the fights of the revolution' ('*Milton a forradalom harcaiban*') merges the discussion of Milton's political prose works with the consideration of the sonnets written during the interregnum.[63] Lutter's teleological approach does have some virtues: his tracing of Milton's radicalism in the Horton years (conventionally regarded as a period of studious retirement) chimes well with some recent trends in Milton criticism.[64] Yet by redirecting all phases and elements of Milton's career to the service of opening a clear path to *Paradise Lost*, he remains blind to important aspects of both the original Miltonic texts and their reception.

Another telling (perhaps the most telling) example of this critical blindness is again related to Milton's prose. In the article (discussed above) about 'bourgeois trends' in literary history, Lutter sarcastically mentions the 'characteristically American size' of the critical apparatus in the Yale edition of Milton's prose as an indication of the American 'conquest' of the discipline.[65] Ironically, it is exactly the Yale prose edition, and specifically the volume Lutter singled out (Don Wolfe's edition of volume 1 in the series, published in 1953), which was pioneering a more socially engaged, 'presentist' approach to Milton as 'a rebuke to the project of decontextualizing and depoliticizing that were the enabling intellectual conditions of the Cold War academy', e.g. in the work of the New Critics.[66] Apparently undisturbed by the fact that the American 'conquerors' happened to be closer to his position, Lutter tried to dutifully denigrate their efforts by pointing to a disparaging anonymous review in the *Times Literary Supplement* (which turned out to be by Hugh Trevor-Roper, a figure much reviled by Marxist critics generally). With enemies like these, who needs friends?[67]

The cognitive dissonance detectable in the last example remains the most apparent characteristic of Lutter's work on Milton. He was undoubtedly well versed in Milton's life, work and critical heritage, but his attempt to bring traditional scholarship in line with the official ideology has made much of his work obsolete. What is more, in the light of his writings from around 1955, the very application of the 'Marxist-Leninist' doctrine seems disingenuous, more of a compulsory signalling of conformity than the expression of heartfelt commitment. This impression is supported by what we can learn about his public role as the head of the Eötvös József Collegium – where he was infamous for his ruthless and hardline tactics, but was at the same time under constant surveillance by the communist secret service because of his suspicious views.[68] Recollections of his former students and colleagues suggest that this took a heavy toll on his personal and social life, and it is not a surprise that in a posthumous publication – his translation of a long passage from *Areopagitica* published in 1962 in an anthology of world literature – he seems to approach Milton's prose slightly differently.[69] In the passage Lutter rendered, Milton demonstrates 'that this order of licencing conduces nothing to the end for which it was fram'd' by calling into question both the fitness of the censors and the feasibility of censorship within the state. The closing sentence of the excerpt – 'These things [i.e. dangerous books, pamphlets, songs, etc.] will be, and must be; but how they shall be lest hurtfull, how lest enticing, herein consists the grave and governing wisdom of a State'[70] – seems to hint at a much more tolerant attitude than what Lutter's readers – and the general audience of the age – had been accustomed to. One is left to wonder whether the choice of this passage, and the fact that Lutter himself translated it, may be taken as a statement.

Milton, the 'mirror of the English revolution'

In 1958, when Lutter was already established as *the* Hungarian Miltonist, an article commemorating the three hundred and fiftieth anniversary of Milton's birth was published in the new world literature periodical *Nagyvilág* (founded in 1956). The author, Miklós Szenczi, was six years Lutter's senior, and recently reinstated, after eight years of forced silence, as professor and head of the English Department at Eötvös Loránd University in Budapest, a position he took over from Lutter.[71] The article provides a brief survey of Milton's life and work, stating at the beginning that

> Milton költészetének és prózájának minden sora önvallomás, egy forradalmas korszak eseményeinek vetülete egy rendkívül fogékony, egyre fejlődő nagy erkölcsi és művészi egyéniség tudatában.[72]

(Every line of Milton's poetry and prose is an act of self-confession, the reflection of a revolutionary era in the mind of an extraordinarily receptive, constantly developing great moral and artistic personality.)

At first blush Szenczi seems to strike a familiar note: the interpretation of Milton's life and work in the context of the English revolution brings to mind Lutter's fixation with the 'poet of the English bourgeois revolution' from a couple of years earlier. Our impression might be further strengthened by Szenczi's closing remark, the very last sentence in his study, about the task facing 'Marxist [aka 'socialist'] literary scholarship':

> az angol polgári forradalom legnagyobb írójának alkotását a maga teljességében és társadalmi összefüggéseiben vizsgálja, s a miltoni költészet és próza értékeit szerves részévé tegye az új, szocialista kultúrának.[73]

(. . . it should study the oeuvre of the greatest writer of the English bourgeois revolution in its entirety and in its social context, and to make the values of Miltonic poetry and prose an organic part of the new socialist culture.)

But the first impression might quickly change if we take a closer look at these sentences. The first thing to catch our eye is Szenczi's insistence on reassessing both poetry and prose. Instead of Lutter's forced teleological narrative, in which the main relevance of Milton's works is how they represent some stage in the progress towards the 'revolutionary poetry' of *Paradise Lost* and *Samson Agonistes*, Szenczi emphatically proposes a more balanced view, where it is *the entirety* of his works that makes Milton 'the greatest writer of the English bourgeois revolution'. Further, whereas for Lutter the expression 'the poet of the English bourgeois revolution' was a clear instance of the *objective genitive* (i.e. Milton strove to represent the revolution), in Szenczi's text the interpretation of the phrase 'the greatest writer of the English bourgeois revolution' seems to tilt towards a *subjective genitive* (i.e. the greatest writer that the revolutionary era produced). Observe, furthermore, that in these sentences Szenczi's focus is predominantly on Milton rather than the revolution – in other words, he is interested in the political context only insofar as it sheds further light on the 'great moral and artistic personality' he is about to introduce.

Published two years after the 1956 revolution, during the period of severe retribution, the article is very cautious in its terminology: quoting *Defensio Secunda*, where Milton provides reasons for his return from Italy,

Szenczi translates the phrase *tristis ex Anglia belli civilis nuntius* ('the sad tidings of civil war from England') as 'the sad tidings of the complications in England' (*az angliai bonyodalmak szomorú híre*).[74] Moreover, Szenczi is sometimes at pains to insert turns of phrase familiar from Lutter's writings, as when he states Milton was defending the republic from 'the attacks of internal and external reactionary forces' (*a belső és külső reakció támadásai ellen*).[75] Such elements stick out from the article like patches of misapplied varnish – Szenczi's last sentence quoted above is a prime instance of what might be called a 'Marxist fig leaf', i.e. a compulsory tribute paid to communist ideology even when the writer was clearly not taking a 'Marxist' direction – but they remain largely local and insignificant. If we disregard these embarrassed ideological nods – some of which positively seem to be editorial interpolations – the overall impression is that the article is a balanced appraisal of Milton's work. This is most apparent in Szenczi's well-informed discussion of the prose pamphlets: in his brief discussion and sampling of *Areopagitica*, he paints a compelling picture of Milton's intellectual background by focusing on the freedom of the will, the choice between good and evil, and the necessity of the *vita activa*, while in his reflection on *The Readie and Easie Way to Establish a Free Commonwealth* he does not shy away from pointing out the increasingly aristocratic character of Milton's republicanism and his loss of faith in the masses.[76] All things considered, the article displays in miniature the essential characteristics of Szenczi's later writings: erudition, a sober and pithy style, and the 'ideological mantle' of 'Marxism' worn lightly, though not carelessly.

Szenczi was Lutter's close contemporary (and for some years his colleague), but his career took a markedly different shape from Lutter's.[77] Born in 1904, he started his university years in Budapest, but later transferred to Aberdeen, where he graduated with distinction in English and ancient Greek in 1928. Returning to Budapest, he worked as a teacher in a secondary school and at the Eötvös József Collegium until 1937, when he was entrusted with organising Hungarian studies in London, at the School of Slavonic Studies (later the School of Slavonic and East European Studies, SSEES). Szenczi spent a decade in London (in a period less than ideal for a Hungarian citizen); his published work from these years deals mostly with cultural and literary relations between Britain and Hungary.[78] In 1947 he was offered a professorship at the English Department in Budapest, a position he accepted only to be thrown out, and replaced by Lutter two years later. In the following years he resorted to translation from English and Russian (his rendition of *Pride and Prejudice* is still considered to be the standard Hungarian version). After being reinstated to his former position, he worked at the university until his retirement in 1973, and led, until his death in 1977, the Comparative Literature Research Group of the Institute for Literary Studies of the Hungarian Academy of Sciences.

In the final 20 years of his life Szenczi became a highly respected and much loved member of the academic community in Hungary and internationally; he published on a bewildering variety of subjects ranging through ages and cultures, from antiquity to the eighteenth century and Romanticism to the twentieth century, and between 1970 and 1977 served on the editorial board of the University of Virginia's prestigious journal *New Literary History*. The history of English literature he co-wrote (published in 1972), as well as the anthology of the classics of English poetry he co-edited (published in 1986), were standard sources for Hungarian students of English literature for decades. His most influential work was on early modern drama: he wrote, among other things, a dissertation on Webster, provided serious criticism of Soviet Shakespeare interpretations, and edited an anthology of English Renaissance drama.[79] From the 1960s on he also published widely on the English Romantics, and it was in these years that he also emerged as Hungary's foremost authority on Milton. He edited and annotated István Jánosy's 1969 translation of *Paradise Lost* and, what is perhaps less known, also contributed to the unique staging of the epic in 1970.[80]

What is more, Szenczi seems to have been genuinely interested in Milton's prose: in 1967 he published a study about *The Brief History of Moscovia* in the *New Hungarian Quarterly* in which he not only provided a measured appraisal of Western and Russian scholarship on Milton's treatise, but also offered an important parallel between Milton's description of an envoy and a painting from the early seventeenth century in the holdings of the Hungarian National Museum.[81] Most importantly from our perspective, however, in 1975 he published a selection of excerpts from Milton's prose works entitled *John Milton, the Mirror of the English Revolution* (*John Milton, az angol forradalom tükre*). In short, Szenczi managed to become Milton's critic, editor, translator and biographer during his long career.

The essay 'Milton Agonistes', which was first published as the afterword to István Jánosy's 1969 translation of *Paradise Lost*,[82] provides a comprehensive yet succinct summary of Szenczi's thinking about Milton. The function of this piece is to introduce Milton's work to the wider reading public, hence Szenczi's discussion is not scholarly in the strict sense, but he does reflect on some of the major trends of Milton criticism through the centuries. The title alludes explicitly to Milton's tragedy

Samson Agonistes, and hints at a parallel between Milton the historical figure and the character of Samson. This analogy has long been one of the commonplaces of Milton criticism, but Szenczi's condensing it into a single phrase suggests a complexity of character which goes beyond mere similarities.[83] Szenczi consistently describes Milton, the man and his work, in agonistic terms. This might remind us of Lutter's 'Marxist-Leninist' interpretations (and can be interpreted as a subtle foil to appease such appetites); but in Szenczi's work Milton's combative character is not reduced to direct or indirect representations of the class struggle. Rather, the *agōn* informs Milton's personality, and by extension all aspects of Milton's career from his religious views through his position on divorce to his relationship with his poetic predecessors.

As we saw in Chapter 1 in the discussion of the Hungarian reception of *Paradise Regained*, this approach can be somewhat reductive; however, it is clear that Szenczi here vows allegiance to a tradition of Milton criticism which projects fundamental unity onto the oeuvre. As he himself states, 'Life and work have perhaps never joined together in a poet so organically as in Milton's case' (*Élet és életmű talán egy költőnél sem forrott oly szervesen össze, mint Miltonnál*), quoting the famous passage from *An Apology against a Pamphlet* about how the person who 'would not be frustrate of his hope to write well hereafter in laudable things, ought him selfe to bee a true Poem'.[84]

The Samson of *Samson Agonistes* is, however, a tragic hero, one whose *agōn* involves much more than mere combat. A classicist by education, Szenczi knew this well, and his account of Milton's life and work is shaped accordingly. Although he stresses the unity of Milton's career, he does not conceive of it as one uninterrupted march towards the consummate artefact of *Paradise Lost*. False starts, failures and readjusted or even renegotiated objectives are as much part of Szenczi's story as the inevitable idea of progress that derives from the fact that Milton wrote his greatest poems at the end of his life. Thus, it does not come as a surprise when in the conclusion to his article we read that 'it was Milton's lot to be raised to the highest peak of English poetry as "the reward of a great life filled with pain"' (*Milton egy 'fájdalmas, nagy élet jussán' emelkedett fel az angol költészet legmagasabb csúcsára*).[85] Here Szenczi quoted a line from the poem 'I live in youthful souls' ('*Ifjú szívekben élek*') written by the turn-of-the-century Hungarian poet Endre Ady, not only to indicate that behind Milton's fame lies a life's work ridden with tensions and contradictions, but perhaps also to suggest that through his agonistic character Milton is, if not exactly our contemporary, then at least within reach for twentieth-century audiences.

The consideration of Milton's prose works in Szenczi's essay also follows an agonistic pattern. According to Szenczi, the pamphlets are central to understanding Milton as a writer:

> Két évtizeden át, 1640 és 1660 között Milton közvetlenül is az angol polgári forradalom tükre, eszményeinek megszólaltatója, politikájának védelmezője. Ekkor válik igazán elkötelezett íróvá.[86]

> (Through the two decades between 1640 and 1660 Milton is directly the mirror of the English bourgeois revolution, who lends his voice to the service of the revolution's ideals and the defence of its politics. This is when he becomes a truly committed writer.)

Szenczi provides brief reflections on the major prose works, highlighting those aspects of the individual pieces which he deems the most important from the perspective of Milton's development. In *Of Reformation* he points out the 'lyrical passion' (*lírai szenvedély*) and the 'national pride' (*nemzeti büszkeség*) that seem to him to be 'more important than all polemical intentions' (*Minden polemikus szándéknál fontosabb*).[87] In *Areopagitica*, he stresses nationalism, the question of free will and the problem of good and evil, whereas in the *Defences* he appreciates Milton's rhetorical virtuosity.[88] A multifaceted discussion emerges – Szenczi is clearly well versed in both the text of Milton's pamphlets and their critical heritage – with sporadic and ad hoc reflections on Marxist perspectives. In his attempt to bring a 'Marxist' edge to his survey Szenczi draws exclusively on the later work of Christopher Hill, underlining in each citation that it is a *Marxist* critic whose work he presents. This leads to a positively absurd effect in the passage about *Areopagitica* where Szenczi points out that 'among others Christopher Hill has shown that [Milton's pamphlet] contributed to preparing the French and the American revolutions' (*amint erre Ch. Hill rámutat, hozzájárultak az amerikai és francia forradalom előkészítéséhez is*). He then goes on to quote from Milton's text the famous sentences 'Give me the liberty to know, to utter, and to argue freely' and 'Truth is strong next to the Almighty,'[89] only to conclude:

> *A marxista kritikus idézeteit* szinte vég nélkül folytathatnánk; az érvelés erejéből mit sem von le az eseményeknek... az iróniája.[90]

> (We could continue *the quotes of the Marxist critic* almost endlessly; the irony of the circumstances [that Milton himself became a licenser in the Cromwell administration] in no way diminishes the force of the argument.)

This awkward tribute to 'the Marxist critic' – in which Szenczi quotes well-known commonplaces from Milton's pamphlet, but credits Christopher Hill for selecting them – is paralleled by similarly superficial – and apparently uncomfortable – gestures elsewhere in Szenczi's work. For example, in an important English-language study he published on Milton's 'dialectic' in *Paradise Lost* (discussed in more detail in Chapter 1), he quotes the famous passage from *Areopagitica* about Truth 'hewd . . . into a thousand peeces' and 'scatter'd . . . to the four winds',[91] remarking that Milton here tries

> to prove the thesis, fundamental also to Marxist epistemology, that the discovery of truth is possible only by constant approximation, that absolute truth is reached by an unbroken succession of relative truths.[92]

Szenczi continues with a faint version of Engels's sartorial metaphor about Milton's 'philosophical idea . . . clothed . . . in poetical and religious images', but this is as far as his 'Marxist' approach extends. From his commentary on the quoted passage it becomes clear that, just like in 'Milton Agonistes', he is much more intrigued by the historical, intellectual and religious contexts of *Areopagitica* (and, in this particular study, how they anticipate some of the problems raised in *Paradise Lost*) than the opportunities to apply 'Marxist' doctrine. Nor are such tributary references a permanent feature of Szenczi's writings: much of the Milton chapter in his 1972 *History of English Literature* is adapted from 'Milton Agonistes', but most of the references to Marxist criticism are seamlessly edited out. In this work Szenczi seems to be much more interested in providing a picture of what he calls 'the Miltonic synthesis', a distinctly Baroque closure to the literature of the Jacobean age and the bourgeois revolution, than presenting an 'ideologically sound' interpretation.[93]

It seems, then, that Szenczi's interpretation of Milton's life and work, and Miltonic prose in particular (as expressed in 'Milton Agonistes' and some of his other scholarship), is at best only nominally 'Marxist': apart from a few strategically placed references, there is no sign of a deep engagement with the works of Marxist critics (either from the West or from the Eastern bloc). What readers get instead is standard, old-school, mostly historicist scholarship alert to a number of significant aspects – the theology, the morality, the nationalism, the classicism – of the Miltonic oeuvre. Viewed from the perspective of international Milton studies, Szenczi cannot be said to break much new ground, but his emphasis on the complex 'agonistic' element in Milton's career serves as an important corrective to Lutter's critical legacy. Intriguingly, his attempt to present a more complex picture of Milton's life and work than what is available in Lutter's monograph finally came to fruition not in a volume of criticism, but in the anthology of Milton's prose he edited and published in 1975.

The slim volume entitled *Milton, the Mirror of the English Revolution* (*Milton, az angol forradalom tükre*) was published by the Gondolat Publishing House in the series European Anthology (*Európai Antológia*), which presented important intellectual contexts for European history and culture (e.g. 'everyday life in Greece', or 'the German Enlightenment'). The emphasis on the revolutionary character of Milton's work in the title and the blurb is probably the strongest attempt in the whole volume to bring Milton up to date with the ideological preferences of the Kádár era – and not very obtrusively at that:

> *1641-ben lobbant fel a forradalom lángja Angliában, s néhány év múlva a győztes angol polgárok halálos ítéletet mondtak ki királyuk fölött. E forradalom tevékeny résztvevője, lángeszű gondolkodója és publicistája volt John Milton.*[94]
>
> (The flame of revolution flared up in England in 1641, and after a few years the victorious English bourgeoisie pronounced a death sentence on their king. John Milton was an active participant, genius thinker and publicist of this revolution.)

If we turn the page to the brief preface (*Előszó*),[95] we find a more nuanced picture. Szenczi states that 'Milton's views and his philosophy of life are based on solid foundations: they had developed organically, are complex and complete' (*Milton gondolatvilága, életszemlélete szilárd alapokon nyugvó, szervesen fejlődő, összetett és teljes*). Consequently, the prose works, 'so far virtually unknown in our country' (*Szinte teljesen ismeretlen maradt... nálunk*), are 'an organic part of his work as a writer, and several important aspects of his poetry can be understood only with their help' (*szerves alkotórészei írói munkásságának, a költemények számos lényeges mozzanatát csak segítségükkel érthetjük meg*). In contrast to Lutter, for whom Milton's pamphlets were important mostly insofar as they represented some stage in Milton's development culminating in *Paradise Lost* and *Samson Agonistes*, Szenczi conceives of the relationship of Milton's prose and poetry as essentially complementary, as 'the prose writings provide the clearest record of the development of Milton's views' (*A prózai írások tárják fel legvilágosabban Milton szemléletének fejlődését*).

According to Szenczi,

> Világnézete, személyes felfogása is ezekben az írásokban nyilatkozik meg közvetlenül, ugyanakkor a költői alkotásokban a klasszikus mitológia és a keresztény hitvilág képei és hagyományai, valamint a különféle műfajok szolgálnak nyersanyagul és keretül Milton egyéni mondanivalója számára.[96]

(These writings [i.e. the prose works] reflect his world view and his personal opinions directly, while in his poetry the images and traditions of classical mythology and Christian belief, as well as the different genres serve as raw material and context for Milton's personal ideas.)

Szenczi's selection of Milton's prose is faithful to its title to the extent that the 'backbone' (*gerince*) of the volume is made up of the works published during the revolutionary years. Yet the anthology commands a far wider horizon: Szenczi provides a complete survey of Milton's development as a prose writer, starting from his Latin college exercises (the *Prolusions*) through the not explicitly political pamphlets of the 1640s (the anti-prelatical writings, *Areopagitica*, *Of Education*, the divorce tracts), Milton's historical work (*The History of Britain*, *A Brief History of Moscovia*), down to a succinct summary of *De Doctrina Christiana*. Special attention is paid to the development of Milton's self-presentation throughout his career. The excerpts were translated into Hungarian by a team of experienced translators and young scholars (Péter Dávidházi, Tibor Szepessy, István Géher and Pál Vámosi), each section briefly introduced by Szenczi. He also included a compact summary of the critical tradition in the bibliography, where he mentioned Lutter together with R. M. Samarin as scholars who 'analyse Milton's oeuvre from a Marxist point of view' (*Milton művét marxista nézőpontból elemzi*).[97] Apart from this passing reference, the obligatory 'Marxist' perspective is virtually absent from the volume. What readers get instead is a comprehensive, well-proportioned survey of Milton's Latin and English writings with some of the most important sections translated into elegant Hungarian prose.

The selection and editing of these excerpts was an unquestionable critical feat, but the very brevity of the volume has not done it much service. Nor has the fact, we might add, that it does not contain any of Milton's prose works in their entirety, but functions more or less like a commonplace book, gathering long quotations arranged under different topics (e.g. 'Milton on education') without giving precise references to their original titles or contexts. The volume has probably served many readers well, and it has become a testimony to the strength and breadth of Szenczi's scholarship, but it has also remained a mere preview of what might have been expected from this excellent Miltonist – had he been able to commence work on this project at an earlier time or under different circumstances. To make things worse, the volume has been in a critical limbo ever since its publication – which, as the critic and writer Albert Gyergyai remarked as early as 1975, was true for the reception of much of Szenczi's work[98] – as a result of which it has failed to become what its blurb promised, a 'lasting monument' (*maradandó emlék*).[99]

*

The differences between Lutter's and Szenczi's careers and their work on Milton seem to reflect two radically different intellectual dispositions – indeed, different personae. Both strove to present a complete picture of Milton and both believed in the essential unity of the oeuvre. In the period under discussion both tried, to different extents and with differing degrees of intensity and enthusiasm, to interpret Milton's works in the 'Marxist' contexts prescribed in the communist cultural policy of their day, but while Lutter repeatedly vowed allegiance to current ideological trends, Szenczi's interest in these versions of 'Marxism' seems to have been mostly cursory, and, one might suspect, largely nominal. Ideological commitment is, however, only part of their story: our interpretation of their work is also shaped by how they were able to use and adapt the prevailing critical idiom to achieve their purposes. In this respect, Lutter comes through as ostentatiously proficient, yet he keeps failing to impress with his one-eyed focus, whereas Szenczi's occasional gestures to Marxist critical positions strike us as politely diplomatic at best, and amusingly clumsy at worst.

The image the two men presented of Milton differs accordingly. For Lutter, Milton was 'the poet of the English bourgeois revolution', essentially a propagandist of the 'leftist' ideas of the interregnum period. Szenczi, on the other hand, introduced a Milton who was 'the mirror of the English revolution', i.e. someone whose personality reflected the dynamic, often conflicting tendencies of his age in depth and with precision. Not surprisingly, these ideas also show in the presentation of their books: Lutter's monograph features the portrait of the young Milton (painted during the poet's years at Cambridge, now in the National Portrait Gallery), presumably to evoke the air of youthful revolutionary fervour, while the image on the cover of Szenczi's anthology is based on

William Faithorne's portrait of the 62-year-old Milton, a quietly confident person whose posture exudes a proud sense of achievement. Given Lutter's and Szenczi's vastly different careers, one may wonder to what extent their interpretations of Milton's life and works were also indirect, perhaps unconscious, acts of self-fashioning.[100]

As for Milton's prose works, it seems clear from the discussion above that the four decades of communism were not able not provide a comprehensive context in which they could be fully appreciated by the Hungarian public. Their 'revolutionary' aspect could only partially be brought in line with Lutter's critical programme, and even then they had to be heavily doctored – sometimes to the point of distortion. When, on the other hand, Szenczi undertook to present a more complex account which included not only Milton's 'progressive thoughts', but also the Miltonian ideas on education, organisation of the church, or Christian liberty (and so on), then – due to the anthology format, and possibly Szenczi's age – his attempt could not be but partial, a selection of highlights, which explains why it remained more or less hidden from critics' eyes. The progressive 'Cold War Milton' of the Yale edition that emerged in the United States failed to emerge on the other side of the Iron Curtain. In this respect Hungary was not exceptional among the countries of the Eastern bloc.[101] István Gál's animadversions from 1947 about the revitalising potential of seventeenth-century English prose still rang true in 1989.

Notes

1. Gál was an important figure in Hungarian English studies. He was the secretary of the Hungarian-English Association, and from 1948 he was the librarian of the British Embassy in Budapest. Before the war he founded the periodical *Apollo* (1934–9), where young academics and intellectuals with a background in English studies published (among them Gábor Halász or László Cs. Szabó, whose work is also cited in this book).
2. Gál 1946, 10.
3. Fest, Országh and Szenczi 1941, 55–6.
4. Milton 2013, 206.
5. Frank 2017, 35.
6. McDowell 2016, 218–19.
7. See Szenczi 1975.
8. Milton 2013, 88.
9. See Czigány 1990, 48.
10. Sonnet 'To Mr Cyriack Skinner Upon his Blindness', line 12.
11. For the earliest reception, see, among others, von Maltzahn 1995 and Peacey 2016.
12. See Gömöri 1989, 78–9.
13. Gömöri 1989, 79.
14. 16 March 1792.
15. See Tarnai 1965, and Péti 2017, 330–1.
16. N. A. 1837, 186–7.
17. Danielik 1847, 75.

18. See Péter 2011.
19. Macaulay 1825, 306; See Szigeti 1970, 211–12. See also Csukássi's 1876 article on Milton as a poet and a statesman; and Gángó 2004.
20. Petrochevich 1846, 103, 102. Petrochevich Horváth was heavily influenced by Chateaubriand (whom he actually met in Paris), and regarded Milton as a forerunner of the French Revolution.
21. Milton 1904, 7–9.
22. Kisfaludy 1858, 2404.
23. Although their arguments for the freedom of the press are often similar, Táncsics does not quote Milton in his pamphlet.
24. Wlislocki 1884; for the libel suit case, see Prusinszky 2014, 149.
25. See e.g. Németh 1974, 98–146.
26. Yolland 1912, 504–5.
27. Voinovich 1926, 79–80.
28. Bernát 1921; on Bernát's politics see Hanebrink 2006, 30–1; on the intolerant side of Milton, see Walker 2014.
29. Halász (1901–1945) was another young intellectual in the pre-war era with a strong interest in English literature. He was a prolific essayist who contributed to many literary periodicals, and became the chief critic of the periodical *West* (*Nyugat*). Being of Jewish descent, like many of his contemporaries and fellow intellectuals he was made to join a forced labour unit in 1944, where he died in 1945.
30. Miklós Szentkuthy (1908–1988) was one of the most important Hungarian writers of the twentieth century. He graduated in English and French from Pázmány Péter University, and after a two-year scholarship in London, he submitted and defended a doctoral dissertation on Ben Jonson (the first of its kind in Hungary) in 1931. The title of the thesis is 'The relationship of reality and irreality in the classical naturalism of Ben Jonson' (*Realitás és irrealitás viszonya Ben Jonson klasszikus naturalizmusában*). Szentkuthy was on friendly terms with all the major figures in this chapter: Gál, Halász, Lutter and Szenczi.
31. Halász 1942, 90. For the original of the excerpt translated, see Milton 2013, 206–8.
32. István Gál, for example, discussed this passage in an English-language article in the *Hungarian Quarterly* in 1939. See Gál 1939, 251–2.
33. On Gusztáv Jánosi's translation and influence, see Chapter 1.
34. Lutter 1960a, 101.
35. Loewenstein 2013, 273.
36. *OED* s. v. 'Fantastic', A1.
37. On the basis of their correspondence, in the holdings of the Petőfi Literary Museum, Budapest. Szentkuthy was also a friend of Miklós Szenczi, the other scholar whose work on Milton this chapter explores.
38. Fodor 1991, 91.
39. In post-war Hungarian academia a three-tier system of degrees was introduced after the Soviet model. After graduating from their MA studies (which usually took five years), young academics obtained a doctorate (often abbreviated as *dr.univ.* and referred to as 'small doctorate') issued by the university, which could be followed by a CSc (the equivalent of a PhD) issued by the Hungarian Academy of Sciences, and then a DSc (the so-called 'great doctorate'), also issued by the Hungarian Academy of Sciences. This system changed in 1993 when the Western-style PhD was introduced, and the issuing of both 'small doctorate' and 'CSc' degrees was discontinued.
40. Lutter's reports are preserved in the Petőfi Literary Museum (V.3829/58/1–2; V.3819/311/1–4). The ones he wrote in 1949 are especially interesting, since they recommend the publishing of several English and American works with prefaces 'for correct appreciation' (*helyes értékelésére*) by the public.
41. His writings before and during World War II, although free from hardline communist ideology, reflect the need to engage with current developments (Lutter 1935), larger social and historical processes (Lutter 1944) and ideas of politcal commitment (Lutter 1947).
42. Reader's report, 6 March 1949 (on a novel by Edwin Seaver), Petőfi Literary Museum, V.3829/58/1.
43. Kardos 1952, 3–4.
44. Lutter 1952, 216.

45. Lutter 1952, 215.
46. Lutter 1952, 220; emphases in the original.
47. Lutter 1952, 212–3, emphases in the original.
48. Lutter 1952, 230. For Milton's views on the Levellers, see Dzelzainis 2005. See also Chapter 2 for modern attempts to mix Milton with the Levellers.
49. Lutter 1951, 6.
50. See Lutter 1955a; Lutter 1960b.
51. Lutter 1955b, 56.
52. Lutter 1956b, 188.
53. Gáldi 1955, 384–5, *passim*.
54. Lutter 1956a, 12.
55. Lutter 1956a, 101.
56. Milton 2013, 86.
57. Lutter 1956a, 101–2.
58. Dunn 1994, 58.
59. Lutter 1956a, 104–5.
60. Milton 2013, 250.
61. Lutter 1956a, 105. Cf. also Szenczi 1975, 99: 'in trust from the people for the benefit of them all' (*a nép bizalmából valamennyiük közös érdekében*).
62. Cf. Chernaik 2017, 89.
63. About the post-war career of Milton's sonnets, see Chapter 4.
64. See e.g. Jones 2013.
65. Lutter 1955b, 50.
66. Achinstein 2008, 830.
67. Lutter's ambivalence towards Western scholarship is a fine example of 'systemic relativism', i.e. the attempt of Soviet and communist elites to present 'the social world of state socialism as something essentially different from that of capitalism or any other social formation' even at the expense of inconsistency or self-contradiction. See Péteri 2006, 6.
68. See, e.g. Pál 2010.
69. Sőtér 1962, 202–5.
70. Milton 2013, 196.
71. As reported by Ádám Nádasdy, on the first day Szenczi walked into his office he told Lutter: '*Kifelé!*' ('Get out!') – using a restrained, yet authoritative behest very much befitting his character. This change of guard is significant, since between 1950 and 1957 the Budapest English Department was the only place where English was taught at university level in Hungary (the English department at Debrecen, established in 1938, was closed in 1950, and reopened only in 1957).
72. Szenczi 1958, 1815.
73. Szenczi 1958, 1821.
74. Szenczi 1958, 1816; Cf. Szenczi's corrected translation in 1975: *az angol polgárháborúról érkező szomorú hír* ('the sad tidings I received of the English civil war' – Szenczi 1975, 115).
75. Szenczi 1958, 1816.
76. Szenczi 1958, 1818.
77. Drawing on archival material, Frank 2017 provides a detailed account of Szenczi's career.
78. See e.g. Szenczi 1937, Szenczi 1939 and Szenczi 1946.
79. See Szenczi 1932, Szenczi 1961, Szenczi 1965.
80. See Chapter 1.
81. Szenczi 1967. The painting in question is attributed to Szymon Boguszowicz.
82. On this translation, see Chapter 1.
83. On the importance of this essay and its title, see also Chapter 2.
84. Szenczi 1989, 168; Milton 2013, 97–8.
85. Szenczi 1989, 198.
86. Szenczi 1989, 174.
87. Szenczi 1989, 174.
88. Szenczi 1989, 174–8.
89. Milton 2013, 209, 210.
90. Szenczi 1989, 175, emphasis mine.

91. Milton 2013, 205
92. Szenczi 1971, 71.
93. Szenczi, Szobotka and Katona 1972, 200–16.
94. Szenczi 1975, blurb.
95. Szenczi 1975, 5–6.
96. Szenczi 1975, 6.
97. Szenczi 1975, 201.
98. Gyergyai 1975, 1913; apart from Gyergyai's tribute the only mentioning of Szenczi's volume in the year it was published is in Takács 1975.
99. Milton 1975, blurb.
100. Gyergyai 1975, 1912 uses the words 'proud modesty' and 'seriousness' to describe Szenczi's personality.
101. See Lange 2017 and Uzakova 2014.

4
'I rebel quietly': revolution and gender in Hungarian translations of Milton's shorter poems

1958: 'A slim volume' of Milton's poetry selected with 'the best of intentions'

In 1958 the world was celebrating the three hundred and fiftieth anniversary of John Milton's birth. Milton's poetry and prose were issued in new or revised editions (by Helen Darbishire, Walter Skeat, etc.), and several important monographs were published on his works (such as William George Madsen's *The Idea of Nature in Milton's Poetry* and George Whiting's *Milton and this Pendant World*). The World Peace Council – founded, and for a long time funded, by the Soviet Union – also marked the anniversary, and there were commemorations in various forms in communist countries.[1] Hungary was also celebrating the great poet, albeit at a lower key. Miklós Szenczi, freshly rehabilitated to his former position as professor of English, published an article in the new world literature periodical *Nagyvilág*,[2] and several daily and weekly newspapers included short notes on Milton or reported the commemoration by the World Peace Council. There were also plans for a representative volume to be published by the Európa Publishing House, the exclusive forum for world literature in the 1950s.[3] However, as one of the editors of Európa complained in an internal reader's report, there seemed to be a scarcity of available material:

> Vajjon megtehetjük-e, hogy Milton születésének 350. évfordulóját a meglevő magyar fordításokból, akár a legjobb indulattal összeválogatott, de mégiscsak vézna verses-kötettel ünnepeljük? Áltathatjuk-e magunkat azzal, hogy sub specie aeternitatis

dolgozunk, ha a kötet utószavában menthetetlenül hivatkoznunk kell a szerződészárlat okozta szűkös anyagi viszonyainkra? Vagy érthetőbben fogalmazva: nem jobb-e a barátom születésnapjáról véletlenül megfeledkeznem, mintsem, hogy egy nadrággombbal lepjem meg a nagy napon?[4]

(I wonder if we can afford to celebrate the three hundred and fiftieth anniversary of Milton's birth with a slim volume of poetry of poems selected (even with the best of intentions) from the existing Hungarian translations. Can we still pretend to work *sub specie aeternitatis* if in the afterword we have to refer to our financial difficulties caused by the ban on new contracts? Or, to put it more plainly: is it not better to forget my friend's birthday by mistake than to surprise him with a button for his trousers on his big day?)

The reader then goes on to enumerate the existing translations of Milton's works but dismisses them for aesthetic as well as political reasons: Gusztáv Jánosi's translation of *Paradise Lost* is so poor that it is better forgotten; Lőrinc Szabó's new translation of the epic is incomplete; *Samson* was translated by Tihamér Dybas, a defector, and is of low quality.[5] There are no versions of *Comus* or the Latin and Italian poems. Thus caught between a rock and a hard place, the reader concludes:

Két kibuvó látszik, hogy ne kiadónk szegénységi bizonyítványát jelentessük meg Milton versei gyanánt: egyik lehetőség, hogy a gyomai Knerr nyomdában megjelent Tóth Árpád Milton fordításait adjuk ki ugyanolyan alakban, betűtípussal és záródíszekkel. Másik, hogy a Janus-sorozatban jelentessük meg Milton kisebb verseit, de még így is óhatatlan a minimális kiegészítés.[6]

(There seem to be two ways out of the situation so that we wouldn't publish Milton's poems as our company's certificate of poverty. One of them is to republish Árpád Tóth's translations of Milton, published by Knerr in Gyoma, in the same format, typeface and tailpieces. The other is that we publish Milton's shorter poems in the Janus series [a bilingual series], but even so minimal additions are inevitable.)

The publisher eventually chose the latter option. In the second half of 1958, Európa published a collection of Milton's shorter poetry selected and edited by Tibor Bartos (one of the prominent literary translators of the age) and supplied with a preface by Tibor Lutter. Elegantly presented in a bilingual format (with the original text on the verso facing the translation on the recto), the little volume entitled *Poems (Versek)* contained 15 poems the great majority of which were translated before the communist era. In 1958 memories of the bloody end of the 1956 uprising (in communist jargon: 'counter-revolution') were fresh and the regime of János Kádár was still carrying on with retributions; the volume was, therefore, presented cautiously. While Lutter's preface tried to steer readers into the 'correct' direction of interpreting Milton's works, on the basis of the poems selected Milton emerges as a classic poet whose beautiful poems are mostly about traditional themes such as love, the beauty of nature, time, etc. In the preface, Lutter duly quotes Wordsworth about the 'trumpet-like' quality of Milton's sonnets, and goes on to conflate the traditional image of Milton as the poet-prophet with his own interpretation of Milton as a revolutionary:[7]

> *Egyidőben Milton líráját a kritika élesen elhatárolta epikájától, s szinte egészen külön emberként tárgyalta Miltont, a prózaírót. Ma már jól látjuk, hogy Milton nagyságát legmélyebben egységes fejlődés-képében érthetjük meg, mert csakis ebben az értelmezésben jutunk közel ahhoz a költőhöz, aki a költészetet szent hivatásának tekintette, melynek oltárához a költő csak bíbor palástban léphet, s úgy vélte, hogy ezen az oltáron a legtisztább tömjén illata a forradalom füstölőjéből száll az ég felé.*[8]

(There was a time when critics sharply separated Milton's lyric from his epic, and discussed Milton the prose writer as a virtually separate person. Today we know better: the most thorough understanding of Milton's greatness is through an integrated idea of his development, for this is the only interpretation bringing us close to the poet who considered poetry his sacred vocation; poetry, to whose altar the poet can only step in his purple robes: he believed that on this altar it is from the incense boat of the revolution that the purest fragrance rises to the sky.)

Lutter also gives an example of how this 'integrated idea' of Milton's oeuvre can be put into practice. Quoting extensively from Milton's sonnets on his blindness, he argues that even in his most soul-searching mode Milton is concerned with the cause of the revolution. Lutter's proof is hinged on the expression 'I fondly ask' in Sonnet 19 ('When I consider how my light is spent'), which he discusses on the basis of its Hungarian translation. The early twentieth-century translator Árpád

Tóth interpreted the phrase (rather freely) as *lázongok halkan* ('I rebel quietly'); for Lutter this means that the sonnet 'contemplates the memories of "quiet rebellion"' (*[a] "halk lázongás" emlékén tűnődik*).⁹

The phrase 'quiet rebellion' is, however, almost the maximum of what readers of the volume received of Milton's public role and political activity. Despite Lutter's emphasis on the overarching theme of revolution in Milton's oeuvre, the volume's actual selection of the shorter poems is largely apolitical. It starts with Sonnet 1 ('O Nightingale'), and includes 'On Shakespeare', Sonnets 7, 8 and 20 ('How soon hath time'; 'Captain, Colonel, or Knight in Arms'; 'Lawrence of virtuous Father'), 'L'Allegro' and 'Il Penseroso', 'Lycidas', Milton's sonnets on his blindness (Sonnets 19, 22, 23), 'The Morning Prayer of Adam and Eve' (from Book 4 of *Paradise Lost*), and the invocation to Holy Light (from Book 3 of *Paradise Lost*). Of these poems, only Sonnet 22 ('Cyriack, this three years day') features explicit references to Milton's political activity; however, these are invested into the speaker's attempt to redeem the personal tragedy of blindness. From the remaining two, more apparently public poems included in the collection, Sonnet 18 ('On the late Massacher in Piemont') goes beyond seventeenth-century politics (and Milton's personal indignation) to present 'a specific example of the efficacy of faith in relation to wisdom and zeal'.¹⁰ Sonnet 16 ('To Oliver Cromwell'), is, thus, the only poem in the volume which stands as an explicit representative of Milton' revolutionary or 'heroical' lyric (Sonnets 15–17).¹¹ This is hardly surprising. Neither Sonnet 15 ('Fairfax, whose name'), which raises the sensitive issue of 'new rebellions rais[ing] / Thir Hydra heads', nor Sonnet 17 ('Vane, young in yeares'), which ends proclaiming Sir Henry Vane religion's 'eldest son', would have been acceptable in the tension-ridden years of the late 1950s. Sonnet 16's emphasis on the necessity of suppressing internal and external enemies, by contrast, harmonised with the politics of the early Kádár era well, not to mention the fact that István Vas's translation rendered the phrase 'peace hath her victories' as 'the fight of/for peace is more beautiful' (*a béke harca szebb*), which evoked one of the key motifs of international communism, 'the fight for peace'.¹²

Poems was, then, a heavily curated volume which tried to steer on the safe side. Fears about commemorating the anniversary year 'with a slim volume of poetry of poems selected (even with the best of intentions) from the existing Hungarian translations' came true; ironically, however, this modest collection – beset from the beginning by financial, practical and even ideological difficulties – went a long way to conserve the canon of Milton's shorter poetry that was formed in the first half of the twentieth century. The core of the selection was formed by eight poems translated by Árpád Tóth, a poet from the first generation of the *Nyugat* periodical (published between 1908 and 1941). They were originally published in 1921 in a sumptuously presented quarto-sized volume designed 'in the spirit of seventeenth-century printing'.[13] These eight poems are some of the most well known and arguably the most important short pieces among Milton's poetical works: besides 'Lycidas' and 'L'Allegro' and 'Il Penseroso' Tóth also translated two sonnets on blindness: Sonnet 19 ('When I consider how my light is spent') and Sonnet 22 ('Cyriack, this three years day'). From the time of their first publication, Tóth's translations were noted for their melodiousness – according to Mihály Babits, a leading poet and critic of the *Nyugat*, these poems make the impression 'as if a virtuoso violinist was filtering Beethoven's symphonies through his instrument and soul' (*mint a hegedűvirtuóz, aki Beethoven szimfoniáit szűri át hangszerén és a lelkén*)[14] – and have been considered, by contemporaries and posterity alike, an unsurpassable tour de force. In all fairness, however, the brilliance of Tóth's versions comes at a price, since the translation's faithfulness to Milton's original text is often compromised. Very much in line with his own poetry, Tóth adapts – or, using a musical metaphor, reorchestrates – Milton's pieces so that they sound like symbolist poems: a case in point is his translation of 'Lycidas', which at times reads like Paul-Marie Verlaine's 'Chanson d'automne' (a poem Tóth also translated).[15] As György Rába pointed out in 1969: 'These are superb Hungarian poems, but they undeniably "unravel" the original' (*Remek magyar versek, de tagadhatatlanul „felbontják" az eredetit*).[16]

The 1958 volume cemented these idiosyncratic but powerful translations of Milton's shorter poems in the canon of Hungarian literature, and also complemented them with a few pieces translated by Tóth's younger colleagues from the *Nyugat* circle – such as 'On Shakespeare' by Lőrinc Szabó; 'On Time' and Sonnet 16 ('To Oliver Cromwell') by István Vas; and Sonnet 18 ('On the late Massacher in Piemont') by Géza Képes. Two further volumes published in the communist era – Milton's selected poetical works published in 1978, and the 1989 anthology of English Baroque lyric poets[17] – also reprinted Tóth's translations as the core of their collection of Milton's lyric poetry. These new editions also included a few other short poems translated by young Hungarian poets (Dezső Tandori, István Jánosy, Gyula Tellér or László Kálnoky),[18] but the impact of these later additions wanes in comparison to the influence of Tóth's translations, which to this day are part of 'world literature' curricula in Hungarian secondary and higher education as specimens of 'Baroque poetry'. A prime example of the prevalence of the pre-war translations is Péter Egri's essay from 1975, which presents a close reading of Sonnets

18 ('On the late Massacher in Piemont', translated by Géza Képes) and 19 ('When I consider how my light is spent', translated by Árpád Tóth) from a comparative perspective. Egri compares Milton's sonnets to pieces of Baroque painting and music (especially the fugue form) and considers Milton's refashioning of the Petrarchan sonnet structure as an expression of the 'dynamic tension' that he detects across the sister arts. Characteristically for the age, Egri (a disciple of Georg Lukács) derives this 'Baroque' tension from what he terms the 'social and historical contexts': it is the result, he claims, of the 'paradox of history' in which the repressed drama of the Puritan revolution is channelled into the 'dramatic sonnets'.[19]

The post-war reception history of Milton's shorter poetry, thus, could be characterised as rather static, and, in comparison to the critical and creative responses to other segments of the Miltonic oeuvre (notably the two epics and *Samson Agonistes*),[20] also remarkably conservative of the earlier traditions of poetry and literary translation. The 1958 volume *Poems* is in many ways emblematic of this conservatism; importantly, however, it also features the translation of a single poem which, although it went unnoticed in Lutter's preface, seems to challenge many aspects of Milton's Hungarian reception.[21] The poem in question is Sonnet 23 ('Methought I saw my late espoused Saint'); it was translated by Ágnes Nemes Nagy, one of the most important Hungarian poets of the second half of the twentieth century and the only Hungarian woman translator of Milton's works to date.[22] As I shall show below, Nemes Nagy's translation engages critically not only with its original, but also with the predominantly patriarchal contexts of Milton's Hungarian reception which had been prevalent in Hungarian culture since the eighteenth century and continued to be endorsed during the four decades of communism.

As Nemes Nagy knew, translation is never a unidirectional process: not only does it reorient the reception of the original, but it also has an effect on the target language, the translator's primary context. Thus, the Hungarian version of Milton's sonnet – published originally in 1957, after more than a decade during which Nemes Nagy was silenced by the communist regime and could only resort to translation as a means to publish – also provides an important contrast to the image of Nemes Nagy (officially cultivated by her contemporaries and often endorsed by herself too) as a 'masculine', 'objectivist' lyric poet. In the early reception of Nemes Nagy's work, her fellow poets and critics often resorted to the cultural stereotype of 'masculinity' to refer to certain qualities of her lyric: its restrained technical mastery and analytic thrust as well as its dense precision and lack of pathos. Thus, she was cited as a 'more masculine', even 'the most masculine poet of her generation'.²³ As we shall see, her translation of Sonnet 23, through its presentation of a powerful, active female figure simultaneously affirms and challenges this stereotypical (self-)representation. What is more, Nemes Nagy's creative engagement with Milton's original also found its way to her poetry and resulted in the critical revision of Sonnet 23 in two important, posthumously published poems. The following account is therefore about the interaction between gender and cultural policy not only in Milton's postwar Hungarian reception, but also in Nemes Nagy's poetic career. First, however, let us take a brief look at the gendered context from which this remarkable writer and translator, and her truly 'revolutionary' translation, had to emerge.

'As a child follows his father': patriarchal traditions in Milton's Hungarian reception, and the curious case of Sonnet 23

Spanning almost three centuries, Milton's reception in Hungary has been dominated by male critics and translators who have emphasised the masculinist tendencies in the poet's life and his works (often proposing direct connections between the two). This is apparent already in the first translation of the complete text of *Paradise Lost* and *Paradise Regained* (1796), rendered into prose by Sándor Bessenyei, a former member of Empress Maria Theresa's Royal Hungarian Guard.²⁴ Bessenyei, who translated from Nicolas-François Dupré de Saint-Maur's French version, described in his preface how he 'contemplated . . . Milton excelling on his bloodfoamed Pegasus around me' (*MILTONT vérrel tajtékzó Pegazusán körültem déltzegeskedni . . . szemléltem*), then recalled how the 'Muse' advised him:

> *Ha MILTON-nal mint Poëta verset akarsz futni, vele nem érsz; mert az, ollyan mint Ő, érzed hogy nem vagy: de ha mint Philosophus tisztelettel késéred, mint a' gyermek Attya utánn hogy szokott indúlni, így gondolatit magyarázhatod; ebben nemtsak Apolló, de még Márs-is, kinek híve voltál, segedelmedre lehet.*²⁵

> (If you [i.e. the translator] want to run a race with MILTON as a Poet, you will not reach him, because you can feel that you are not like him, but if you follow him with respect as a philosopher, and start out after him as a child follows his father, you can explain his thoughts; not only Apollo, but also Mars, to whose retinue you used to belong, can help you.)

True to his double profession as a soldier and a man of letters, Bessenyei described Milton both as an unsurpassable military hero and a father-like master or teacher. The next 150 years saw the emergence of similarly patriarchal, yet not as manifestly militant perspectives on Milton and his work. In 1890 Gusztáv Jánosi, a Catholic priest and the translator of the second complete Hungarian version of *Paradise Lost*, expatiated upon Milton's 'sad matrimony' (*szomorú házasélete*), which, according to him, was to be blamed upon Mary Powell, that 'somewhat frivolous, base-spirited woman' (*kissé ledér, köznapi lelkű nő*). Supporting his point from the text of *Paradise Lost*, Jánosi quoted at length from Adam's diatribe against Eve and women (*PL* 10. 880–908) to illustrate that Milton 'poured his heartfelt complaints and unhappiness [into that passage] when he [i.e. Milton] upbraids Eve' (*saját szíve panaszát, boldogtalanságát önti ki..., midőn Évának szemrehányást tesz*).[26] When Jánosi's translation was republished in 1930, László Ravasz, a prominent bishop of the Reformed Church, supplied a new preface in which he plainly stated that Milton 'was born a patriarch, one who tends his flock, lives with his people, both absorbs and pours into their life, and a terrible distance was stretching between him and his children' (*Pátriárkának született, aki nyáját terelgeti, népével él, annak életét felszívja és annak életébe átömlik és rettentő távolság tátongott közötte és gyermekei között*).[27] In the second half of the twentieth century, this picture inevitably diversified: the author of the 1969 translation of *Paradise Lost*, István Jánosy, for example, found creative tension between Milton's 'manifest identity: the Old Testament or ancient Greek patriarchal world' (*manifeszt tudata: ószövetségi vagy antik-görög atyajogú világa*) and the counteracting forces of what he calls 'Miltonic romanticism' (*miltoni romantika*).[28] Even in recent decades the idea of a 'masculinist' Milton persisted in the parallels drawn between the poet's life and that of his character Samson (and the simultaneous elevation of the latter to the status of a communist hero),[29] and as recently as 2019 the new prose translation of *Paradise Regained* was praised as a 'serious, masculine short epic that regards itself as equal to the Bible' (*komoly, férfias, a Bibliát partnernek tekintő kiseposz*).[30]

It was not only the late masterpieces (*Paradise Lost, Paradise Regained* and *Samson Agonistes*) that received such critical treatment: the reception of Milton's sonnets has proceeded along very similar lines. In the preface to his anthology *English Baroque Lyric* (*Angol barokk líra*, 1946), István Vas pointed out that 'not even three marriages, one divorce, and the death of two of his wives changed that fact that his [Milton's] real muse was politics and political religion' (*három házassága, egy elválása és két feleségének halála sem változtatott azon, hogy igazi múzsája a politika volt és a politikus vallás*).³¹ It is not only Vas's erroneous recollection of Milton's divorce (which Milton sought, but never obtained) that should be the focus of our attention here, but also that he bundles together Milton's sonnets under the category of the 'political' and the 'politically religious'.³² Ten years after Vas's verdict, Tibor Lutter, attempting to present a 'consistent' Marxist interpretation of Milton's whole oeuvre in his monograph, emphasised revolutionary content and form in Milton's sonnets, pointing out that 'none of Milton's sonnets is about love' (*szonettjeinek egyike sem szerelmi tárgyú*).³³ According to Lutter, these poems 'condense those thoughts which inspired Milton's spirit in some crucial moments of the revolution' (*azokat a gondolatokat tömöríti[k], amelyek Milton lelkét a forradalom egy-egy sorsdöntő pillanatában ihlették*).³⁴ It is thus not a surprise that Lutter, who quoted most of Milton's sonnets in full in his book, does not even mention Sonnet 23 in his discussion.

Writing a dozen years after Lutter, during the period of 'consolidation', Miklós Szenczi sets a different tone in his essay 'Milton Agonistes' (first published in 1969). In this piece, which became the canonical Hungarian account of Milton's life and works for the rest of the century (it was republished several times in editions of Milton's works),³⁵ Szenczi clearly provided a long overdue account of the variety of Milton's sonnets, but, steering clear of Lutter's sweeping generalisations, he introduced new ones: 'These powerful, masculine poems break the droning, single-stringed late Elizabethan and Jacobean tradition of love, traces of which can be detected in Milton's own earlier Italian sonnets' (*ezek az erőteljes, férfias versek szakítanak a késő Erzsébet-kor és a Jakab-kor döngicsélésbe fulladó, egyhúrú szerelmi hagyományával, melynek nyomai Milton saját korai, olasz nyelvű szonettjeiben is fellelhetők*).³⁶ Although Szenczi does mention in parentheses Milton's sonnet on his deceased wife, his main interest lies with the political sonnets, and especially Sonnet 18 ('On the Late Massacher in Piemont'), the 'most poetic expression of Milton's Protestant piety, and moral outrage' (*Milton protestáns vallásosságának, erkölcsi felháborodásának legköltőibb kifejezése*).³⁷ It seems that Szenczi, just like Lutter in the preface to the 1958 volume *Poems*, was clearly inspired by Wordsworth's 'Scorn not the Sonnet', which attributes epic significance to the 'soul-animating strains' of Milton's sonnets by defining them in terms of a traditional metaphor (as Wordsworth says, 'in his [Milton's] hand / The Thing became a trumpet'). It took a further 20 years to introduce a perspective that could fully accommodate Sonnet 23: in the 1989 volume *Donne, Milton and the Poets of the English Baroque* (*Donne, Milton és az angol barokk költői*), Győző Ferencz highlights in his brief note on Milton that 'his deeply personal, moving sonnets [written around 1652] are the masterpieces of the English sonnet tradition' (*ekkoriban [1652 körül] írott, mélyen személyes, megrendítő szonettjei az angol szonettköltészet remekei*).[38] Ferencz included Sonnet 23 as well as the sonnet to Cyriack Skinner in the latter group.

'I am not "masculine". I am weak': Sonnet 23 in Ágnes Nemes Nagy's poetic career

The critical tradition sketched above provides the historic context for Ágnes Nemes Nagy's translation of Sonnet 23 (the first translation of this sonnet into Hungarian). In the 1958 bilingual volume (*Poems*) it was placed between Sonnet 20 ('Lawrence of virtuous Father virtuous Son') and Sonnet 16 ('To Oliver Cromwell'). This (roughly chronological) placing of the poem undoubtedly serves to demonstrate the rich variety of Milton's sonnets, but, in keeping with the 1958 volume's cautious arrangement, it also works towards neutralising the openly political tone of the sonnet to Cromwell. Ironically, however, the sonnet's position in the volume might also produce a contrary effect. For Nemes Nagy and many of her contemporaries the sonnet form with its tight, traditional structure was a means of 'protest against societal and political aggression and barbarism' (*társadalmi-politikai erőszak és barbárság elleni tiltakozás*),[39] and the presence of Sonnet 23 near one of Milton's explicitly political sonnets is bound to establish a sobering contrast between the ideologically charged interpretations of Milton's revolutionary poetry (as expressed in e.g. Lutter's work) and the body of work Milton actually left behind.

This is, however, not the only context in which Nemes Nagy's translation has proved remarkably subversive. As mentioned before, the poem was first published at the end of a long period of forced silence. After her debut in 1946 with the volume *In a Double World* (*Kettős világban*), Nemes Nagy was silenced for over a decade by the communist regime for not complying with the party line and the cultural policy of dictatorship. The only form of creative outlet for such writers was translation, and roughly a third of *Dry Lightning* (*Szárazvillám*, 1957), the first book of poetry Nemes Nagy was allowed to publish, consisted of translations. Sonnet 23 was also published in this volume: it is printed on a recto page facing one of Ronsard's sonnets from the 'Sur la mort de Marie' sequence ('Comme on voit sur la branche au mois de May la rose'), also addressing a dead lover.[40] If Ronsard's poem testifies to 'the poet's ability to transcend loss through language' and symbolic action (such as offering a basket full of flowers in the deceased lover's memory),[41] Milton's sonnet provides a stark reminder that attempts to rescue the beloved 'from death by force' are viable only in myth and will always remain incomplete. The juxtaposition of the two sonnets might well be accidental,[42] but the progress from Ronsard to Milton on the printed page seems to herald the shift of focus in Nemes Nagy's own poetry. It was in these years that she reoriented her preoccupation with material objects of the world to confront what she called 'the realm of the nameless'.[43]

Szárazvillám received mixed reviews: critics praised Nemes Nagy's technical mastery and intellectual rigour, but they also voiced their doubts about her individualistic, intellectual voice, and urged a deeper engagement with the 'people' and the 'achievements of the new world' of communist Hungary.[44] The richly allusive text and the strong religious tone of Sonnet 23 must have been mildly objectionable to such critics: it seems that not even in translations could Nemes Nagy comply with the requirements of the ruling ideology. On the other hand, the poem's openly personal recollection of a private event might have seemed somewhat alien to Nemes Nagy, whose 'objective' lyric and 'detached impersonality' otherwise tended to avoid the direct representation of private emotions and experiences.[45] It is also worth recalling the image that had emerged of Nemes Nagy as a poet in her lifetime, one that she seemed to endorse tacitly throughout her career. From her earliest works to her death, the poetry of Nemes Nagy was often represented as embodying 'a "masculine" type of objectivity',[46] and she was herself seen as a stern Puritan (she had Calvinist ancestry). Sonnet 23 seems simultaneously to reinforce and challenge this stereotype: by ventriloquising a male voice, Nemes Nagy undoubtedly presents the feminine at a critical distance, yet she also complicates the recollected experience by intensifying the vulnerability of the male speaker. Indeed, Nemes Nagy's ambivalence towards both masculinity and translation can be detected in the intriguing connection she makes between the two in one of her posthumously published essays, which was written around the time her translation of Sonnet 23 was published:

> *Minden barátom azzal szokott dicsérni, hogy milyen erős, milyen férfias vagyok. Ez hízeleg is nekem, igyekszem is azt domborítani, amit dicsérnek bennem. De igaz-e?*
>
> *Jó, mentségemül szolgálhat, hogy sokat kellett – más értelemben – dolgoznom, hivatal, bélyegzés, értekezlet; tanítás, vad kamasz fiúkba fektetett fölösleges energiák; fordítás, fordítás, tízezer sorok, végeláthatatlan homokrágcsálás . . . Versenyen kívül kellett volna futnom, s elfáradtam, mielőtt a pályára jutottam volna. De hát össze*

kéne szednem magam! Mi mást tehetnék az életben még? Mi más élni, mint 'egy célra elhajítva lenni'? Mi más kötelesség van – néhány erkölcsi normán kívül – mint saját képességeink végigfutása? Mért nem teszem? Mert nem vagyok erős. Nem vagyok 'férfias'.

Gyönge vagyok.

1958. július 14.[47]

(All my friends praise me for my strength, my masculinity. This flatters me, I try to bring into relief what I am praised for. But is this true?

A good excuse might be that I had to work (in another sense) a lot: the office, stamping, meetings, teaching, energies wasted on wild adolescent boys; translation, translation, tens of thousands of lines, endless chewing of sand . . . I should have run *hors concours*, and I got tired even before stepping on the track. But I should pull myself together! What else could I do in life? What else is life but 'being thrown at one target'? What other obligations are there – except for some moral norms – than running the course of our abilities? Why am I not doing this? Because I am not strong. I am not 'masculine'.

I am weak.

14 July 1958)

In this excerpt, the act of translation is at the focus of several opposing forces. It is unpleasant drudgery, along with a number of other menial tasks such as teaching or office work, but its labours of constraint have actually contributed to the poet's performance of 'strength' and 'masculinity'. At the same time, this facade of power conceals an uncertain, debilitated self who has been exhausted and dragged down by the very activities that have contributed to her strength and kept her afloat. Nemes Nagy's awareness of her own 'shortcomings', however, also provides a powerfully ironic reflection on social and cultural expectations and stereotypes of 'strength' and 'masculinity'. One is justly reminded of the Pauline motto Milton adopted in his blind period: 'My strength is made perfect in weakness'.[48] Composed in the same period as the note above, Nemes Nagy's translation of Sonnet 23 also reflects on these contradictory dynamics as it mediates the original's richly allusive engagement with dream and reality, death and life, weakness and strength, and blindness and insight.

Alcestis as 'victim' and 'sacrifice': Sonnet 23 in Hungarian

Methought I saw my late espoused Saint
Brought to me like *Alcestis* from the grave,
Whom *Joves* great Son to her glad Husband gave,
Rescu'd from death by force though pale and faint.
Mine as whom washt from spot of child-bed taint,
Purification in the old Law did save,
And such, as yet once more I trust to have
Full sight of her in Heaven without restraint,
Came vested all in white, pure as her mind:
Her face was vail'd, yet to my fancied sight,
Love, sweetness, goodness, in her person shin'd
So clear, as in no face with more delight.
But O as to embrace me she enclin'd
I wak'd, she fled, and day brought back my night.

Ugy tetszett: láttam régholt szentemet,
mint Alkestist, a sír áldozatát,
kit Zeusz fia férjének visszaádd,
halálból tépve, halvány-reszketeg.
Lemosva gyermekágyi szennyeket
jött, rajta ős-törvényű tisztaság,
ugy, hogy bíznom kell mindörökkön át:
a mennyben látnom gáttalan lehet.
Lelke színe fehérlett köntösén.
Arcán fátyol; s átsejlett fátyolán
a báj, a vágy, a jóság; ennyi fény
az ő arcáról tündököl csupán.
Már rámhajolt, s jaj, fölriadtam én,
elszállt, s a nap meghozta éjszakám.[49]

(It seemed to me that I saw my long-deceased saint, / [she was] like Alcestis, a sacrifice for/a victim of the grave, / whom Zeus' son gives back to her husband, torn from death, pale and trembling. / Having washed off child-bed taints, / she came, the purity of the ancient law was on her, / in such a way that I must trust for ever / I will be able to see [her] in Heaven without restraint, / the colour of her soul was reflected in the whiteness on her robe: / her face had a veil on, yet it seemed through her veil / grace, desire, goodness [were visible]; so much light / could shine from her face only. / She was leaning over me; alas, I started up / she flew away, and day brought my night.)

As far as the sonnet form and the Hungarian language allow, Nemes Nagy remains faithful to the original content: the poem's 'plot' is the same as in Milton, and the translation faultlessly reproduces the first quatrain's classical allusion as well as the second quatrain's reaching back to the 'deep past of the Israelites' and reaching forward to the 'promise of Heaven' in 'decorous humility' (to use Gordon Teskey's words).[50] There are, however, certain subtle changes in phrasing or emphasis, which introduce new possibilities of interpretation, or amplify existing ones. By choosing to render 'late-espoused' as 'long-deceased', for example, the translator highlights the extraordinary nature of the visitation – as if a long-forgotten memory had unexpectedly surfaced – and extends the significance of the verb *láttam* ('saw') to evoke Milton's sighted period.[51] This ambiguity between the recollection of actual visual material and 'fancied' sight is present in several elements of Nemes Nagy's translation: in contrast to the visual vagueness characterising the original, in the Hungarian version we are confronted with rather more clear-cut images, such as the 'trembling' of the wife's figure in line 4, the speaker's strong focus on the veil covering her face, or the way this veil, rather than the 'person' (in Milton), radiates all the virtues.[52] What Sándor Radnóti proposed as a governing principle of Nemes Nagy's poetry, that it is informed by a dualism between what is visible and what is envisioned, seems to be true of this translation, too. This dualism, however, never freezes into mechanical analogies or correspondences: 'the image remains one and the same and there is only passion vibrating between what is seen and what is given as a vision' (*a kép azonos, és csak az indulat vibrál a befogadásban a látvány és a látomás között*).[53]

This tension between what is seen and what is given to one as a vision is also explored in Milton's original: the way the poem's speaker recollects the ancient myth of Alcestis and fades it into the 'pale and faint' figure of the wife is a classic example of Miltonic montage.[54] The simile's relatively narrow focus on how the wife's figure is presented ('Brought') as well as the traditional typological association of Hercules and Christ means that the illustrative imagery never really tears away from the poem's actual subject. As in some of Milton's most memorable similes (the Vallombrosa simile in *Paradise Lost*, for example), the vehicle ultimately collapses into the tenor. By contrast, in Nemes Nagy's rendition 'Brought to me' is omitted, allowing for a much more extended differentiation between tenor and vehicle, the vision described and the myth evoked. In her critical work Nemes Nagy naturally recognised the necessity of a close affinity of tenor and vehicle in similes; however, she also underlined that 'the creation of a new sign' in a simile is based on 'the unity of the two signs *in mutual recognition*'.[55] Indeed, the translator's use of the present tense in *visszaadd* ('gives back') in line 3 similarly strengthens the separation of the two narrative levels, creating the impression that in the Hungarian text we read a recollection of a mythological scene inserted within the recollection of a dream (I saw her like I saw Alcestis), a miniature recapitulation of Euripides' *Alcestis*. One cannot help but feel that Nemes Nagy (who was educated as a classicist) pored over Euripides' drama while translating Milton's sonnet: the phrase *a sír áldozatát* – which could mean either a sacrifice for, or a victim of, the grave – at least strongly evokes the self-presentation of Euripides' Alcestis as both a victim and a sacrifice in her dying speech.

Just like Euripides, Nemes Nagy's version greatly enhances the agency of Alcestis, and, by extension, the figure of the deceased wife. In Milton's sonnet both female figures are notably passive: Alcestis is 'Brought' and 'Rescu'd' (by Hercules), and the wife is 'washt' and 'save[d]' in a passive sense by purification in the Old Law. In the Hungarian version, by contrast, the verbs and participles characterising Alcestis and the wife are markedly more active: *lemosva* suggests 'having washed off'; 'came' is brought to the forefront from line 9 to line 6; and even the passive participle, *tépve* ('torn'), describing Alcestis, is ambiguous enough to hint at a general state of being unsettled in body and mind as well as being rescued. Perhaps the most tantalising element in Nemes Nagy's representation of the female figure is in the last but one line: the wife is represented as 'leaning over' (*rámhajolt*) the speaker, whom, as a consequence, we must imagine lying down. Milton's wording does not rule out this possibility: the verb 'incline' means to bend or tilt 'forward and downward' (*OED* 1a), but it can also imply a mental inclination (completely absent from the Hungarian). What is more, the distinct and well-documented classical resonances of the Miltonic scene – Orpheus rescuing Eurydice, Aeneas trying to embrace Creusa, or Odysseus doing the same to Antikleia in Book 11 of the *Odyssey* (and so on)[56] – are more likely to evoke the image of the speaker as an active, standing figure. Nemes Nagy's version trades these ancient tropes for the similarly powerful image of an incapacitated speaker who is dreaming that he is lying down. The figure of the wife, in contrast, moves about confidently: even in the last line she 'flew away' (*elszállt*) rather than 'fled' (as in Milton's original). The 'late-espoused Saint' in Nemes Nagy's translation is not just *like* Alcestis, but she *is* Alcestis, insofar as this Greek name can punningly suggest 'someone strong' (ἀλκῆς τις).

Nemes Nagy's version of Milton's sonnet thus presents a paradoxical situation in which a traditionally 'fleeting/shadowy dream'[57] is more active, more potent than its observer. The overwhelming sense of the speaker's helplessness at the closure of the poem (curiously resonant with Nemes Nagy's own confession of weakness discussed above) is thus built up from within the dream narrative: the speaker remains supine as the vision fades into reality with the departure of the wife's image. The dramatic tension achieved in this way is further intensified in the superb rhyming triplets of the sestet: *köntösén – ennyi fény – fölriadtam én* ('on her robe – so much light – I started up') and *fátyolán – csupán –éjszakám* ('through her veil – only – my night'). These, in a fashion characteristic of Nemes Nagy's poetry, highlight the poem's emotional trajectory from hopeful vision to disheartening reality through a strong focus on material objects. Readers of the 1958 bilingual volume of Milton' poems (*Versek/Poems*), whose interpretations were likely to be shaped by the Hungarian critical tradition's insistence on Milton's 'masculine' voice and 'revolutionary' content in the sonnets, might well have found a curious counterpoint to their expectations in the private vision of what could be perceived as an emasculated speaker as presented in Nemes Nagy's translation. The quiet pathos of the poem certainly provided a new context for reading Milton's other, equally stylised, but differently oriented writings on his blindness, such as Sonnets 19 and 22, the invocation to Book 3 of *Paradise Lost* (1–55), which were all included in the same volume, or the 'autobiographical' parts of *Samson Agonistes*, which were first made available to the Hungarian audience in 1956.

Ultimately, Nemes Nagy's translation of Sonnet 23 had contributed to the reshaping of the Hungarian canon of Milton's works: in the 1978 edition of Milton's selected poetical works,[58] and in Győző Ferencz's 1989 anthology cited above,[59] the poem is placed at an emphatic position as the last piece of the minor poems.[60] For Hungarian readers, however, the translation also allowed a glimpse into a completely unknown side of Nemes Nagy, the translator-poet herself. Milton's intensely personal poem provided a stark contrast to the poet's self-presentation in her published poetry as well as her reception by contemporaries as a 'disciplined, strict, pithy, conscious, objective, ethereal, reclusive, masculine woman poet' (*fegyelmezett, szigorú, tömör, tudatos, objektív, átszellemült, rejtőző, férfias költőnő*).[61] As a piece of literary translation, Sonnet 23 might have baffled some of Nemes Nagy's contemporaries; as one of her poems it would probably have been considered an anomaly.

'When she looked back': Sonnet 23 in the context of Nemes Nagy's poetry

Twenty-first-century readers are in a different position than Nemes Nagy's contemporary audience. The dominant perception of Nemes Nagy as 'the most masculine' poet of her generation and of the second half of the twentieth century has changed significantly in recent decades. Since her death in 1991, the Hungarian reading public has been exposed to a body of Nemes Nagy's poetry which she collected in notebooks throughout her career, but never actually published, and which cannot conveniently be described with the labels of 'discipline', 'objectivism' or 'masculinity' that she herself tacitly, if critically, endorsed. These poems feature an unmistakably private and often passionate voice and focus unapologetically on the female experience: they provide a striking counterpoint to Nemes Nagy's published poetry. The reasons why Nemes Nagy decided not to publish these pieces can only be guessed, but critics and readers have certainly acknowledged their sheer volume, which roughly equals in volume the poetry published in her lifetime, and the remarkable contrast they provide to the received image (and self-presentation) of the author. These 'new' poems have greatly unsettled the canon of Nemes Nagy's poetry – similarly (but on a larger scale) to how her translation of Sonnet 23 reshaped the dominant image of Milton in Hungary in the 1960s and 1970s. In hindsight we can see that this other side of Nemes Nagy's poetry is often reflected in the wide range of her translations, and we can certainly find important traces of this hidden oeuvre in her rendering of Milton's sonnet. One may justly wonder whether some of the poems among these long-unpublished pieces were at least partly inspired by Milton's vision. Two rather famous poems stand out and offer themselves for reflection: as a conclusion to this chapter I will present them with minimal commentary. The undated poem 'This I have seen . . .' ('Én láttam ezt') reads as if it were recording the visitation described in Milton's sonnet from the deceased wife's perspective:

> Én láttam ezt. (Még sose láttam.)
> Én jártam itt. (Még sose jártam.)
> Egy másik életben talán
> Erre a földre rátaláltam.

Egy másik életben talán
(Vagy valamely másik halálban),
Amikor öntudatlanul
S elfátyolozva erre jártam.

Vagy el se mentem én soha.
Itt voltam mindig, földbe-ástan.
S most itt állok, még szédelegve
E vértelen feltámadásban.

This I have seen (This I have never seen)
Here I have been (Here I have never been)
Perhaps in some other life
I simply stumbled on the scene.

Perhaps in some other life
(Some other dying, possibly)
Wearing veils, I came this way,
Or strayed here unconsciously.

Perhaps I never went away,
Have always been here, earth enfolded,
And stand here lost, without direction
In this bloodless resurrection.[62]
(translation by George Szirtes)

The situation described uncannily resembles the setting of Sonnet 23, but with some important differences. While, as we have seen above, Nemes Nagy's translation of Sonnet 23 develops an active Alcestis-like character in the figure of the 'late-espoused Saint', 'This I have seen ...' actually adopts the voice of a female character (one cannot but help being reminded here of Nemes Nagy's forced silence). Finding a voice allows the speaker to reflect, and the sense of permanent and total helplessness and uncertainty (resulting from a general lack of direction as well as being caught in an endless loop of 'bloodless resurrection') provides a stark alternative to the mythologically and religiously stylised teleological narrative in Milton's dream vision. Indeed, in Nemes Nagy's poem the speaker's own experiences are themselves 'pale and faint', as, positively ghost-like, she hints at being repeatedly 'Rescu'd from death by force'.

Another poem, entitled 'The departing one' ('A távozó'; in George Szirtes's translation, 'When she looked back . . .') was originally written around 1960, but was copied by Nemes Nagy into one of her draft-books on 16 January 1990.[63] It is often taken to be her great 'death poem', collecting into a single focus the past of the narrative, the present of the narration and future departure.[64] The poem registers a fleeting vision of a 'departing one' – an unidentified, and in the Hungarian ungendered, but personified being which could be the speaker's soul, hope, life, guardian angel, etc. – not in a dream vision, but in the speaker's confrontation with an X-ray photograph. The experience represented, with its emphasis on looking back, is strongly evocative of the final parting of Orpheus and Eurydice, but the facelessness of the 'departing one', not to mention George Szirtes's decision to render the genderless subject of the poem into a female figure in the English version, calls to mind Milton's vision in Sonnet 23.

> *Hogy visszanézett, nem volt arca már,*
> *Hogy visszanézett –*
> *Akikben itt lakott, a maszkok,*
> *földdé mosódtak zöldek és a kékek,*
> *szétkent kupacban arcok, homlokok,*
> *hogy utoljára visszanézett.*
>
> *S amikor hátat fordított,*
> *két szárnya*
> *röntgennel átvilágított*
> *tüdőszárny, olyan ezüst –*
> *és szét-szétnyílott – centiméteres*
> *kis repülési szándék – s összezárult*
> *kilélegezve.*
>
> *És láttam én,*
> *láttam akkor, hogy az enyém,*
> *nem másé, sajna, az enyém,*
> *két vállam közül távozott,*
> *akár az átvilágított,*
> *s a maszk nem takarta már, hogy visszanézett.*

When she looked back her face had disappeared.
When she looked back.
The masks that she inhabited
dissolved in earth; green, blue and black
in smeary piles of brow and head
the very last time she looked back.

As soon as she had turned away
two wings, her wings,
began to glow beneath the ray,
the purest silver, wings and lungs
which slowly opened as to fly
an inch or so, then closed again
as she breathed out.

I saw it all,
I saw then they belonged to me,
not others, sadly, but to me:
between my shoulder-blades she flew
like something light had shivered through,
no mask to stunt her backward view.
(translation by George Szirtes)[65]

If 'This I have seen . . .' presented the situation of Sonnet 23 'from the other side', i.e. from the point of view of a hitherto silenced female figure, 'When she looked back . . .' rewrites Milton's sonnet in a way that allows a powerful female voice to reflect on a similar experience to Milton's dream vision. Importantly, however, the painful departure, which in Milton's sonnet is registered by the shock of waking up from a dream, here becomes the process of waking up to the reality of terminal illness. Although the 'full sight' that Milton's speaker hopes for is here achieved ('I saw it all'), it comes with the ironic and resigned realisation that with the loss of masks the departing one's face also disappears.

In one of her short poems, Nemes Nagy presents the reflections of a translator on the original:

Fordítás közben

Nézlek, nézlek.
Látom a lángelmén a fércet,
a lágy koponya-varratot.
Csak így lehetek cinkosod:
köszönöm a nagylelküséged.

While translating

I watch you. I detect
loose stitches on a glorious intellect,
soft skull-sutures. Only this

can make us accomplices.
Many thanks and my deep respect.
(translation by Peter Zollman)[66]

On the one hand, the poem's speaker analytically observes, and ironically comments on, the process of translating: in turning a text into another language, the translator cannot help but notice the signs of 'stitching' or repair to the original (importantly, the Hungarian word for 'stitch', *férc*, is often used to refer to 'botched' work). On the other hand, the poem also registers the translator's sense of wonder, her admiration for how such 'stitches' become organic parts of the original and how they assume a vital function like babies' flexible cranial sutures. This ambivalence is then complemented by a sense of complicity and grateful appreciation, the implicit claim of belonging with the original. Although she is a world apart from Keats's ecstatic look into Chapman's Homer, Nemes Nagy reflects on a similar experience: translation is bound to change the target language, but it also completely transforms received conceptions of the original. Accordingly, Nemes Nagy's translation of Sonnet 23 and her two poems discussed above manage to achieve both a critical distance from, and a special complicity with, Milton's original. As we have seen, during her lifetime Nemes Nagy's poetry and personality were often characterised as 'rigorous', 'ethereal', 'masculine' – terms that sound as if they had been taken from the critical heritage of Milton and his works. In her rendering of Sonnet 23, however, Nemes Nagy used these qualities of her poetry to empower the 'pale and faint' female character of Milton's original, while in the poems 'This I have seen . . .' and 'When she looked back . . .' she endowed this character with a voice and a personal history. These pieces show us a striking example of how literary translation actually *complements* the original, and in this process Nemes Nagy, a Central European woman writer from the twentieth century writing under communist dictatorship, became Milton's unlikely but equal partner, one of the 'sad friends of Truth'.[67]

Notes

1. See e.g. Uzakova 2014, 23–4; Hao 2016, 571–2.
2. Szenczi 1958; on this article, and Szenczi's work, see Chapter 3.
3. On publishing in the communist era in general, and the Európa Publishing House in particular, see the Introduction.
4. Anon. 1958c, 1.
5. On Jánosi's and Szabó's translations, see Chapter 1; on Hungarian versions of *Samson* (including the one mentioned by the reader), see Chapter 2.

6. Anon. 1958c, 2.
7. On Lutter's critical work, see Chapter 3.
8. Milton 1958, 11.
9. Milton 1958, 11.
10. Jones 1977, 167.
11. See Schlueter 1995 for the term 'heroical sonnets' and the discussion of Milton's three poems that fall into this category.
12. For the idea of the 'fight for peace', see Browder 1936, 131–8. Vas's translation was originally published in Vas 1946.
13. Milton 1921, 31. This is the volume 'published by Knerr in Gyoma' that the reader's report refers to above.
14. Babits 1934, 1:264.
15. See Péti 2017, 340.
16. Rába 1969, 427.
17. Milton 1978; Ferencz 1989.
18. The 1978 edition of the selected poetical works already contained all three of Milton's revolutionary or 'heroical' sonnets.
19. Egri 1975, 88, 108–9. Just like Lutter, Egri uses Tóth's translation to draw far-reaching conclusions about the public dimension of Milton's sonnet. For a contemporary critique of Egri's rather narrow theoretical focus, see Csetri 1977.
20. See Chapters 1 and 2.
21. The rest of this chapter is adapted from Péti 2021c.
22. Some of Nemes Nagy's work is available in English; see Nemes Nagy 1988, 2004 and 2007, as well as Lehóczky 2011, which is a monograph-length discussion of her oeuvre in English.
23. Menyhért 2013, 25, 73, 79.
24. On this translation, see Péti 2017, 329–32.
25. Milton 1796, sig. b1^{r-v}.
26. Milton 1890, 10.
27. Milton 1930, xii.
28. Milton 1969, 417.
29. See Chapter 2.
30. Milton 2019, blurb written by Ádám Nádasdy.
31. Vas 1946, 9–10.
32. This critical manoeuvre seems tailored for the sonnet to Cromwell (Sonnet 16), one of the two poems by Milton included in Vas's collection, but is a more problematic fit for the youthful sense of belatedness in Sonnet 7 ('How soon hath Time'), the other poem in the anthology.
33. Lutter 1956a. On Lutter and his monograph, see Chapter 3.
34. Lutter 1956a, 124, 126.
35. On Szenczi and this essay, see Chapter 1 and Chapter 3.
36. Milton 1969, 349.
37. Milton 1969, 350.
38. Ferencz 1989, 360.
39. Pataky 2016, 7–8.
40. Nemes Nagy 1957, 126–7.
41. Birkett and Kearns 1997, 29.
42. As Győző Ferencz reminded me, translators of the day were commissioned by the publishing houses: they were not in the position to select what works they preferred to translate.
43. Nemes Nagy 1988, 8–9; see also Lehóczky 2011, 44–5.
44. Kardos 1957; Sík 1958.
45. Ferencz and Hobbs 1998, xv.
46. Pető 2001, 241.
47. Nemes Nagy 2008, 600.
48. See Kerrigan 1983, 134.
49. Milton 1958, 71.
50. Teskey 2015, 238.
51. This use of 'long-deceased' also seems to imply that in Nemes Nagy's interpretation it is Mary Powell rather than Catherine Woodcock who is the subject of the poem.

52. *Pace* Teskey who reads 'her person' as referring to the wife's 'entire body' (a sense in *OED* 4a; see Teskey 2015, 237), I would claim that the phrase suggests a more abstract sense of 'self', 'individuality' (*OED* 3a) or 'presence' (*OED* 3b).
53. Radnóti 1974, 1302, emphasis in the original.
54. On Milton's montage technique, see Péti 2014.
55. 'A költői kép' ('The poetic image), quoted in Lehóczky 2011, 46–7.
56. See Ulreich 1974, Stroup 1960, and Milton 1998, 700, respectively.
57. *Odyssey* 19.562.
58. Milton 1978.
59. Ferencz 1989.
60. Milton 1978, 48–9; Ferencz 1989, 234.
61. Menyhért 2013, 74.
62. Nemes Nagy 2004, 81.
63. Nemes Nagy 2016, 679.
64. Kántás 2014, 12.
65. Nemes Nagy 2004, 84.
66. Nemes Nagy 2004, 101.
67. Milton 2013, 205.

Epilogue

In 1989 state socialism came to end in Hungary (and the whole of Eastern Europe) not with a bang but with a whimper. Still the sudden arrival of freedom sent profound shockwaves through all aspects of life – the cultural sphere not excepted.[1] In academia remnants of the old 'Marxist-Leninist' modes of scholarship – slowly grinding to a halt in the previous decade – were rapidly discarded to open the field for a plethora of international theoretical influences, and the book publishing industry promptly started to move towards a market-oriented model. Paradoxically, but with hindsight predictably, in Milton's Hungarian reception the disappearance of censorship and ideological constraints did not result in a renaissance, but rather an almost complete silence of more than two decades. Literary critics were busy catching up with the latest developments in literary and cultural theory and publishers could not, or did not want to, cater for the needs of the relatively 'few' (*PL* 7.31) that usually form Milton's audience. The translations published in the previous decades remained in (or, rather, out of) use in their old 'socialist' editions. So did the scholarship and criticism that used to accompany them, and it was only in the new millennium that new renditions of Milton's prose and poetry started to appear, together with novel critical approaches and apparatuses.[2] These new publications generally represent more of a restart of Milton's reception than a continuation or revision of the post-war trends: even when they draw on the translations and the criticism of the communist era, they do so with a strong critical distance, and from contexts that are informed by international scholarship and recent developments in Milton studies.

It might seem, then, that the various post-war Hungarian interpretations of Milton's work can be aptly described with Jesus' words in *Paradise Regained*: 'Long in preparing, soon to nothing brought' (*PR* 3.389). Although the critical works I have introduced certainly add to the ways in which Milton's works were appropriated in the twentieth century, they represent a discontinued and not very successful branch of Milton's reception. The translations and adaptations of Milton's works from the period, by contrast, have not been as quickly dispensed with or forgotten, but they are now inevitably replaced by newer versions catering for new audiences. Furthest from Milton's words, the poems of Ágnes Nemes Nagy (inspired as they were by her translation of Sonnet 23) have an afterlife of their own, quite apart from the Miltonic heritage. The intellectual landscape charted in this book thus resembles a long-abandoned city: its plan is still discernible, some of its structures strike us with their quaintness or impracticality, others with their imposing presence or dazzling beauty, but all of them bear the signs of irreversible disintegration and the whole complex is devoid of the life it once accommodated. Is such a place worth a visit for anyone other than the tourist interested in historical curiosities? Or, in other words, can the interpretations of Milton's works documented in the previous chapters have any significance (for Miltonists or students of reception studies, for example), beyond the obvious fact that they are a part of the history of Milton's international reception?

This is a difficult question to resolve, and I certainly would not venture to provide a definitive answer. It seems that one of the recurring (and for me one of the most intriguing) aspects of the story recounted in the chapters above is the tension-ridden complexity of responses to Milton's oeuvre, which also testifies to the complex, often contradictory uses Miltonic texts allow.[3] Supported and/or prompted by the various cultural agents of communist cultural policy (party ideologues, censors, publishers, the academic environment), the critics whose work we encountered above published commentaries on Milton's works which were tendentious and selective to varying degrees, but almost always explicitly signalled the author's (heartfelt or superficial) loyalty to the prevailing ideology.[4] The way this was performed remotely resembles what Daniel Shore calls the 'bizarre kind of curatorial labour' in *Paradise Lost*,[5] a well-known and outstanding example of which is the 'Mulciber episode' where, in describing Satan's chief architect, the narrator evokes the story of Hephaistos from Homer:

> Nor was his name unheard or unador'd
> In ancient *Greece*; and in *Ausonian* land
> Men call'd him *Mulciber*; and how he fell
> From Heav'n, they fabl'd, thrown by angry *Jove*
> Sheer o're the Chrystal Battlements: from Morn
> To Noon he fell, from Noon to dewy Eve,
> A Summers day; and with the setting Sun
> Dropt from the Zenith like a falling Star,

> On *Lemnos* th'*Ægean* Ile: thus they relate,
> Erring; for he with this rebellious rout
> Fell long before. (*PL* 1.738–48)

In this passage the epic narrator highlights, but also explicitly corrects ('thus they relate, / Erring) a pagan myth. Nor is this a single occurrence: *Paradise Lost* features many other instances where Milton questions, refutes or lambasts non-Christian (or, if Christian, non-Protestant) cultural and religious traditions. Shore himself suggests the curious example of 'the museums of scientific atheism' in Lenin's Soviet Union as a close parallel to this narratorial strategy in *Paradise Lost*, but some of the critical works documented in this book test the validity of this comparison. While in the Mulciber episode the narrator's comments on the fundamental erroneousness of ancient myth involve the splendid poetic evocation and recreation of the material to be discarded, in hard-line 'Marxist-Leninist' Hungarian Milton criticism (most notably, in the works of Tibor Lutter), the ideological content never manages to organically complement the Miltonic text. In reading Milton's account of the fall of Mulciber we cannot but recall Homer; in reading the wildest attempts of post-war Hungarian critics to prove the revolutionary potential of Milton's works, we tend to lose sight of Milton.[6]

At the same time, the powerful translations and adaptations of Milton's works that emerged during the four decades of state socialism readily testify to the what Daniele Monticelli and Anne Lange have pointed out about translation under totalitarian regimes: it has 'the power to detach readers from their socio-historical situation by transporting them into a different territory'.[7] Although many of the translations discussed in the chapters above contain embarrassed nods to 'Marxist-Leninist' ideology, and sometimes even elements of contemporary propaganda, their chief interest lies in the ways they open wider horizons for interpretation, and thus, perhaps inadvertently, challenge received wisdom and official critical strains. As I have tried to show, this is more or less characteristic of all translations discussed in this volume, but nowhere is the subversive potential of interpreting Milton more apparent than in the seriously Miltonic feats of Ágnes Nemes Nagy's bold rendition of Sonnet 23, or Károly Kazimir's 1970 stage production of *Paradise Lost* based on István Jánosy's then-fresh translation. In retrospect it seems that in such crucial instances Hungarian interpretations of Milton's words 'Suspended [the] Hell' (*PL* 2.554) of the Cold War. Just like the Berlin Wall, the Iron Curtain functioned in a twofold way: for Easterners it was an insurmountable, tragic barrier to an imagined utopia, while for

Western Europeans it worked as a flattering mirror reflecting their own fortunate position.[8] Nemes Nagy and Kazimir managed to make it, if not disappear, at least become temporarily transparent from both sides.

However tempting it would be to cast the difference outlined above between the critical and the creative responses to Milton's works as a story of opposing motives, interests and objectives, the material collected in this volume provides solid evidence for a more complicated state of affairs. As we have repeatedly seen, critics of the age were not only active collaborators of translators, but they themselves occasionally ventured to render Milton's works into Hungarian. Conversely, some of the translators wrote spirited prefaces or afterwords in the 'Marxist-Leninist' vein, but produced versions of Milton's works which had little or nothing to do with their commentaries. The most bewildering case is, again, the 1970 stage production of *Paradise Lost*, where the director, Károly Kazimir, worked closely together with both the translator, István Jánosy, and Hungary's foremost Milton critic of the time, Miklós Szenczi. In 1970 these three men were at very different stages of their careers – and their relationship to state socialism varied accordingly. Although often sidelined by the various communist regimes, Kazimir was reputed to be 'most talented' in navigating his way through communist bureaucracy.[9] Szenczi, an accomplished university professor, who was silenced for eight years from 1948 to 1956, was understandably cautious in all his moves, as witnessed by his polite gestures to 'Marxism' in his critical works. Jánosy, a Lutheran theologian and preacher by profession, remained out of politics and chose 'studious retirement'[10] by translating ancient and early modern classics. Astonishingly, these different career paths might be put in close parallel with different periods in Milton's own life. Was it then the Miltonic text (and the intellectual kinship these people might have felt with Milton) that brought the theatre director, the translator and the critic together and guaranteed their success? Or should we rather conceive of their collaboration as one of the more fortunate (by-)products of an otherwise stifling cultural policy? In a true Miltonic manner, the picture that emerges is compelling not only for the insights it provides, but also the questions it raises.

Notes

1. See Hankiss 1994, 119 for the idea of the 'shock of freedom' in Eastern Europe.
2. The complete text of *Areopagitica* has been translated twice recently: Zsolt Komáromy, András Kiséry and Árpád Mihály completed the first version (still unpublished), while Miklós Könczöl published his rendition of the text in 2018. A new prose translation of *Paradise Regained* (done by the author of this volume) was published in 2019, and a new translation of *Paradise Lost* (by

Viktor Horváth and the author of this volume providing 'scholarly background') is underway. Most of the prose, the Latin poems and *Comus* remain untranslated at the time of publication.
3. Cf. Feisal Mohamed's recent monograph in which he explores the complexity of the Miltonic oeuvre and its modern reception, confronting 'pre-secularity and post-secularity on their own terms' (Mohamed 2011, 18).
4. For the concept of Milton's 'curatorial' work, see Shore 2012.
5. Shore 2012, 35.
6. Such critical attempts would be considered 'not good' by Kermode, since they 'divert from [the objects valued or their value] the special forms of attention they have been accorded' (Kermode 1985, 92).
7. Monticelli and Lange 2014, 106.
8. See Rév 1994, 160.
9. Léner 2015.
10. Milton 2013, 461.

Appendix

John Milton:

ELVESZETT PARADICSOM[1]

Fordította:

Jánosy István

[Színpadra alkalmazta:

Jánosy István és Kazimir Károly]

Szereplők:

Sátán
Ádám
Éva
Mihály
Rafael
Gábriel
Atya
Fiú
1. Angyal
2. Angyal
3. Angyal
Bűn
Halál
Belzebub
Moloch
Béliál
Mammon
Abdiel
Ördögök

John Milton

PARADISE LOST

Translated into Hungarian by

István Jánosy

[Adapted to the Stage by

István Jánosy and Károly Kazimir

Rendered back into Milton's English by

Miklós Péti]

Dramatis Personae:

Satan
Adam
Eve
Michael
Raphael
Gabriel
God
The Son
Angel 1
Angel 2
Angel 3
Sin
Death
Beelzebub
Moloch
Belial
Mammon
Abdiel
Devils

1. Rész

ÁDÁM:	Az ember legelső bűnét, s a tiltott
	fa gyümölcséből kóstolást, amely
	halált hozott a földre.
ÉVA:	Bűnt reánk,
ÁDÁM:	s kivetett az Édenből, míg egy különb
	Ember megváltott, s visszahozta üdvünk.
MIND:	Zengd, Múzsa,
ÁDÁM:	– világosítsd
	elmém ködét, elestemből emelj,
	védj, hogy a téma fenségéhez illőn [10]
	hirdessem az örök Gondviselést,
	s embernek igazoljam Isten útját.
BÉLIÁL:	Mi vitte
	ős-szüleinket rá, hogy Alkotójuk
	elárulják, és megszegjék tilalmát,
MOLOCH:	Ki űzte őket undok pártütésre?
SÁTÁN:	Pokol Kigyója! Ő, ki álnokul
	és sanda bosszuból az ember anyját
	elcsábitotta, miután az Égből
	gőgje lelökte őt s egész hadát: [20]
	az angyal-pártütőket, kiknek útján
	kivánt kerülni dicsben társai
	fölé, hogy az Úrral egyenlő legyen.
MIHÁLY:	Hiú merénylet! A Mindenható
	leszórta őt fejest a légi égből,
	perzselve lánggal, szörnyü pusztulással
	feneketlen romlásba: lakjon ott
	acél-láncban, a büntetés tüzén,
	ki a Nagy Istent harcra hívta ki. [30]
RAFAEL:	Sátán veszett hadával; bárha halhatatlan –
	letörve most,
MIHÁLY:	ám szörnyűbb szenvedés
	van szabva rá, hisz gyötri őt a tűnt
	boldogság és az örök kíntudat:

Part 1

ADAM:	OF Mans First Disobedience, and the Fruit
	Of that Forbidden Tree, whose mortal tast
	Brought Death into the World,
EVE:	and all our Sin,[2]
ADAM:	With loss of *Eden*, till one greater Man
	Restore us, and regain the blissful Seat.
ALL:	Sing, Muse,
ADAM:	What in me is dark
	Illumin, what is low raise and support;
	That to the highth of this great Argument [10]
	I may assert Eternal Providence,
	And justifie the wayes of God to men.
BELIAL:	What cause
	Mov'd our Grand Parents in that happy State,
	Favour'd of Heav'n so highly, to fall off
	From thir Creator, and transgress his Will,
MOLOCH:	Who first seduc'd them to that foul revolt?
SATAN:	Th' infernal Serpent; he it was, whose guile
	Stird up with Envy and Revenge, deceiv'd
	The Mother of Mankind, what time his Pride [20]
	Had cast him out from Heav'n, with all his Host
	Of Rebel Angels, by whose aid aspiring
	To set himself in Glory above his Peers,
	He trusted to have equal'd the most High.
MICHAEL:	Vain attempt! Him the Almighty Power
	Hurld headlong flaming from th' Ethereal Skie
	With hideous ruine and combustion down
	To bottomless perdition, there to dwell
	In Adamantine Chains and penal Fire,
	Who durst defie th' Omnipotent to Arms. [30]
RAPHAEL:	Satan with his horrid crew; though immortal –
	Confounded now,
MICHAEL:	but his doom
	Reserv'd him to more wrath; for now the thought
	Both of lost happiness and lasting pain
	Torments him:

GÁBRIEL:	Míly más e hely, mint honnan estek ők!
RAFAEL:	Erőben-bűnben fő hatalmi társa –
BELZEBUB:	A nevem Belzebub.
	Szent Fény. Ég elsőszülött sarja, üdv!
	Az Örökkévalóval egy-örök tűz,
	zenghetlek bűntelen? [40]
MOLOCH:	Isten szavára
	mintegy köpennyel födözted be a
	mély, tiszta vizek támadó világát,
	mely lett üres, ormótlan végtelenből.
SÁTÁN:	Még vakmerőbb szárnyakkal fölkereslek,
	más dallal, mint hajdan Orpheus –
	újra fölkereslek
	bizton, s érzem királyi élet-mécsed,
	habár te nem keresed föl szemem,
	mely hasztalan forog, hogy megtalálja [50]
	szúrós sugárod, pirkadatra nem lel.
ÁDÁM:	Ám szüntelen bolyongok ott, hol a
	múzsák időznek tiszta csermely, árnyas
	berek ölén, napszőtte dombokon
	szent dal-szerelme-babonázva.
SÁTÁN:	Így az évvel
	négy évszak visszatér, de vissza nem tér
	hozzám a nappal, este-reggel édes
	közelgése, tavasz-virág varázsa,
	nyár rózsája, nyáj, isten ember arca; [60]
	helyettük köd, s örök-sötét borult
	reám, s zárva vagyok az emberek
	vidám körétől, és a tudomány
	szép könyve nékem fehér lap csupán:
	természet művei lemosva róla,
	tudás ez egy kapúja zárva nékem.
ÉVA:	Annál inkább bensőmbe, Égi fény,
	te fényeskedj, s eszem minden hatalmát
	te ragyogd bé, ültess szemet belé,
	söpörd ki szennyét, látva hogy kitárjak [70]
	halandó-szem-nem-látta dolgokat.
KÓRUS:	Halandó-szem-nem-látta dolgokat.
RAFAEL:	A Mindenható atya,
	hol trónol minden magasság fölött

GABRIEL:	O how unlike the place from whence they fell!
RAPHAEL:	One next himself in power, and next in crime –
BEELZEBUB:	My name is Beelzebub.
	Hail holy Light, offspring of Heav'n first-born, [40]
	Or of th' Eternal Coeternal beam
	May I express thee unblam'd?
MOLOCH:	At the voice
	Of God, as with a Mantle didst invest
	The rising world of waters dark and deep,
	Won from the void and formless infinite.
SATAN:	Thee I revisit now with bolder wing,
	With other notes then to th' *Orphean* Lyre –
	thee I revisit safe,
	And feel thy sovran vital Lamp; but thou [50]
	Revisit'st not these eyes, that rowle in vain
	To find thy piercing ray, and find no dawn.
ADAM:	Yet not the more
	Cease I to wander where the Muses haunt
	Cleer Spring, or shadie Grove, or Sunnie Hill,
	Smit with the love of sacred Song.
SATAN:	Thus with the Year
	Seasons return, but not to me returns
	Day, or the sweet approach of Ev'n or Morn,
	Or sight of vernal bloom, or Summers Rose, [60]
	Or flocks, or heards, or the human face of God;[3]
	But cloud in stead, and ever-during dark
	Surrounds me, from the chearful wayes of men
	Cut off, and for the Book of knowledg fair
	Presented with a Universal blanc
	Of Nature's works to mee expung'd and ras'd,
	And wisdome at one entrance quite shut out.
EVE:	So much the rather thou Celestial light
	Shine inward, and the mind through all her powers
	Irradiate, there plant eyes, all mist from thence [70]
	Purge and disperse, that I may see and tell
	Of things invisible to mortal sight.
CHORUS:	Of things invisible to mortal sight.
RAPHAEL:	The Almighty Father from above,

	a kristály Empyreumból, hol ül,	
	alátekint, hogy lássa alkotását,	
	s teremtményeiét.	
GÁBRIEL:	Körötte állnak,	
	sürűn mint csillagok, az Égi szentek,	
	őt látva véghetetlen boldogan.	[80]
ÖRDÖG:	Jobbján dicső sugár-képmása áll,	
	Egyszülötte.	
ATYA:	Egyszülöttem, nézd csak, ellenfelünk mikép dühöng.	
	Sem a szabott határ, sok lánc, sem az	
	ásitó szakadék nem fogja vissza: úgy csi-	
	gázza őt a veszekedett bosszú,	
	mi pártütő fejére száll utóbb!	
MIHÁLY:	Az Úr legelőször	
	ősszüleinket pillantotta meg,	
	az embernem két zsengéjét az Üdv	[90]
	kertjébe plántáltatva, szerelem	
	s öröm örök gyümölcseit szakasztva	
	vetélytárstalan szerelemben és	
	örök örömben, üdv-magányban.	
RAFAEL:	Aztán átfürkészi a Poklot és a köztes	
	űr-szakadékot, s látja, ím a Sátán	
	veszett hadával; bárha halhatatlan –	
	letörve most.	
SÁTÁN:	Vészben megedzett drága társaim	
	Nézzétek azt az elvadult, kopár sikot,	[100]
	az iszonyat helyét,	
	Gyerünk oda	
	e hányódó tüzárból –	
	Szétszórt erőink szedjük össze ott,	
	s főzzük ki, mint sérthetjük legkivált	
	ellenfelünk, bukásunk mint javítsuk,	
	e szörnyüségen urrá mint legyünk;	
	mi bátorítást adhat a remény,	
	s ha nem: mi elhatározást a kín?	
	Üdv, Alvilág! Iszony s te Vég-Pokol!	[110]
	Fogadd be új urad, kinek szivét	
	nem változtatja meg hely és idő.	
	E szív önnön helye, és benne támaszt	
	Pokolból Mennyet és Mennyből Pokolt.	

	From the pure Empyrean where he sits
	High Thron'd above all highth, bent down his eye,
	His own works and their works at once to view.
GABRIEL:	About him all the Sanctities of Heaven
	Stood thick as Starrs, and from his sight receiv'd
	Beatitude past utterance. [80]
DEVIL:	On his right
	The radiant image of his Glory stands,[4]
	His onely Son.
GOD:	Onely begotten Son, seest thou what rage
	Transports our adversarie.
	Him no bounds prescrib'd, nor all the chains, nor yet
	the main Abyss wide interrupt can hold; so bent
	he seems on desparate reveng,
	that shall redound upon his own rebellious head.
MICHAEL:	The Lord first beheld [90]
	Our two first Parents, yet the onely two
	Of mankind, in the happie Garden plac't,
	Reaping immortal fruits of joy and love,
	Uninterrupted joy, unrivald love
	In blissful solitude.
RAPHAEL:	He then survey'd
	Hell and the Gulf between, and Satan there
	with his horrid crew; though immortal –
	Confounded now.
SATAN:	O now in danger tri'd, now known in Armes [100]
	See you yon dreary Plain, forlorn and wilde,
	The seat of desolation,
	Thither let us tend
	From off the tossing of these fiery waves –
	There reassembling our afflicted Powers,
	Consult how we may henceforth most offend
	Our Enemy, our own loss how repair,
	How overcome this dire Calamity,
	What reinforcement we may gain from Hope,
	If not what resolution from despare. [110]
	Hail horrours, hail
	Infernal world, and thou profoundest Hell
	Receive thy new Possessor: One who brings
	A mind not to be chang'd by Place or Time.
	The mind is its own place, and in it self
	Can make a Heav'n of Hell, a Hell of Heav'n.

| | Mit számit, hol, ha ugyanaz vagyok?
| | Legyek akármi, de kisebb Nála nem.
| | Itt végre szabadok leszünk!
| ÖRDÖGÖK: | Szabadok leszünk.
| MIHÁLY: | Ördögsereg!
| | Ez néktek fegyelem, vállalt hüség, [120]
| | katona-függelem, hogy a Vezérhez,
| | s Törvényhez vagytok engedetlenek?
| | S te fondor tettető, te kérkedel most
| | a szabadság védőjeként, aki
| | egykor hajbókló szolgaként imádtad
| | az Ég erős urát?! Miért, ha nem
| | remélve, hogy megdöntöd őt, s király leszel?
| SÁTÁN: | Inkább Pokolban úr, mint szolga, Égben . . .
| BELZEBUB: | De mért hagynánk hites barátainkat,
| | bukásunk cimboráit így heverni [130]
| | merülve Feledés tavába, mért
| | ne hívjuk őket, s osszuk meg velük
| | e nyomorú lakot, vagy újra még
| | tegyünk próbát, mit nyerhetünk a Mennyben
| | új fegyverrel, s mit veszthetünk Pokolban?
| SÁTÁN: | Hatalmak, hercegek,
| | virágai az Égnek, mely tiétek
| | volt egykor, s most veszett! Íly döbbenet
| | megrázhat örök lényeket?
| | Ocsúdjatok, vagy bukjatok örökre! [140]
| | Erők, Hatalmak, Égi istenek,
| | ha üdv-ölébe mély nem temethet
| | örök erőt, így bukva, elcsigázva
| | sem mondok le a Mennyről!
| | Ez egység, egyetértés, és hüség
| | fölényével, mi több itt, mint az Égben,
| | most indulunk pörölni ősi jussunk.
| | Azt vitassuk, mi a jobb út:
| | nyilt harc, vagy titkos ármány.
| | Ki jó tanácsot adhat, szóljon az! [150]
| 1. ANGYAL: | Titkos gyűlés?
| 2. ANGYAL: | Zárt tanácskozás?

	What matter where, if I be still the same,	
	And what I should be, all but less then he	
	Here at least we shall be free!	
DEVILS:	We shall be free!	[120]
MICHAEL:	Armie of Fiends,	
	Was this your discipline and faith ingag'd,	
	Your military obedience, to dissolve	
	Allegeance to th' acknowledg'd Power supream?	
	And thou sly hypocrite, who now wouldst seem	
	Patron of liberty, who more then thou	
	Once fawn'd, and cring'd, and servilly ador'd	
	Heav'ns awful Monarch? wherefore but in hope	
	To dispossess him, and thy self to reigne?	
SATAN:	Better to reign in Hell, then serve in Heav'n . . .	[130]
BEELZEBUB:	But wherefore let we then our faithful friends,	
	Th' associates and copartners of our loss	
	Lye thus astonisht on th' oblivious Pool,	
	And call them not to share with us their part	
	In this unhappy Mansion, or once more	
	With rallied Arms to try what may be yet	
	Regaind in Heav'n, or what more lost in Hell?	
SATAN:	Princes, Potentates,	
	Warriers, the Flowr of Heav'n, once yours, now lost,	
	Can such astonishment sieze	[140]
	Eternal spirits?	
	Awake, arise, or be for ever fall'n.	
	Powers and Dominions, Deities of Heav'n,	
	For since no deep within her gulf can hold	
	Immortal vigor, though opprest and fall'n,	
	I give not Heav'n for lost.	
	With this advantage then	
	To union, and firm Faith, and firm accord,	
	More then can be in Heav'n, we now return	
	To claim our just inheritance of old,	[150]
	By what best way,	
	Whether of open Warr or covert guile,	
	We now debate; who can advise, may speak.	
ANGEL 1:	A secret conclave?	
ANGEL 2:	In close recess?	

1. ANGYAL:	Menjünk, jelentsük.
MOLOCH:	Én nyilt csatára voksolok! Nem értek
	cselhez – ezzel nem kérkedem;
	pokollánggal, haraggal fegyverezve
	törjünk szabad utat az Ég-toronyba,
	csürvén kínunkból iszonyú dzsidát
	Gyötrönk ellen, trónját s magát
	is lássa elborítva furcsa tűzzel [160]
	pokol-kénkővel, önmaga-eszelte
	kínnal! [ELLENKEZÉS]
	Avagy riaszt a vég? Kihívjuk ismét
	a Bajnokabbat? Dühe lel ujabb, még
	rosszabb utat bajunkra? – Félhetünk
	Pokolban még gyötrőbb nyomort? Mi rosszabb,
	mint az üdvből kiűzve ittlakozni?
	végkínra ítéltetve szörnyü Mélyben,
	ennél jobban összetörni
	csak végromlásunk bír, Halál! Miért [170]
	féljünk?
BÉLIÁL:	A nyílt, vagy rejtett háborút azért
	én nem javallom. Kény, erő, csalás
	vele szemben mit ér? Eszén ki jár túl,
	hiszen szeme mindent lát! Az Ég-tetőről
	látja s kacagja minden moccanásunk;
	kik tenni tudnánk,
	tudjunk most tűrni; nem törvénytelen
	ez a parancs – ha lettünk volna bölcsek,
	így határoztunk volna, nemhogy íly nagy [180]
	Ellent kihívjunk, íly kockázatot
	vállalva.
	Ez hát sorunk, amit ha szenvedünk,
	Ellenfelünk haragja megcsitul tán,
	ha tőlünk messze van, s nem sértjük őt,
	feled minket, elégli büntetésünk,
	hozhat reményt Jövő
	örök foIyása, véletlen, csere,
	mit várni érdemes, mivel mai sorsunk –
	boldognak rossz, de rossznak nem a végső, [190]
	ha magunk nem hozunk fejünkre több bajt.
MAMMON:	Tegyük föl, megszelídül és kegyelmet
	hirdet nekünk ujabb alázkodás
	igéretére – míly szemekkel állunk
	színe elé, s fogadjuk ránkszabott,

ANGEL 1:	Let's go and report it!
MOLOCH:	My sentence is for open Warr: Of Wiles,
	More unexpert, I boast not:
	Let us rather choose arm'd with Hell flames and fury all at once
	O're Heav'ns high Towrs to force resistless way, [160]
	Turning our Tortures into horrid Arms
	Against the Torturer; he shall see his Throne it self
	Mixt with *Tartarean* Sulphur, and strange fire,
	His own invented Torments. **[DISAPPROVAL]**
	Th' event is fear'd; should we again provoke
	Our stronger, some worse way his wrath may find
	To our destruction: if there be in Hell
	Fear to be worse destroy'd: what can be worse
	Then to dwell here, driv'n out from bliss, condemn'd
	In this abhorred deep to utter woe; [170]
	More destroy'd then thus
	We should be quite abolisht and expire.
	What fear we then?
BELIAL:	Warr therefore, open or conceal'd, alike
	My voice disswades; for what can force or guile
	With him, or who deceive his mind, whose eye
	Views all things at one view? he from heav'ns highth
	All these our motions vain, sees and derides;
	To suffer, as to doe,
	Our strength is equal, nor the Law unjust [180]
	That so ordains: this was at first resolv'd,
	If we were wise, against so great a foe
	Contending, and so doubtful what might fall.
	This is now
	Our doom; which if we can sustain and bear,
	Our Supream Foe in time may much remit
	His anger, and perhaps thus farr remov'd
	Not mind us not offending, satisfi'd
	With what is punish't;
	Besides what hope the never-ending flight [190]
	Of future dayes may bring, what chance, what change
	Worth waiting, since our present lot appeers
	For happy though but ill, for ill not worst,
	If we procure not to our selves more woe.
MAMMON:	Suppose he should relent
	And publish Grace to all, on promise made
	Of new Subjection; with what eyes could we
	Stand in his presence humble, and receive

	kemény törvényeit hajbókolón:	
	zengjük trónját csicsergő himnuszokkal,	
	isten-voltát kényszer-alellujákkal,	
	míg ő Úrként feszít. Unalmas	
	öröklét ez annak imádatával	[200]
	mulatva, kit utálunk! Ne akarjuk	
	erővel a lehetetlent, mi ingyen	
	se kéne – bár Mennyben, a csillogó	
	rablétet, –ám inkább keressük üdvünk	
	önnönmagunkban, és magunknak éljünk	
	csak a miénkből, bár e zord magányban,	
	de szabadon, senkitől se függve, [HELYESLÉS]	
	itt miben különb az Ég?	
BELZEBUB:	Trónok, hatalmak, Ég szülöttei!	
	Mért töprengünk: háború	[210]
	vagy béke? A háború rabságba vitt,	
	s buktunk javíthatatlan.	
	S míly békét adhatunk, ha nem ami	
	tőlünk telik: gyülölséget, csatát,	
	nem törhető dacot, alattomos	
	folyton-főzött bosszút.	
SÁTÁN:	És ha valami könnyü módra lelnénk?	
	Mert van egy hely (ha nem csal ősi jóslat),	
	másik világ, új faj boldog hona –	
	a neve:	[220]
ABDIEL:	Ember,	
MOLOCH:	ezidőtt teremti	
	az Úr:	
BÉLIÁL:	hozzánk hasonló,	
1. ÖRDÖG:	bár erőben gyarlóbb,	
2. ÖRDÖG:	ám a fenti Úrnál	
	nagyobb kegyben leend.	
BELZEBUB:	Kisérhetünk talán kalandot itt	
	vad rajtaütéssel: kiűzzük apró	
	lakossát, mint minket az Úr, s ha mégse,	[230]
	elcsábítjuk, hogy légyen ellenévé	
	Isten, s müvét megbánva, enkezével	
	törölje el.	

	Strict Laws impos'd, to celebrate his Throne	
	With warbl'd Hymns, and to his Godhead sing	[200]
	Forc't Halleluiah's; while he Lordly sits	
	How wearisom Eternity so spent in worship paid	
	To whom we hate. Let us not then pursue	
	By force impossible, by leave obtain'd	
	Unacceptable, though in Heav'n, our state	
	Of splendid vassalage, but rather seek	
	Our own good from our selves, and from our own	
	Live to our selves, though in this vast recess,	
	Free, and to none accountable, [**APPROVAL**]	
	What can Heav'n shew more?	[210]
BEELZEBUB:	Thrones and Imperial Powers, off-spring of heav'n,	
	What sit we projecting peace and Warr?	
	Warr hath determin'd us, and foild with loss	
	Irreparable.	
	What peace can we return,	
	But to our power hostility and hate,	
	Untam'd reluctance, and revenge though slow.	
SATAN:	What if we find	
	Some easier enterprize? There is a place	
	(If ancient and prophetic fame in Heav'n	[220]
	Err not) another World, the happy seat	
	Of some new Race call'd	
ABDIEL:	Man,	
MOLOCH:	About this time	
	To be created,	
BELIAL:	Like to us,	
DEVIL 1:	Though less in power and excellence,	
DEVIL 2:	But favour'd more	
	Of him who rules above.	
BEELZEBUB:	Here perhaps	[230]
	Som advantagious act may be achiev'd	
	By sudden onset, to drive as we were driven,	
	The punie habitants, or if not drive,	
	Seduce them to our Party, that thir God	
	May prove thir foe, and with repenting hand	
	Abolish his own works.	

GÁBRIEL:	Pokolfőknek tetszett e vakmerő terv.
	Örömszikrás szemek! Egyhanguan
	meg is szavazták.
SÁTÁN:	Istenzsinat! Méltón itéltetek
	Ámde kit bocsássunk,
	hogy kifürkéssze ezt az új világot,
	ki képes erre? Minő fortély, erő [240]
	képes kiútat lelni körbe sűrün
	figyelő angyal-őrszemek között?
	Óvatos kell legyen, s mi is: vajon kit
	válasszunk.
	Kit küldünk, most azon
	áll, vagy bukik minden: a végreményünk!
1. ANGYAL:	Várakozás villan szemén: ki vállalja e vészes
	merényletet; de mind kukán lapul.
SÁTÁN:	Ó, Menny-szülöttek, Égi Trónok! Íly mély
	csönd, habozás méltán nyügöz le titeket. [250]
	Ám engem nem riaszt. Nagy út vezet
	s nehéz a Pokolból a fénybe. Biztos
	e tömlöcünk, kilencszer zár körül
	mohón-nyelő iszonyu tűzburok.
	De nem érdemleném e trónt, Urak,
	ha elriasztna
	valami is annak kisérletétől,
	mi terv közjót szolgálni itéltetik,
	habár nehéz, veszélyes.
	Velem e vad kalandra ne jöjjön senki! [260]
1. ANGYAL:	Gyűlés végeztével a visszamaradók szétszélednek.
	Sátán szárnyra kap, s Pokolkapuk felé
	veszi magános röptét.
BŰN:	A kapu két szögén egy-egy iszony-lény:
	derékig bájos nőszerű az egyik,
	ám lent sokágu, pikkelyes, tömérdek
	tekergő kigyóteste van, halálos
	fullánkkal végükön.
	Ez alvilági kulcsot jog szerint
	s a mindenható Ég-király parancsa [270]
	szerint én őrzöm; tiltva van kinyitnom
	e páncél ajtót: készen áll Halál, hogy
	erő ellen hatalmát kö[zbe]vesse,

GABRIEL:	The bold design	
	Pleas'd highly those infernal States, and joy	
	Sparkl'd in all thir eyes; with full assent	
	They vote.	[240]
SATAN:	Well have ye judg'd, well ended long debate,	
	Synod of Gods! But first whom shall we send	
	In search of this new world, whom shall we find	
	Sufficient? What strength, what art can then	
	Bear him safe through the strict Senteries and Stations thick	
	Of Angels watching round? Here he had need	
	All circumspection, and we now no less	
	Choice in our suffrage; for on whom we send,	
	The weight of all and our last hope relies.	
ANGEL 1:	His look suspence, awaiting who appeer'd	[250]
	To undertake the perilous attempt; but all sat mute.	
SATAN:	O Progeny of Heav'n, Empyreal Thrones,	
	With reason hath deep silence and demurr	
	Seis'd you, though I remain undismaid:[5] long is the way	
	And hard, that out of Hell leads up to light;	
	Our prison strong, this huge convex of Fire,	
	Outrageous to devour, immures us round	
	Ninefold, and gates of burning Adamant	
	Barr'd over us prohibit all egress.	
	But I should ill become this Throne, O Peers,	[260]
	If aught propos'd and judg'd of public moment, in the shape	
	Of difficulty or danger could deterr	
	Mee from attempting.	
	This enterprize none shall partake with me.	
ANGEL 1:	The Councel thus ended, the rest betake them several wayes.[6]	
	Satan puts on swift wings, and towards the Gates of Hell	
	Explores his solitary flight.	
SIN:	On either side a formidable shape;	
	The one seem'd Woman to the waste, and fair,	
	But ended foul in many a scaly fould	[270]
	Voluminous and vast, a Serpent arm'd	
	With mortal sting.	
	The key of this infernal Pit by due,	
	And by command of Heav'ns all-powerful King	
	I keep, by him forbidden to unlock	
	These Adamantine Gates; against all force	
	Death ready stands to interpose his power,[7]	

	s nem fél, hogy rajta győz élő erő.	
HALÁL:	Másik alak – ha épp	
	alaknak hivható, melyen tagot,	
	izűletet se látni, vagy valónak,	
	mi árnynak tetszik (ilyennek is, olyannak	
	is látszik) éj-sötéten áll, miként tíz	
	fúria; mérges, szörnyü, mint Pokol; ráz	[280]
	iszonyu lándzsát, s fejszerü dudorán	
	királykoronafélét hord.	
SÁTÁN:	Honnan, mi faj vagy, átkozott alak, hogy	
	utamba merted vetni torz fejed?	
	Pokolfaj: égi szellemmel ne küzdj!	
HALÁL:	Te vagy az áruló kherúb, aki	
	először tört békét, hitet az Égben,	
	mit meg nem törtek még, s az Égfiak	
	harmadját lázadó fegyverbe hívtad	
	az Isten ellen, mért is téged ő	[290]
	és csürhédet kiebrudalt, s ide	
	számkivetett: örök tűz-kínban élni?	
	Ég-szellemnek hiszed magad, Pokolra-	
	itélt, és itt dacot meg gúnyt lihegsz,	
	hol én vagyok király – hogy még dühösb légy! –,	
	Urad, királyod?	
	Vissza börtönödbe,	
	csalárd szökevény, s kotródásodnak adj	
	szárnyat, nehogy késésed skorpió-	
	korbáccsal űzzem, és dzsidám suhintva	[300]
	még meg nem élt kínt bocsássak reád!	
BŰN:	Apám, miért veted kezed	
	egyetlen magzatodra, és mi düh szállt	
	meg, sarjam, hogy halál-fegyveredet	
	saját apád fejére szegzed?	
SÁTÁN:	Miért hívsz apádnak engem s ez Iszonyt fiamnak?	
	Nem ismerek, nem láttam én soha	
	nálad és nála szörnyebb látományt!	
BŰN:	Felejtettél? Szemedben oly csunyának	
	tetszem ma? Én, kit hajdan ott az Égben	[310]
	oly szépnek láttál, sűrü lángot	
	lövelt fejed, s baloldalán nagy űr nyílt,	

	Fearless to be o'rmatcht by living might.	
DEATH:	The other shape,	
	If shape it might be call'd that shape had none	[280]
	Distinguishable in member, joynt, or limb,	
	Or substance might be call'd that shadow seem'd,	
	For each seem'd either; black it stood as Night,	
	Fierce as ten Furies, terrible as Hell,	
	And shook	
	A dreadful Dart; what seem'd his head	
	The likeness of a Kingly Crown had on.	
SATAN:	Whence and what art thou, execrable shape,	
	That dar'st, though grim and terrible, advance	
	Thy miscreated Front athwart my way?	[290]
	Retire, Hell-born, don't contend with Spirits of Heav'n.	
DEATH:	Art thou that Traitor Angel, art thou hee,	
	Who first broke peace in Heav'n and Faith, till then	
	Unbrok'n, and in proud rebellious Arms	
	Drew after him the third part of Heav'ns Sons	
	Conjur'd against the highest, for which both Thou	
	And they outcast from God, are here condemn'd	
	To waste Eternal dayes in woe and pain?	
	And reck'n'st thou thy self with Spirits of Heav'n,	
	Hell-doom'd, and breath'st defiance here and scorn	[300]
	Where I reign King, and to enrage thee more,	
	Thy King and Lord? Back to thy punishment,	
	False fugitive, and to thy speed add wings,	
	Least with a whip of Scorpions I pursue	
	Thy lingring, or with one stroke of this Dart	
	Strange horror seise thee, and pangs unfelt before.	
SIN:	O Father, what intends thy hand, she cry'd,	
	Against thy only Son? What fury O Son,	
	Possesses thee to bend that mortal Dart	
	Against thy Fathers head?	[310]
SATAN:	Why thou call'st	
	Me Father, and that Fantasm call'st my Son?	
	I know thee not, nor ever saw till now	
	Sight more detestable then him and thee!	
SIN:	Hast thou forgot me then, and do I seem	
	Now in thine eye so foul, once deemd so fair	
	In Heav'n, thy head flames thick and fast	
	Threw forth, till on the left side op'ning wide,	

	honnan kiszöktem én. A teljes Ég-had	
	ámulva megriadt, szükölve vissza-	
	hőkölt, Bűnnek hivott, s baljóslatú	
	jelnek itélt; de rokonnak szokva meg,	
	tetszettem, és bájam megnyerte még	
	a legfőbb zsémbelőket is, kivált	
	Téged, ki bennem legtökéletesebb	
	képmásod lelve meg, belémszerettél,	[320]
	s doromboltál velem titokba, míg	
	méhem növő terhet fogant.	
SÁTÁN:	Lányom, édes, ha igényelsz apádnak,	
	s mutatod szép fiam, méz zálogát	
	Menny-élveinknek – nem jövök, mint	
	ellen, tudd meg, de hogy a kín e rémes	
	fekete házából megváltsalak	
	kettőtöket, magam megyek e durva küldetésbe,	
	csakhogy vándor-fürkészve megkeressem	
	a megjósolt helyet, jelek szerint mely	[330]
	alkotva már –és új lakók raja	
	plántáltatott beléje megürült	
	helyünket pótlandó – sietek	
	megtudni, és ha látom, visszatérek,	
	s elviszlek Téged és Halált oda,	
	hogy élvben éljetek, s a sűrű légben	
	illatbalzsamban ringjatok titokban,	
	halkan; lesz ott mit ennetek dugig,	
	véghetetlen: minden zsákmányotok lesz!	
HALÁL:	A Pokol-ajtószárnyak szétcsapódnak,	[340]
	a sarkokon csikorognak,	
	s fenekestül megrendül a sötétség.	
GÁBRIEL:	A Sátán az Ég-falnál surran a barna légben	
	az éj ezoldalán, s leszállni készül.	
3. ANGYAL:	Őt nézi Isten fönti őrhelyéről,	
	honnan figyel multat, jelent, jövőt.	
	Jövőbelátva mondja Egy-fiának:	
ATYA:	Egyszülöttem, nézd csak, ellenfelünk.	
	Minden sorompót szétzúzva íme szárnyal útjain	
	az épp megalkotott Világ felé,	[350]
	a beleplántált emberhez, hogy azt,	
	ha tudja: kénnyel, vagy mi még gonoszb:	
	fortéllyal rontsa meg – kiveszti őt,	

	Out I sprung; amazement seis'd	
	All th' Host of Heav'n back they recoild affraid	[320]
	At first, and call'd me *Sin*, and for a Sign	
	Portentous held me; but familiar grown,	
	I pleas'd, and with attractive graces won	
	The most averse, thee chiefly, who full oft	
	Thy self in me thy perfect image viewing	
	Becam'st enamour'd, and such joy thou took'st	
	With me in secret, that my womb conceiv'd	
	A growing burden.	
SATAN:	Dear Daughter, since thou claim'st me for thy Sire,	
	And my fair Son here showst me, the dear pledge	[330]
	Of dalliance had with thee in Heav'n, know	
	I come no enemie, but to set free	
	From out this dark and dismal house of pain,	
	Both him and thee, I go this uncouth errand sole,	
	To search with wandring quest a place foretold	
	Should be, and, by concurring signs, ere now	
	Created vast and round, a place of bliss	
	In the Pourlieues of Heav'n, and therein plac't	
	A race of upstart Creatures, to supply	
	Our vacant room, I haste to know,	[340]
	And this once known, shall soon return,	
	And bring ye to the place where Thou and *Death*	
	Shall dwell at ease, and up and down unseen	
	Wing silently the buxom Air, imbalm'd	
	With odours; there ye shall be fed and fill'd	
	Immeasurably, all things shall be your prey!	
DEATH:	Op'n flie th' infernal dores,	
	And on thir hinges grate	
	Harsh Thunder, that the lowest bottom shook	
	Of Darkness.[8]	[350]
GABRIEL:	Satan coasts the wall of Heav'n on this side Night	
	In the dun Air sublime, and ready now to stoop.	
ANGEL 3:	Him God beholding from his prospect high,	
	Wherein past, present, future he beholds,	
	Thus to his onely Son foreseeing spake:	
GOD:	Only begotten Son, seest thou our adversarie,	
	Through all restraint broke loose he wings his way	
	Directly towards the new created World,	
	And Man there plac't, with purpose to assay	
	If him by force he can destroy, or worse,	[360]
	By some false guile pervert; and shall pervert.	

	mert csábszavára fület hajt az ember,	
	s az egy-parancsot könnyen megszegi,	
	így ő, s hitetlen sarjadéka vész!	
	Ki lesz a vétkes ebben? Csak maga.	
	Az első pártütők	
	önként buktak maguk-kisértve-rontva!	
	Az embert ezek tőre csalja el:	[360]
	ezért az ember irgalomra lel.	
	De nem azok! Dicsfényem Földön, Égen	
	ragyogjon igazságban, irgalomban!	
	De kezdet és vég: irgalmam tüze!	
FIÚ:	Atyám, a szó kegyes volt, mely királyi	
	Igéd zárta: embernek irgalom.	
	Ám az embernek veszni kell vajon,	
	kedvencednek, legkisebb fiadnak?	
	Vagy lelje célját, s hiúsítsa terved	
	ellenfeled?! Ártó cselét betöltse,	[370]
	s jóságodat sorvassza semmivé?! Magad kivánod	
	kiveszteni egész műved miatta,	
	amit dicsőségedre alkotál?	
	Kétségbe vonhatják jóságod így,	
	nagyságod is, s mentséged nincs reá!	
ATYA:	Szivem fia, ki magad vagy Igém,	
	tudásom s cselekvő hatalmam – ezzel	
	kimondtad ennen gondolatomat,	
	mit rendelt örök Végezésem is.	
	Minden ember ne vesszen el: aki	[380]
	akar, megváltassék, nem érdeméből,	
	de szívem szabad irgalmábul.	
	Beléjük plántálom vezérükül	
	bírámat, a Lelkiismeret szavát;	
	ha jól használják, fülelnek reá:	
	fényt fényre lelnek, s hittel üdvözülnek.	
FIÚ:	Ima, megtérés, köteles	
	hüség előtt, ha igaz szándék szítja	
	ezt, füled nem süket,	
	szemed se zárt.	[390]
MIHÁLY:	Atyánk, Mindenható!	
	Végleges, halhatatlan, végtelen.	
SÁTÁN:	Felsőbb dicsőség koronása, Nap,	
	Tudd meg: gyűlölöm sugárodat,	
	mely fölidézi, míly hatáskörből	
	zuhantam, mely dicsőbb volt,	
	mint a tiéd; míg gőg és törtetés	

	For man will hark'n to his glozing lyes,	
	And easily transgress the sole Command,	
	So will fall, hee and his faithless Progenie!	
	Whose fault? Whose but his own?	
	The first sort by thir own suggestion fell,	
	Self-tempted, self-deprav'd: Man falls deceiv'd	
	By the other first: Man therefore shall find grace,	
	The other none: in Mercy and Justice both,	
	Through Heav'n and Earth, so shall my glorie excel,	[370]
	But Mercy first and last shall brightest shine.	
SON:	O Father, gracious was that word which clos'd	
	Thy sovran sentence, that Man should find grace.	
	For should Man finally be lost, should Man	
	Thy creature late so lov'd, thy youngest Son?	
	Or shall the Adversarie thus obtain	
	His end, and frustrate thine, shall he fulfill	
	His malice, and thy goodness bring to naught?! or wilt thou thy self	
	Abolish thy Creation, and unmake,	
	For him, what for thy glorie thou hast made?	[380]
	So should thy goodness and thy greatness both	
	Be questiond and blaspheam'd without defence.	
GOD:	Son who art alone	
	My word, my wisdom, and effectual might,	
	All hast thou spok'n as my thoughts are, all	
	As my Eternal purpose hath decreed:	
	Man shall not quite be lost, but sav'd who will,	
	Yet not of will in him, but grace in me	
	Freely voutsaft.	
	And I will place within them as a guide	[390]
	My Umpire Conscience, whom if they will hear,	
	Light after light well us'd they shall attain,	
	And to the end persisting, safe arrive.	
SON:	To Prayer, repentance, and obedience due,	
	Though but endevord with sincere intent,	
	Thine ear shall not be slow, thine eye not shut.	
MICHAEL:	Father Omnipotent,	
	Immutable, Immortal, Infinite.	
SATAN:	O thou with surpassing Glory crownd,	
	O Sun, how I hate thy beams	[400]
	That bring to my remembrance from what state	
	I fell, how glorious once above thy Spheare;	
	Till Pride and worse Ambition threw me down	

	le nem taszított Mennyekből, az Ég
	királya ellen lázadót.
MIHÁLY:	Örök Király, Mindennek Alkotója, [400]
	Fény Forrása – dicsfényed szemvakító:
SÁTÁN:	Nem érdemelte tőlem ezt, hiszen
	Ő emelt íly magasztos polcra, és e
	jótettét sosem hánytorgatta föl.
	Tisztem se volt nehéz. Mi volna könnyebb:
	viszonoznom magasztalással és
	hálával? Ám jó volta ingerelt?
	sarkallt a gonoszra? Hatalmak, Hercegek,
	virágai az égnek,
MIHÁLY:	nem közelíthet senki trónusodhoz, [410]
	hacsak teljes tüzed nem árnyékolod be,
	s szentségtartóként nem borítsz magadra
	felhőt,
SÁTÁN:	fő vezérül is gyülöltem szolgasort; hittem,
	ha egyet lépek, a legfelsőbb leszek, s lerovom
	a hála nagy adóját perc alatt.
	Teher fizetni csak, s tartozni még:
MIHÁLY:	sugár özönében ruhád
	sötétnek tetszik, ám így is vakul a
	Menny: [420]
SÁTÁN:	Bár súlyos rendelése alantasabb
	angyalnak küldött volna! Boldogan
	hív lettem volna, féktelen remény
	nem hajszolt volna törtetésre.
MIHÁLY:	A legfénylőbb szeráfok is
	eléd csak szárnyuk-födte szemmel állnak!
SÁTÁN:	Vádolnod kit vagy mit van jogod?
	Csak Isten egyenlőn osztott szerelmét,
	mely átkozott legyen! . . . Jóság, gyülölség –
	nekem mindegy, örök gyötrelmet oszt! [430]
	Nyomorult! Merre fussak el a végtelen düh és kétség elől?
	Menekvésem: Pokol! Magam vagyok
	Pokol! Legbelül vadabb üresség
	riaszt,
	Gyötrelmeimhez képest a Pokol
	Mennynek tetszik! Ó, szűnj! Hát nincs

	Warring in Heav'n against Heav'ns matchless King:	
MICHAEL:	Eternal King; Author of all being,	
	Fountain of Light, thy self invisible	
	Amidst the glorious brightness.	
SATAN:	He deservd no such return	
	From me, whom he created what I was	
	In that bright eminence, and with his good	[410]
	Upbraided none; nor was his service hard.	
	What could be less then to afford him praise,	
	The easiest recompence, and pay him thanks,	
	How due! Did all his good prove ill in me	
	And wrought but malice? Princes, Potentates, the Flowr of Heav'n,	
MICHAEL:	where thou sit'st	
	Thron'd inaccessible, but when thou shad'st	
	The full blaze of thy beams, and through a cloud	
	Drawn round about thee like a radiant Shrine,	
SATAN:	lifted up so high	[420]
	I sdeind subjection, and thought one step higher	
	Would set me highest, and in a moment quit	
	The debt immense of endless gratitude,	
	So burthensome, still paying, still to ow;	
MICHAEL:	dark with excessive bright thy skirts appeer,	
	Yet dazle Heav'n,	
SATAN:	O had his powerful Destiny ordaind	
	Me some inferiour Angel, I had stood	
	Then happie; no unbounded hope had rais'd	
	Ambition.	[430]
MICHAEL:	The brightest Seraphim	
	Approach not, but with both wings veil thir eyes!	
SATAN:	Whom hast thou then or what to accuse,	
	But Heav'ns free Love dealt equally to all?	
	Be then his Love accurst! . . . love or hate,	
	To me alike, it deals eternal woe.	
	Me miserable! which way shall I flie	
	Infinite wrauth, and infinite despaire?	
	Which way I flie is Hell; my self am Hell;	
	And in the lowest deep a lower deep	[440]
	Still threatning to devour me opens wide,	
	To which the Hell I suffer seems a Heav'n.	

	helye számomra a megbánásnak, irgalomnak?
	Csak megalázkodással! Ezt a szót
	eltiltja gőgöm, és irtózatom
	a szégyentől. [440]
	S ha bánnám bűnöm, s visszanyerném
	kegyelemből előbbi polcomat? – Nincs kibékülés,
	halálos gyűlölet hol mély sebet szúrt;
	szörnyebb visszaesésbe, vészbe vinne,
	s drágán fizetném meg, kettős kinokkal
	e rövid felvonásközt. Tudja ezt
	Számonkérőm is, és dehogy ajánl
	békét nekem, de én se koldulok!
ATYA:	Hosszútűrésem, irgalom-napom
	ki megveti, soha nem ízleli. [450]
SÁTÁN:	Remény tehát nincs?
ATYA:	A zord még zordabb lesz, vak még vakabb, hogy
	botoljanak, mélyebbre essenek –
	csak ezek nem nyerik kegyelmemet.
SÁTÁN:	Remény tehát nincs?
ATYA:	Ezzel nincs vége: az ember vétkezik
	az Egek felsőbbsége ellen, amint
	istenné lenni tör, s mindent veszít . . .
	halnia kell magának és nemének!
	Hacsak nem akad más, ki őhelyette önként [460]
	váltságot adna – halálért halált . . .
	De hol van íly szeretet, Égiek?
	Mellyőtök lesz halandó, hogy az ember
	bűnét megváltsa, és ártatlanul
	mentse a bűnöst? Íly önáldozó
	jóság a Mennyekben kinél lakik?
SÁTÁN:	Remény tehát nincs?
FIÚ:	Itt vagyok íme én!
	Magam ajánlom érte föl magam:
	életért életet! Szálljon rám dühöd! [470]
	Tekints embernek!
	Halálnak most alávetem magam,
	s halandó voltommal adósa lészek;
	ám ha a tartozás fizetve: – győztesen
	föltámadok, s talpam alá vetem
	legyőzőmet, majd a megváltott sokasággal Égbe

	O then at last relent: is there no place	
	Left for Repentance, none for Pardon left?	
	None left but by submission; and that word	
	Disdain forbids me, and my dread of shame.	
	But say I could repent and could obtaine	
	By Act of Grace my former state –	
	Never can true reconcilement grow	
	Where wounds of deadly hate have peirc'd so deep:	[450]
	Which would but lead me to a worse relapse	
	And heavier fall: so should I purchase deare	
	Short intermission bought with double smart.	
	This knows my punisher; therefore as farr	
	From granting hee, as I from begging peace:	
GOD:	This my long sufferance and my day of grace	
	They who neglect and scorn, shall never taste.	
SATAN:	All hope excluded thus?	
GOD:	But hard be hard'nd, blind be blinded more,	
	That they may stumble on, and deeper fall;	[460]
	And none but such from mercy I exclude.	
SATAN:	All hope excluded thus?	
GOD:	But yet all is not don; Man disobeying,	
	Disloyal breaks his fealtie, and sinns	
	Against the high Supremacie of Heav'n,	
	Affecting God-head, and so loosing all . . .	
	He with his whole posteritie must dye,	
	Unless for him som other able, and as willing, pay	
	The rigid satisfaction, death for death.	
	Say Heav'nly Powers, where shall we find such love,	[470]
	Which of ye will be mortal to redeem	
	Mans mortal crime, and just th' unjust to save,	
	Dwels in all Heaven charitie so deare?	
SATAN:	All hope excluded thus?	
SON:	Behold mee then, mee for him, life for life	
	I offer, on mee let thine anger fall;	
	Account mee man;	
	Now to Death I yield, and am his due	
	All that of me can die, yet that debt paid,	
	I shall rise Victorious, and subdue	[480]
	My vanquisher, Then with the multitude of my redeemd	
	Shall enter Heaven	

	szállok sok távollét után, Atyám,	
	hogy lássam arcodat, melyen harag	
	felhője sem maradt, csak szűntelen	
	béke s engesztelés.	[480]
MIHÁLY:	Atyánk, mindenható, végleges, halhatatlan, végtelen . . .	
SÁTÁN:	Isten hozzád remény és rettegés,	
	szív-furdalás! Minden jó veszve nékem!	
	Hisz helyünkbe, kik	
	átok alá estünk, alkotta ujabb	
	kegyencét: az embert s az ő világát.	
	Rossz, légy te üdvöm! Általad osztozom	
	az Ég királyával országain,	
	s felénél többön úr leszek talán!	
	Megtudja még az ember, s új világa!	[490]
	Így értem az Éden széléhez, az édes Paradicsomhoz.	
	Újarcu, furcsa élőlények!	
ÉVA:	A férfi erőre, eszmélésre termett,	
ÁDÁM:	szelídségre a nő, csinos varázsra.	
	A férfi Istené,	
ÉVA:	a nőnek ő az Istene; nagy tiszta homloka,	
	magasztos szeme uralomra vall;	
	választott üstökén jácintosan	
	alágyürűztek játszi fürtjei,	
	de csak erős válláig érnek el.	[500]
ÁDÁM:	A nőnek dísztelen arany haja,	
	mint fátyol, karcsu derekáig omlik,	
	s borzas csigákban hullámzik alá,	
	mint szőlő kaccsa kunkorul.	
ÉVA:	E kép alázatot sugall, melyet azért	
	gyengéd parancsra ád a nő,	
ÁDÁM:	s a férfi hálával vesz el.	
SÁTÁN:	Pokol! Mit látnak szemeim borúsan?	
	Helyünkbe ilyen üdvezült magasra	
	az Úr másfajta lényeket teremtett:	[510]
	föld sarjai, nem szellemek, de mégis	
	alig alábbvalók az Égieknél.	

	Long absent, and returne,	
	Father, to see thy face, wherein no cloud	
	Of anger shall remain, but peace assur'd,	
	And reconcilement.	
MICHAEL:	Father Omnipotent, Immutable, Immortal, Infinite . . .	
SATAN:	So farwel Hope, and with Hope farwel Fear,	
	Farwel Remorse: all Good to me is lost;	
	Behold in stead	[490]
	Of us out-cast, exil'd, his new delight,	
	Mankind created, and for him this World.	
	Evil be thou my Good; by thee at least	
	Divided Empire with Heav'ns King I hold	
	By thee, and more then half perhaps will reigne;	
	As Man ere long, and this new World shall know.	
	So on I fare, and to the border come	
	Of *Eden*, to delicious Paradise,	
	All kind of living Creatures new to sight and strange!	
EVE:	For contemplation hee and valour formd,	[500]
ADAM:	For softness shee and sweet attractive Grace,	
	Hee for God only,	
EVE:	Shee for God in him:	
	His fair large Front and Eye sublime declar'd	
	Absolute rule; and Hyacinthin Locks	
	Round from his parted forelock manly hung	
	Clustring, but not beneath his shoulders broad:	
ADAM:	Shee as a vail down to the slender waste	
	Her unadorned golden tresses wore	
	Disheveld, but in wanton ringlets wav'd	[510]
	As the Vine curles her tendrils,	
EVE:	Which impli'd	
	Subjection, but requir'd with gentle sway,	
	And by her yielded,	
ADAM:	By him best receivd.	
SATAN:	O Hell! what doe mine eyes with grief behold,	
	Into our room of bliss thus high advanc't	
	Creatures of other mould, earth-born perhaps,	
	Not Spirits, yet to heav'nly Spirits bright	
	Little inferior.	[520]

Mezítlen járnak; bánják is ha látja
Isten vagy angyal, nem gondolva rosszra,
járkálnak kéz a kézbe, drága pár.
Susogó árny-lugas alatt a zöldben
üde forrásnál csak leülnek, és
az édes kerti munkából elég
annyi, hogy élvezzék a hűs zefirt
s a pihenést, és ízesebb legyen [520]
étel, ital: oldalvást feküdnek
virágokkal teleszőtt, enyhe lankán;
gyümölcshúst esznek, és ha szomjuhoznak,
a héjával mernek a dús folyóból.
Foly nyájas szó, kedveskedő mosoly,
kamaszos kelletés, amint az illik
hitvesi nászban egybekelt, magános párhoz.
    Köröttük ugrándozva játszik
az összes állat (azóta elvadultak),
az oroszlán mókázva szökken, és a [530]
gidát ringatja mancsában, s a medve,
tigris, párduc előttük mórikázik,
ormótlan elefánt nagy buzgalommal,
hogy mulattassa őket, ruganyos
ormányát tekeri.

SÁTÁN: Fondor kígyó közel lopódzik.
Ámulva nézem őket; tán szeretni
is tudnám... Arcukon az Isten arca
élőn sugárzik, s oly sok bájt szitált
rájuk az Alkotó keze. Nemes pár! [540]
Nem is sejted, milyen közel vagyon
színváltozásod, mikor mind e szépség
vész- s búra válik.

ÁDÁM: Egyetlen társam mind e sok gyönyörben!
Drágább, mint minden! Az Erő, amely
teremtett minket s nékünk ez Világot, nem kivánt
mást tőlünk, csak: tegyük szerény egyetlen
parancsát, hogy az Éden mindenik
ízes-gyümölcs fájáról vegyünk,
csak a Tudás fájáról nem. [550]
A Halál, bármi légyen,
szörnyű lehet! Hisz tudod, mondta Isten:
halállal halsz, ha eszel ez gyümölcsből!
Ez egy, miben engednünk kell neki,

            So pass they naked on, nor shun the sight
            Of God or Angel, for they think no ill:
            So hand in hand they pass, the lovliest pair.
            Under a tuft of shade that on a green
            Stood whispering soft, by a fresh Fountain side
            They sit them down, and after no more toil
            Of thir sweet Gardning labour then suffic'd
            To recommend coole *Zephyr*, and made ease
            More easie, wholsom thirst and appetite more grateful,
            They sit recline on the soft downie Bank damaskt
            with flours: [530]
            The savourie pulp they chew, and in the rinde
            Still as they thirsted scoop the brimming stream;
            Nor gentle purpose, nor endearing smiles
            Wanted, nor youthful dalliance as beseems
            Fair couple, linkt in happie nuptial League,
            Alone as they.
            About them frisking play
            All Beasts of th' Earth, since wilde, and of all chase.
            Sporting the Lion ramps, and in his paw
            Dandles the Kid; Bears, Tygers, Ounces, Pards   [540]
            Gambol before them,
            Th' unwieldy Elephant
            To make them mirth us'd all his might, and wreathd
            His Lithe Proboscis.
SATAN: Close the Serpent sly
            Insinuating, wove his breaded train . . .
            Them my thoughts pursues
            With wonder, and could love, so lively shines
            In them Divine resemblance, and such grace
            The hand that formd them on thir shape hath pourd.   [550]
            Ah gentle pair, yee little think how nigh
            Your change approaches, when all these delights
            Will vanish and deliver ye to woe.
ADAM: Sole partner and sole part of all these joyes,
            Dearer thy self then all; the Power
            That made us required
            From us no other service then to keep
            This one, this easie charge, of all the Trees
            In Paradise that bear delicious fruit
            So various, not to taste that onely Tree   [560]
            Of knowledge.
            What ere Death is,
            Som dreadful thing no doubt; for well thou knowst
            God hath pronounc't it death to taste that Tree,
            The only sign of our obedience left

| | ki az uralom annyi más jelét
ruházta ránk, s kezünkbe adta a
többi lényt földön, légben, tengeren.
Ne tartsuk zordnak ezt az egy tilalmat:
minden másban szabadságunk vagyon,
s választhatunk tenger gyönyör között! [560]
ÉVA: Te, kiért s kiből
alkottak: hús husodból, nélküled
nem volna célom. Őrizőm, uram!
Amit szóltál, igaz, helyes, hisz Istent
hálával magasztalni tartozunk
naponta, én kivált, ki a boldogabb
részt élvezem, téged bírván, ki nálam
százszor különb vagy, míg te énvelem
magadhoz méltó társra nem találsz.
A napra sokszor emlékszem, midőn [570]
ocsúdtam álmomból, s árnyékban a
virág-ágyon kerestem ámulón, ki
vagyok, s ide honnan, hogyan kerültem.
Nem messze egy barlangból zümmögő
víz csordogált, majd egy mezőn megállt
tóvá terülve mozdulatlanul,
tisztán, miként az Égbolt. Arra mentem
gyanútlanul, a zöld parton ledőltem,
s belépillantottam a tiszta, bársony
tóba, mely másik Égnek nyílt nekem. [580]
Amint ráhajlom, a szikrás vizen
szemből másik alak hajol felém
s rám bámul.
Visszahőkölök. Az is.
Hogy mosolyogva visszatérek, ő is
jő mosolyogva kérdező szemekkel,
szerető rokonszenvvel. Rá szögezném
mind mostanig szemem, s hiún epedve
bámulnám, ha nem intett volna szó:
ATYA: Magad vagy az, mit látsz ott, szép teremtmény. [590]
Veled jön, s tűnik. Ám kövess, vezetlek
oda, hol nemcsak árnyék várja jöttöd
s szived – de az, kinek képmása vagy:
benne, ki elválaszthatatlanul
tiéd, lelsz élvet, s néki szülsz magadhoz
hasonlókat, sokat, ezért neveznek
Emberfaj anyjának.

            Among so many signes of power and rule
            Conferrd upon us, and Dominion giv'n
            Over all other Creatures that possess
            Earth, Aire, and Sea. Then let us not think hard
            One easie prohibition, who enjoy   [570]
            Free leave so large to all things else, and choice
            Unlimited of manifold delights!

EVE: O thou for whom
            And from whom I was formd flesh of thy flesh,
            And without whom am to no end, my Guide
            And Head, what thou hast said is just and right.
            For wee to him indeed all praises owe,
            And daily thanks, I chiefly who enjoy
            So farr the happier Lot, enjoying thee
            Præeminent by so much odds, while thou   [580]
            Like consort to thy self canst no where find.
            That day I oft remember, when from sleep
            I first awak't, and found my self repos'd
            Under a shade of flours, much wondring where
            And what I was, whence thither brought, and how.
            Not distant far from thence a murmuring sound
            Of waters issu'd from a Cave and spread
            Into a liquid Plain, then stood unmov'd
            Pure as th' expanse of Heav'n; I thither went
            With unexperienc't thought, and laid me downe   [590]
            On the green bank, to look into the cleer
            Smooth Lake, that to me seemd another Skie.
            As I bent down to look, just opposite,
            A Shape within the watry gleam appeard
            Bending to look on me, I started back,
            It started back, but pleas'd I soon returnd,
            Pleas'd it returnd as soon with answering looks
            Of sympathie and love; there I had fixt
            Mine eyes till now, and pin'd with vain desire
            Had not a voice thus warnd me: [600]

GOD: What thou seest,
            What there thou seest fair Creature is thy self,
            With thee it came and goes: but follow me,
            And I will bring thee where no shadow staies
            Thy coming, and thy soft imbraces, hee
            Whose image thou art, him thou shalt enjoy
            Inseparablie thine, to him shalt beare
            Multitudes like thy self, and thence be call'd
            Mother of human Race.

ÉVA:	Mit is tehetnék?
	Láthatatlan vezéremet követem,
	míg meg nem látlak egy platán alatt. Futok [600]
	vissza, követsz te, rámkiáltasz:
ÁDÁM:	Éva!
	Térj vissza! Kitől szöksz? Belőle vagy:
	húsa-csontja! Hogy élj, az oldalamból,
	szivem mellől kölcsönöztem neked
	élet-létet, hogy itten, oldalamnál
	légy édes vigaszom: csak az enyém!
	Kereslek, lelkem része! Jussom is van
	másik felemhez!
ÉVA:	S gyöngéd kézzel ekkor megfogtál, [610]
	engedek, azóta érzem: különb a szépségnél
	a férfi-kellem s a bölcsesség, az szép csak igazán!
SÁTÁN:	Szólt ősanyátok, s szemében tiszta lángu
	hitvesi vonzalom csillant, szelíd ragaszkodás,
	míg félig átkarolva simult ős-Atyátokhoz
	Gyötrő, gyülölt látvány! Egymást ölelve
	Édenre lelt e kettő:
	mig én Poklokra vesztve, hol gyönyör
	s szerelem nincs, csak hasgató sovárgás
	gyötör örök betelhetetlenül. – [620]
	De ne felejtsem, mit nyerék saját
	szájukból! Nincs is minden a kezükben!
	Egy végzetes fa van – Tudás nevű –,
	melyhez nem érhetnek. Tudás tilos?
	S halál? S csak íly tudatlanság a létük
	feltétele? Ez üdvük nyitja, és
	bizonysága alázatos hitüknek?
	Ó szép alap: reá építhető
	bukásuk. Mig élhetsz,
	élj, boldog pár! Szíjj visszajöttömig [630]
	rövidke kéjt . . . hisz vár rád hosszu kín.
	Beköszöntött az est.
	Csönd járt vele: nyugodni tért az állat
	füágyára, fészkére a madár,
	csupán az éber csalogány dalolta
	egész éjjel szerelmi énekét
	csendet büvölve.

EVE:	What could I doe,	[610]
	But follow strait, invisibly thus led?	
	Till I espi'd thee, fair indeed and tall,	
	Under a Platan. Back I turnd,	
	Thou following cryd'st aloud,	
ADAM:	Return faire *Eve*,	
	Whom fli'st thou? whom thou fli'st, of him thou art,	
	His flesh, his bone; to give thee being I lent	
	Out of my side to thee, neerest my heart	
	Substantial Life, to have thee by my side	
	Henceforth an individual solace dear;	[620]
	Part of my Soul I seek thee, and thee claim	
	My other half!	
EVE:	With that thy gentle hand	
	Seisd mine, I yielded, and from that time see	
	How beauty is excelld by manly grace	
	And wisdom, which alone is truly fair.	
SATAN:	So spake your[9] general Mother, and with eyes	
	Of conjugal attraction unreprov'd,	
	And meek surrender, half imbracing leand	
	On your first Father,	[630]
	Sight hateful, sight tormenting! thus these two	
	Imparadis't in one anothers arms	
	The happier *Eden*, shall enjoy thir fill	
	Of bliss on bliss, while I to Hell am thrust,	
	Where neither joy nor love, but fierce desire,	
	Still unfulfill'd with pain of longing pines;	
	Yet let me not forget what I have gain'd	
	From thir own mouths; all is not theirs it seems:	
	One fatal Tree there stands of Knowledge call'd,	
	Forbidden them to taste: Knowledge forbidd'n?	[640]
	Can it be death? and do they onely stand	
	By Ignorance, is that thir happie state,	
	The proof of thir obedience and thir faith?	
	O fair foundation laid whereon to build	
	Thir ruine! Live while ye may,	
	Yet happie pair; enjoy, till I return,	
	Short pleasures, for long woes are to succeed.	
	Now came still Eevning on,	
	Silence accompanied, for Beast and Bird,	[650]
	They to thir grassie Couch, these to thir Nests	
	Were slunk, all but the wakeful Nightingale;	
	She all night long her amorous descant sung;	
	Silence was pleas'd.	

ÁDÁM:	Szép párom, Éva, itt az éji óra,	
	minden pihen, és ez bennünket is	
	könnyű álomra hí; fölváltva rendelt	[640]
	nekünk az Úr munkát, nyugvást, miként	
	éjt és napot;	
	holnap, mihelyt hajnalsugár csikozza	
	kelet egét, fölserkenünk, s legott	
	munkához látunk, ott virágos fákat	
	nyesünk, emitt a zöldelő fasort,	
	Természet útján elnyugoszt az éj.	
ÉVA:	Uram, parancsolóm, amit kivánsz,	
	teszem tüstént, mert így akarta Isten.	
	Ő a Törvény Neked, s nekem te vagy!	[650]
	Nem tudni többet – ez a nő legbüvösb	
	tudománya, disze. Veled csevegve	
	időt felejtek. Évszakok s mulásuk	
	mind kedves. Édes a hajnal fuvalma,	
	kora madárdal bája, szép a Nap, ha	
	e bűvös tájon hinti szét kelő	
	sugárait harmatszikrás virágra, fű-fára,	
	de sem a pitymalló hajnal lehe,	
	kora madárdal bája, sem e kéjes	
	tájon kelő nap, sem harmatsziporkás	[660]
	gyümölcs, virág, fű, sem esők utáni	
	illat, se méz-szelíd est, néma éj	
	fenkölt madárdalával, holdsugáros,	
	csillagos séta nélküled nem édes!	
	De éjjel mért ragyognak? Vajh kiért	
	e büszke kép, ha álom zár szemet?	
ÁDÁM:	Isten, s ember tökéletes leánya!	
	Járniuk kell utuk a Föld körül	
	reggel és este, helyről helyre rendben,	
	hogy a még nem született nemzeteknek	[670]
	fénnyel szolgáljanak.	
	Ezek, bár éjt nem nézi senki őket	
	nem hiába fénylenek; s ne hidd, ha ember	
	nem volna, úgy nem volna bámulója	
	az Égnek s Istennek magasztalója.	
	Millió szellemlény bolyong a Földön	
	láttatlanul, ha ébredünk, ha alszunk,	
	szemlélik müveit magasztalással	
	éjt-nappal.	
MIHÁLY:	Miért ülsz lesben magad álcázva,	[680]
	mint az ellen várakozván a szunnyadók felett?	

ADAM:	Fair Consort, th' hour
	Of night, and all things now retir'd to rest
	Mind us of like repose, since God hath set
	Labour and rest, as day and night to men
	Successive;
	To morrow ere fresh Morning streak the East [660]
	With first approach of light, we must be ris'n,
	And at our pleasant labour, to reform
	Yon flourie Arbors, yonder Allies green,
	Mean while, as Nature wills, Night bids us rest.
EVE:	My Author and Disposer, what thou bidst
	Unargu'd I obey; so God ordains,
	God is thy Law, thou mine: to know no more
	Is womans happiest knowledge and her praise.
	With thee conversing I forget all time,
	All seasons and thir change, all please alike. [670]
	Sweet is the breath of morn, her rising sweet,
	With charm of earliest Birds; pleasant the Sun
	When first on this delightful Land he spreads
	His orient Beams, on herb, tree, fruit, and flour,
	But neither breath of Morn when she ascends
	With charm of earliest Birds, nor rising Sun
	On this delightful land, nor herb, fruit, floure,
	Glistring with dew, nor fragrance after showers,
	Nor grateful Eevning mild, nor silent Night
	With this her solemn Bird, nor walk by Moon, [680]
	Or glittering Starr-light without thee is sweet.
	But wherfore all night long shine these, for whom
	This glorious sight, when sleep hath shut all eyes?
ADAM:	Daughter of God and Man, accomplisht *Eve*,
	Those have thir course to finish, round the Earth,
	By morrow Eevning, and from Land to Land
	In order, though to Nations yet unborn,
	Ministring light prepar'd, they set and rise;
	These then, though unbeheld in deep of night,
	Shine not in vain, nor think, though men were none, [690]
	That heav'n would want spectators, God want praise;
	Millions of spiritual Creatures walk the Earth
	Unseen, both when we wake, and when we sleep:
	All these with ceasless praise his works behold
	Both day and night.
MICHAEL:	Why satst thou like an enemie in waite
	Here watching at the head of these that sleep?

SÁTÁN:	Nem ismersz meg?
	Egykor ismertetek: nem mint komátok
	ültem, hová ti nem szállhattatok.
	Nem ismertek? E nemtudástok annak
	jele, hogy csürhétek legalja vagytok.
GÁBRIEL:	Miért akartad álmukat zavarni,
	kiknek Isten itt adta üdvhelyét?
SÁTÁN:	Gábriel! Az Égben bölcsnek tartanak,
	magam is annak hittelek. De most [690]
	kétely fog el.
	Ki nem szeretne szökni a Pokolból,
	kit oda zárt itélet?
	Ím a válasz!
MIHÁLY:	Hordd el magad
	oda, honnan szöktél! Ha ezután
	megszentelt honhoz ólálkodol,
	én vonszollak vissza láncban
	a Pokolba.
	S bezárlak: majd többé nem gúnyolódhatsz, [700]
	hogy könnyű zárra nyílik a Pokol!
	Képmutatók papoljanak akármit
	ártatlanságról, szűziességről, és
	szidják tisztátalannak, mit az Úr
	tisztának mond, parancsol egyeseknek,
	s megenged mindeneknek. Sarjadást
	rendelt urunk.
	Üdv, tiszta nász! Titok-Szabály:
	embersarjadzás forrása, a köztulajdon
	Éden egyetlen magántulajdona. [710]
	Aludj, szép pár, ne törj még boldogabb
	létre, tanuld meg, hogy többet ne tudj!
ÁDÁM:	Ébredj, bűvös menyasszonyom, utóbb talált
	kincsem, utolsó Ég-ajándok, első
	vigalmam! Ím Hajnal ragyog, s a friss föld
	hív minket: elszalasztjuk megfigyelni,
	hogy palántáink mennyit nőttek és
	citromliget mint illatoz, miképp ül
	virágon méh, mint szíjja méz-levét.
ÉVA:	Egyetlenem, ki gondom elcsitítod, [720]
	fölényem, tökélyem, látnom arcodat
	s az új reggelt míly boldogság! Ez éjjel
	(nem értem még ily éjet!) álmot láttam,
	nem milyet szoktam rólad, múlt napunk
	szorgalmáról, s hogy holnap mit teszünk,

SATAN:	Know ye not mee? ye knew me once no mate	
	For you, there sitting where ye durst not soare;	
	Not to know mee argues your selves unknown,	[700]
	The lowest of your throng.	
GABRIEL:	Why dost thou violate sleep, and those	
	Whose dwelling God hath planted here in bliss?	
SATAN:	*Gabriel*, thou hadst in Heav'n th' esteem of wise,	
	And such I held thee; but this question askt	
	Puts me in doubt.	
	Who would not, finding way, break loose from Hell,	
	Though thither doomd?	
	Thus much what was askt.	
MICHAEL:	Flie thither whence thou fledst: if from this houre	[710]
	Within these hallowd limits thou appeer,	
	Back to th' infernal pit I drag thee chaind,	
	And Seale thee so, as henceforth not to scorne	
	The facil gates of hell too slightly barrd.	
	Whatever Hypocrites austerely talk	
	Of puritie and place and innocence,	
	Defaming as impure what God declares	
	Pure, and commands to som, leaves free to all.	
	Our Maker bids increase, who bids abstain	
	But our Destroyer, foe to God and Man?	[720]
	Haile wedded Love, mysterious Law, true source	
	Of human ofspring, sole proprietie,	
	In Paradise of all things common else.	
	Sleep on	
	Blest pair; and O yet happiest if ye seek	
	No happier state, and know to know no more.	
ADAM:	Awake my fairest, my espous'd, my latest found,	
	Heav'ns last best gift, my ever new delight,	
	Awake, the morning shines, and the fresh field	
	Calls us, we lose the prime, to mark how spring	[730]
	Our tended Plants, how blows the Citron Grove,	
	How the Bee sits on the Bloom extracting liquid sweet.	
EVE:	O Sole in whom my thoughts find all repose,	
	My Glorie, my Perfection, glad I see	
	Thy face, and Morn return'd, for I this Night,	
	Such night till this I never pass'd, have dream'd,	
	If dream'd, not as I oft am wont, of thee,	
	Works of day pass't, or morrows next designe,	

	de bajról, sérelemről, mit e szörny	
	éjjel előtt nem képzeltem. Mikéntha	
	fülembe sustorogna, valaki	
	sétára hívott nyájasan. Te vagy,	
	gondoltam. Így szólt:	[730]
ÉVA:		
SÁTÁN: [ISM]	„Mért is alszol, Éva?"	
	„Míly bűvös most az óra, hűs a csend,"	
SÁTÁN:	ha nem csapong a csalogány dala –	
	az most van ébren, s vágya énekét	
	gyötrődve zengi, most király	
	a telehold, sugára kedvesebbé	
	árnyal mindent. Hiába, hogyha senki	
	nem nézi!	
	Kél az ég ezer szemével.	
ÉVA: [ISM]	„Kit nézzen, ha nem engem", a természet	[740]
	sóvárgottját? „Láttamra minden ujjong."	
	"Bájomtól elbüvölve nézni vágyik."	
SÁTÁN:	Éva! Éva!	
ÉVA:	Szavadra keltem, s nem leltem reád.	
	Elindultam, hogy megtaláljalak,	
	s róttam – azt hittem, egyedül – utam, mely	
	az eltiltott Tudás-fához vezérelt.	
	Képzeletemnek még bübájosabb volt,	
	mint nappal. Mialatt csodálkozva néztem,	
	mellém került egy szépformáju, szárnyas	[750]
	alak, olyan, milyennek látni szoktuk	
	az Égből szálltakat.	
SÁTÁN:	Csodás fa!	
	Gyümölcstől roskadó! Senki se méltat,	
	isten, ember, s ízlelje mézed? A tudás ilyen	
	lenézett? Vagy irigység, vagy mi tiltja	
	megkóstolásod? Tiltsa bárki, nem	
	tart vissza engem fölkinált javadtól:	
	Mi másért ültettek? –	
ÉVA:	S nem nyughatott,	[760]
	szakított róla vakmerő kezekkel, s ette!	
	Jég-borzadás nyilalt belém:	
	ilyen pimasz tettel kisért pimasz beszéd!	
SÁTÁN:	Tündér teremtmény, angyal Éva!	

	But of offence and trouble, which my mind	
	Knew never till this irksom night; methought	[740]
	Close at mine ear one call'd me forth to walk	
	With gentle voice, I thought it thine; it said,	
EVE:		
SATAN: [REPEATING]		
	"*Why sleepst thou Eve? now is the pleasant time,*	
	The cool, the silent, save where silence yields"	
SATAN:	To the night-warbling Bird, that now awake	
	Tunes sweetest his love-labor'd song; now reignes	
	Full Orb'd the Moon, and with more pleasing light	
	Shadowie sets off the face of things; in vain,	
	If none regard!	
	Heav'n wakes with all his eyes,	[750]
EVE: [REPEATING]	"*Whom to behold but mee,*" Natures	
	desire, "*In my sight all things joy,*	
	with ravishment attracted by my beauty still to gaze."	
SATAN:	Eve! Eve!	
EVE:	I rose as at thy call, but found thee not;	
	To find thee I directed then my walk;	
	And on, methought, alone I pass'd through ways	
	That brought me on a sudden to the Tree	
	Of interdicted Knowledge: fair it seem'd,	
	Much fairer to my Fancie then by day:	[760]
	And as I wondring lookt, beside it stood	
	One shap'd and wing'd like one of those from Heav'n	
	By us oft seen.	
SATAN:	O fair Plant!	
	with fruit surcharg'd!	
	Deigns none to ease thy load and taste thy sweet,	
	Nor God, nor Man; is Knowledge so despis'd?	
	Or envie, or what reserve forbids to taste?	
	Forbid who will, none shall from me withhold	
	Longer thy offerd good, why else set here?	[770]
EVE:	This said he paus'd not, but with ventrous Arme	
	He pluckt, he tasted; mee damp horror chil'd	
	At such bold words voucht with a deed so bold!	
SATAN:	Here, happie Creature, fair Angelic *Eve*,	

	Egyél te is! Bár boldog vagy, lehetsz	
	még boldogabb, de persze nem különb:	
	istennő léssz az istenek között,	
	többé nem földre bilincselve, de	
	a légben néha, mint mi; néha meg	
	szállj föl a Mennybe érdemed nyomán, s lásd,	[770]
	mint élnek istenek, s ugy élj te is!	
ÉVA:	Így szólt, felém szaladt, s amit szakasztott,	
	annak darabját ajkamhoz tevé.	
	Étvágyamat az édes, ízes illat	
	úgy fölcsigázta, hogy nem álltam ellen,	
	megízleltem. Ugy rémlett, fellegekbe	
	szálltam vele, megpillantottam ott lenn	
	az órjás földi tájat: tarka, tágas	
	kilátást. Megcsodálva röptömet	
	s a magasztos átváltozást, vezérem	[780]
	elillant; így éreztem, süllyedek,	
	s elszunnyadok. Felébredvén, de boldog	
	vagyok, hogy mindez álom...	
ÁDÁM:	Legszebb képmásom, édes egyfelem!	
	Nekem is épp úgy fáj az éji álmod	
	kuszált eszméje, én se szívlelem	
	a rossz-álmot: gonosztól jön, gyanítom.	
ÉVA:	Honnan e rossz?	
ÁDÁM:	Nem fészkelhet tebenned,	
	tisztán teremtettben! Tudd meg tehát:	[790]
	a lélekben sok rossz hajlam lakik	
	melyek ura az ész.	
	Isten s ember eszébe a gonosz	
	jöhet, tűnhet, ha megtagadjuk, úgy	
	nem hágy szennyet, nyomot; ez ád reményt,	
	hogy mitől álmodban megriadtál,	
	azt ébren sem helyesled, nem teszed.	
ATYA:	Rafael, látom, az éji szakadékból	
	szökött Sátán a földön míly zavart	
	támasztott.	[800]
ÁDÁM:	Lássunk tehát újdonsült dolgainknak,	
	ligetben, forrásnál.	
RAFAEL:	Így vigasztalja bájos kedvesét.	
	Az megcsitul, de egy-egy könny gurul	

	Partake thou also; happie though thou art,	
	Happier thou mayst be, worthier canst not be:	
	Taste this, and be henceforth among the Gods	
	Thy self a Goddess, not to Earth confin'd,	
	But somtimes in the Air, as wee, somtimes	
	Ascend to Heav'n, by merit thine, and see	[780]
	What life the Gods live there, and such live thou.	
EVE:	So saying, he drew nigh, and to me held,	
	Even to my mouth of that same fruit held part	
	Which he had pluckt; the pleasant savourie smell	
	So quick'nd appetite, that I, methought,	
	Could not but taste. Forthwith up to the Clouds	
	With him I flew, and underneath beheld	
	The Earth outstretcht immense, a prospect wide	
	And various: wondring at my flight and change	
	To this high exaltation; suddenly	[790]
	My Guide was gon, and I, me thought, sunk down,	
	And fell asleep; but O how glad I wak'd	
	To find this but a dream!	
ADAM:	Best Image of my self and dearer half,	
	The trouble of thy thoughts this night in sleep	
	Affects me equally; nor can I like	
	This uncouth dream, of evil sprung I fear;	
EVE:	Yet evil whence?	
ADAM:	In thee can harbour none,	
	Created pure. But know that in the Soule	[800]
	Are many lesser Faculties that serve	
	Reason as chief;	
	Evil into the mind of God or Man	
	May come and go, so unapprov'd, and leave	
	No spot or blame behind: Which gives me hope	
	That what in sleep thou didst abhorr to dream,	
	Waking thou never wilt consent to do.	
GOD:	*Raphael*, I see what stir on Earth	
	Satan from Hell scap't through the darksom Gulf	
	Hath raisd.	[810]
ADAM:	And let us to our fresh imployments rise	
	Among the Groves, the Fountains, and the Flours.	
RAPHAEL:	So cheard he his fair Spouse, and she was cheard,	
	But silently a gentle tear let fall	

| | szeméből, és hajával eltörölte.
| | Ám készen állt két újabb könny szeme
| | kristályzsilipjén: mielőtt lecsöppent,
| | lecsókolgatja Ádám szeretet
| | s szelíd önvád jeléül.
| | Így minden földerült. A rétre szöknek. [810]
| ATYA: | Menj hát, s fél napon át, barát baráttal,
| | beszélgess Ádámmal, bárhol leled:
| | emlékeztessed boldog helyzetére,
| | ez hatalmában hagyta meg saját
| | szabad akaratát, mely bár szabad,
| | de változékony. Intsed őt: ne térjen
| | tévútra magabiztosan; mi les rá,
| | minő veszély, s kitől, míly ellen az,
| | ki lebukván az Égből most a mások
| | boldogságból-bukásán sántikál. [820]
| | Tudja meg, nehogy akarva vétkezvén, azt hozza föl,
| | hogy nem intették, s gyanútlanul bukott.
| ÁDÁM: | Siess ki, Éva, látnod érdemes,
| | kelet felől a fák közt míly dicső
| | alak közelg, úgy tetszik, délidőn
| | új hajnal kélne; hoz talán az Égből
| | parancsot nékünk, és kegyeskedik
| | e nap vendégünk lenni. Menj, siess,
| | és minden készletünket hozd elő,
| | s tetézd meg jól, hogy méltóan fogadjuk [830]
| | szent vendégünk!
| ÉVA: | Szaladok, s indáról ág-, bokorról
| | gyümölcseik szinét-javát szakasztom,
| | hogy vendégünk tetézve lássam el.
| ÁDÁM: | Ó, égi Sarj, hisz Ég lehet csak
| | hazája íly magasztosnak. Ha már
| | leszálltál égi trónodról, s e boldog
| | helyet jelenlétedre méltatod,
| | úgy méltóztass velünk e lugas árnyán megpihenni, [és]
| | megízlelni e kert gyümölcseit [840]
| RAFAEL: | Ádám, ezért jövök,
| | hol van árnyas kunyhód, vezess oda!
| | Egészen estig most szabad vagyok.

	From either eye, and wip'd them with her haire;
	Two other precious drops that ready stood,
	Each in thir Chrystal sluce, hee ere they fell
	Kiss'd as the gracious signs of sweet remorse
	And pious awe, that feard to have offended.
	So all was cleard, and to the Field they haste. [820]
GOD:	Go therefore, half this day as friend with friend
	Converse with *Adam*, in what Bowre or shade
	Thou find'st him: advise him of his happie state,
	Happiness in his power left free to will,
	Left to his own free Will, his Will though free,
	Yet mutable; whence warne him to beware
	He swerve not too secure: tell him withall
	His danger, and from whom, what enemie
	Late falln himself from Heav'n, is plotting now
	The fall of others from like state of bliss; [830]
	This let him know,
	Least wilfully transgressing he pretend
	Surprisal, unadmonisht, unforewarnd.
ADAM:	Haste hither *Eve*, and worth thy sight behold
	Eastward among those Trees, what glorious shape
	Comes this way moving; seems another Morn
	Ris'n on mid-noon; som great behest from Heav'n
	To us perhaps he brings, and will voutsafe
	This day to be our Guest. But goe with speed,
	And what thy stores contain, bring forth and poure [840]
	Abundance, fit to honour and receive
	Our Heav'nly stranger.
EVE:	I will haste and from each bough and break,
	Each Plant and juiciest Gourd will pluck such choice
	To entertain our Angel guest.
ADAM:	Native of Heav'n, for other place
	None can then Heav'n such glorious shape contain;
	Since by descending from the Thrones above,
	Those happie places thou hast deignd a while
	To want, and honour these, voutsafe with us [850]
	To rest, and what the Garden choicest bears
	To taste.
RAPHAEL:	*Adam*, I therefore came,
	Lead on then where thy Bowre
	Oreshades; for these mid-hours, till Eevning rise
	I have at will.

	Embernem anyja, üdv!	
	Kinek gyümölcsös méhe majd a Földet	
	még több fiúval tölti, mint amennyi	
	gyümölccsel Isten fái ezt az asztalt	
	elhalmozták.	
ÁDÁM:	Ó, kóstold meg, Égi vándor,	
	a jót, mit Tápadónk nagylelkűsége –	[850]
	kitől méretlen száll minden kiváló	
	javunk – adat nekünk a Földanyával	
	étkül s élvül; talán a szellemeknek	
	ízetlen étek; én csak azt tudom:	
	mindünknek adja egyetlen Atyánk.	
RAFAEL:	Ha mit ő a félig szellem-	
	embernek ád, nem lehet megvetendő	
	színtiszta szellemnek, hisz ennek is	
	kell táplálék, mint magadfajta földi	
	embernek; mindkettőbe adva vannak	[860]
	alantas érzékszervek, melyek által	
	látnak, hallnak, tapintanak, szagolnak,	
	ízlelnek, és emésztenek a testi	
	valót átalakítva testetlenné, hát ne hidd,	
	hogy átallom a kóstolót.	
	Az asztalnál Éva mezítlenül	
	szolgált, csordultig töltve meg habos	
	kupáikat nektárral.	
ATYA:	Tisztaság, méltó az Édenhez!	
RAFAEL:	Ha valaha	
	mentsége volna Isten sok fiának,	[870]
	hogy megpillantva nőt, belészeret –	
	úgy most lehetne! . . . Ám az ő szivükben	
	nem úr a szenvedély, nem ismerik	
	poklát a megcsalt féltékeny sziveknek.	
ÁDÁM:	Ó, Ég-lakó! Kegyelmed érzem abban,	
	ahogy megtiszteléd emberfajunk:	
	méltóztattál szerény lakába lépni,	
	s megízlelni e föld gyümölcseit,	
RAFAEL:	Egy a Mindenható, kiből kiáradt	[880]
	minden dolog, s kihez majd visszatér, ha	
	el nem fajult.	
	Így ne ámulj,	
	ha mit Isten jónak itélt neked,	
	nem lököm vissza, de átlényegítem	
	sajátommá. Jöhet még oly idő,	

	Haile Mother of Mankind, whose fruitful Womb	
	Shall fill the World more numerous with thy Sons	
	Then with these various fruits the Trees of God	
	Have heap'd this Table.	[860]
ADAM:	Heav'nly stranger, please to taste	
	These bounties which our Nourisher, from whom	
	All perfet good unmeasur'd out, descends,	
	To us for food and for delight hath caus'd	
	The Earth to yield; unsavourie food perhaps	
	To spiritual Natures; only this I know,	
	That one Celestial Father gives to all.	
RAPHAEL:	Therefore what he gives	
	To man in part	
	Spiritual, may of purest Spirits be found	[870]
	No ingrateful food: and food alike those pure	
	Intelligential substances require	
	As doth your Rational; and both contain	
	Within them every lower facultie	
	Of sense, whereby they hear, see, smell, touch, taste,	
	Tasting concoct, digest, assimilate,	
	And corporeal to incorporeal turn,	
	To taste think not I shall be nice.	
	Mean while at Table *Eve*	
	Ministerd naked, and thir flowing cups	[880]
	With pleasant liquors crown'd.	
GOD:	O innocence Deserving Paradise!	
RAPHAEL:	If ever, now	
	Had the Sons of God excuse to be	
	Enamour'd at this sight!...[10]	
	But in those hearts	
	Love unlibidinous reign'd, nor jealousie	
	Was understood, the injur'd Lovers Hell.	
ADAM:	Inhabitant with God, now know I well	
	Thy favour, in this honour done to man,	[890]
	Under whose lowly roof thou hast voutsaf't	
	To enter, and these earthly fruits to taste,	
RAPHAEL:	One Almightie is, from whom	
	All things proceed, and up to him return,	
	If not deprav'd from good.	
	Wonder not then, what God for you saw good	
	If I refuse not, but convert, as you,	
	To proper substance; time may come when men	

| | midőn az ember angyalokkal együtt
| | eszik, s nem érzi étkük léginek.
| | E testi tápláléktól testetek
| | talán egyszer átszellemül, s idővel | [890]
| | megjobbul, szárnyasan a légbe röppen,
| | mint mi, és kénye-kedve szerint lakik
| | itt, vagy az égi szent Paradicsomban:
| | ha engedelmesek maradtok és
| | annak szerelmében hivek, kinek
| | családja vagytok.
| ÁDÁM: | De mondd,
| | ez óvásod: „Ha engedelmesek
| | maradtok" – mit jelent? Dacolhatunk mi
| | Ővéle, elveszítve kedvezését, | [900]
| | ki minket porból gyúrt, s e helyre plántált.
| RAFAEL: | Ég s Föld fia, jegyezd meg!
| | Boldog vagy? – Istennek köszönheted.
| | Ám magadnak köszönd, ha az maradsz,
| | engedelmességednek. Erre int
| | óvásom! Szívleld meg! Tökéletesnek
| | teremtett Isten, ám változhatónak.
| | Jónak, de úgy, hogy csak terajtad áll,
| | hogy jó maradj.
| | Önkéntes hódolat: ez óhaja, | [910]
| | nem kényszermunka – ezt nem kedveli,
| | s nem is kedvelheti! Hisz szolgaszívet
| | miképp tegyen ki próbának: vajon
| | önként szolgál, vagy csak mivel a kényszer
| | űzi, s nincs módja mást választani?
| | Mi, angyalok, kik színről színre látjuk,
| | szerencsénkben csak úgy maradhatunk meg
| | mi is, ha mint ti, tesszük rendelését –
| | Szeretjük, vagy se, tőlünk függ. Ez éltet
| | vagy ront. Vannak, akik engedetlenül | [920]
| | lebuktak már az Égből a Pokolba.
| | Mily végső üdvből míly kínokba estek.
| ÁDÁM: | A Mennyben lett viszály,
| | miről szóltál, kétséget önt belém;
| | annál inkább szeretnék hallani
| | mindent, ha jónak látod.
| RAFAEL: | Nagy dolgot kérsz, emberfaj őse, tőlem!
| | Mint fedjem föl egy más
| | világ titkát, amit talán nem is
| | jogos kitárnom? Ám ha javadra végzem, | [930]

	With Angels may participate, and find	
	No inconvenient Diet, nor too light Fare:	[900]
	And from these corporal nutriments perhaps	
	Your bodies may at last turn all to Spirit,	
	Improv'd by tract of time, and wingd ascend	
	Ethereal, as wee, or may at choice	
	Here or in Heav'nly Paradises dwell;	
	If ye be found obedient, and retain	
	Unalterably firm his love entire	
	Whose progenie you are.	
ADAM:	But say,	
	What meant that caution joind, *if ye be found*	[910]
	Obedient? can we want obedience then	
	To him, or possibly his love desert	
	Who formd us from the dust, and plac'd us here?	
RAPHAEL:	Son of Heav'n and Earth,	
	Attend: That thou art happie, owe to God;	
	That thou continu'st such, owe to thy self,	
	That is, to thy obedience; therein stand.	
	This was that caution giv'n thee; be advis'd.	
	God made thee perfet, not immutable;	
	And good he made thee, but to persevere	[920]
	He left it in thy power.	
	Our voluntarie service he requires,	
	Not our necessitated, such with him	
	Findes no acceptance, nor can find, for how	
	Can hearts, not free, be tri'd whether they serve	
	Willing or no, who will but what they must	
	By Destinie, and can no other choose?	
	Myself and all th' Angelic Host that stand	
	In sight of God enthron'd, our happie state	
	Hold, as you yours, while our obedience holds;	[930]
	To love or not; in this we stand or fall:	
	And Som are fall'n, to disobedience fall'n,	
	And so from Heav'n to deepest Hell; O fall	
	From what high state of bliss into what woe!	
ADAM:	What thou tellst	
	Hath past in Heav'n, som doubt within me move,	
	But more desire to hear, if thou consent.	
RAPHAEL:	High matter thou injoinst me, O prime of men,	
	How shall I relate	
	The secrets of another world, perhaps	[940]
	Not lawful to reveal? yet for thy good	

| | elnézi Isten; – egy napon, minőt
a Menny nagy éve hoz,
az angyalhadakat egybehívta királyi szó.
És megjelentek számtalan sokan
az Isten trónjánál a négy világtáj
felől fény-rendekben vezéreikkel, a végtelen Atya,
ki mellett üdvözülten ült fia
mintha tüzes hegyről beszélne, melynek
csúcsa vakít: nem látható: | |
| ATYA: | Halljátok, sugárszülte angyalok, | [940] |
| | trónok, hatalmak, országok s erények
örökérvényü végezésemet!
E nap teremtettem, kit Egyszülött
Fiamnak nyilvánítok ím e szent
hegyen fölkenve; őt, kit jobbomon
itt láttok, állitom vezéretekké,
– s magamra esküszöm, hogy meghajol
neki a Mennyben minden térd, s királynak
vallja! Ki nem hajt | |
| | szavára, ellenem dacol, s kötést tör: | [950] |
| | Isten-látásból mélybe vettetik,
a legkülső sötétre hull, s helye
ott lesz örökre meg nem válthatóan! | |
| RAFAEL: | Az összes angyal
látszólag egyetért – nem mind valóban.
Sátán erőivel
szárnyon már messze száguldott, trónjára száll
Istennel egyenlő
rangot áhítva, majmolván a Szent | |
| | hegyet, melyen a Messiás király lett | [960] |
| | az Ég láttára. Ide vonta össze
hadait oly ürüggyel, hogy parancsot
kapott: hányják-vessék meg, mint fogadják
királyukat, s igazságot tettetve
fülüket így töltötte rágalommal: | |
| SÁTÁN: | Trónok, erények, uralmak, és hatalmak,
ha csak nem puszta címek e magasztos
rangok immár, mióta új parancs
szerint mellőzve minket, más nyeré el | |
| | a főhatalmat fölszentelt király | [970] |
| | nevén, hogy vegyen
tőlünk térdrebukás-adót, mi nem volt
eddig, hitvány hajbókolást, mi egynek
is sok! Hogy tűrjük most kettőnek adva?! | |

	This is dispenc't; – on a day	
	On such day	
	As Heav'ns great Year brings forth, th' Empyreal Host	
	Of Angels by Imperial summons call'd,	
	Innumerable before th' Almighties Throne	
	Forthwith from all the ends of Heav'n appeerd	
	Under thir Hierarchs in orders bright, the Father infinite,	
	By whom in bliss imbosom'd sat the Son,	
	Amidst as from a flaming Mount, whose top	[950]
	Brightness had made invisible, thus spake:	
GOD:	Hear all ye Angels, Progenie of Light,	
	Thrones, Dominations, Princedoms, Vertues, Powers,	
	Hear my Decree, which unrevok't shall stand.	
	This day I have begot whom I declare	
	My onely Son, and on this holy Hill	
	Him have anointed, whom ye now behold	
	At my right hand; your Head I him appoint;	
	And by my Self have sworn to him shall bow	
	All knees in Heav'n, and shall confess him Lord:	[960]
	Him who disobeyes	
	Mee disobeyes, breaks union	
	Cast out from God and blessed vision, falls	
	Into utter darkness, deep ingulft, his place	
	Ordaind without redemption, without end.	
RAPHAEL:	All seemd well pleas'd, all seem'd, but were not all.	
	Satan with his Powers	
	Far was advanc't on winged speed, came to his Royal seat	
	Affecting all equality with God,	
	In imitation of that Mount whereon	[970]
	Messiah was declar'd in sight of Heav'n.	
	Thither he assembl'd all his Train,	
	Pretending so commanded to consult	
	About the great reception of thir King,	
	Thither to come, and with calumnious Art	
	Of counterfeted truth thus held thir ears.	
SATAN:	Thrones, Dominations, Princedoms, Vertues, Powers,	
	If these magnific Titles yet remain	
	Not meerly titular, since by Decree	
	Another now hath to himself ingross't	[980]
	All Power of King anointed	
	To receive from us	
	Knee-tribute yet unpaid, prostration vile,	
	Too much to one, but double how endur'd,	
	To one and to his image now proclaim'd?	

	Egyeduralmat ki vehet magára	
	ésszel vagy joggal az egyenjogúak	
	fölött, mégha ezek fényben s erőben	
	kisebbek is, de egyként szabadok?	
	És ki szabhat törvényt nekünk, akik	
	törvény nélkül se vétkezünk? S mi több,	[980]
	urunk legyen, s alázkodást akarjon	
	királyi cimünket megcsufolva, mely	
	uralomra, nem szolgaságra rendelt?	
ABDIEL:	Gaz, káromló hazugság!	
	Szavak, miket egy fül se várt az Égben,	
	legkevésbé tőled, hálátalan,	
	kit oly magasra társaid fölé	
	plántált! Te szabsz törvényt az Úrnak?	
	Tapasztalatból tudjuk, Ő mily jó,	
	méltóságunkra mint munkál s javunkra:	[990]
	szándéka nem, hogy kisebbé tegyen	
	bennünket, inkább szeretné emelni	
	szerencsénket, még jobban egyesítve	
	egy fő alatt.	
	Becsülheted egyenlőnek magad –	
	bármily nagy és dicső vagy – s minden angyalt	
	együtt Isten Fiával?	
	Fojtsd el gonosz dühöd!	
	Ezeket ne kisértsd! A dühre gerjedt	
	Atyát s Fiát siess megcsöndesíteni,	[1000]
	míg – időben – irgalmuk nyerheted!	
SÁTÁN:	Teremtmények vagyunk – mondtad –, s mi több:	
	másodkéz művei? Hisz átruházta fiára ezt a	
	munkát az Atya?	
	Bolond újság!	
1. ÖRDÖG:	No halljuk, hol tanultad?	
	S ki látta, mikor volt?	
MAMMON:	Emlékszel-e teremtésedre,	
	mikor gyúrt a Mester?	
SÁTÁN:	Mi nem tudunk időt, mikor nem éltünk.	[1010]
	Magunkból sarjasztott önéltető	
	erőnk. Hatalmunk	
	magunkban van, saját karunk tanít	
	dicső tettekre, hogy próbát tegyünk:	
	ki egyenlő velünk?	
	Vidd a Fölkent Királynak	
	e szónk, s kotródj, míg röptöd bajtalan!	

	Who can in reason then or right assume	
	Monarchie over such as live by right	
	His equals, if in power and splendor less,	
	In freedome equal?	
	Or can introduce	[990]
	Law and Edict on us, who without law	
	Erre not, much less for this to be our Lord,	
	And look for humiliation[11] to th' abuse	
	Of those Imperial Titles which assert	
	Our being ordain'd to govern, not to serve?	
ABDIEL:	O argument blasphemous, false and proud!	
	Words which no eare ever to hear in Heav'n	
	Expected, least of all from thee, ingrate	
	In place thy self so high above thy Peeres.	
	Shalt thou give Law to God?	[1000]
	By experience taught we know how good,	
	And of our good, and of our dignitie	
	How provident he is, how farr from thought	
	To make us less, bent rather to exalt	
	Our happie state under one Head more neer	
	United. Thy self though great and glorious dost thou count,	
	Or all Angelic Nature joind in one,	
	Equal to him begotten Son? Cease this impious rage,	
	And tempt not these; but hast'n to appease	
	Th' incensed Father, and th' incensed Son,	[1010]
	While Pardon may be found in time besought.	
SATAN:	That we were formd then saist thou? and the work	
	Of secondarie hands, by task transferd	
	From Father to his Son? strange point and new!	
DEVIL 1:	Doctrin which we would know whence learnt?	
	Who saw when this creation was?	
MAMMON:	Rememberst thou	
	Thy making, while the Maker gave thee being?	
SATAN:	We know no time when we were not as now;	
	Know none before us, self-begot, self-rais'd	[1020]
	By our own quick'ning power.	
	Our puissance is our own, our own right hand	
	Shall teach us highest deeds, by proof to try	
	Who is our equal:	
	These tidings carrie to th' anointed King;	
	And fly, ere evil intercept thy flight.	

ABDIEL:	Istentől pártolt szellem, átkozott,	
	minden jóból kizárt! Bukásodat	
	már elvégezve látom, és veszését	[1020]
	nyomorult bandádnak, kiket bevontál	
	árulásodba. De nem rémítgetésre	
	repülök el ez átok-sátoroktól,	
	de hogy a tüstént lángba buggyanó düh	
	nehogy itt érjen, mely nem válogat.	
	Fejedre várhatod villámai	
	nyelő tüzét, s jajongva megtudod,	
	ki teremtett – s ki az, ki elveszíthet!	
RAFAEL:	Szólt Abdiel, hitetlenek között ki	
	egyedül hű, a számtalan hamis közt	[1030]
	rettenetlen, csábíthatatlanul	
	szilárd. Megőrzé buzgalmát, hüségét,	
	szeretetét, bár egymagában állt,	
	nem téritette el se szám, se példa	
	az Igaztól, és nem ingatta meg	
	szilárd hitét. Közöttük elvonult,	
	bár rázudult az ellen gúnya, mit	
	fölénnyel tűrt, s harctól se rettegett.	
	Gúnnyal felelve hátat forditott	
	a vészre itélt, hetvenkedő titánnak.	[1040]
ABDIEL:	Bukásod már elvégezve látom	
	S vesztését nyomorult bandádnak.	
SÁTÁN:	Vészben megedzett drága társaim,	
	megmutattátok: méltók	
	nem csak a szabadságra vagytok – ez	
	csekély óhaj –, de mit inkább áhítunk:	
	dicsőségre, uralkodásra is.	
ATYA:	Menj, Mihály, Menny-hadak hercege,	
[MAGNÓ]:	e sok fiamat ma győztes	
	harcra vigyétek, hősi szenteket!	[1050]
	Csapjatok reájuk,	
	tűzzel, fegyverrel bátran, és az Ég	
	partjáig űzzétek ki őket, üdvtől,	
	Istentől el a büntetés helyére.	
MIHÁLY:	Hát rád leltünk, pimasz!	
	Hát azt remélted, ellenállás nélkül	
	elérheted Isten trónját őrizetlen,	
	mert övéi,	
	elálltak tőle, rettegvén erődtől	

ABDIEL:	O alienate from God, O spirit accurst,
	Forsak'n of all good; I see thy fall
	Determind, and thy hapless crew involv'd
	In this perfidious fraud. [1030]
	Yet not for thy advise or threats I fly
	These wicked Tents devoted, least the wrauth
	Impendent, raging into sudden flame
	Distinguish not: for soon expect to feel
	His Thunder on thy head, devouring fire.
	Then who created thee lamenting learne,
	When who can uncreate thee thou shalt know.
RAPHAEL:	So spake *Abdiel* faithful found,
	Among the faithless, faithful only hee;
	Among innumerable false, unmov'd, [1040]
	Unshak'n, unseduc'd, unterrifi'd
	His Loyaltie he kept, his Love, his Zeale;
	Nor number, nor example with him wrought
	To swerve from truth,
	Or change his constant mind
	Though single. From amidst them forth he passd,
	Long way through hostile scorn, which he susteind
	Superior, nor of violence fear'd aught;
	And with retorted scorn his back he turn'd
	On that proud Titan[12] to swift destruction doom'd. [1050]
ABDIEL:	I see thy fall determind,
	And thy hapless crew involv'd.
SATAN:	O now in danger tri'd, now known in Armes
	Found worthy not of Libertie alone,
	Too mean pretense, but what we more affect,
	Honour, Dominion, Glorie, and renowne.
GOD:	Go *Michael* of Celestial Armies Prince,
[TAPE]	Lead forth to Battel these my Sons
	Invincible, lead forth my armed Saints,
	Them with Fire and hostile Arms [1060]
	Fearless assault, and to the brow of Heav'n
	Pursuing drive them out from God and bliss,
	Into thir place of punishment.
MICHAEL:	Proud, art thou met? thy hope was to have reacht
	The highth of thy aspiring unoppos'd,
	The Throne of God unguarded, and his side
	Abandond at the terror of thy Power

	s vad nyelvedtől?	[1060]
	Bolond!
	Nem vetted észbe, hogy céltalan
	fogsz fegyvert Isten ellen.
SÁTÁN:	Azt hittem eddig,
	hogy ég s szabadság egyenlőn
	jár minden mennybélinek.
	Most látom, legtöbb lomha:
	szolga inkább, dallal edzvén magát
	s lakmározással. Őket övezted föl,
	menybéli dalárdát, hogy vívjon	[1070]
	szabadsággal szolgaság. Ma lesz a
	döntő nap! Beszél a tett!
MIHÁLY:	Királykodj a Pokolban, s hadd az Égben
	szolgálnom örök-áldott Istenünket,
	s tennem szavát, mert hódolatra méltó.
	Pokolban nem trón – bilincs vár reád.
SÁTÁN:	Amit te bűnnek tartasz, mi glóriának.
	Erőd keményítsd,
	Én nem futok! Téged
	kerestelek.	[1080]
	Szaladj segélyért a Mindenhatódhoz!
	Miért nem jönnek e büszke győztesek?
	Elébb kérkedve jöttek. És ha most
	nyílt szívvel, homlokkal fogadjuk őket
	(többet mit tehetnénk?), s elébük adjuk
	békefeltételünket, ime mást akarnak,
	bolond bakugrásokkal elszaladnak.
	Táncolni szottyant kedvük? Táncnak ez
	bohócos kissé s túl vad is. Talán a
	kínált békén ujongnak? Azt gyanítom,	[1090]
	ha ismét hallanák javaslatunkat
	az őket gyors döntésre ösztökélné.
	Miért nem jönnek e büszke győztesek?
RAFAEL:	Így szórakoztak csúfolódva ők.
	Nem volt szemernyi kételyük sem a
	sikerben.
	Úgy remélték, könnyü már
	az Örök Úrral harcot állniuk,
	mennydörgését gunyolták és nevették
	hadseregét. De nem sokáig.	[1100]
ATYA:	Dicsőségem tükörmása, szerelmes
	fiam, kinek orcáin látható
	a láthatatlan: isten-lényegem,

SATAN:	Or potent tongue; fool, not to think how vain
	Against th' Omnipotent to rise in Arms.
SATAN:	At first I thought that Libertie and Heav'n [1070]
	To heav'nly Soules had bin all one; but now
	I see that most through sloth had rather serve,
	Ministring Spirits, traind up in Feast and Song;
	Such hast thou arm'd, the Minstrelsie of Heav'n,
	Servilitie with freedom to contend,
	As both thir deeds compar'd this day shall prove.
MICHAEL:	Reign thou in Hell thy Kingdom, let mee serve
	In Heav'n God ever blest, and his Divine
	Behests obey, worthiest to be obey'd,
	Yet Chains in Hell, not Realms expect. [1080]
SATAN:	The strife which thou call'st evil, but wee style
	The strife of Glorie:
	Mean while thy utmost force,
	I flie not,
	But have sought thee farr and nigh.
	And join him nam'd *Almighty* to thy aid!
	Why come not on these Victors proud?
	Ere while they fierce were coming, and when wee,
	To entertain them fair with open Front
	And Brest, (what could we more?) propounded terms [1090]
	Of composition, strait they chang'd thir minds,
	Flew off, and into strange vagaries fell,
	As they would dance, yet for a dance they seemd
	Somwhat extravagant and wilde, perhaps
	For joy of offerd peace: but I suppose
	If our proposals once again were heard
	We should compel them to a quick result.
	Why come not on these Victors proud?
RAPHAEL:	So they among themselves in pleasant veine
	Stood scoffing, highthn'd in thir thoughts beyond [1100]
	All doubt of victorie, eternal might [630]
	To match with thir inventions they presum'd
	So easie, and of his Thunder made a scorn,
	And all his Host derided; but they stood not long.
GOD:	Effulgence of my Glorie, Son belov'd,
	Son in whose face invisible is beheld
	Visibly, what by Deitie I am,

	s kinek kezével terveim betöltöm.	
	Másod-mindenható! Két napja múlt,	
	mióta Mihály s erői mentek	
	megtörni a lázadót. Nyilván kemény	
	volt a harcuk, hogyha két íly fegyveres	
	csap össze, mert magukra hagytam őket.	
	Így nem születve döntés. Az emésztő	[1110]
	háboru véghez vitte, mit tehet,	
	és őrjöngésig féket engedett,	
	és fegyverül hegyet dobált, az Égben	
	barbár romlás pusztított.	
	Elmúlt két nap. Harmadik tiéd!	
FIÚ:	Égi trónok Legfőbbje, ó, Atyám!	
	A kormánypálcát tőled átveszem, erőddel	
	fölfegyverezve a Mennyből kiűzöm	
	e pártütőket megkészitett lakukba.	
	Csak álljatok figyelve,	[1120]
	Isten dühét miként árasztja ki	
	általam e gazokra.	
RAFAEL:	Így szólt és arca iszonyúra vált.	
MIHÁLY:	Robognak a zord szekér kerékei, miként ár	
	zubogó zajja, vagy sereg. Rohan	
	egyenest istentelen ellenére	
	éjkomoran. A lángkerék alatt	
	a szilárd mennybolt is beléremeg,	
	csak Isten trónja nem.	
	Pokol méltó lakuk, kiolthatatlan	[1130]
	tüzével rakva, kín és jaj hona.	
RAFAEL:	Ellen üzéséből, egyedül győztes,	
	szekerével megtért a Messiás.	
	Ő diadalmenetben	
	száll a Mennyben a fennen trónoló	
	szent Atya udvarában, templomába,	
	hol dicsőségbe Isten béfogadja.	
ÁDÁM:	Égi Tolmács! Isten kegyelme küldött	
	hogy még időben óvjon attól, mi vesztünk hona,	
	ha nem ismerjük, s mit emberész nem ér föl;	[1140]
	miért az örök Jónak halhatatlan	
	hálával tartozunk, és megfogadjuk	
	intését ünnepélyesen: magasztos	
	parancsát tartjuk, hisz avégre lettünk.	

	And in whose hand what by Decree I doe,	
	Second Omnipotence, two dayes are past,	
	Since *Michael* and his Powers went forth to tame	[1110]
	These disobedient; sore hath been thir fight,	
	As likeliest was, when two such Foes met arm'd;	
	For to themselves I left them,	
	And no solution will be found:	
	Warr wearied hath perform'd what Warr can do,	
	And to disorder'd rage let loose the reines,	
	With Mountains as with Weapons arm'd, which makes	
	Wild work in Heav'n, and dangerous to the maine.	
	Two dayes are therefore past, the third is thine!	
SON:	O Father, O Supream of heav'nly Thrones,	[1120]
	Scepter and Power, thy giving, I assume,	
	And rid heav'n of these rebell'd,	
	To thir prepar'd ill Mansion.	
	Stand onely and behold	
	Gods indignation on these Godless pourd.	
RAPHAEL:	So spake the Son, and into terrour chang'd	
	His count'nance.	
MICHAEL:	The Orbes of his fierce Chariot rowld, as with the sound	
	Of torrent Floods, or of a numerous Host.	
	Hee on his impious Foes right onward drove,	[1130]
	Gloomie as Night; under his burning Wheeles	
	The stedfast Empyrean shook throughout,	
	All but the Throne it self of God.	
	Hell thir fit habitation fraught with fire	
	Unquenchable, the house of woe and paine.	
RAPHAEL:	Sole Victor from th' expulsion of his Foes	
	Messiah his triumphal Chariot turnd:	
	He celebrated rode	
	Triumphant through mid Heav'n, into the Courts	
	And Temple of his mightie Father Thron'd	[1140]
	On high: who into Glorie him receav'd.	
ADAM:	Divine interpreter, by favour sent	
	Down from the Empyrean to forewarne	
	Us timely of what might else have bin our loss,	
	Unknown, which human knowledg could not reach:	
	For which to the infinitly Good we owe	
	Immortal thanks, and his admonishment	
	Receave with solemne purpose to observe	
	Immutably his sovran will, the end	
	Of what we are.	[1150]

ÁDÁM ÉS ÉVA IMÁJA: Jó Atya, dicső műved mindez itt,
Mindenható! E Mindenség tiéd,
e csudaszép! S milyen csudás lehetsz te,
Kimondhatatlan! – Ülsz az Ég fölött,
s nem láthatunk, csak így homályosan,
legkisebb műveidben; mégis ők [1150]
jóságod és hatalmad hirdetik.
Üdv, Mindenség ura! Légy bőkezű,
csak jót adj nékünk, és ha valami
gonoszt fogant az éj vagy rejteget:
szórd szét, mint szórja szét a fény az éjt!

THE PRAYER OF ADAM AND EVE:

These are thy glorious works, Parent of good,
Almightie, thine this universal Frame,
Thus wondrous fair; thy self how wondrous then!
Unspeakable, who sitst above these Heavens
To us invisible or dimly seen
In these thy lowest works, yet these declare
Thy goodness beyond thought, and Power Divine:
Hail universal Lord, be bounteous still
To give us onely good; and if the night
Have gathered aught of evil or conceald, [1160]
Disperse it, as now light dispels the dark.

2. rész

RAFAEL: Dicsőség Istennek, s az
embernek jószándék, s lakának Béke!
Dicsőség Néki, kinek jogos boszúja
elűzte a Gonoszt szine elől, s onnan záporozza minden
világra, korra végtelen szerelmét.
ÉVA: Fülnek csodás, magasztos dolgokat
tártál föl, mik világunktól elütnek,
égi Tolmács!
ÁDÁM: Isten kegyelme küldött,
hogy még időben óvjon attól, mi vesztünk hozza, ha   [10]
nem ismerjük, s mit emberész nem ér föl;
miért az örök Jónak halhatatlan
hálával tartozunk, és megfogadjuk
intését ünnepélyesen: magasztos
parancsát tartjuk, hisz avégre lettünk.
RAFAEL: Fordítsd javadra, hogy hallottad,
mi szörnyü a lázadás gyümölcse.
Ők állhattak volna híven, s elbuktak.
Emlékezz, s remegd a bűnt!
ÁDÁM: Fenn jár még a Nap; lásd,   [20]
mit eszeltem ki, csak hogy itt maradj,
megkérve: vedd füledbe, mit mesélek:
most halld tőlem históriám, amit
talán nem ismersz.
RAFAEL: Beszéld tehát el,
mert távol voltam aznapon ködös,
és furcsa küldetésben, a Pokol-
kapukhoz útban, harcinégyszögű
légióban.
De most beszélj te! Nem kisebb örömmel   [30]
fülelek szódra, mint az enyémre te!
ÁDÁM: Mintha bódulatból
ocsúdnék: halk virágokon hevertem
balzsamos izzadásban, mit a Nap
fölszikkasztott páráival betelve.
Mennybe forgattam ámuló szemem,
s bámultam csak a tág eget.

PART 2

RAPHAEL:	Glorie to the most High, good will
	To future men, and in thir dwellings peace:
	Glorie to him whose just avenging ire
	Had driven out th' ungodly from his sight
	And thence diffuse
	His good to Worlds and Ages infinite.
EVE:	Great things, and full of wonder in our eares,
	Farr differing from this World, thou hast reveal'd
	Divine interpreter!
ADAM:	By favour sent [10]
	Down from the Empyrean to forewarne
	Us timely of what might else have bin our loss,
	Unknown, which human knowledg could not reach:
	For which to the infinitly Good we owe
	Immortal thanks, and his admonishment
	Receave with solemne purpose to observe
	Immutably his sovran will, the end
	Of what we are.
RAPHAEL:	Let it profit thee to have heard
	By terrible Example the reward [20]
	Of disobedience; firm they might have stood,
	Yet fell; remember, and fear to transgress.
ADAM:	Day is yet not spent; till then thou seest
	How suttly to detaine thee I devise,
	Now hear mee relate
	My Storie, which perhaps thou hast not heard.
RAPHAEL:	Say therefore on;
	For I that Day was absent, as befell,
	Bound on a voyage uncouth and obscure,
	Farr on excursion toward the Gates of Hell; [30]
	Squar'd in full Legion.
	But thy relation now; for I attend,
	Pleas'd with thy words no less then thou with mine.
ADAM:	As new wak't from soundest sleep
	Soft on the flourie herb I found me laid
	In Balmie Sweat, which with his Beames the Sun
	Soon dri'd, and on the reaking moisture fed.
	Strait toward Heav'n my wondring Eyes I turnd,
	And gaz'd a while the ample Skie, till rais'd

	Sebes ösztönös mozdulattal fölszökelltem,	
	mintha oda indulnék; lábra álltam.	
	Köröttem láttam völgyet és hegyet,	[40]
	árnyas erdőt, napszőtte síkokat,	
	zsongó vizek áttetsző szökdelését:	
	itt lények éltek, álltak, vagy röpültek,	
	ágon madár csatinázott,	
	mosolygott minden; szivemben illat és öröm!	
	Magam kezdtem fürkészni – tagjaim:	
	nekilendültem, nekifutamodtam	
	rugós izűletekkel, friss irammal.	
	Nem tudtam még: ki volnék, hol, mi okból.	
	Próbáltam szólni, s szóltam: íme nyelvem	[50]
	követte óhajom, nevén neveztem,	
	mit láttam, könnyedén. Mondtam: „Te Nap –	
	gyöngy fény. Sugáros Föld: vidám, üde."	
	Mig így ujongtam, jártam, azt se tudtam,	
	honnan szíttam első lehelletem,	
	s láttam ez üdvös fényt – de semmi válasz;	
	fejemnél hirtelen álomjelenség	
	állt meg, kinek belső feltünte szendén	
	meggyőzte képzelésem, hogy vagyok,	
	még élek. Úgy gondoltam, égi lény, ki	[60]
	így szólt:	
ATYA:	Lakásod vár, serkenj föl, Ádám,	
	első ember, ki számtalan tömegnek	
	lettél ősatyja. Hívtál, itt vagyok, hogy	
	helyedre az Üdv-kertbe vigyelek.	
	Én vagyok, kit keressz –	
	– Mindennek alkotója,	
	amit magad körül, alul, fölül látsz.	
	Neked adom ez Édent, tudd tiédnek!	
	Gondozd, müveld, és edd gyümölcseit!	[70]
	E kert minden fájáról szabadon,	
	boldog szívvel ehetsz, ne félj hiánytól,	
	ám amelynek gyümölcse-ízlelése	
	a jó és rossz tudását hozza meg,	
	emlékezz, mire intelek: ne ízleld,	
	irtózz keserves zsoldjától, eszedbe	
	vésd: mely napon parancsomat szeged,	
	s eszel róla, halállal halsz legott!	
	Neked s utódaidnak nemcsak e	
	kertet adom – az egész Földet is;	[80]
	bírd mint ura, s mindazt, mi rajta él:	
	légben, vízben, szárnyast, vadat, halat!	

By quick instinctive motion up I sprung, [40]
As thitherward endevoring, and upright
Stood on my feet; about me round I saw
Hill, Dale, and shadie Woods, and sunnie Plaines,
And liquid Lapse of murmuring Streams; by these,
Creatures that livd, and movd, and walk'd, or flew,
Birds on the branches warbling; all things smil'd,
With fragrance and with joy my heart oreflow'd.
My self I then perus'd, and Limb by Limb
Survey'd, and sometimes went, and sometimes ran
With supple joints, as lively vigour led: [50]
But who I was, or where, or from what cause,
Knew not; to speak I tri'd, and forthwith spake,
My Tongue obey'd and readily could name
What e're I saw. Thou Sun, said I, faire Light,
And thou enlight'nd Earth, so fresh and gay.
While thus I call'd, and stray'd I knew not whither,
From where I first drew Aire, and first beheld
This happie Light, when answer none return'd,
When suddenly stood at my Head a dream,
Whose inward apparition gently mov'd [60]
My fancy to believe I yet had being,
And livd: One came, methought, of shape Divine,
And said:

GOD: Thy Mansion wants thee, *Adam*, rise,
First Man, of Men innumerable ordain'd
First Father, call'd by thee I come thy Guide
To the Garden of bliss, thy seat prepar'd.
Whom thou soughtst I am,
Author of all this thou seest
Above, or round about thee or beneath. [70]
This Paradise I give thee, count it thine
To Till and keep, and of the Fruit to eate:
Of every Tree that in the Garden growes
Eate freely with glad heart; fear here no dearth:
But of the Tree whose operation brings
Knowledg of good and ill,
Remember what I warne thee, shun to taste,
And shun the bitter consequence: for know,
The day thou eat'st thereof, my sole command
Transgrest, inevitably thou shalt dye! [80]
Not onely these fair bounds, but all the Earth
To thee and to thy Race I give; as Lords
Possess it, and all things that therein live, .
Or live in Sea, or Aire, Beast, Fish, and Fowle.

ÁDÁM:	Miképp imádjalak, Szerzője mind e Létnek
	és ennyi jónak, mellyel ím az embert
	oly bőkezűen, oly nagylelküen
	elhalmozod? De senki sincs, kivel
	megosztanám! Mi boldogságot ád
	e nagy magány? Ki élvez egymaga?
ATYA:	Mit hívsz magánynak? Nincs a Föld s az Ég
	tele élő teremtményekkel, és nem [90]
	parancsodra járulnak mind eléd
	és játszadoznak?
	Mulass velük,
	s vezesd őket! Országod épp elég tág!
ÁDÁM:	Szavam ne sértsen, égi szent Erő! A nem hasonlók,
	nem férnek össze, egymást csakhamar
	megutálják. Társas viszonyra vágyom:
	részt kapni minden ésszerű gyönyörben;
	Nem társulhat barommal a madár,
	vagy hal madárral, ökörrel majom, [100]
	legkevésbé az állattal az ember!
ATYA:	Látom, Ádám, kényes, finom szerencsét
	kivánsz magadnak, kiszemelve társad,
	s gyönyört szakítni nem kivánsz magadban.
	Mit gondolsz hát felőlem s helyzetemről?
	Úgy látod, én elég boldog vagyok
	örök magányomban? Társat magamhoz
	méltót nem lelek, egyenlőt mégkevésbé.
	Kit leljek csevegőtársnak, ha csak nem
	egy-egy lényt alkotásaim közül, [110]
	kik nálam végtelen alábbvalóbbak,
	mint hozzád képest többi műveim.
	Nem ilyen társakat
	szántam neked; mindez csak próba volt,
	hogy lássam, mint itélsz jóról, helyesről.
ÁDÁM:	Elnémult, vagy nem hallottam, mivel
	legyőzte égi volta földi énem,
	az álmomban kerestem enyhülést,
	amely a lét segélyszavára hullt rám,
	s szemem bezárta. De nyitva hagyta benső [120]

ADAM: How may I adore thee, Author of this Universe,
And all this good to man, for whose well being
So amply, and with hands so liberal
Thou hast provided all things: but with mee
I see not who partakes. In solitude
What happiness, who can enjoy alone? [90]

GOD: What call'st thou solitude, is not the Earth
With various living creatures, and the Aire
Replenisht, and all these at thy command
To come and play before thee?
With these
Find pastime, and beare rule; thy Realm is large!

ADAM: Let not my words offend thee, Heav'nly Power,
in disparitie the one intense, the other still remiss
Cannot well suite with either, but soon prove
Tedious alike: Of fellowship I speak [100]
Such as I seek, fit to participate
All rational delight,
Much less can Bird with Beast, or Fish with Fowle
So well converse, nor with the Ox the Ape;
Wors then can Man with Beast, and least of all.

GOD: A nice and suttle happiness I see
Thou to thyself proposest, in the choice
Of thy Associates, Adam, and wilt taste
No pleasure, though in pleasure, solitarie.
What think'st thou then of mee, and this my State, [110]
Seem I to thee sufficiently possest
Of happiness, or not? who am alone
From all Eternitie, for none I know
Second to mee or like, equal much less.
How have I then with whom to hold converse
Save with the Creatures which I made, and those
To me inferiour, infinite descents
Beneath what other Creatures are to thee?
I no such companie
Intended thee, for trial onely brought, [120]
To see how thou could'st judge of fit and meet.

ADAM: Hee ended, or I heard no more, for now
My earthly by his Heav'nly overpowerd,
I sought repair
Of sleep, which instantly fell on me, call'd
By Nature as in aide, and clos'd mine eyes.
Mine eyes he clos'd, but op'n left the Cell

	látásom képzelet-szemét, amellyel	
	szinte önkívületben láttam alva,	
	hol fekszem, s láttam a fénysugár-Dicsőt,	
	ki előtt ébren álltam. Ő fölém	
	görnyedve oldalam nyitotta, és	
	kivett egy szív-hevétől még meleg	
	bordát, még élet-vértől lüktetőt.	
	Nagy volt a seb, de hirtelen betöltvén	
	hússal, begyógyította, két kezével	
	bordámat gyúrva. Alkotó keze	[130]
	alatt teremtmény támadt: mint a férfi	
	olyan, de másnemű, s tündéri szép,	
	hogy mind, mi szépnek tetszett ez világban,	
	most csúfnak tűnt.	
ATYA:	Kit most eléd hozok, tetszik bizonnyal;	
	másik éned, hasonmásod, segéded, s szived	
	vágyát betölti teljesen.	
ÁDÁM:	Ez mindent jóra vált! Szavad, Teremtő,	
	betöltötted, jóságos, bőkezű	
	adója minden szépnek! Ám a legszebb	[140]
	ajándok: ő! Tőlem ne vondd el! Érzem:	
	csont csontomból, husomból hús, magam	
	lelem meg benne.	
ATYA:	Nő a neve!	
ÁDÁM:	Mert a férfiból nőtt:	
ATYA:	ezért a férfi hagyja	
	el szüleit, s ragaszkodjék nejéhez,	
	s lesznek egy hús, egy lélek, érzelem!	
ÁDÁM:	S bevallom, élvezek	
	mindent köröttem, ami feltünik	[150]
	s ha nincs: nem támaszt változást,	
	gyötrő sóvárgást –íly gyönyörnek érzem	
	az ízlelést, látást, szaglást, gyümölcsöt,	
	virágot, sétát, madarak dalát . . .	
	Ám ő egészen más! Imádva nézem,	
	cirógatom, itt éltem át először	
	a furcsa szenvedélyt, megrendülést,	
	hisz ura voltam más minden gyönyörnek	
	rendíthetetlen. Vagy silánynak	
	teremtődtem, ki nem tud ellenállni	[160]
	íly támadásnak, vagy az Isten	

	Of Fancie my internal sight, by which	
	Abstract as in a transe methought I saw,	
	Though sleeping, where I lay, and saw the shape	[130]
	Still glorious before whom awake I stood;	
	Who stooping op'nd my left side, and took	
	From thence a Rib, with cordial spirits warme,	
	And Life-blood streaming fresh; wide was the wound,	
	But suddenly with flesh fill'd up and heal'd:	
	The Rib he formd and fashond with his hands;	
	Under his forming hands a Creature grew,	
	Manlike, but different sex, so lovly faire,	
	That what seemd fair in all the World, seemd now	
	Mean.	[140]
GOD:	What next I bring shall please thee, be assur'd,	
	Thy likeness, thy fit help, thy other self,	
	Thy wish, exactly to thy hearts desire.	
ADAM:	This turn hath made amends; thou hast fulfill'd	
	Thy words, Creator bounteous and benigne,	
	Giver of all things faire, but fairest this	
	Of all thy gifts, nor enviest. I now see	
	Bone of my Bone, Flesh of my Flesh, my Self	
	Before me;	
GOD:	Woman is her Name.	[150]
ADAM:	Of Man extracted.	
GOD:	For this cause he shall forgoe	
	Father and Mother, and to his Wife adhere;	
	And they shall be one Flesh, one Heart, one Soule.	
ADAM:	I enjoy, and must confess to find	
	In all things else delight indeed, but such	
	As us'd or not, works in the mind no change,	
	Nor vehement desire, these delicacies	
	I mean of Taste, Sight, Smell, Herbs, Fruits and Flours,	
	Walks, and the melodie of Birds; but here	[160]
	Farr otherwise, transported I behold,	
	Transported touch; here passion first I felt,	
	Commotion strange, in all enjoyments else	
	Superiour and unmov'd, here onely weake	
	Against the charm of Beauties powerful glance.	
	Or Nature faild in mee, and left some part	
	Not proof enough such Object to sustain,	
	Or God on her bestow'd	

	túl széppé tette! Persze, értem én, hogy
	a Természet szándéka szerint a Nő
	észben csekélyebb rendű és a fő
	lelki tulajdonokban is.
	De ha bájához járulok,
	magában az olyan tökéletesnek
	tetszik, ön-lényét híven ismerőnek,
	hogy amit mond, csinál: hiszem leginkább
	illőnek, bölcsnek, erényesnek. Ha ő [170]
	jelen van, omlik a magas tudás.
RAFAEL:	Miért csodálod, mivel bűvöl el?
	Külsejével? Igaz, hogy szemre szép,
	méltó rá, hogy becézd, tiszteld, szeresd!
	De ne légy rabja! Mérd magadhoz őt,
	s itélj! S ha az emberfaj tenyészetét
	célzó viszony varázsát mindenen túl
	gyönyörnek érzed, vésd eszedbe jól:
	megadatott ez mindegyik baromnak.
	Ha társaságában olyanra lelsz, [180]
	mi magasabb, vonzóbb, értelmesebb:
	szeresd! Csupán a szenvedélyt kerüld:
	nem igaz szerelem.
	Leszállt a Nap
	távozásra int.
	Tebenned
	dől el magad s minden fiad üdve, veszte!
	Tarts ki! Üdvöd és
	veszted szabad szándékodban van adva.
	Bévül teljes, ne várj külső segélyre! [190]
	Kisértő bűnnel állj csatát magad!
ÉVA:	Légy jó emberfajunkhoz, jöjj gyakorta!
RAFAEL:	Atyám, ha valaha
	mentsége volna Isten sok fiának,
	hogy megpillantva nőt, belészeret –
	úgy most lehetne! . . .
ATYA:	Ne többet!
GÁBRIEL:	Ti szárnyra kelve
	lessétek ki e kert minden zugát,
	főleg, ahol a két kedvenc lakik, [200]
	s most ártalmat nem sejtve álmodik.

	Too much of Ornament.	
	For well I understand in the prime end	[170]
	Of Nature her th' inferiour, in the mind	
	And inward Faculties.	
	Yet when I approach	
	Her loveliness, so absolute she seems	
	And in her self compleat, so well to know	
	Her own, that what she wills to do or say,	
	Seems wisest, vertuousest, discreetest, best;	
	All higher knowledge in her presence falls.	
RAPHAEL:	What transports thee so,	
	An outside? fair no doubt, and worthy well	[180]
	Thy cherishing, thy honouring, and thy love,	
	Not thy subjection: weigh with her thy self;	
	Then value: but if the sense of touch whereby mankind	
	Is propagated seem such dear delight	
	Beyond all other, think the same voutsaf't	
	To Cattel and each Beast;	
	What higher in her societie thou findst	
	Attractive, human, rational, love still;	
	In loving thou dost well, in passion not,	
	Wherein true Love consists not.	[190]
	But the Sun set my Signal to depart.	
	Thine and of all thy Sons	
	The weal or woe in thee is plac't!	
	Stand fast; to stand or fall	
	Free in thine own Arbitrement it lies.	
	Perfet within, no outward aid require;	
	And all temptation to transgress repel.	
EVE:	Thou to mankind	
	Be good and friendly still, and oft return.	
RAPHAEL:	Father, if ever,	[200]
	now had the Sons of God excuse to be	
	Enamour'd at this sight!...	
GOD:	No more!	
GABRIEL:	Search through this Garden, leave unsearcht no nook,	
	But chiefly where those two fair Creatures Lodge,	
	Now laid perhaps asleep secure of harme.	

2. ANGYAL:	Ez éjt nyugatról angyal érkezett,
	királyi mozgású, de megfakult lény:
	ádáz szeme s zord lépte a Pokol
	urára vall.
GÁBRIEL:	Vigyázzatok!
	Uzziel, a felét vezesd ki délnek
	portyára, míg északra tér a más fél,
SÁTÁN:	s e körútuk majd nyugatnál egyesül.
GÁBRIEL:	Vigyázzatok! [210]
1. ANGYAL:	Ez éjt nyugatról angyal érkezett,
	királyi mozgású, de megfakult lény:
	ádáz szeme s zord lépte a Pokol
	urára vall.
SÁTÁN:	Vigyázzatok!
	Ó, Föld, az Éghez míly hasonlatos, ha
	nem szebb... Különb hely isteneknek is,
	Tebenned míly gyönyörrel
	sétálhatnék, ha tudnék még örülni!
	Édes-felváltva völgy, halom, folyó, [220]
	erdő, sík, tenger és vadon-övezte
	part, szirt, barlang – be szép! De egyikükben
	sem lelem nyughelyem, s magam körül
	minél több szépet látok, antul inkább
	emészt a kín belül, ellenkezések
	gyülölt csatájaként.
	De lakni nem vágyom sem itt, sem Égben,
	mígnem a Menny csucsán úr nem leszek!
	Csak rontásban találok enyhülést
	kétségeimre: ha veszve látom az embert. [230]
	Pokol erői közt enyém lesz az
	érdem, hogy egy nap elveszítem azt,
	mit hat nap-éjt egyvégtiben csinált
	az úgynevezett Mindenható. Az angyalok
	vigyázását félem, de hogy kijátsszam:
	éjféli ködbe burkolózva csúszom,
	leskelve kúszom minden egy bokorba:
	föllelni ott a szunnyadó kigyót, hogy
	rejtsem magam gyűrött gyűrűbe.
	Sötét aláztatás! egy vadba bújni [240]
	szoríttatom,
	hogy lényem testet öltsön egy baromban –

ANGEL 2:	This Eevning from the Sun's decline arriv'd	
	Who tells of som infernal Spirit seen	
	Hitherward bent (who could have thought?) escap'd	
	The barrs of Hell.	[210]
GABRIEL:	Stand firm!	
	Uzziel, half these draw off, and coast the South	
	With strictest watch; these other wheel the North,	
SATAN:	Their circuit meets full West.	
GABRIEL:	Stand firm!	
ANGEL 2:	This Eevning from the Sun's decline arriv'd	
	Who tells of som infernal Spirit seen	
	Hitherward bent (who could have thought?) escap'd	
	The barrs of Hell.	
SATAN:	Stand firm!	[220]
	O Earth, how like to Heav'n, if not preferr'd	
	More justly . . . Seat worthier of Gods.	
	With what delight could I have walkt thee round,	
	If I could joy in aught, sweet interchange	
	Of Hill, and Vallie, Rivers, Woods and Plaines,	
	Now Land, now Sea, and Shores with Forrest crownd,	
	Rocks, Dens, and Caves; but I in none of these	
	Find place or refuge; and the more I see	
	Pleasures about me, so much more I feel	
	Torment within me, as from the hateful siege	[230]
	Of contraries.	
	But neither here seek I, no nor in Heav'n	
	To dwell, unless by maistring Heav'ns Supreame;	
	For onely in destroying I find ease	
	To my relentless thoughts; and him destroyd,	
	To mee shall be the glorie sole among	
	The infernal Powers, in one day to have marr'd	
	What he *Almightie* styl'd, six Nights and Days	
	Continu'd making.	
	The vigilance of his angels	[240]
	I dread, and to elude, thus wrapt in mist	
	Of midnight vapor glide obscure, and prie	
	In every Bush and Brake, where hap may finde	
	The Serpent sleeping, in whose mazie foulds	
	To hide me, and the dark intent I bring.	
	O foul descent! that I am now constraind	
	Into a Beast,	
	This essence to incarnate and imbrute,	

	én, ki az Úr helyébe törtem egykor!	
	De mibe nem alázkodnék boszú	
	és törtetés! Ki nagyra vágyik, oly	
	mélyre bukjék, milyen magasra szállt,	
	s fanyalodjék a legrútabbra is!	
	Bosszú – először édes, majd keservvel	
	csap vissza önmagára! Légyen! Eh,	
	mi gondom rá, csak nyerjem célomat.	[250]
ÉVA:	Ádám, Adj tanácsot, vagy	
	hallgasd meg, mi jutott eszembe épp!	
	Dolgunkat osszuk el! Te menj oda,	
	hová tetszik, vagy hol nagyobb a szükség,	
	kötözz indát fatörzs köré, irányítsd	
	a nyujtózó borostyánt; én pedig	
	amott a mirtuszlomb közé fonódott	
	rózsát fejtem ki – délig tán bevégzem . . .	
	Mert míg mindennap így együtt fogunk	
	dologhoz, vajh csoda, ha íly közel	[260]
	– egymást lessük, mosolygunk csak, vagy új tárgy	
	beszélgetésre hív, s halasztva már	
	napi munkánk: ha kezdjük is korán,	
	meddő marad, s vacsoránk nem érdemeljük!	
ÁDÁM:	Egyetlen társam, minden földi élő	
	közül legkedvesebb, Éva, jól	
	intettél, jól eszmélkedél, miképp	
	töltsük be dolgunk. Ám Isten nem gürcölésre	
	szerzett, de ésszel párosult gyönyörre.	
	Hanem ha már unod	[270]
	a sok beszédet, ám legyünk külön.	
	Olykor magány a legjobb társaság.	
	Kis távollét – édes találkozás.	
	Más kételyem van: féltelek, nehogy	
	baj érjen épp, ha válunk. Hisz tudod,	
	mitől óvtak: hogy ádáz ellenünk	
	üdvünk irígyli.	
	Vagy az a terve, hogy törjük meg az	
	Istennek tett eskünket, vagy lerontsa	
	hitves-szerelmünket, mit legkivált	[280]
	irigyel a nekünk adott gyönyörből.	
	Akárhogy . . . Tarts ki férjed oldalán,	
	A nő – ha vész és szégyen les reá –	
	legjobb oltalmat ott lel férje mellett,	
	ki őrzi, vagy vele kiáll pokolt!	

	That to the hight of Deitie aspir'd;	
	But what will not Ambition and Revenge	[250]
	Descend to? who aspires must down as low	
	As high he soard, obnoxious first or last	
	To basest things.	
	Revenge, at first though sweet,	
	Bitter ere long back on it self recoiles;	
	Let it; I reck not, so it light well aim'd,	
EVE:	*Adam*, now advise	
	Or hear what to my minde first thoughts present,	
	Let us divide our labours, thou where choice	
	Leads thee, or where most needs, whether to wind	[260]
	The Woodbine round this Arbour, or direct	
	The clasping Ivie where to climb, while I	
	In yonder Spring of Roses intermixt	
	With Myrtle, find what to redress till Noon:	
	For while so near each other thus all day	
	Our taske we choose, what wonder if so near	
	Looks intervene and smiles, or object new	
	Casual discourse draw on, which intermits	
	Our dayes work brought to little, though begun	
	Early, and th' hour of Supper comes unearn'd.	[270]
ADAM:	Sole *Eve*, Associate sole, to me beyond	
	Compare above all living Creatures deare,	
	Well hast thou motion'd, well thy thoughts imployd	
	How we might best fulfill the work.	
	Yet not to irksom toile, but to delight	
	He made us, and delight to Reason joyn'd.	
	But if much converse perhaps	
	Thee satiate, to short absence I could yield.	
	For solitude somtimes is best societie,	
	And short retirement urges sweet returne.	[280]
	But other doubt possesses me, least harm	
	Befall thee sever'd from me; for thou knowst	
	What hath bin warn'd us, what malicious Foe	
	Envies our happiness.	
	Whether his first design be to withdraw	
	Our fealtie from God, or to disturb	
	Conjugal Love, then which perhaps no bliss	
	Enjoy'd by us excites his envie more;	
	Or this, or worse, leave not the faithful side	
	That gave thee being.	[290]
	The Wife, where danger or dishonour lurks,	
	Safest and seemliest by her Husband staies,	
	Who guards her, or with her the worst endures.	

ÉVA:	Van ellenünk, ki rontásunkra tör –
	ezt hallottam. Ám hogy férjem és az Úr
	iránti hűségem kétségbevond,
	mert ellenünk kisérthet – hallani
	nem vártam ezt! Íly gond [290]
	szivedbe hogy hatolhatott be, Ádám,
	kedvesedről ilyen komisz gyanú?!"
ÁDÁM:	Nem bizalmatlanságból elleneznem
	szemem-elől-tűntöd, de hogy kerüld
	a kísértést magát s ravasz ellenünket.
	Ne nézd le más segélyét.
	Tekinteted varázsától nyerek
	erőt minden erényre; hogyha nézel,
	bölcsebb, vigyázóbb, bajnokabb vagyok.
ÉVA:	Ha az a végzetünk, hogy egyrakáson [300]
	szorongjunk, mert lopódzkodik a Gaz,
	ki oly ravasz vagy durva, hogy egyenként
	nem is tudunk, ha ránkcsap, védekezni –
	lehetnénk vész-remegve boldogok?!
	Erény, hit, szeretet, mit ér maga
	próbálatlan, ha csak külső segély
	támasztja?
ÁDÁM:	Nem bizalomhiány, de szeretet
	serkent, hogy gyakran intselek s te engem.
	Kisértést ne keress! [310]
	Jön a kisértés nemkeresve is,
	Kerülni jobb, s elkerülöd,
	ha velem maradsz.
ÉVA:	Engedelmeddel, így megintve
	még vígabban megyek. Bár nem hiszem, hogy
	a Gőgös elsőbb rám, gyengébbre les . . .
	Mégis? Annál nagyobb szégyen bukása!
ÁDÁM:	Gyere vissza hamar.
ÉVA:	Délre.
HALÁL:	Ó, nyomorult, rászedett, [320]
	megtértedben hiún hivő, esendő
	Éva! Ó, sanda vég! Te már soha
	nem lelsz az Édenben se édes étket,
	se mély szunyát! Édes virágok, árnyak
	közt pokol gyűlölet les rád: hogy útad

EVE:	That such an Enemie we have, who seeks	
	Our ruin, I over-heard	
	But that thou shouldst my firmness therfore doubt	
	To God or thee, because we have a foe	
	May tempt it, I expected not to hear.	
	Thoughts, which how found they harbour in thy brest	
	Adam, misthought of her to thee so dear?	[300]
ADAM:	Not diffident of thee do I dissuade	
	Thy absence from my sight, but to avoid	
	Th' attempt itself,	
	Misdeem not then, If such affront I labour to avert.	
	I from the influence of thy looks receave	
	Access in every Vertue, in thy sight	
	More wise, more watchful, stronger.	
EVE:	If this be our condition, thus to dwell	
	In narrow circuit strait'nd by a Foe,	
	Suttle or violent, we not endu'd	[310]
	Single with like defence, wherever met,	
	How are we happie, still in fear of harm?	
	And what is Faith, Love, Vertue unassaid	
	Alone, without exterior help sustaind?	
ADAM:	Not mistrust, but tender love enjoynes,	
	That I should mind thee oft, and mind thou me.	
	Seek not temptation,	
	Trial will come unsought which to avoide	
	Were better, and most likelie if from mee	
	Thou sever not.	[320]
EVE:	With thy permission then, and thus forewarnd	
	The willinger I goe, nor much expect	
	A Foe so proud will first the weaker seek,	
	So bent, the more shall shame him his repulse.	
ADAM:	Come back soon.	
EVE:	By noon.	
DEATH:	O much deceav'd, much failing, hapless *Eve*,	
	Of thy presum'd return! event perverse!	
	Thou never from that houre in Paradise	
	Foundst either sweet repast, or sound repose;	[330]
	Such ambush hid among sweet Flours and Shades	
	Waited with hellish rancour imminent	

	szegje, vagy visszaküldjön elrabolva	
	hitedet és ártatlan üdvödet.	
BŰN:	Íly ritka véletlen! Íme egymagában Éva,	
SÁTÁN:	Mint ki városba zárva él,	
	ahol zsufolt házak, sürű csatornák	[330]
	döglesztik a leget, s kiszabadul	
	nyár-reggel, hogy szép faluban, tanyán	
	fellélegezzen . . . szín gyönyörre lel:	
	kéj a vetés-, tehén-, petrence-, tej-szag,	
	minden falusi kép, falusi hang;	
	s ha nimfa-léptű szép szűz csöppen arra:	
	mi szépnek látszott, még szebb lesz neki,	
	főleg a lány, kiben minden gyönyör	
	összpontosul.	
	Alakja égi, de angyalnál gyöngédebb nőies;	[340]
	ártatlan bája, minden moccanása, nyilvánulása.	
	Mi báj igéz, hogy elfeledtem, mi hozott	
	ide? Ármány, s nem szeretet.	
	Gyönyör nekem csupán a rontás.	
HALÁL:	Magában a nő, kiszolgáltatva támadásnak!	
BŰN:	Messze látok körül: nincs itt ura,	
SÁTÁN:	kinek inkább félem különb eszét, más öröm nekem	
	mind veszve már: nem hagyhatom szaladni	
	a rám mosolygó alkalmat.	
	Íly korán egyedül? Szép nő. Isteni szerelemre méltó!	[350]
	Ne ámulj, ha ámulni tudsz, királynő!	
	Hisz csak te vagy csoda! Ne fegyverezd	
	szelíd szép Mennyed: szemed megvetéssel,	
	hogy így közelgek hozzád, legszebb mása alkotódnak!	
ÉVA:	Ez mit jelentsen? Emberek szavával szól	
	állat, emberi érzéseket!	
SÁTÁN:	Méltón ott látszanál,	
	hol mindenek csodálnak! Ám e vad,	
	zárt térben, barmok közt, kik oktalan	
	szemlélőid, s félig se képesek	[360]
	meglátni, mi benned szép – kivéve egy	
	férfit . . . ki lát? (de egy: mi az!) –	

	To intercept thy way, or send thee back
	Despoild of Innocence, of Faith, of Bliss.
SIN:	Such rare chance! *Eve* separate.
SATAN:	As one who long in populous City pent,
	Where Houses thick and Sewers annoy the Aire,
	Forth issuing on a Summers Morn to breathe
	Among the pleasant Villages and Farmes
	Adjoynd, from each thing met conceaves delight, [340]
	The smell of Grain, or tedded Grass, or Kine,
	Or Dairie, each rural sight, each rural sound;
	If chance with Nymphlike step fair Virgin pass,
	What pleasing seemd, for her now pleases more,
	She most, and in her look summs all Delight.
	Her Heav'nly forme
	Angelic, but more soft, and Feminine,
	Her graceful Innocence, her every Aire
	Of gesture or lest action transported to forget
	What hither brought us, hate, not love, [350]
	Save what is in destroying, other joy
	To me is lost.
DEATH:	Behold alone
	The Woman, opportune to all attempts,
SIN:	Her Husband, for I view far round, not nigh,
SATAN:	Whose higher intellectual more I shun,
	other joy to me is lost: then let me not let pass
	Occasion which now smiles.
	Alone so early? Shee fair, divinely fair, fit Love for Gods!
	Wonder not, sovran Mistress, if perhaps [360]
	Thou canst, who art sole Wonder, much less arm
	Thy looks, the Heav'n of mildness, with disdain,
	Displeas'd that I approach thee thus,
	Fairest resemblance of thy Maker faire.
EVE:	What may this mean? Language of Man pronounc't
	By Tongue of Brute, and human sense exprest?
SATAN:	There best beheld
	Where universally admir'd; but here
	In this enclosure wild, these Beasts among,
	Beholders rude, and shallow to discerne [370]
	Half what in thee is fair, one man except,
	Who sees thee? (and what is one?)

ÉVA:	A tagolt beszédet, hittem, megtagadta
	Isten az állattól, kit alkotása
	napján beszédre némának teremtett.
	Lehet érzése – sejtem, hisz szemükben,
	tettükben gyakran csillan értelem.
SÁTÁN:	Pedig istennőt istenek közt kéne látni,
	imádni kéne számtalan angyaloknak,
	szolgálva néked kíséröidül. [370]
ÉVA:	Tudtam, te vagy, kigyó, a legravaszabb
	állat, de nem, hogy emberszót beszélsz!
	Ismételd e csodát, és mondd, hogyan
	lettél némából szólóvá, s irántam
	kedvesebb, mint a többi állat, amelyet
	naponta látok?
SÁTÁN:	E szép Föld császárnője, Éva
	Miként a többi füevő barom,
	elsőbb én is alantaslelkü voltam,
	étkem szerint: csak páromat, étkemet [380]
	ismertem, semmi más magasztosat.
	Ám egy nap a mezőn bolyongva,
	csodás fa tűnt szemembe, rakva szép
	vegyes-szinü gyümölccsel;
	Hogy tüzes vágyam oltsam, eltökéltem,
	a szép almát tüstént megízlelem;
	éh, szomj – nagy rábeszélők – ezek ösztökéltek,
	s a bájoló gyümölcs-szag ingerelt.
	Fölkúsztam hát, hogy szakajtsak –
	ilyen gyönyört [390]
	étel-italban eddig nem lelék.
	Jóllakva végre furcsa változást
	vettem magamban észre: szellemem
	az ész fokát elérte, és legott
	beszéltem is, de formám ez maradt.
	és szemléltem immár fogékony ésszel
	megannyi dolgot, szépet, jót, de minden
	szépet és jót is egyesülve látom
	isteni jelenésed s bájaid
	arany-sugarában, ez ösztökélt, [400]
	hogy bár talán terhedre, erre térjek,
	s bámuljalak, imádjalak, ki méltán
	vagy királynője minden alkotottnak!

EVE:	Language of Man of these I thought deni'd
	To Beasts, whom God on thir Creation-Day
	Created mute to all articulat sound;
	Sense I demurre, for in thir looks
	Much reason, and in thir actions oft appeers.
SATAN:	You shouldst be seen
	A Goddess among Gods, ador'd and serv'd
	By Angels numberless, thy daily Train. [380]
EVE:	Thee, Serpent, suttlest beast of all the field
	I knew, but not with human voice endu'd;
	Redouble then this miracle, and say,
	How cam'st thou speakable of mute, and how
	To me so friendly grown above the rest
	Of brutal kind, that daily are in sight?
SATAN:	Empress of this fair World, resplendent *Eve*,
	I was at first as other Beasts that graze
	The trodden Herb, of abject thoughts and low,
	As was my food, nor aught but food discern'd [390]
	Or Sex, and apprehended nothing high:
	Till on a day roaving the field, I chanc'd
	A goodly Tree farr distant to behold
	Loaden with fruit of fairest colours mixt,
	To satisfie the sharp desire I had
	Of tasting those fair Apples, I resolv'd
	Not to deferr; hunger and thirst at once,
	Powerful perswaders, quick'nd at the scent
	Of that alluring fruit, urg'd me so keene.
	About the mossie Trunk I wound me soon, [400]
	To pluck and eat my fill.
	Such pleasure till that hour
	At Feed or Fountain never had I found.
	Sated at length, ere long I might perceave
	Strange alteration in me, to degree
	Of Reason in my inward Powers, and Speech
	Wanted not long, though to this shape retain'd.
	And with capacious mind
	Considerd all things fair and good;
	But all that fair and good in thy Divine [410]
	Semblance, and in thy Beauties heav'nly Ray
	United I beheld; which compel'd
	Mee thus, though importune perhaps, to come
	And gaze, and worship thee of right declar'd
	Sovran of Creatures, universal Dame.

ÉVA:	Túlzó dicséreted kétséget ébreszt	
	a gyümölcs erénye felől, amit először	
	te próbáltál ki. De mondd, hol nőtt e fa,	
	míly messze?	
SÁTÁN:	Ha vezérletem	
	meg nem veted, hozzá viszlek hamar.	
ÉVA:	Vezess!	[410]
	Kár volt a fáradás, hiába-út,	
	– kigyó! E fa nekem gyümölcstelen,	
	bármíly dusan terem. Erényei	
	hite maradjon így csupán veled!	
	Csodás, ha így hat. Ám e fát mi nem	
	érinthetjük – az Úr parancsolá!	
SÁTÁN:	Azt mondta hát az Isten, hogy e Kert	
	egy fájának gyümölcséből se egyél,	
	s föld, lég urának tett kettőtöket?	
ÉVA:	A kertben minden fának gyümölcséből ehetsz,	[420]
	hanem a kertközépi tetszetős	
	fának gyümölcséből ne egyél – az Úr szólt –,	
	ingyen se illesd, hogy belé ne halj!	
ÁDÁM [KINT]:	Éva! Éva!	
SÁTÁN:	Mindenség Királynője! Ó, ne higgy	
	halálriasztásnak! Nem lész halott!	
	Mitől is? A gyümölcstől? A tudás	
	életet ád. Tekints rám!	
	Én érintettem, ettem, s élek ím,	
	sőt különb létet nyertem tőle, mint	[430]
	amit kirótt a Végzet, még magasabbra	
	merészkedtem. Embernek zárva van,	
	mi nincs baromnak?	
	Mért tiltja hát? Hogy megriasszon, és	
	alantas és tudatlan állapotban	
	tartson szolgáinak? Hisz tudja, mely nap	
	ízlelitek, látónak hitt, de mégis	
	vak szemetek megnyílik teljesen,	
	s lát élesen, és lesztek istenekkel	
	egyenlőkké: jó s rossz tudóivá,	[440]
	mint ők! Ti istenekké, hogyha én	
	belül emberré lettem – így arányos.	
	S mért bűn, ha az	
	ember eképp tudást nyer? És mit árt	
	az Istennek tudástok, ha	

EVE:	Serpent, thy overpraising leaves in doubt
	The vertue of that Fruit, in thee first prov'd:
	But say, where grows the Tree, from hence how far?
SATAN:	The way is readie, and not long,
	If thou accept my conduct, I can bring thee
	thither soon. [420]
EVE:	Lead then.
	Serpent, we might have spar'd our coming hither,
	Fruitless to mee, though Fruit be here to excess,
	The credit of whose vertue rest with thee,
	But of this Tree we may not taste nor touch;
	God so commanded.
SATAN:	Indeed? hath God then said that of the Fruit
	Of all these Garden Trees ye shall not eate,
	Yet Lords declar'd of all in Earth or Aire?
EVE:	Of the Fruit [430]
	Of each Tree in the Garden we may eate,
	But of the Fruit of this fair Tree amidst
	The Garden, God hath said, Ye shall not eate
	Thereof, nor shall ye touch it, least ye die.
ADAM [OUTSIDE]:	Eve! Eve!
SATAN:	Queen of this Universe, doe not believe
	Those rigid threats of Death; ye shall not Die:
	How should ye? by the Fruit? it gives you Life
	To Knowledge. Look on mee,
	Mee who have touch'd and tasted, yet both live, [440]
	And life more perfet have attaind then Fate
	Meant mee, by ventring higher then my Lot.
	Shall that be shut to Man, which to the Beast
	Is open?
	Why then was this forbid? Why but to awe,
	Why but to keep ye low and ignorant,
	His worshippers; he knows that in the day
	Ye Eate thereof, your Eyes that seem so cleere,
	Yet are but dim, shall perfetly be then
	Op'nd and cleerd, and ye shall be as Gods, [450]
	Knowing both Good and Evil as they know.
	That ye should be as Gods, since I as Man,
	Internal Man, is but proportion meet.
	Wherein lies th' offence,
	That Man should thus attain to know?
	What can your knowledge hurt him, or this Tree

	minden övé? Vagy tán irígy? Lakozhat	
	irígység Istenben? Szükségtek van e	
	gyümölcsre. Ember-istennő! Szakajtsd le!	
ÉVA:	Szóval mit is tilt? A tudást, a jót,	
	és hogy bölcsek legyünk! Íly tilalom	[450]
	nem köthet! Ám ha a Halál utóbb	
	csak úr lesz rajtunk, mit segít e benső	
	szabadságunk? Amely napon eszünk	
	e gyümölcsből, az ítélet szerint	
	halállal bűnhődünk. Halott a kígyó?	
	Evett és él. Vagy csak nekünk	
	fundálták a halált? E kígyó	
	ki először ette, mégsem irígy: örömmel	
	ajánlja föl a nyert előnyt nekünk;	
	álnok gyanútól ment emberbarát.	[460]
	Mit féljek én? Hogy is tudnám, mitől	
	féljek, ha nem tudom, mi a jó, a rossz,	
	Isten, Halál, törvény, vagy büntetés?	
	Itt nől az ír, az isteni gyümölcs –	
	s harapni ingerel! Ugyan mi gátol,	
	hogy testemet s elmémet élesítse?	
	Királyi fa! Az Éden fái közt	
	te legkülönb! Tudásra elvezérlő,	
	eddig rágalmazott, homályba vont!	
	Mint céltalant, gyümölcsöd csüngni hagyták.	[470]
	Mától fogva legfőbb ügyem nekem,	
	hogy minden reggel én gondozzalak	
	méltó dalos magasztalással, és	
	megkönnyítsem tenyésző terhedet.	
SÁTÁN:	Mindenható, letépte és eszi.	
	Sebét a Föld megérzi, és a Tenyészet	
	szivéből felsóhajt minden müve,	
	és följajong, hogy minden elveszett.	
HALÁL:	Mohón csak ette,	
	nem tudva, hogy halált nyel.	[480]
BŰN:	Végül eldőlt,	
	mint borba részegült.	
2. ANGYAL:	Ó Gábriel! Rád bízatott az őrség,	
	hogy ébren vigyázd az Édenhez	
	gonosz ne közelítsen.	
GÁBRIEL:	Az imént egy szellem jött	

	Impart against his will if all be his?	
	Or is it envie, and can envie dwell	
	In Heav'nly brests? You need this fair Fruit.	
	Goddess humane, reach then, and freely taste.	[460]
EVE:	What forbids he but to know,	
	Forbids us good, forbids us to be wise?	
	Such prohibitions binde not. But if Death	
	Bind us with after-bands, what profits then	
	Our inward freedom? In the day we eate	
	Of this fair Fruit, our doom is, we shall die.	
	How dies the Serpent? hee hath eat'n and lives,	
	For us alone	
	Was death invented? Yet that one Beast which first	
	Hath tasted, envies not, but brings with joy	[470]
	The good befall'n him, Author unsuspect,	
	Friendly to man, farr from deceit or guile.	
	What fear I then, rather what know to feare	
	Under this ignorance of good and Evil,	
	Of God or Death, of Law or Penaltie?	
	Here grows the Cure of all, this Fruit Divine,	
	Inviting to the Taste, what hinders then	
	To reach, and feed at once both Bodie and Mind?	
	O Sovran, vertuous, precious of all Trees	
	In Paradise, of operation blest	[480]
	To Sapience, hitherto obscur'd, infam'd,	
	And thy fair Fruit let hang, as to no end	
	Created; but henceforth my early care,	
	Not without Song, each Morning, and due praise	
	Shall tend thee, and the fertil burden ease.	
SATAN:	God Almighty, she pluck'd, she eat:	
	Earth feels the wound, and Nature from her seat	
	Sighing through all her Works gives signs of woe,	
	That all is lost.	
DEATH:	Greedily she ingorg'd without restraint,	[490]
	And knew not eating Death	
SIN:	Satiate at length,	
	And hight'nd as with Wine, jocond and boon.	
ANGEL 2:	*Gabriel*, to thee thy course by Lot hath giv'n	
	Charge and strict watch that to this happie place	
	No evil thing approach or enter in.	
GABRIEL:	This day came to my Spheare	

	hogy lássa a Mindenható műveit	
	észrevettem: lénye nem égi	
	egy volt a számüzött bandából.	
	Félek, felszökött a Mélyből,	[490]
	hogy szítson új viszályt.	
1. ANGYAL:	Vigyázz! Keresd meg!	
	Itt e kapun át nem enged senkit	
	az ide rendelt őr; csak azt,	
	kit ismer: égből jött.	
2. ANGYAL:	De senki nem jött	
	déltől ilyen.	
GÁBRIEL:	Biztos lehetsz, hogy számot adsz	
	küldőnknek, kinek tiszte: védeni	
	minden bajtól e szent helyet s az embert.	[500]
ÉVA:	Mint kerüljek Ádám	
	szeme elé? Áruljam el neki	
	változásom, és béavassam őt	
	üdvöm teljébe, vagy ne? Bölcseségem	
	előnyeit megtartsam en-kezemben,	
	társ nélkül: így pótoljam nő-nemem	
	hiányait, s szerelmét fölcsigázva	
	legyek vele egyenlővé – utóbb tán	
	(mit úgy óhajtok) felsőbbrendüvé?	
	Alsóbbrendű miképp lehet szabad?	[510]
	Ez szép – de hátha észrevett az Úr,	
	s zsoldom: halál? Én többé nem leszek,	
	Ádám elvesz más Évát, s él vele	
	boldog gyönyörben, hogyha már kihúnytam.	
	Halálos gondolat! Nos eltökéltem,	
	osszon meg Ádám kínt, gyönyört velem!	
	úgy szeretem: vele minden halált	
	kibírok, s nélküle nem kell a Lét!	
[ÁDÁMHOZ MEGY]		
	Nem ámultál, miért maradtam el?	
	Különös volt az ok,	[520]
	s csodálatos a hallomása – mert	
	nem igaz, mi mondatott nekünk: hogy nem szabad	
	a fát érintenünk, nem is nyit útat	
	még nem tudott gonosznak, hanem épp	
	erénye égi, mert szemünk kinyitja,	
	s istenné teszi azt, ki ízleli.	
	Ma megtörtént ez, mert a bölcs kígyó –	

	A Spirit to know more of th' Almighties works,	
	I soon discernd his looks	
	Alien from Heav'n, one of the banisht crew	[500]
	I fear, hath ventur'd from the deep, to raise	
	New troubles.	
ANGEL 1:	Him thy care must be to find.	
	In at this Gate none pass	
	The vigilance here plac't, but such as come	
	Well known from Heav'n;	
ANGEL 2:	and since Meridian hour	
	No Creature thence.	
GABRIEL:	Be sure, thou shalt give account	
	To him who sent us, whose charge is to keep	[510]
	This place inviolable, and these from harm.	
EVE:	But to *Adam* in what sort	
	Shall I appeer? shall I to him make known	
	As yet my change, and give him to partake	
	Full happiness with mee, or rather not,	
	But keep the odds of Knowledge in my power	
	Without Copartner? so to add what wants	
	In Femal Sex, the more to draw his Love,	
	And render me more equal, and perhaps,	[520]
	A thing not undesireable, somtime	
	Superior: for inferior who is free?	
	This may be well: but what if God have seen	
	And Death ensue? then I shall be no more,	
	And *Adam* wedded to another *Eve*,	
	Shall live with her enjoying, I extinct;	
	A death to think. Confirm'd then I resolve,	
	Adam shall share with me in bliss or woe:	
	So dear I love him, that with him all deaths	
	I could endure, without him live no life.	
[GOES TO ADAM]		
	Hast thou not wonderd, *Adam*, at my stay?	[530]
	But strange	
	Hath bin the cause, and wonderful to heare:	
	This Tree is not as we are told, a Tree	
	Forbidden to Taste,[13] nor to evil unknown	
	Op'ning the way, but of Divine effect	
	To open Eyes, and make them Gods who taste;	
	And hath bin tasted such: the Serpent wise,	

| | vagy el nem tiltva, mint mi, vagy dacolva –
| | evett az almából, s nem lett halott,
| | és ettem és valónak éltem át   [530]
| | hatását: volt ködös szemem kinyílt,
| | szivem kitágult, szellemem sugárzik,
| | s istenné nőttem, mind csupán teérted!
| | Ingyen se kéne nélküled! Egyél,
| | hogy egyenlő sors kössön össze minket,
| | egyenlő szerelem, gyönyör! Különben
| | ha nem eszel, más és más fokozat
| | rekeszt el minket, s isten-voltomat
| | el kéne dobnom érted – ámde már
| | késő: a Végzet ezt nem engedi!   [540]
ÁDÁM: | Isten legjobb, legszebb végalkotása,
| | tökélye mindannak, mi gondolatba,
| | látványba önthető: mi istenes,
| | szent, jó, édes, imádandó – miképp
| | buktál el, íly hamar-romlásba, arcod,
| | virágod vesztve, most halálra szánt!?
| | Hogy szeghetted meg a kemény tilalmat,
| | beszeplőzvén a tiltott szent gyümölcsöt?
| | Egy ismeretlen ellenség csele
| | csalt vesztedbe, s magaddal engem is   [550]
| | romlásba vert, mert szikla-szándokom,
| | hogy veled haljak! Nélküled hogy is
| | élhetnék? Édes társaságodat
| | hogy nélkülözném, egybekelt frigyünket?
| | Hogy élnék e vadonban egymagam?
| | Isten talán teremtne másik Évát, ujabb bordámból,
| | ám hiányodat szivem sosem tudná feledni! Nem!
| | Érzem: a természet bilincse von;
| | csont a csontomból, hús husomból – ez vagy!
| | Érjen üdv,kín, tőled nem válhatok!   [560]
| | Nem hiszem, hogy a bölcs nagy Alkotó,
| | bár fenyeget, valóban elsöpörne
| | minket, kiket oly nagyra méltatott.
| | Mindegy. Hozzád kötöttem sorsomat.
| | Itéletedben osztozom. Ha meghalsz,
| | halok veled! Halál lesz nékem élet!
ÉVA: | Ha gondolnám, hogy e merényletemnek
| | halál a zsoldja, úgy csak egymagam
| | tűrném a legszörnyűbbet, s tégedet
| | nem bújtanálak, ám ugy érzem én, egész más   [570]
| | sarjad belőle: nem halál, de fölsőbb
| | élet, nyíltabb szem, új öröm, remény
| | s oly isteni íz, mihez képest az eddig

	Or not restraind as wee, or not obeying,	
	Hath eat'n of the fruit, and is become,	
	Not dead. I Have also tasted, and have also found	[540]
	Th' effects to correspond, opener mine Eyes	
	Dimm erst, dilated Spirits, ampler Heart,	
	And growing up to Godhead; which for thee	
	Chiefly I sought, without thee can despise.	
	Thou therefore also taste, that equal Lot	
	May joyne us, equal Joy, as equal Love;	
	Least thou not tasting, different degree	
	Disjoyne us, and I then too late renounce	
	Deitie for thee, when Fate will not permit.	
ADAM:	O fairest of Creation, last and best	[550]
	Of all Gods works, Creature in whom excell'd	
	Whatever can to sight or thought be formd,	
	Holy, divine, good, amiable, or sweet!	
	How art thou lost, how on a sudden lost,	
	Defac't, deflourd, and now to Death devote?	
	Rather how hast thou yeelded to transgress	
	The strict forbiddance, how to violate	
	The sacred Fruit forbidd'n! som cursed fraud	
	Of Enemie hath beguil'd thee, yet unknown,	[560]
	And mee with thee hath ruind, for with thee	
	Certain my resolution is to Die;	
	How can I live without thee, how forgoe	
	Thy sweet Converse and Love so dearly joyn'd,	
	To live again in these wilde Woods forlorn?	
	Should God create another Eve, and I	
	Another Rib afford, yet loss of thee	
	Would never from my heart; no no, I feel	
	The Link of Nature draw me: Flesh of Flesh,	
	Bone of my Bone thou art, and from thy State	
	Mine never shall be parted, bliss or woe.	[570]
	Nor can I think that God, Creator wise,	
	Though threatning, will in earnest so destroy	
	Us his prime Creatures, dignifi'd so high.	
	However I with thee have fixt my Lot,	
	Certain to undergoe like doom, if Death	
	Consort with thee, Death is to mee as Life.	
EVE:	Were it I thought Death menac't would ensue	
	This my attempt, I would sustain alone	
	The worst, and not perswade thee, rather die.	
	Farr otherwise th' event, not Death, but Life	[580]
	Augmented, op'nd Eyes, new Hopes, new Joyes,	
	Taste so Divine, that what of sweet before	

	érzékelt minden édesség nekem	
	silánynak tűnt. Kövesd példámat, Ádám!	
	Egyél, szórd szélbe halálfélelmedet!	
SÁTÁN:	Mindenható, letépte és eszi.	
	Sebét a Föld megérzi, és a Tenyészet	
	szivéből felsóhajt minden müve,	
	és följajong, hogy minden elveszett.	[580]
GÁBRIEL:	Tudták, kellett tudniuk	
	a szent parancsot: bárki is kisért,	
	ne izleljék az almát, mit ha meg-	
	szegnek, jön a büntetés.	
	Sokszor bűnösek, bukásra méltók!	
3. ANGYAL:	Mint tudott a fondor Ellen	
	besettenkedni.	
GÁBRIEL:	Mentsük magunkat, hisz éberen vigyáztunk.	
ÁDÁM:	Kinyílt szemünk, tudjuk, mi jó, mi rossz.	
	Veszett a jó, nyakunkon a gonosz;	[590]
	tudás gonosz gyümölcse, hogyha ezt kell	
	tudnunk, mi lecsupaszít, becsületünktől	
	megfoszt, ártatlanságunktól, hitünktől,	
	hajdani díszünktől, mi már mocsok!	
	És arcunkon a rút sóvár gyönyör	
	nyilván jele, honnan a bűn zudul	
	s bűn vége, szégyen! Vesztünkről tehát	
	biztos lehetsz már. Mint viseljem el	
	eztán Isten orcáját, angyalét,	
	mit eddig néztem elragadtatással?	[600]
	Rejtsetek el, fenyők, ezernyi ágú	
	cédrusfák, hogy többé ne lássam őket!	
	Most azt eszeljük ki: gyalázatunkban	
	egymás elől illetlen részeinket	
	hogy rejtsük el, miket szemlélni szégyen,	
	mert csúfak!	
ÉVA:	Tán akad néhány fa, melynek	
	nagy, puha lombjait egymásba fűzve	
	felövezzük csípőnket; elfedik	
	e részeket, hogy a szégyen ott ne üljön,	[610]
	ez új jövevény, s ne tárjon fel csunyát.	

	Hath toucht my sense, flat seems to this, and harsh.
	On my experience, *Adam*, freely taste,
	And fear of Death deliver to the Windes.
SATAN:	God Almighty, he pluck'd, he eat:
	Earth feels the wound, and Nature from her seat
	Sighing through all her Works gives signs of woe,
	That all is lost.
GABRIEL:	They knew, and ought to have still remember'd [590]
	The high Injunction not to taste that Fruit,
	Whoever tempted; which they not obeying,
	Incurr'd, what could they less, the penaltie,
	And manifold in sin, deserv'd to fall.
ANGEL 3:	How the suttle Fiend had stoln
	Entrance unseen.
GABRIEL:	Towards the Throne Supream
	Accountable let's haste to make appear
	With righteous plea, our utmost vigilance.
ADAM:	Our Eyes [600]
	Op'nd we find indeed, and find we know
	Both Good and Evil, Good lost, and Evil got,
	Bad Fruit of Knowledge, if this be to know,
	Which leaves us naked thus, of Honour void,
	Of Innocence, of Faith, of Puritie,
	Our wonted Ornaments now soild and staind,
	And in our Faces evident the signes
	Of foul concupiscence; whence evil store;
	Even shame, the last of evils; of the first
	Be sure then. How shall I behold the face [610]
	Henceforth of God or Angel, earst with joy
	And rapture so oft beheld?
	Cover me ye Pines,
	Ye Cedars, hide me, where I may never see them more.
	But let us now, as in bad plight, devise
	What best may for the present serve to hide
	The Parts of each from other, that seem most
	To shame obnoxious, and unseemliest seen.
EVE:	Some Tree whose broad smooth Leaves together sowd,
	And girded on our loyns, may cover round [620]
	Those middle parts, that this new commer, Shame,
	There sit not, and reproach us as unclean.

ÁDÁM:	Hallgattál volna szavaimra, és
	maradtál volna velem – Hogy kértelek! –
ÉVA:	. . . és ha maradok veled,
	ki tudja, vajh nem esett volna meg
	előtted is, vagy épp veled? Ha ott vagy,
	vagy itt ront rád a kígyó, hátha te
	sem gyanitottál volna cselt, ha úgy
	szól, mint beszélt?! Köztünk gyülölködésre
	nem volt ok, mért hihettem volna, hogy [620]
	károm kivánja? S ha az vagyok,
	aki vagyok, mint főm, határozottan
	mért nem parancsoltad: ne menjek el
	veszélybe úgy, mint mondtad?
	Ha tiltásodban sziklaszilárd maradsz,
	nem buktam volna el, s te sem velem!
ÁDÁM:	Ez a szerelmed? Zsoldja az enyémnek,
	hálátlan Éva. Nem eléggé zordonul
	tiltottalak. Ezen fölül erőszak
	lett volna hátra. Szabad akaratnál [630]
	nincs helye annak.
	Így jár, aki fejére hagyja nőni
	a nőt, értékét túlbecsülve . . . a nő
	nem tűr korlátot, és magára hagyva
	ha vész, okolja férje gyönge voltát!
FIÚ:	Vádolja csak egyik a másikát
	sok meddő órán, önmagát egyik sem
	itéli el – s nincs vége hiú pöruknek.
ATYA:	Bukott. S mi más van hátra? Lássa bűne
	halálitéletét; kimondatott [640]
	aznap, habár hivé üres beszédnek,
	mert nem azonnal szállt fejére, mint
	rettegte ő. Nem múlik még e nap
	s megtudja: tűrés nem feloldozás!
	Az Igazság nem szenved gúnyt,
	nem úgy, miként a jóság szenvedett.
	De kit küldjek itéletére? Téged?
	Fiam-helyettesem. Reád ruháztam
	Ég-Föld-Pokol minden itéletét.
	Értsék hamar: szándékom az, hogy az [650]
	igazsággal irgalmat társitok.
	emberré kell lenned, hogy rajtuk ítélj!

ADAM:	Would thou hadst heark'nd to my words, and stai'd
	With me, as I besought thee!
EVE:	. . . Who knows but might as ill have happ'nd thou being by,
	Or to thy self perhaps: hadst thou been there,
	Or here th' attempt, thou couldst not have discernd
	Fraud in the Serpent, speaking as he spake;
	No ground of enmitie between us known,
	Why hee should mean me ill, or seek to harme? [630]
	Being as I am, why didst not thou the Head
	Command me absolutely not to go,
	Going into such danger as thou saidst?
	Hadst thou bin firm and fixt in thy dissent,
	Neither had I transgress'd, nor thou with mee.
ADAM:	Is this the Love, is this the recompence
	Of mine to thee, ingrateful *Eve*, exprest?
	Not enough severe,
	It seems, in thy restraint: what could I more?
	Beyond this had bin force, [640]
	And force upon free Will hath here no place.
	Thus it shall befall
	Him who to worth in Women overtrusting
	Lets her will rule; restraint she will not brook,
	And left to her self, if evil thence ensue,
	Shee first his weak indulgence will accuse.
SON:	Thus they in mutual accusation spend
	The fruitless hours, but neither self-condemning,
	And of thir vain contest appears no end.
GOD:	But fall'n he is, and now [650]
	What rests but that the mortal Sentence pass
	On his transgression Death denounc't that day,
	Which he presumes already vain and void,
	Because not yet inflicted, as he fear'd,
	By some immediate stroak; but soon shall find
	Forbearance no acquittance ere day end.
	Justice shall not return as bountie scorn'd.
	But whom send I to judge them? whom but thee
	Vicegerent Son, to thee I have transferr'd
	All Judgement whether in Heav'n, or Earth, or Hell. [660]
	Easie it might be seen that I intend
	Mercie collegue with Justice, sending thee
	Destin'd Man himself to judge Man fall'n.

FIÚ:	Örök Atyám, tiéd a rendelés,
	enyém, hogy Égen-Földön megtegyem
	végső parancsod, hogy rajtam, szerelmes
	fiadon lelked boldogan nyugodjék.
ATYA:	Várj! Megyek, magam megítélem törvényszegőid.
FIÚ:	Ám tudod, bármi légyen az itélet,
	vállalnom kell a legszörnyűbbet – így
	fogadtam ezt előtted, meg se bántam. [660]
	Így jogot nyertem, hogy magamra véve,
	enyhítsem büntetésük irgalommal,
	az igazságot úgy vegyítve, hogy ők is
	kielégüljenek, s te is megenyhülj.
ATYA:	Ádám, hol vagy? Ki máskor messziről
	futottál már, hogy láss! Nem tetszel így
	magányba bujdokolva. Máskor a
	kész kötelesség keresetlenül
	előhozott. Nem veszel észre ma?
	Mi változás tart távol? Jöjj elő! [670]
ÁDÁM:	Hallgattalak a kertben, és szavadtól
	megfélemlék, mivel mezítelen
	vagyok.
ATYA:	Szavamat gyakran hallhattad, s nem riadtál –
	örültél néki! Most egyszerre mint
	lett szörnyüvé? Ki mondta, hogy mezítlen
	vagy? Ettél tán a fáról, a gyümölcsből,
	amelytől eltiltottalak: ne edd?
ÁDÁM:	E nő, kit alkotál segélyemül,
	oly szép, tökéletes, kivánatos [680]
	Ég-adománya volt, hogy semmi rosszra
	nem gyanakodtam tőle. Bármi tette
	már önmagában igazolni látszott,
	amit tett. Ő szakajtott, s ettem én!
ATYA:	Hát ő volt istened, hogy az én igémet
	mellőzve őt követted? Mesteredül
	teremtetett, különbnek, vagy veled
	egyrangunak, hogy férfivoltodat
	reáruházd s a posztot, melyre Isten
	fölébe helyezett? [690]
	Mit cselekedtél, asszony, mondd csak el?

SON:	Father Eternal, thine is to decree,	
	Mine both in Heav'n and Earth to do thy will	
	Supream, that thou in mee thy Son belov'd	
	Mayst ever rest well pleas'd.	
GOD:	Wait, I go to judge	
	On Earth these thy transgressors.	
SON:	But thou knowst,	[670]
	Whoever judg'd, the worst on mee must light,	
	For so I undertook before thee; and not repenting, this obtaine	
	Of right, that I may mitigate thir doom	
	On me deriv'd, yet I shall temper so	
	Justice with Mercie, as may illustrate most	
	Them fully satisfied, and thee appease.	
GOD:	Where art thou *Adam*, wont with joy to meet	
	My coming seen far off? I miss thee here,	
	Not pleas'd, thus entertaind with solitude,	
	Where obvious dutie erewhile appear'd unsaught:	[680]
	Or come I less conspicuous, or what change	
	Absents thee, or what chance detains? Come forth.	
ADAM:	I heard thee in the Garden, and of thy voice	
	Affraid, being naked, hid my self.	
GOD:	My voice thou oft hast heard, and hast not fear'd,	
	But still rejoyc't, how is it now become	
	So dreadful to thee? that thou art naked, who	
	Hath told thee? hast thou eaten of the Tree	
	Whereof I gave thee charge thou shouldst not eat?	
ADAM:	This Woman whom thou mad'st to be my help,	[690]
	And gav'st me as thy perfet gift, so good,	
	So fit, so acceptable, so Divine,	
	That from her hand I could suspect no ill,	
	And what she did, whatever in it self,	
	Her doing seem'd to justifie the deed;	
	Shee gave me of the Tree, and I did eate.	
GOD:	Was shee thy God, that her thou didst obey	
	Before his voice, or was shee made thy guide,	
	Superior, or but equal, that to her	
	Thou did'st resigne thy Manhood, and the Place	[700]
	Wherein God set thee above her made of thee?	
	Say Woman, what is this which thou hast done?	

ÉVA:	A kígyó áltatott el. Ettem én!	
1. ANGYAL:	Elsőnek a kígyót itélte meg	
ATYA:	Mert ezt tetted, légy átkozott e Föld összes barma közül te egymagad! Csússz hasadon, s vak élted napjain egyed a port! Teközted és e nő közt ellenkezést szerzek, közötted és sarja között!	
1. ANGYAL:	Az asszonyon meg így itélkezett:	[700]
ATYA:	Megsokasítom szenvedésedet, méhed kínját: szüld fájdalomban a magzatjaid, s legyél alávetett urad kényének; ő legyen királyod!	
1. ANGYAL:	Végül Ádám fejére szólt szava:	
ATYA:	E Föld tövisset és bogáncsot teremjen néked, edd a rét füvét! Arcod verítékével edd kenyered. Míg földdé léssz, mert abból vétettél; tudd meg, miből születtél: por vagy és porrá kell lenned itt!	[710]
FIÚ:	Itélt az Úr, Biró is egyben, az e napra igért halált halasztva. Szánta őket.	
SÁTÁN:	Trónok, hatalmak, hercegségek, erények, erők! Beléhelyeztetett kertjébe az ember, ki elűzetésünk árán lett boldog. Mesterétül őt elcsábitottam csellel, Isten ezen megorrolván (kacagjatok csak!) átadta kedves emberét s világát prédául a Halálnak, Bűnnek –így nekünk, hogy kockázat, törettetés nélkül bírván meglakjuk, és urak legyünk az emberen, amint neki kellett volna uralkodni mindenen. Igaz, megítélt engem is, vagy inkább nem is engem, de a kigyót, kinek	[720]

EVE:	The Serpent me beguil'd and I did eate.
ANGEL 1:	Which when the Lord God heard, without delay
	To Judgement he proceeded on th' accus'd
	Serpent.
GOD:	Because thou hast done this, thou art accurst
	Above all Cattle, each Beast of the Field;
	Upon thy Belly groveling thou shalt goe,
	And dust shalt eat all the dayes of thy Life. [710]
	Between Thee and the Woman I will put
	Enmitie, and between thine and her Seed!
ANGEL 1:	And to the Woman thus his Sentence turn'd:
GOD:	Thy sorrow I will greatly multiplie
	By thy Conception; Children thou shalt bring
	In sorrow forth, and to thy Husbands will
	Thine shall submit, hee over thee shall rule.
ANGEL 1:	On *Adam* last thus judgement he pronounc'd.
GOD:	Thou in sorrow shalt eate all the days of thy Life;
	Thorns also and Thistles the ground shall bring
	thee forth [720]
	Unbid, and thou shalt eate th' Herb of th' Field,
	In the sweat of thy Face shalt thou eat Bread,
	Till thou return unto the ground, for thou
	Out of the ground wast taken, know thy Birth,
	For dust thou art, and shalt to dust returne.
SON:	So judg'd he Man, both Judge and Saviour sent,
	And th' instant stroke of Death denounc't that day,
	Pittying them.
SATAN:	Thrones, Dominations, Princedoms, Vertues, Powers,
	Man was plac't in a Paradise, by our exile [730]
	Made happie: Him by fraud I have seduc'd
	From his Creator; he thereat
	Offended, worth your laughter, hath giv'n up
	Both his beloved Man and all his World,
	To Sin and Death a prey,
	And so to us,
	Without our hazard, labour, or allarme,
	To range in, and to dwell, and over Man
	To rule, as over all he should have rul'd.
	True is, mee also he hath judg'd, or rather [740]
	Mee not, but the brute Serpent in whose shape

	álcájában áltattam el az embert.	
	Gyülölködést szerez közöttem és az	[730]
	ember között; sarkát marom meg én,	
	utóda meg fejem bezúzza (nincs	
	kimondva, hogy mikor). Ki nem szerezne	
	fejbezuzás árán egész világot.	
	Vagy nyakatok lesúnnyjátok, s kivántok	
	térdelni inkább? Nem! Ha mint remélem,	
	jól ismerem valótok, és ti is	
	ismeritek! Ég-szülte ős fiak	
	vagyunk, akik nem voltak senkié,	
	s ha nem is egyenlők, de szabadok,	[740]
	egyenlőn szabadok.	
ÖRDÖGÖK:	Egyenlőn szabadok.	
SÁTÁN:	Egyeduralmat ki vehet magára	
	ésszel vagy joggal az egyenjogúak	
	fölött, mégha ezek fényben s erőben	
	kisebbek is, de egyként szabadok?	
	És ki szabhat törvényt nekünk, akik	
	törvény nélkül se vétkezünk? S mi több,	
	urunk legyen, s imádatot kivánjon	
	király cimünket megcsufolva, mely	[750]
	uralomra, nem szolgaságra rendelt?	
ÖRDÖGÖK:	Nem szolgaságra rendelt.	
SÁTÁN:	Mi van még hátra, istenek?	
	A teljes üdvbe lépjetek be! Föl!	
1. ANGYAL:	Gyalázhatod bitang szitokkal	
	Isten méltányos döntését,	
	Szerinted	
	jogtalan, hogy törvénnyel kösse meg	
	valaki azt, ki szabad, és egyenlők	
	fölött uralkodjék egy mind fölött	[760]
	örökjogon?	
3. ANGYAL:	Te szabsz törvényt az Úrnak?	
GÁBRIEL:	És a szabadság pontjait vele	
	épp te vitatod meg, kinek személyét	
	ő gyúrta s mind az Ég hatalmait	
	szabad kedvére, és kiszabta lényük?	
2. ANGYAL:	Tapasztalatból tudjuk, Ő milyen jó,	
	méltóságunkra mint munkál s javunkra:	
	szándéka nem, hogy kisebbé tegyen	

	Man I deceav'd: that which to mee belongs,
	Is enmity, which he will put between
	Mee and Mankinde; I am to bruise his heel;
	His Seed, when is not set, shall bruise my head:
	A World who would not purchase with a bruise?
	Will ye submit your necks, and chuse to bend
	The supple knee? ye will not, if I trust
	To know ye right, or if ye know your selves
	Natives and Sons of Heav'n possest before [750]
	By none, and if not equal all, yet free,
	Equally free,
DEVILS:	Equally free.
SATAN:	Who can in reason then or right assume
	Monarchie over such as live by right
	His equals, if in power and splendor less,
	In freedome equal? or can introduce
	Law and Edict on us, who without law
	Erre not, much less for this to be our Lord,
	And look for adoration to th' abuse [760]
	Of those Imperial Titles which assert
	Our being ordain'd to govern, not to serve?
DEVILS:	Not to serve!
SATAN:	What remains, ye Gods,
	But up and enter now into full bliss.
ANGEL 1:	Canst thou with impious obloquie condemne
	The just Decree of God?
	Unjust, saist thou
	To binde with Laws the free,
	And equal over equals to let Reigne, [770]
	One over all with unsucceeded power?
ANGEL 3:	Shalt thou give Law to God?
GABRIEL:	Shalt thou dispute
	With him the points of libertie, who made
	Thee what thou art, and formd the Pow'rs of Heav'n
	Such as he pleasd, and circumscrib'd thir being?
ANGEL 2:	By experience taught we know how good,
	And of our good, and of our dignitie
	How provident he is, how farr from thought

	bennünket, inkább szeretné emelni	[770]
	szerencsénket.	
1. ANGYAL:	Törvénye törvényünk, s ránk visszaszáll,	
	ha tiszteljük. Fojtsd el gonosz dühöd!	
	Ezeket ne kisértsd! A dühre gerjedt	
	Atyát s Fiát siess megcsöndesítni,	
	míg – időben – irgalmuk nyerheted!	
SÁTÁN:	Inkább Pokolban úr, mint szolga Égben.	
	Szép lányom, és te unokám-fiam!	
	Bizonyságát adtátok, hogy a Sátán	
	faja vagytok. Most szálljatok a	[780]
	Paradicsomba, s királykodjatok	
	nagy üdvben ott, a Földön és a Légben	
	s főképp az emberen, ki mindenek	
	urának mondatott. Elébb tegyétek	
	rabbá, aztán öljétek meg! A Földre	
	teljhatalmú helyettesül bocsátlak	
	benneteket, nem rontható hatalmam	
	belétek öntve! Egyesült erőtök	
	megtarthatja most nekem ez új uralmat,	
	mit Bűn Halálnak ád merényletem	[790]
	nyomán. Ha győztök együtt, a Pokol	
	dolgát ne féltsük!	
BŰN:	Sátán másod-szülötte, mindenen	
	győztes Halál! Mit szólsz újabb honunkhoz?	
HALÁL:	Nekem, akit örök éhség gyötör,	
	mindegy, hogy Pokol, Paradicsom, Ég.	
	Legjobb, ahol legtöbb a martalékom.	
BŰN:	Faljál előbb virágot, fát, gyümölcsöt,	
	aztán vadat, madarat és halat!	
	Menj, hová végzeted s vad ösztönöd	[800]
	vezet, tőled nem tágitok, s az útat	
	sem vétem el, ha vonsz; hisz számtalan	
	ölés, zsákmány szagát szivom, s Halál	
	izét érzem mindenben, ami él.	
	Merész kalandodban nem hagylak el,	
	fej-fej mellett hiven segítelek!	
ÁDÁM:	Üdvből nyomorba hulltam. Rejtsetek	
	az Úr orcájától, kit látni akkor	
	üdvöm csúcspontja volt! Ha véget érne	
	itt nyomorom . . . megszolgáltam, tehát	[810]
	elszenvedném.	

	To make us less, bent rather to exalt	[780]
	Our happie state.	
ANGEL 1:	His Laws our Laws, all honour to him done	
	Returns our own.	
	Cease then this impious rage,	
	And tempt not these; but hast'n to appease	
	Th' incensed Father, and th' incensed Son,	
	While Pardon may be found in time besought.	
SATAN:	Better to reign in Hell, then serve in Heav'n.	
	Fair Daughter, and thou Son and Grandchild both,	
	High proof ye now have giv'n to be the Race	[790]
	Of *Satan*. You two this way, down to Paradise descend;	
	There dwell and Reign in bliss, thence on the Earth	
	Dominion exercise and in the Aire,	
	Chiefly on Man, sole Lord of all declar'd,	
	Him first make sure your thrall, and lastly kill.	
	My Substitutes I send ye, and Create	
	Plenipotent on Earth, of matchless might	
	Issuing from mee: on your joynt vigor now	
	My hold of this new Kingdom all depends,	
	Through Sin to Death expos'd by my exploit.	[800]
	If your joynt power prevailes, th' affaires of Hell	
	No detriment need feare.	
SIN:	Second of *Satan* sprung, all conquering *Death*,	
	What thinkst thou of our Empire now?	
DEATH:	To mee, who with eternal Famin pine,	
	Alike is Hell, or Paradise, or Heaven,	
	There best, where most with ravin I may meet.	
SIN:	Thou therefore on these Herbs, and Fruits, and Flours	
	Feed first, on each Beast next, and Fish, and Fowle,	
	Goe whither Fate and inclination strong	[810]
	Leads thee, I shall not lag behinde, nor erre	
	The way, thou leading, such a sent I draw	
	Of carnage, prey innumerable, and taste	
	The savour of Death from all things there that live:	
	Nor shall I to the work thou enterprisest	
	Be wanting, but afford thee equal aid.	
ADAM:	O miserable of happie! hide me from the face	
	Of God, whom to behold was then my highth	
	Of happiness: yet well, if here would end	
	The miserie, I deserv'd it, and would beare	[820]
	My own deservings.	

HALÁL:	De mindez nem segít!
ÁDÁM:	Amit eszem, iszom, mit szaporítok,
	csak továbbplántált átok! Egykoron
	oly élvvel hallott hang: „Sokasodjatok!" –
	halálos hallomás ma. Így ugyan
	mit szaporítsak? Átkot enfejemre?!
	Érezve a tőlem rá háruló
	gonoszt, jövő idők mely sarja nem
	átkozza főm: „Vesszen tisztátlan ősünk! [820]
	Ádám, neked köszönhetjük . . . " De e
	köszönet átok! Kértelek, Teremtő,
	hogy sárból emberré gyúrj? Esdekeltem,
	hogy a sötétből hívj elő, s e bűvös
	kertbe helyezz? Megérthetetlen
	igazságod. Az igazat bevallva
	későn tusázom véle. Visszalöknöm
	feltételeit akkor kellett volna,
	amikor adta.
	Elismerem: igaz itélete, [830]
	hogy por vagyok, s a porba visszatérek.
	Bármint jön, boldog óra. Mért halasztja
	keze, mit mára tűzött rendelése?
	Mért élek még, miért gunyol halállal,
	és nyújtja kínomat? Még riogat egy
	nagy kétely: hátha meg se halhatok
	egészen – az élet-szellem, melyet
	Isten lehellett belém, talán nem oszlik
	el e testi röggel. Vajh ki tudja, sírban,
	vagy más szörnyű helyen, nem kell-e halnom [840]
	élő halált? Tegyük fel:
	a Halál nem egy ütés, de végtelen
	nyomor, mit e naptól fogva itt belül
	bennem s kivül érezni kezdtem, és
	örökre így lesz. Jaj, e rettegés
	e szörnyü fordulattal visszahull
	dörögve védtelen fejemre. Én
	s a Halál örökké egy testben leledzünk.
	Nem egymagam, de minden nemzedék
	átkozva bennem! Ó, lelkiismeret! [850]
	Míly szörnyüség-örvénybe tántorítsz!
	Jaj, nincs kiút! Mind mélyebb mélybe hullok!
	Mért nem jössz, Halál,
	hogy egy – de háromszor kívánt – csapással
	végezz velem?

DEATH: But this will not serve!
ADAM: All that I eat or drink, or shall beget,
Is propagated curse. O voice once heard
Delightfully, *Encrease and multiply*,
Now death to hear! for what can I encrease
Or multiplie, but curses on my head?
Who of all Ages to succeed, but feeling
The evil on him brought by me, will curse
My Head, Ill fare our Ancestor impure, [830]
For this we may thank *Adam*; but his thanks
Shall be the execration.
Did I request thee, Maker, from my Clay
To mould me Man, did I sollicite thee
From darkness to promote me, or here place
In this delicious Garden? inexplicable
Thy Justice seems; yet to say truth, too late,
I thus contest; then should have been refusd
Those terms whatever, when they were propos'd:
His doom is fair, [840]
That dust I am, and shall to dust returne:
O welcom hour whenever! why delayes
His hand to execute what his Decree
Fixd on this day?
Why do I overlive,
Why am I mockt with death, and length'nd out
To deathless pain? Yet one doubt
Pursues me still, least all I cannot die,
Least that pure breath of Life, the Spirit of Man
Which God inspir'd, cannot together perish [850]
With this corporeal Clod; then in the Grave,
Or in some other dismal place who knows
But I shall die a living Death?
But say that Death be not one stroak, as I suppos'd,
Bereaving sense, but endless miserie
From this day onward, which I feel begun
Both in me, and without me, and so last
To perpetuitie; Ay me, that fear
Comes thundring back with dreadful revolution
On my defensless head; both Death and I [860]
Am found Eternal, and incorporate both,
Nor I on my part single, in mee all
Posteritie stands curst!
O Conscience, into what Abyss of fears
And horrors hast thou driv'n me; out of which
I find no way, from deep to deeper plung'd!
Why comes not Death with one thrice acceptable stroke?

[ÉVA MEGJELENIK]

                Kigyó, te!
                Kívánom, bárha hozzá
                hasonló termet és kígyó szine
                mutatná meg csalárd szived, hogy így
                minden teremtmény óvakodna tőled,   [860]
                nehogy nagyon is égi termeted,
                mely ördögi hamisságot takar,
                csapdába ejtse őket! Én bizony
                nélküled boldog lettem volna, ha
                gőgöd s hiú nagyzási vágyad – épp a
                legfőbb veszély idején – meg nem veti
                intő szavam, méltatlannak találva
                kétségeimet. Te páváskodni akartál
                Sátán előtt, nagy fölfuvalkodottan
                rászedni őt, de midőn eléd került   [870]
                a kígyó, ő szedett rá, és te engem. Az Úr,
                a bölcs Teremtő, ki az Ég csucsát
                sürűn megrakta férfi-szellemekkel,
                e furcsaságot vajon mért teremté,
                ki a Természet tünde tévedése?
                Mért nem töltötte meg – mint angyaloknál –
                a Földet férfiakkal nők helyett, más
                utat lelvén, hogy embert sokszorozzon?

ÉVA: Ne hagyj el, ó Ádám! Tanum az Ég,
                mily őszinte szerelmes tisztelet   [880]
                ég szívemben irántad, s akaratlan
                vétettem csúful rászedetve. Kérlek
                esdőn, a térded kulcsolom, ne fossz meg
                miért élek – kedves tekintetedtől,
                segélyedtől, tanácsodtól e végső
                inségben, egyetlen valóm, erőm!
                Ha eldobsz, hova menjek? Ketten hibáztunk,
                te Isten ellen, én az Isten és
                teellened!

ÁDÁM: De jöjj, egymást ne vádoljuk, ne marjuk,   [890]
                ugyis vádolnak már – a szeretet
                szolgálatán serénykedjünk: miként
                könnyítsük egymás terheit, bajunkat
                megosztva, mert e napra rótt halál
                nem jön hamar,
                s átszáll szegény
                fajunkra is.

ÉVA: ... ha már, silányt,
                visszavettél kegyedbe, s így remélem,

[EVE APPEARS]

	Thou Serpent,	
	Nothing wants, but that thy shape,	
	Like his, and colour Serpentine may shew	[870]
	Thy inward fraud, to warn all Creatures from thee	
	Least that too heav'nly form, pretended	
	To hellish falshood, snare them. But for thee	
	I had persisted happie, had not thy pride	
	And wandring vanitie, when lest was safe,	
	Rejected my forewarning, and disdain'd	
	Not to be trusted, longing to be seen	
	Though by the Devil himself, him overweening	
	To over-reach, but with the Serpent meeting	
	Fool'd and beguil'd, by him thou, I by thee.	[880]
	O why did God, Creator wise, that peopl'd highest Heav'n	
	With Spirits Masculine, create at last	
	This noveltie on Earth, this fair defect	
	Of Nature, and not fill the World at once	
	With Men as Angels without Feminine,	
	Or find some other way to generate	
	Mankind?	
EVE:	Forsake me not thus, *Adam*, witness Heav'n	
	What love sincere, and reverence in my heart	
	I beare thee, and unweeting have offended,	[890]
	Unhappilie deceav'd; thy suppliant	
	I beg, and clasp thy knees; bereave me not,	
	Whereon I live, thy gentle looks, thy aid,	
	Thy counsel in this uttermost distress,	
	My onely strength and stay: forlorn of thee,	
	Whither shall I betake me? both have sin'd,	
	But thou	
	Against God onely, I against God and thee.	
ADAM:	But rise, let us no more contend, nor blame	
	Each other, blam'd enough elsewhere, but strive	[900]
	In offices of Love, how we may light'n	
	Each others burden in our share of woe;	
	Since this days Death denounc't,	
	Will prove no sudden,	
	And to our hapless Seed deriv'd.	
EVE:	Restor'd by thee, vile as I am, to place	
	Of new acceptance, hopeful to regaine	

visszanyerem szerelmedet, szivem [900]
egyetlen üdvét, tőled élve-halva
nem rejtem el, hogy nyugtalan szivemben
mi eszme támadt, tán e végnyomorban
segít, vagy végét szegi ... Ha utódaink
gondja öl legkivált, kiknek születni
biztos nyomorra kell, s végül halál
nyeli el őket, s ha utálat az,
hogy okai legyünk a más bajának,
ki magzatunk, s ágyékunkból fakad,
hatalmadban van még fogantatása, [910]
születése előtt kiveszteni
ez átok-fajt: maradj gyerektelen,
mint most vagy, így megcsalatik Halál
a zsákmányával, s kénytelen velünk
kettőnkkel vad-mohó belét betömni.
De ha nehéznek véled, gyötrelemnek,
hogy társalogva, vágyva, nézve egymást,
lemondj szerelem szertartásiról,
oly édes nász-ölelésről, s vágyakozva
csak epekedj reménytelen, velem [920]
szemközt, ki épp oly vágyban senyvedek,
s ez kínzóbb kín, mint melytől rettegünk –
úgy tegyünk pontot: Keressük a Halált, vagy
ha nem találjuk, hajtsuk végre tisztét
önnön kezünkkel.
ÁDÁM: Ha a halált hajhászod, és e kín
szüntét, s úgy véled, a kimért boszútól
így szabadulsz, kétséged ne legyen:
bölcsebben fegyverezte bosszuló
dühét az Úr, semhogy kijátszd, az ilyen dacoskodás [930]
csak felbőszíti őt, hogy a halált
élővé váltsa bennünk. Hadd keressünk
bölcsebb döntést! Már rémlik is!
Munkával nyerjem kenyerem! Baj ez?
Tunyaság rosszabb volna. Művem éltet.
Mi jobbat tehetnénk? Ha visszamennénk
az ítélet helyére, s ha leborulnánk
előtte hódolón, s bevallanánk
alázattal bűnünket, és kegyelmet
kérnénk, ő megenyhül, s bosszusága [940]
elfordul tőlünk, hisz derült szemében,
még mikor zordnak véltük is, komornak,
csak kegyes irgalom fényeskedett.
Uram, nem tudom, míly szavakkal esdekeljek.

                Thy Love, the sole contentment of my heart
                Living or dying, from thee I will not hide
                What thoughts in my unquiet brest are ris'n,   [910]
                Tending to some relief of our extremes,
                Or end . . .
                If care of our descent perplex us most,
                Which must be born to certain woe, devourd
                By Death at last, and miserable it is
                To be to others cause of misery,
                Our own begotten, and of our Loines,
                In thy power it lies, yet ere Conception to prevent
                The Race unblest, to being yet unbegot.
                Childless thou art, Childless remaine: [920]
                So Death shall be deceav'd his glut, and with us two
                Be forc'd to satisfie his Rav'nous Maw.
                But if thou judge it hard and difficult,
                Conversing, looking, loving, to abstain
                From Loves due Rites, Nuptial imbraces sweet,
                And with desire to languish without hope,
                Before the present object languishing
                With like desire, which would be miserie
                And torment less then none of what we dread,
                Then let us make short,   [930]
                Let us seek Death, or he not found, supply
                With our own hands his Office on our selves.

ADAM: If thou covet death, as utmost end
                Of miserie, so thinking to evade
                The penaltie pronounc't, doubt not but God
                Hath wiselier arm'd his vengeful ire then so
                To be forestall'd; rather such acts
                Of contumacie will provoke the highest
                To make death in us live: Then let us seek
                Some safer resolution, which methinks   [940]
                I have in view. With labour I must earne
                My bread; what harm? Idleness had bin worse;
                My labour will sustain me,
                What better can we do, then to the place
                Repairing where he judg'd us, prostrate fall
                Before him reverent, and there confess
                Humbly our faults, and pardon beg, he will relent and turn
                From his displeasure; in whose look serene,
                When angry most he seem'd and most severe,
                What else but favor, grace, and mercie shon?   [950]
                Lord, I am unskilful with what words to pray.

ÉVA:	Uram, nem tudom, míly szavakkal esdekeljek.
FIÚ:	Nézd, ó Atyám, mi zsengét hajt a Föld
	emberbe plántált irgalmadból! Ez
	ima-sóhaj, mit arany füstölőmben
	tömjénnel én, papod, eléd hozok,
	drágább izű gyümölcs – hisz ezt szivébe [950]
	megbánással te ültetted –, különb
	Éden minden kezed-gondozta fa
	gyümölcsinél, melyek a bűneset
	előtt lettek. Könyörgésére hajtsd most
	füled, halld – bárha néma – sóhaját!
	Nem tudja, míly szavakkal esdekeljen.
ÁDÁM:	Uram, nem tudom, míly szavakkal esdekeljek.
FIÚ:	Engedd, legyek tolmácsa, védnöke,
	s engesztelője.
	Fogadj el engem s tőlük általam [960]
	az ember iránti béke illatát.
	Engesztelődj!
ATYA:	Mit kérsz, legyen, Szerelmetes Fiam!
	Minden, mit kérsz, parancsom volt, de ők
	nem élhetnek az Édenben tovább:
	Mihály, hajtsd végre megbizásomat!
	Válassz a kherubok közül nehány
	lobogó-láng vitézt, nehogy az ellen
	embert segítve, vagy betörve az
	üres birtokba keltsen új zavart. [970]
	Siess, és hajtsd ki Isten Édenéből
	a bűnös párt kimélet nélkül, a
	szentelt helyről e két szentségtelent.
	Ha fogadják szavad türelmesen,
	vigasztalan ne űzd el őket! Ádám
	csak tudja meg, tőled, mi lesz a sorsa.
	Közöld velük: szövetségem megújitom
	a nő magvával. Búsan űzd ki őket,
	de békével!
ÁDÁM:	Mióta imával sürgettem csitítani [980]
	a sértett Istent, előtte bensőmet alázva,
	már bízom abban,
	hogy kegyesen meghallgat; visszatért
	keblembe béke, a Halál keserve
	elmúlt, s mi élni fogunk. Üdv néked, Éva,
	kit joggal hívnak így, embernem anyja!

EVE:	Lord, I am unskilful with what words to pray.
SON:	See Father, what first fruits on Earth are sprung
	From thy implanted Grace in Man, these Sighs
	And Prayers, which in this Golden Censer, mixt
	With Incense, I thy Priest before thee bring,
	Fruits of more pleasing savour from thy seed
	Sow'n with contrition in his heart, then those
	Which his own hand manuring all the Trees
	Of Paradise could have produc't, ere fall'n [960]
	From innocence. Now therefore bend thine eare
	To supplication, heare his sighs though mute;
	Unskilful with what words to pray,
ADAM:	Lord, I am unskilful with what words to pray.
SON:	Let mee interpret for him, mee his Advocate
	Accept me, and in mee from these receave
	The smell of peace toward Mankinde,
	Be reconcil'd!
GOD:	All thy request for Man, accepted Son,
	Obtain, all thy request was my Decree: [970]
	But longer in that Paradise to dwell,
	The Law I gave to Nature him forbids:
	Michael, this my behest have thou in charge,
	Take to thee from among the Cherubim
	Thy choice of flaming Warriours, least the Fiend
	Or in behalf of Man, or to invade
	Vacant possession som new trouble raise:
	Hast thee, and from the Paradise of God
	Without remorse drive out the sinful Pair,
	From hallowd ground th' unholie. [980]
	If patiently thy bidding they obey,
	Dismiss them not disconsolate; reveale
	To *Adam* what shall come in future dayes, intermix
	My Cov'nant in the womans seed renewd;
	So send them forth, though sorrowing, yet in peace.
ADAM:	Since I saught
	By Prayer th' offended Deitie to appease,
	Kneel'd and before him humbl'd all my heart,
	Perswasion in me grew
	That I was heard with favour; peace returnd [990]
	Home to my brest, the bitterness of death
	Is past, and we shall live. Haile to thee,
	Eve rightly call'd, Mother of all Mankind,

	Minden élőnek anyja: általad
	él az ember s az emberért a többi!
ÉVA:	E névre méltó nem vagyok, hiszen
	vétkeztem én, akit segélyedül [990]
	rendeltek, lettem végzeted, szidás,
	gáncs, gyanu illet inkább! Végtelen
	kegyelmes volt Birám, hogy engem ítélt
	az Élet kútfejének, ki halált
	hoztam mindenre; jó voltál te is:
	méltóztattál ily magasztos neven
	hívni kit más név illet.
	Ám a rét hív verítékes dologra, de
	oldaladtól sosem bolyongok el,
	bármi messze legyen napi munkánk, itt élj [1000]
	bukva, bár, de elégedetten!
ÁDÁM:	Ó, Éva, várj. A dombon ott
	–úgy veszem ki – egy égi vendég jő,
	nem is alantas,
	járásából itélve nem riasztó, hogy rettegjem,
	de nem is oly baráti, mint Rafael. Hogy ne sértsem,
	alázattal elémegyek. Te menj el!
MIHÁLY:	Bevezetésre nem szorul az Ég
	parancsa; elég az, hogy a fülébe vette az
	Úr imád, s bünöd nyomán a méltó [1010]
	bosszú – a halál – elesik zálogától.
	Kegyelemből sok nap van adva néked,
	hogy térj meg, és tedd jóvá egy bünöd
	sok jótettel. Lehet, hogy megcsitul
	Urad s megvált Halál rabló jogától.
	De az Édenben te nem lakhatsz tovább.
	Nem tűri. Jöttem, és kitiltalak
	a kertből, hogy – amelyből vétetél –
	a földet túrd, hozzád illőbb talajt!
ÉVA:	Nemvárt csapás, halálnál is borúsabb! [1020]
	Éden, el kell, hogy hagyjalak, szülő-
	földem – boldog séták, árnyak, melyek
	Istennek illenek lakul? Reméltem,
	nyugodtan – bár busan – itt élem éltem
	a kettőnkre kimért halál-napig.
	Virágok, mik nem nyiltok máshelyütt,
	ki fordít napnak bennetek.
	Mi, kik szoktunk halhatatlan gyümölcshöz,
	tisztátlanabb leget miként szivunk?

EVE:	Mother of all things living, since by thee
	Man is to live, and all things live for Man.
	Ill worthie I such title should belong
	To me transgressour, who for thee ordaind
	A help, became thy doom;[14] to mee reproach
	Rather belongs, distrust and all dispraise:
	But infinite in pardon was my Judge, [1000]
	That I who first brought Death on all, am grac't
	The sourse of life; next favourable thou,
	Who highly thus to entitle me voutsaf'st,
	Farr other name deserving. But the Field
	To labour calls us now with sweat impos'd,
	I never from thy side henceforth to stray,
	Wherere our days work lies,
	Here let us live, though in fall'n state, content.
ADAM:	O *Eve*, I descrie from yonder Hill
	One of the heav'nly Host, and by his Gate [1010]
	None of the meanest, yet not terrible,
	That I should fear, nor sociably mild,
	As *Raphael*, that I should much confide,
	Whom not to offend, with reverence I must meet, and thou retire.
MICHAEL:	Heav'ns high behest no Preface needs:
	Sufficient that thy Prayers are heard, and Death,
	Then due by sentence when thou didst transgress,
	Defeated of his seisure many dayes
	Giv'n thee of Grace, wherein thou may'st repent,
	And one bad act with many deeds well done [1020]
	Mayst cover: well may then thy Lord appeas'd
	Redeem thee quite from Deaths rapacious claime;
	But longer in this Paradise to dwell
	Permits not; to remove thee I am come,
	And send thee from the Garden forth to till
	The ground whence thou wast tak'n, fitter Soile.
EVE:	O unexpected stroke, worse then of Death!
	Must I thus leave thee Paradise? thus leave
	Thee Native Soile, these happie Walks and Shades,
	Fit haunt of Gods? where I had hope to spend, [1030]
	Quiet though sad, the respit of that day
	That must be mortal to us both. O flours,
	That never will in other Climate grow,
	Who now shall reare ye to the Sun,
	How shall we breath in other Aire
	Less pure, accustomd to immortal Fruits?

MIHÁLY:	Éva, ne sírj, de tűrve mondj le arról,	[1030]
	mit jogosan vesztettél el, s ne kösd	
	szived balgán ahhoz, mi nem tiéd!	
	Nem egymagad mégy, véled jár urad;	
	Ott van szülőhelyed, hol ő lakik.	
ÁDÁM:	Parancsának alávetem magam.	
	Az fáj leginkább, hogy kimenve innét	
	rejtve lesz tőlem arca, tiltva-zárva	
	áldott alakja.	
	Amaz alsóbb világban hol keressem	
	sugár előtünését, lábnyomát?	[1040]
MIHÁLY:	Országodul a teljes Földet adta,	
	nem megvetendő adományt. Ne hidd,	
	jelenlétét az Éden szűk határa	
	magába zárja: völgyön és síkon	
	jelen van Isten, mint itt, megleled	
	és jelenléte sok jellel követ, előbb, hogy innen	
	elmégy, tudd meg jövőd, mi vár reád s	
	utódaidra.	
	Ádám, nyisd föl szemed, s szemléld, mit is	
	terem utóbb eredendő bünöd	[1050]
	sarjadban, ki hozzá sem ér a tiltott	
	fához, s kigyóval sem szövetkezik,	
	s vétked se véti, mégis száll bünödből	
	rá romlás, hogy még zordabb bűnt tegyen	
	Káin, Ábel! Ágyékodból fakadt fivér e kettő,	
	Ádám, s igazat ölt igaztalan –	
	irígységből, mert öccse ajándokit	
	tetszéssel vette az Ég; ám bosszu száll	
	e véres tettre.	
ÁDÁM:	Jaj, szörnyü tett, jaj, szörnyü volt oka!	[1060]
	Most a halált láttam? Szülő poromba	
	így kell majd visszatérnem?	
MIHÁLY:	A halált láttad itt	
	első alakjában ez emberen.	
	De sok alakja, számos útja van	
	bősz barlangjában.	
	Látok kórházat: fertőzött, komor,	
	Benne szorongott számtalan beteg:	
	kisértetes görcs, kínpad-kín, szivet-	
	törő agónia, megannyi láz,	[1070]
	vonaglás.	

MICHAEL:	Lament not *Eve*, but patiently resigne	
	What justly thou hast lost; nor set thy heart,	
	Thus over-fond, on that which is not thine;	
	Thy going is not lonely, with thee goes	[1040]
	Thy Husband, him to follow thou art bound;	
	Where he abides, think there thy native soile.	
ADAM:	To his great bidding I submit.	
	This most afflicts me, that departing hence,	
	As from his face I shall be hid, deprivd	
	His blessed count'nance;	
	In yonder nether World where shall I seek	
	His bright appearances, or foot step-trace?	
MICHAEL:	All th' Earth he gave thee to possess and rule,	
	No despicable gift; surmise not then	[1050]
	His presence to these narrow bounds confin'd	
	Of Paradise or *Eden*: doubt not but in Vallie and in plaine	
	God is as here, and will be found alike	
	Present, and of his presence many a signe	
	Still following thee. Ere thou from hence depart, know	
	What shall come in future dayes to thee and to thy Ofspring.	
	Adam, now ope thine eyes, and first behold	
	Th' effects which thy original crime hath wrought	
	In some to spring from thee, who never touch'd	
	Th' excepted Tree, nor with the Snake conspir'd,	[1060]
	Nor sinn'd thy sin, yet from that sin derive	
	Corruption to bring forth more violent deeds.	
	Cain, Abel: these two are Brethren, *Adam*, and to come	
	Out of thy loyns; th' unjust the just hath slain,	
	For envie that his Brothers Offering found	
	From Heav'n acceptance; but the bloodie Fact	
	Will be aveng'd.	
ADAM:	Alas, both for the deed and for the cause!	
	But have I now seen Death? Is this the way	
	I must return to native dust?	[1070]
MICHAEL:	Death thou hast seen	
	In his first shape on man; but many shapes	
	Of Death, and many are the wayes that lead	
	To his grim Cave.	
	Before my eyes appears a Lazar-house, wherein were laid	
	Numbers of all diseas'd, all maladies	
	Of gastly Spasm, or racking torture, qualmes	
	Of heart-sick Agonie, all feavorous kinds,	
	Convulsions, Epilepsies, fierce Catarrhs,	

	Szörnyű e rángás, fulladás! Iszony
	ápolta őket: ágyról ágyra járt,
	s fölöttük rázta győztesen Halál
	dzsidáját: ütni késik, bár be sokszor
	esengtek érte, végreményükért!
ÁDÁM:	Ó nyomorú ember, milyen bukásba
	aljasodtál? Mi vár reád, mi szörny-sors?
	Jobb volna nem születni.
MIHÁLY:	Isten arcát nem tisztelték magukban	[1080]
	Ezért oly undok büntetésük im;
	nem Isten arca torzult – az övék! . . .
ÁDÁM:	De hát a kín ösvényein kívül
	Nincs más irány, hogy a halálhoz érjünk?
	Nem futok haláltól,
	s nem vágyom létem húzni, azon leszek:
	e terhes nyűgöt mint tegyem le könnyen . . .
MIHÁLY:	Ne szeresd léted, ne gyülöld, de míg
	élsz, szépen élj! Hogy meddig? Bízd az Égre!
	Most láss Ádám tágas teret, különb-	[1090]
	különb-szín sátrakat. Olyik körül
	füvellő nyájak. Másból hangszerek
	zenéje hallatszott ki: orgona, hárfa,
	ki játszik rajtuk, röpke ujja
	ihletre szállt magas, mély hangokon,
	űzvén dalos fugát.
	Zeng zenével mind a sátor.
ÁDÁM:	Boldog együttlét, szerelmi élmény,
	ifjúság, dal, virágok, koszorúk.
MIHÁLY:	Ám szép nemet nevelnek.	[1100]
	Szépek e nők, istennőknek hihetnéd,
	kiket látsz: vidámak, bájosak,
	de híjjával a jóknak, mik a nő
	házi erénye, s fő illem-disze.
	Ezeket csak a kéjvágyó közízlés
	nevelte táncra, dalra, cicomára,
	nyelv-pergetésre és szemforgatásra.
	Az ember józan faja
	elszórja erkölcsét, hirét ebül
	e szép istentagadó tündérekért.	[1110]

	Dire was the tossing, deep the groans, despair	[1080]
	Tended the sick busiest from Couch to Couch;	
	And over them triumphant Death his Dart	
	Shook, but delaid to strike, though oft invokt	
	With vows, as thir chief good, and final hope.	
ADAM:	O miserable Mankind, to what fall	
	Degraded, to what wretched state reserv'd!	
	Better end heer unborn.	
MICHAEL:	Since they	
	Gods Image did not reverence in themselves,	
	Therefore so abject is thir punishment,	[1090]
	Disfiguring not Gods likeness, but thir own . . .	
ADAM:	But is there yet no other way, besides	
	These painful passages, how we may come	
	To Death, and mix with our connatural dust?	
	I flie not Death, nor would prolong	
	Life much, bent rather how I may be quit	
	easiest of this combrous charge . . .	
MICHAEL:	Nor love thy Life, nor hate; but what thou livst	
	Live well, how long or short permit to Heav'n.	
	Now see a spacious Plaine, whereon	[1100]
	Were Tents of various hue; by some were herds	
	Of Cattel grazing: others, whence the sound	
	Of Instruments was heard, of Harp and Organ; and who moovd	
	Thir stops and chords: his volant touch	
	Instinct through all proportions low and high	
	Fled and pursu'd transverse the resonant fugue.	
	With Feast and Musick all the Tents resound.	
ADAM:	Such happy interview and fair event	
	Of love and youth not lost, Songs, Garlands, Flours!	
MICHAEL:	Yet they a beauteous ofspring shall beget;	[1110]
	For that fair femal Troop thou seest, so blithe, so smooth, so gay,	
	Yet empty of all good wherein consists	
	Womans domestic honour and chief praise;	
	Bred onely and completed to the taste	
	Of lustful appetence, to sing, to dance,	
	To dress, and troule the Tongue, and roule the Eye.	
	To these that sober Race of Men,	
	Shall yield up all thir vertue, all thir fame	
	Ignobly, to these fair Atheists.	

ÁDÁM:	Ó, szégyen, szánalom! Kik éltüket
	oly szépen kezdték, ím bal útra tértek,
	vagy féluton aléltak. Látom én:
	egyenlő hévvel tart tovább az ember
	kínja, s oka utóbb is épp a nő!
MIHÁLY:	Oka a férfi nőies, puhány volta.
	Mihelyt az ész az emberben ködös lesz,
	s nem úr, a zagyva vágyak, szenvedélyek
	elorozzák az észtül a jogart,
	s rabbá teszik, ki szabad volt, az embert. [1120]
	Így hát, mivel eltűri, hogy silány
	erők uralkodjanak szivében az ész
	fölött, az Úr igaz itélete
	aláveti a kinti kényuraknak,
	kik jogtalanul tőle elragadják
	külső szabadságát. Szükségszerű
	a zsarnok. Bár zsarnoknak nincs bocsánat!
	De készülj újabb látomásra!
GÁBOR:	Ki a végetlen űrt kimérted,
	Anyagot alkotván beléje, [1130]
MIHÁLY:	Ki az örökké változandót,
	S a Változatlant egyesíted,
RÁFÁEL:	Ki boldogságot áradoztatsz,
	A testet öntudatra hozva.
	És bölcseséged részesévé
	Egész világot felavatva:
	Hozsána néked, Jóság!
ÚR:	S te, Lucifer, hallgatsz, önhitten állsz,
	Dicséretemre nem találsz-e szót,
	Vagy nem tetszik tán, amit alkoték? [1140]
LUCIFER:	S mi tessék rajta, – Hogy nehány anyag
	Nehány golyóba összevissza gyúrva,
	Most vonzza, űzi és taszítja egymást?
	Nehány féregben öntudatra kél,
	Az ember ezt, ha egykor ellesi,
	Vegykonyhájában szintén megteszi.
RABSZOLGA:	Miért él a pór? A gúlához követ
	Hord az erősnek, s állítván utódot
	Jármába, meghal. – Milljók egy miatt.

ADAM:	O pittie and shame, that they who to live well	[1120]
	Enterd so faire, should turn aside to tread	
	Paths indirect, or in the mid way faint!	
	But still I see the tenor of Mans woe	
	Holds on the same, from Woman to begin.	
MICHAEL:	From Mans effeminate slackness it begins,	
	Reason in man obscur'd, or not obeyd,	
	Immediately inordinate desires	
	And upstart Passions catch the Government	
	From Reason, and to servitude reduce	
	Man till then free. Therefore since hee permits	[1130]
	Within himself unworthie Powers to reign	
	Over free Reason, God in Judgement just	
	Subjects him from without to violent Lords;	
	Who oft as undeservedly enthrall	
	His outward freedom: Tyrannie must be,	
	Though to the Tyrant thereby no excuse.	
	And now prepare thee for another sight.	
GABRIEL:	Thou who compassed the infinitudes,[15]	
	Creating matter out of nothing,	
MICHAEL:	Thou who fused the changeless and the changing,	[1140]
RAPHAEL:	Thou flood and fountain of our happiness,	
	Bringer of the body to self-consciousness,	
	Allowing the entire world to partake	
	Of thy Wisdom, we offer to Thee	
	Our hosannas, Virtue Eternal.	
GOD:	You there, Lucifer, proudly standing apart,	
	No word of praise from you? Are you still silent?	
	Does something in my work, perhaps, displease you?	
LUCIFER:	And what should please me? That certain substances,	
	Are now screwed up into these tiny globes	[1150]
	That chase, attract or else repel each other?	
	Awaking a few worms to consciousness,	
	If man's at all observant he'll concoct	
	Some hash like this with his poor instruments.	
SLAVE:	A slave? Why does he live – to carry stones	
	And raise his master's pyramid, to breed	
	His own successor for the yoke, and die.	
	A million souls for one.	

PÉTER:	El fogsz pusztulni, korcsult nemzedék,	[1150]
	E nagy világ most tisztuló szinéről.	
PÁTRIÁRKA:	E gonoszhitűek	
	A szentháromság rejtélyes tanában	
	A homoiusiont hirdetik,	
	Mig az egyház a homousiont	
	Alapítá meg a hit cikkeül.	
CSONTVÁZ:	Én az vagyok, ki ott lesz	
	Minden csókodban, minden ölelésben.	
RUDOLF:	Állítsd fel, Kepler, horoszkópomat,	
	Rossz álmam volt az éjjel, rettegek...	[1160]
ÉVA:	János, nekem szükségem volna pénzre...	
ÁDÁM:	Egy fillérem sincs, mind elhordtad immár.	
ROBERSPIERRE:	Egyenlőség, testvériség, szabadság,	
	A felséges nép majd itél fölötted.	
KÉJHÖLGY:	A mámor elszállt, a festék lement,	
	Itt oly hideg van: jobb-e odalent?	
ELÍTÉLT:	Maradj, bilincs, a hitvány por felett.	
NYEGLE:	Egymást szedtük rá azzal, hogy tudunk,	
	Most a valónál mind elámulunk.	
ÁDÁM:	Miért bánsz így a művészettel, ember!	[1170]
	Mondd, tetszik-é, amit húzasz, magadnak?	
ZENÉSZ:	Dehogy tetszik, dehogy! Sőt végtelen kín	
	Ezt húzni napról napra, s nézve nézni,	
	Miként mulatnak kurjongatva rajta.	
	E vad hang elhat álmaimba is.	
	De mit tegyek, élnem kell, s nem tudok mást.	
AGGASTYÁN:	Hogy ébren légy, borsón fogsz térdepelni.	
PLÁTÓ:	Még a borsón is szépet álmodom.	
ESZKIMÓ:	Ha isten vagy, tegyed,	
	Könyörgök, hogy kevesb ember legyen,	[1180]
	S több fóka.	
LUCIFER:	Miért is kezdtem emberrel nagyot,	

ST. PETER:	Base generation! you shall pass away	
	In the vast purification of the world.	[1160]
PATRIARCH:	These wicked infidels	
	Proclaim the idea of Homoiusion	
	In the mystic doctrine of the Trinity,	
	Although the True Church has declared the doctrine	
	of Homousion an article of faith.	
SKELETON:	[I am the] One who is sure to be	
	Present at all your kisses and embraces.	
RUDOLF:	Kepler, draw my horoscope for me,	
	I had a bad dream last night and I fear . . .	
EVE:	Johann, my dear, I'm rather short of money.	[1170]
ADAM:	I haven't a farthing, you've had everything.	
ROBERSPIERRE:	Liberty, Equality, Fraternity! –	
	The noble people will pass judgment on you.	
WHORE:	All passion spent, my skin stripped bare	
	I feel cold: what's it like down there?	
THE CONDEMNED MAN:	The chains remain, my clay is poor.	
QUACK-DOCTOR:	We each claimed wisdom as our own	
	But truth astounds all once it's known.	
ADAM:	Why do you waste your talent on this rubbish!	
	Tell me, do you like what you are playing?	[1180]
MUSICIAN:	Like it? Good heavens, no! It's endless torture	
	Grinding out this stuff from day to day,	
	To see man dance and hear them bawl for more.	
	This awful racket even haunts my dreams.	
	But what can I do? How else can I live?	
ELDER:	To wake you up we'll make you kneel on grain.	
PLATO:	My dreams are sweet, even on hard grains.	
ESKIMO:	If god you are, I beg you, do this for me,	
	Let there be less of men and more of seals.	
LUCIFER:	Oh why did I embark	[1190]

	Ki sárból, napsugárból összegyúrva
	Tudásra törpe, és vakságra nagy.
AZ ÚR:	Ne kérdd tovább a titkot, mit jótékonyan
	Takart el istenkéz vágyó szemedtől.
ÁDÁM:	Ó, gyász: előre látni ezt!
	Be jobban élnék jövő-tudatlan:
	tűrve csak a bajtól a magam
	zsoldját. Elég az egyes napok nyüge. [1190]
	Ne fürkéssze eztán ember, mi lesz
	vele és gyermekével – végzetes rossz,
	mit ha előre tud, nem űzhet el.
	Eljön az.
	Jóslásod, áldott Jós, milyen hamar
	megmérte a muló Világot, Évek
	pályáját, mígnem az idő megáll.
	Rajt túl az Úr, Öröklét, szem se látja
	végét. Nagyon okulva elmegyek:
	elmém nagy békességgel, tudással teljes, [1200]
	bolondság hajtott ennél többre vágyni.
MIHÁLY:	Ha ezt tudod, a tudomány egészét
	érted; ne hajhássz többet, bárha ismerj
	névről minden csillagot, Ég-erőt is,
	minden titkát a Mélynek, a Tenyészet
	s Isten minden müvét; Földön, vizen
	légben s Mennyben a Föld minden javát
	élvezd, minden királyságát, hatalmát –
	csak adj tudásodhoz megillető
	tettet s hitet, erényt, mérsékletet, [1210]
	akkor
	ez Édent itthagynod nem lesz gyülölt:
	sokkal derüsebb Édent lelsz magadban.
	A pontos óra most
	bucsúra int, s figyeld: amit az alsó
	dombon helyeztem el, ott várja már
	az őrség indulását, lángoló kard
	cikáz körül soruk előtt a válás
	jeléül. Nincs időnk. Éva, menjetek.
ÉVA:	Véled megyek – [1220]
	nélküled itt: kiűzetéssel egy!
	Ég alatt mindenem te vagy. Ez erős vigaszt viszem

	On mighty things with man who is mere mud	
	And sunlight rolled into a ball, dwarfish	
	In intellect, gigantic in his blindness.	
GOD:	Do not ask	
	to burrow deeper into the great secret	
	The hand of God, for the very best of motives,	
	Has hidden from your hungry eyes.	
ADAM:	O Visions ill foreseen! better had I	
	Liv'd ignorant of future, so had borne	
	My part of evil onely, each dayes lot	[1200]
	Anough to bear. Let no man seek	
	Henceforth to be foretold what shall befall	
	Him or his Childern, evil he may be sure,	
	Which neither his foreknowing can prevent, it must be.	
	How soon hath thy prediction, Seer blest,	
	Measur'd this transient World, the Race of time,	
	Till time stand fixt: beyond is all abyss,	
	Eternitie, whose end no eye can reach.	
	Greatly instructed I shall hence depart.	
	Greatly in peace of thought, and have my fill	[1210]
	Of knowledge, what this Vessel can containe;	
	Beyond which was my folly to aspire.	
MICHAEL:	This having learnt, thou hast attained the summe	
	Of wisdom; hope no higher, though all the Starrs	
	Thou knewst by name, and all th' ethereal Powers,	
	All secrets of the deep, all Natures works,	
	Or works of God in Heav'n, Aire, Earth, or Sea,	
	And all the riches of this World enjoydst,	
	And all the rule, one Empire; onely add	
	Deeds to thy knowledge answerable, add Faith,	[1220]
	Add vertue, Patience, Temperance, add Love,	
	Then wilt thou not be loath	
	To leave this Paradise, but shalt possess	
	A paradise within thee, happier farr.	
	The hour precise exacts our parting hence;	
	and see the Guards, by mee encampt on yonder Hill, expect	
	Thir motion, at whose Front a flaming Sword,	
	In signal of remove, waves fiercely round;	
	We may no longer stay: *Eve*, go.	
EVE:	With thee to goe,	[1230]
	Is to stay here; without thee here to stay,	
	Is to go hence unwilling; thou to mee	
	Art all things under Heav'n.	

	magammal, bár miattam veszve minden:	
	rám szállt az Úr irgalma, méltatlanra,	
	hogy általam hoz üdvöt az Ígért Mag!	
MIHÁLY:	. . . hamar az angyal	
	most kézen fogja két riadt szülőnket	
	és úgy vezérli őket egyenest	
	a kelet-kapúhoz, majd sietve le	
	a szirten a síkra, s eltünik. A kettő	[1230]
	még visszanéz, és a Paradicsom	
	kelet-partját szemléli: üdvhazájuk	
	volt még előbb!	
	Fölötte imbolyog	
	a lángoló kard, zordon tömeggel	
	tömött kapú, a vad tüzes dzsidák.	
	Önkéntelen könnyük pereg, de törlik.	
	Előttük a Világ, hol nyughelyet	
	lelnek, s vezérük lesz a Gondviselés.	
	Kéz a kézbe, lassu vándorlépteik	[1240]
	magányban az Édenen át vezetnek.	

– Vége –

	This further consolation yet secure	
	I carry hence; though all by mee is lost,	
	Such favour I unworthie am voutsaft,	
	By mee the Promis'd Seed shall all restore.	
MICHAEL:	. . . In either hand the hastning Angel caught	
	Our lingring Parents, and to th' Eastern Gate	
	Led them direct, and down the Cliff as fast	[1240]
	To the subjected Plaine; then disappeer'd.	
	They looking back, all th' Eastern side beheld	
	Of Paradise, so late thir happie seat,	
	Wav'd over by that flaming Brand, the Gate	
	With dreadful Faces throng'd and fierie Armes:	
	Som natural tears they drop'd, but wip'd them soon;	
	The World was all before them, where to choose	
	Thir place of rest, and Providence thir guide:	
	They hand in hand with wandring steps and slow,	
	Through *Eden* took thir solitarie way.	[1250]

– The End –

Notes

1. The following script was prepared from the typescript in the National Széchényi Library, Budapest (OSZK MM 19.079). It represents István Jánosy's and Károly Kazimir's reworking of the text of *Paradise Lost* into a two-act drama. The play was staged in 1970 in Budapest, in the Theatre in the Round. The Hungarian text is reproduced by permission and courtesy of János Sebestyén Jánosy, heir to the literary estate of István Jánosy. I edited the Hungarian text minimally (obvious typos were silently corrected, and missing punctuation marks were supplied). The English version is based on the text of *Paradise Lost* edited by Barbara Lewalski (2007). Occasionally the Hungarian translator and director altered Milton's original for effect or to accommodate Milton's lines to the performance (see Chapter 1 for specific cases). In such cases, I altered Milton's original as far as it seemed necessary. The lines from Imre Madách's *Tragedy of Man* at the end of the play are quoted in George Szirtes's translation from Imre Madách, *The Tragedy of Man* (Budapest: Corvina, 2000).
2. Jánosy's original translation of Milton's epic (published in 1969, henceforth *1969*) reads *kín* (woe).
3. *1969*: *ember isten-arca* (human face divine).
4. *1969*: *ült* (sat).
5. *1969*: *nyügöz le most / minket, bár nem riaszt* (Seis'd us, though undismaid).
6. From the 'Argument' to Book 2.
7. *1969*: *dzsidáját közbevesse* (to interpose his dart).
8. *1969*: *Erebus*.
9. In the following lines Satan adopts the words of the epic narrator, speaking to the audience in the second person.
10. Raphael here and in 2.200–2 adopts the lines of the narrator to reflect his momentary enchantment with Eve.
11. *1969*: *imádatot* (adoration).
12. *1969*: *Toronynak* (tower).
13. *1969*: *veszélyes* (Of danger tasted).
14. *1969*: *hálód* (snare).
15. From lines 1138 to 1197 Jánosy and Kazimir create a collage from scenes 1, 4, 6, 7, 8, 9, 11, 12, 14 and 15 of Imre Madách's *Tragedy of Man*.

Bibliography

Abody, Béla. 1970. 'Csoda a Ligetben' [A wonder in the city park]. *Élet és Irodalom* 14.31: 12.
Achinstein, Sharon. 1996. '*Samson Agonistes* and the drama of dissent'. *Milton Studies* 33: 133–58.
Achinstein, Sharon. 2008. 'Cold War Milton'. *University of Toronto Quarterly* 77.3: 801–36.
Achinstein, Sharon. 2010. 'Red Milton'. In John T. Shawcross and David. V. Urban, eds, *Visionary Milton: Essays on prophecy and violence*. Pittsburgh: Duquesne University Press, 45–61.
Almási, Miklós. 1970. 'A mű és a jelen birkózása' [The struggle of the work and the present]. *Színház* 3.10: 9–12.
Anon. 1938. 'The editor's comments'. *New International* 4.11: 323–5.
Anon. 1954. 'Irodalmi esemény' [A literary event]. *Szabad Ifjúság*, 11 November, 4.
Anon. 1954/5. 'Lektori Jelentés I' [Reader's report I]. Unpublished reader's report for the Új Magyar Könyvkiadó Publishing House.
Anon. 1958a. 'Küzdő Sámson. John Milton születésének 350. Évfordulójára' [Samson Agonistes. On the 350th anniversary of John Milton's birth]. *Népszabadság*, 9 December 1958, 2.
Anon. 1958b. '"Milton! Thou shouldst be living at this hour"'. *Labour Monthly*, December, 553.
Anon 1958c. 'Feljegyzés a Vállalat Vezetőségének Milton-versek ügyében' [Report to the management concerning Milton's poems]. Unpublished reader's report for the Európa Publishing House, 13 April.
Anon. 1970. 'A rádió mellett' [Beside the radio]. *Magyar Nemzet*, 27 October, 4.
Anon. 1975. 'Lektori Jelentés. John Milton: A küzdő Sámson' [Reader's report. John Milton. Samson Agonistes]. Unpublished reader's report for the Európa Publishing House, 19 April.
Anon. 2021. 'Sámson'. Record in the Hungarian Radio database. http://radiojatek.elte.hu/index.php?title=Sámson_(Milton) (last accessed 22 February 2022).
Ascher, László, and Soma Braun. 1934. 'Irodalom és politika' [Literature and politics]. *Szocializmus* 24.2: 52–5.
Babits, Mihály. 1934. *Az európai irodalom története* [The history of European literature]. Budapest: Nyugat.
Bart, István. 2002. *Világirodalom és könyvkiadás a Kádár-korszakban* [World literature and publishing in the Kádár era]. Budapest: Osiris.
Bartolovich, Crystal. 2012. 'Humanities of scale: Marxism, surface reading – and Milton'. *PMLA* 127.1: 115–21.
Bernát, István. 1921. 'Milton és a sajtó szabadsága' [Milton and the freedom of the press]. *Budapesti Szemle* 187: 49–67.
Birkett, Jennifer, and James Kearns. *A Guide to French Literature: From early modern to postmodern*. New York: Macmillan, 1997.
Blatchford, Robert. 1925. *A varázsműhely* [The sorcery shop]. Trans. Dezső Schöner. *Népszava* 53, 6–7 June.
Blight, David W. 2018. *Frederick Douglass: Prophet of freedom*. New York: Simon & Schuster.
B. Pap, István. 1909. 'Emlékezés Miltonról 1609–1909' [A commemoration of Milton 1609–1909]. *Protestáns Szemle* 21.1: 107–23.
Boss, V. J. 1991. *Milton and the Rise of Russian Satanism*. Toronto: University of Toronto Press.
Browder, Earl. 1936. *What is Communism?* New York: Vanguard Press.
Brown, Deborah, Annie Finch and Maxine Kumin. 2005. *Lofty Dogmas: Poets on poetics*. Fayetteville: University of Arkansas Press.
Caudwell, Christopher. 1937. *Illusion and Reality: A study of the sources of poetry*. London: Macmillan.

Chapman, Alison A. 2017. *The Legal Epic: 'Paradise Lost' and early modern law*. Chicago: University of Chicago Press, 2017.
Chernaik, Warren. 2017. *Milton and the Burden of Freedom*. Cambridge: Cambridge University Press.
Cohen, Milton A. 2010. *Poets and Leftist Critics: Stevens, Cummings, Frost, and Williams in the 1930s*. Birmingham: University of Alabama Press.
Corns, Thomas N. 2016. 'Satan, the son of God, and the brief epic'. In Thomas N. Corns, ed., *A New Companion to Milton*. Chichester: Wiley Blackwell, 517–28.
Császár, Elemér. 1937. 'Pekár Gyula'. *Uj idők* 43.44: 625–7.
Csetri, Lajos. 1977. 'Egri Péter: A költészet valósága. Líra és lírizálódás' [Review of Egri 1975]. *Tiszatáj* 31.8: 82–5.
Csizmadia, Ervin. 2016. 'The Hungarian democratic opposition in the 1980s'. *Intersections: East European Journal of Society and Politics* 1.4: 119–38.
Csorba, Győző. 1978. *Összegyűjtött versek* [Collected poems]. Budapest: Magvető.
Csukássi, László. 1876. 'Milton mint költő és államférfiú' [Milton as a poet and a statesman]. *Divat-Nefelejts* 2: 149–50, 157, 165.
Czigány, Lóránt. 1984. *The Oxford History of Hungarian Literature*. Oxford: Oxford University Press.
Czigány, Lóránt. 1990. *Nézz vissza haraggal* [Look back in anger]. Budapest: Gondolat.
Czigányik, Zsolt. 2011. 'Readers' responsibility: literature and censorship in the Kádár era in Hungary'. In Gárdos Bálint et al., ed. *Confrontations and Interactions. Essays on Cultural Memory*. Budapest and Paris: L'Harmattan. 223–34.
Cs. Szabó, László. 2005. *Kis népek hivatása* [The calling of small nations]. Budapest: Kortárs.
D. P. 1971. '"Jézus Krisztus Szupersztár"' [Jesus Christ Superstar]. *Világosság* 12.12: 744–6.
Danielik, János. 1847. 'A protestantismus-, mint az észvallás és aranyszabadság· képviselőjéről' [On Protestantism as the representative of golden liberty and the religion of reason]. *Religio* 1 August: 73–6.
Darbishire, Helen, ed. 1932. *The Early Lives of Milton*. London: Constable.
Dávidházi, Péter. 1998a. *Per Passivam Resistentiam: Változatok hatalom és írás témájára* [Per passivam resistentiam: Variation on the themes of power and writing]. Budapest: Argumentum.
Dávidházi, Péter. 1998b. *The Romantic Cult of Shakespeare: Literary reception in anthropological perspective*. London: Palgrave Macmillan.
Davies, Sarah. 2018. 'From Iron Curtain to Velvet Curtain? Peter Brook's *Hamlet* and the origins of British–Soviet cultural relations during the Cold War'. *Contemporary European History* 27.4: 601–26.
DeLeon, Daniel. 1903. 'The blind and the seeing Samson'. *Daily People* 4.106: 1–3.
DeLeon, Daniel. 1906. 'Samson Agonistes'. *Daily People* 6.224: 1–2.
DeLeon, Daniel. 1908. 'Try it again, Teddy'. *Daily People* 9.115: 1–2.
Divald, Kornél. 1900. 'A műcsarnok téli kiállítása' [The winter exhibition of the Kunsthalle]. *Magyar Szemle* 12.52: 622–3.
Dunn, Kevin. 1994. *Pretexts of Authority: The rhetoric of authorship in the Renaissance preface*. Stanford, CA: Stanford University Press.
Duran, Angelica. 2014. 'Walter Raleigh, through John Milton, according to William Carlos Williams'. *William Carlos Williams Review* 31.1: 15–31.
Duran, Angelica, Islam Issa and Jonathan Olson, ed. 2017. *Milton in Translation*. Oxford: Oxford University Press.
Dzelzainis, Martin. 2005. 'History and ideology: Milton, the Levellers, and the Council of State in 1649'. *Huntington Library Quarterly* 68.1–2: 269–87.
Egri, Péter. 1975. *A költészet valósága. Líra és lírizálódás* [The reality of poetry. Lyric and lyricisation]. Budapest: Akadémiai Kiadó.
Engels, Frederick. 1847. 'Reform Movement in France – Banquet of Dijon'. *Northern Star*, 18 December, 398.
Faludy, George. 1985. *Selected Poems 1933–80*. Edited and translated by Robin Skelton. Toronto: McClelland and Stewart.
Ferencz, Győző, ed. 1989. *Donne, Milton és az angol barokk költői* [Donne, Milton and the poets of the English Baroque]. Budapest: Európa.
Ferencz, Győző, and John Hobbs, eds. 1998. *Ágnes Nemes Nagy on Poetry: A Hungarian perspective*. Lewiston, NY: Edwin Mellen Press.
Fest, Sándor, László Országh and Miklós Szenczi. 1941. *Angol nyelvkönyv. 4. rész. A gimnázium és leánygimnázium 8. oszt. számára* [English coursebook, part 4. For the eighth grade in secondary schools]. Budapest: Franklin.

Fodor, András. 1991. 'A kollégium. Napló, 1947–1950' [The college. Journal 1947–1950]. *Alföld* 42: 8, 90–4.
Fodor, József. 1963. *Szertelen ünnep* [Unbridled feast]. Budapest: Szépirodalmi Könyvkiadó.
Fodor, József. 1975. *Egy költészet története* [The history of a poetry]. Budapest: Szépirodalmi Könyvkiadó.
Foot, Paul. 2002. 'Workers' movement: The party's just begun'. *Socialist Review* 259, January, 16–17.
Frank, Tibor. 2017. 'A magyar anglisztika nehéz születése: Szenczi Miklós és Országh László' [The difficult birth of Hungarian English studies: Miklós Szenczi and Lászkló Országh]. In Gábor Papp, ed., *Értelmiségi válaszutak 1945 után* [Intellectuals' crossroads after 1945]. Budapest: Kossuth, 25–36.
Gál, István. 1946. 'Angol tankönyveink hiányosságai' [The shortcomings of our English coursebooks]. *Köznevelés* 2: 8–10.
Gál, István. 1939. 'England and Transylvania'. *Hungarian Quarterly* 5.2: 243–55.
Gáldi, László. 1955. 'Lutter Tibor: "John Milton, az angol polgári forradalom költője" című doktori disszertációjának vitája (1955. x. 10.)'. [Minutes of the viva voce examination of Tibor Lutter's CsC dissertation entitled 'John Milton the Poet of the English Bourgeois Revolution', 10 October 1955].
Gángó, Gábor. 2004. 'Trefort Ágoston, az angol forradalom első Magyar történetírója' [Ágoston Trefort, the first Hungarian historian of the English revolution]. In Frank Tibor, ed., *Angliától Nagy-Britanniáig. Magyar kutatók tanulmányai a brit történelemről*. Budapest: Gondolat, 167–75.
Gömöri, György. 1989. *Angol-magyar kapcsolatok a XVI–XVII. században* [English–Hungarian Relationships in the 16th and 17th Centuries]. Budapest: Akadémiai Kiadó.
Greenblatt, Stephen, et al. 1995. 'Introduction'. *Representations* 49: 1–14.
Gregerson, Linda. 2014. 'Milton and the tragedy of nations'. *PMLA* 129.4: 672–87.
Gyergyai, Albert. 1975. 'Arcképvázlat Szenczi Miklósról' [Portrait-sketch of Miklós Szenczi]. *Nagyvilág* 20.12: 1912–13.
Halász, Gábor, ed. 1942. *Az angol irodalom kincseshéza* [The treasure-house of English literature]. Budapest: Athenaeum.
Hammond, Paul. 2014. *Milton and the People*. Oxford: Oxford University Press.
Hanebrink, Paul A. 2006. *In Defense of Christian Hungary: Religion, nationalism, and antisemitism, 1890–1944*. Ithaca, NY: Cornell University Press.
Hankiss, Elemér. 1994. 'European paradigms: East and West, 1945–1994'. *Daedalus* 123.3: 115–26.
Hao, Tianhu. 2016. 'China'. In Thomas N. Corns, ed., *A New Companion to Milton*. Chichester: Wiley Blackwell, 570–2.
Harsányi, Pál. 1837. 'Levelezés' [Correspondence]. *Hírnök* 1.10: 1–3.
Heller, Ágnes. 2007. *Sámson: Erósz és Thanatosz a Bírák könyvében* [Samson: Eros and Thanatos in Judges]. Budapest: Múlt és Jövő.
Hernádi, Miklós. 1967. 'Az angol költészet "új kritikája"' [The 'new criticism' of English poetry]. *Világosság* 10.9: 95–9.
Hernádi, Miklós. 1970. 'Az új Magyar Milton' [The new Hungarian Milton]. *Élet és irodalom* 7.14: 10.
Hill, Christopher. 1949. 'The tercentenary of the English Revolution'. *Modern Quarterly* n.s. 4.2: 97–8.
Hill, Christopher. 1977. *Milton and the English Revolution*. London: Faber & Faber.
Horányi, Károly. 2010. 'Vád és emlékezet: Lezáratlan eljárások Szabó Lőrinc ügyében' [Accusation and memory: unfinished proceedings in the case of Lőrinc Szabó]. *Kortárs* 54.1: 1–26.
Horváth, Károly. 1995. 'Az ember tragédiája szereplőinek és motívumainak bibliai és világirodalmi előzményeiről' [The biblical and literary antecedents of the *Tragedy of Man*]. In Eszter Tarjányi and Csaba Andor, eds. *I. Madách Szimpózium*. [The first Madách Symposium]. Salgótarján and Budapest: Palócföld and Madách Irodalmi Társaság, 10–51.
James, C. L. R. [G. F. Eckstein]. 1949. 'Ancestors of the proletariat'. *Fourth International* 10.8: 254.
Jameson, Fredric. 1986. 'Religion and ideology: A political reading of *Paradise Lost*'. In Francis Barker et al., *Literature, Politics, and Theory*. London: Methuen, 35–56.
Jánosy, István. 1970. '*Paradise Lost* at the Theatre-in-the-Round'. *New Hungarian Quarterly* 11 (winter): 216–21.
Johnson, Samuel. 2009. *The Lives of the Poets: A selection*. Oxford: Oxford University Press.
Jones, Edward, ed. 2013. *Young Milton: The emerging author, 1620–1642*. Oxford: Oxford University Press.

Jones, Nicholas R. 1977. 'The education of the faithful in Milton's Piedmontese sonnet'. *Milton Studies* 10: 167–76.
Kabdebó, Lóránt. 1992. *"A magyar költészet az én nyelvemen beszél": a kései Nyugat-líra összegződése Szabó Lőrinc költészetében* ['Hungarian poetry speaks my language': the summation of the lyric of the late Nyugat in Lőrinc Szabó's poetry]. Budapest: Argumentum.
Kántás, Balázs. 2014. *Fordulópont. Esszék, tanulmányok, kritikák*. [Turning point. Essays, studies, critiques]. Budapest: Napkút.
Kardos, László, ed. 1952. *Világirodalmi évkönyv 1951* [World literature yearbook 1951]. Budapest: Közoktatásügyi Kiadóvállalat.
Kardos, László. 1954. 'Dybas Tihamér Versfordításairól' [About Tihamér Dybas's literary translations]. *Új hang* 3.7: 117.
Kardos, Tibor. 1957. *Nemes Nagy Ágnes: Szárazvillám*. Review. *Kortárs* 1.2: 314–16.
Keeble, N. H. 1987. *The Literary Culture of Nonconformity in Later Seventeenth-Century England*. Leicester: Leicester University Press.
Keeble, N. H. 2016. 'Milton and Puritanism'. In Thomas N. Corns, ed., *A New Companion to Milton*. Chichester: Wiley Blackwell, 124–40.
Kendrick, Christopher. 1986. *Milton: A study in ideology and form*. New York: Methuen.
Kerényi, Károly. 1984. 'Angyali epika' [Angelic epic]. In Géza Komoróczy and János György Szilágyi, eds. *Halhatatlanság és Apolló-vallás. Ókortudományi tanulmányok 1908–1943* [Immortality and Apollo Religion. Studies in classics 1908–1943]. Budapest: Magvető, 7–15.
Kermode, Frank. 1985. *Forms of Attention: Botticelli and Hamlet*. Chicago: University of Chicago Press.
Kerrigan, William. 1983. *The Sacred Complex: On the psychogenesis of Paradise Lost*. Cambridge, MA: Harvard University Press.
Kéry, László. 1956. 'Milton: Sámson'. *Csillag* 10.5: 1039–40.
Kéry, László, and N. J. Szenczi, eds. 1971. *Studies in English and American Philology*. Budapest: English Department of Budapest University.
Kisfaludy, Zsigmond. 1858. 'Milton János. 1608–1674'. *Szépirodalmi Közlöny*, 19 September, 2403–5.
Knight, G. Wilson. 1942. *Chariot of Wrath: The message of John Milton to democracy at war*. London: Faber and Faber.
Kogan, Pauline. 1969. 'The political theme of Milton's *Paradise Lost*'. *Literature and Ideology* 4 (winter): 21–40.
Kontler, László. 1999. *Millenium in Central Europe: A History of Hungary*. Budapest: Atlantisz.
Koopmann, Helmut. 1982. '"German culture is where I am": Thomas Mann in exile'. *Studies in 20th Century Literature* 7.1: 5–16.
Kostihová, Marcela. 2010. *Shakespeare in Transition: Political appropriations in the postcommunist Czech Republic*. London: Palgrave Macmillan.
Kovács, Anna Zsófia. 2012. 'Milton dictating to his daughters: Varieties on a theme from Füssli to Munkácsy'. In Gábor Ittzés and Miklós Péti, eds, *Milton Through the Centuries*. Budapest: KGRE–L'Harmattan, 322–37.
Kovrig, Bennett. 1986. 'Hungarian socialism: The deceptive hybrid'. *East European Politics and Societies* 1.1: 113–14.
Könyves Tóth, Mihály, trans. 1860. 'Milton. Macaulay által jellemezve' [Milton characterised by Macaulay]. *Sárospataki Füzetek* 4: 495–542.
Kriza, János. 1893. *Kriza János költeményei* [The poems of János Kriza]. Budapest: Franklin.
Kühnová, Šárka. 2007. '"Inspired with contradiction": Milton's language of liberty'. In Christophe Tournu and Neil Forsyth, eds, *Milton, Rights and Liberties*. Bern: Peter Lang, 345–54.
Kulcsár-Szabó, Zoltán. 2010. *Tükörszínjátéka agyadnak. Poétikai problémák Szabó Lőrinc költészetében* [A mirror-play of your mind: Poetical problems in Lőrinc Szabó's poetry]. Budapest: Ráció.
Kulcsár-Szabó, Zoltán. 2012. '"A diktátor én vagyok". Szabó Lőrinc' ['I am the dictator': Lőrinc Szabó]. *Irodalomtörténet* 93.4: 445–67.
Kürti, László. 1970. 'A modern Milton' [The modern Milton]. *Film Színház Muzsika* 14.29: 4–6.
Lange, Anne. 2017. 'A vision in times of need: Milton in Estonia'. In Angelica Duran, Islam Issa and Jonathan Olson, eds, *Milton in Translation*. Oxford: Oxford University Press, 185–98.
Lehóczky, Ágnes. *Poetry, the Geometry of the Living Substance*. Newcastle: Cambridge Scholars, 2011.
Lengyel, Lajos. 1942. 'A filozófia alapproblémája "Az Ember tragédiájá"-ban' [The fundamental problem of philosophy in *The Tragedy of Man*]. *Athenaeum* 28.2: 142–65.

Léner, Péter. 2015. 'Színház és morál' [Theatre and morality]. *168 óra*, 17 July.
Lewalski, Barbara K. 2010. 'Milton and the culture wars'. In John T. Shawcross and David V. Urban, eds, *Visionary Milton: Essays on prophecy and violence*. Pittsburgh, PA: Duquesne University Press, 23–44.
Liebert, Elizabeth. 2008. 'Through Eve's looking-glass'. In Charles W. Durham and Kristin A. Pruitt, eds, *Uncircumscribed Mind: Reading Milton deeply*. Cranbury, NJ: Rosemont, 242–61.
Loewenstein, David. 2013. *Treacherous Faith: The specter of heresy in early modern English literature and culture*. Oxford: Oxford University Press.
Lukács, György [Georg Lukács]. 1956. 'Magyar irodalom – világirodalom' [Hungarian literature – world literature]. *Nagyvilág* 1.1: 3–5.
Lukács, Georg. 1968. *Goethe and His Age*. Trans. Robert Anchor. London: Merlin.
Lukácsy, Sándor. 1983. 'Kincsásás V. Álmok a történelemről' [Digging for treasure V. Dreams about history]. *Kortárs* 27.11: 1763–8.
Lutter, Tibor. 1935. *Az újabb angol irodalom nagy kérdőjele: James Joyce* [James Joyce: The great question mark of new English literature]. Budapest: Pázmány Péter Tudományegyetem.
Lutter, Tibor. 1944. *The Spiritual Aspects of Early Quakerism*. Budapest: self-published.
Lutter, Tibor. 1947. 'Metafizikus esztétika' [Metaphysical aesthetics]. *Forum* 1947.8: 615–21.
Lutter, Tibor. 1949. 'Shakespeare és a magyar anglisztika néhány kérdése' [Shakespeare and some questions of Hungarian English studies]. *Irodalomtörténet* 37: 77–97.
Lutter, Tibor. *Milton and Seventeenth Century Literature: A synopsis to a fourteen weeks' course*. Typescript (OSZK 213.218), VKM Jegyzetsokszorosító Iroda, 1951.
Lutter, Tibor. 1952. 'John Milton, "A Paradicsom elveszítése" c. hőskölteménye és a 17. századi angol forradalom' [John Milton's heroic poem *Paradise Lost* and the English Revolution of the seventeenth century]. In Kardos 1952, 212–49.
Lutter, Tibor. 1955a. '"A költészet védelmében" (A Caudwell-vita)' ['In defense of poetry': The Caudwell controversy]. *Filológiai közlöny* 1.2: 245–9.
Lutter, Tibor. 1955b. 'A polgári angol irodalomtörténetírás mai útjai' [Contemporary bourgeois trends in the study of English literary history]. *Filológiai közlöny* 1.1: 47–57.
Lutter, Tibor. 1956a. *John Milton, az angol polgári forradalom költője* [John Milton, the poet of the English Bourgeois Revolution]. Budapest: Akadémiai Kiadó.
Lutter, Tibor. 1956b. 'Angol professzori konferencia Cambridge-ben' [Conference of professors of English in Cambridge]. *Nagyvilág* 1956.1: 185–8.
Lutter, Tibor, ed. 1960a. *Angol irodalom*. [English literature]. Budapest: Tankönyvkiadó.
Lutter, Tibor. 1960b. '"Elkötelezettség" és irodalom' ['Commitment' and literature]. *Nagyvilág* 1960.1: 136–7.
Macaulay, Thomas Babington. 1825. 'Milton'. *Edinburgh Review*, 304–46.
MacDonald, Keith. 2005. 'Christopher Caudwell: A critical evaluation'. PhD thesis, Cardiff University.
Makaryk, Irena R., and Joseph Price, eds. 2006. *Shakespeare in the Worlds of Communism and Socialism*. Toronto: University of Toronto Press.
von Maltzahn, Nicholas. 1995. 'The Whig Milton, 1667–1700'. In David Armitage, Armand Himy and Quentin Skinner, eds, *Milton and Republicanism*. Cambridge: Cambridge University Press, 229–53.
Mark, James. 2005. 'Society, resistance and revolution: The Budapest middle class and the Hungarian Communist State 1948–56'. *English Historical Review* 120.488: 963–86.
Mark, James, and Péter Apor. 2015. 'Socialism goes global: Decolonization and the making of a new culture of internationalism in socialist Hungary 1956–1989'. *Journal of Modern History* 87: 852–91.
Markója, Csilla. 2008. '"Ellentétek keresztezési pontja vagy magad is": Zádor Anna kapcsolatai és a magyar művészettörténet-írás a két háború között' [You yourself are intersection of contraries: Anna Zádor's connections and Hungarian art history in the interwar period]. *Enigma* 55: 25–66.
Marx, Karl. 2000. *Selected Writings*. Oxford: Oxford University Press.
Marx, Karl, and Frederick Engels. 1993. *Collected Works*, vol. 34. New York: International Publishers.
McDowell, Nicholas. 2016. 'Milton's Euripides and the superior rationality of the heathen'. *The Seventeenth Century* 31: 215–37.
McDowell, Nicholas. 2020. *Poet of Revolution: The making of John Milton*. Princeton, NJ: Princeton University Press.

Menyhért, A. 2013. *Női irodalmi hagyomány: Erdős Renée, Nemes Nagy Ágnes, Czóbel Minka, Kosztolányiné Harmos Ilona, Lesznai Anna* [Women's literary tradition: Renée Erdős, Ágnes Nemes Nagy, Minka Czóbel, Ilona Harmos Kosztolányi, Anna Lesznai]. Budapest: Napvilág.

Milton, John. 1796. *Elveszett Paraditsom Milton által. Fordította Frantziából Bessenyei Sándor* [Paradise Lost by Milton. Translated from the French by Sándor Bessenyei], 2 vols. Kassa: Ellinger.

Milton, John. 1890. *Elveszett paradicsom* [Paradise Lost]. Trans. Gusztáv Jánosi. Budapest: Franklin.

Milton, John. 1904. *Elveszett paradicsom* [Paradise Lost]. Trans. Gusztáv Jánosi, 2nd edn. Budapest: Franklin.

Milton, John. 1921. *Kisebb költemények. Fordította Tóth Árpád* [Shorter poems. Translated by Tóth Árpád]. Gyoma: Kner.

Milton, John. 1930. *Elveszett paradicsom* [Paradise Lost]. Trans. Gusztáv Jánosi, preface by László Ravasz. Budapest: Franklin.

Milton, John. 1955. *Sámson* [Samson Agonistes]. Budapest: Új Magyar Könyvkiadó.

Milton, John. 1958. *Versek/Poems*. Budapest: Európa.

Milton, John. 1969. *Elveszett Paradicsom* [Paradise Lost]. Trans. István Jánosy. Budapest: Magyar Helikon.

Milton, John. 1977. *A küzdő Sámson* [Samson Agonistes]. Bucharest: Kriterion.

Milton, John. 1978. *John Milton válogatott költői művei* [Selected poetical works of John Milton]. Budapest: Európa.

Milton, John. 1998. *The Complete Poems*. Ed. John Leonard. Harmondsworth: Penguin.

Milton, John. 2007. *Paradise Lost*. Ed. Barbara K. Lewalski. Oxford: Blackwell.

Milton, John. 2009. *Complete Shorter Poems*. Ed. Stella P. Revard. Chichester: Wiley-Blackwell.

Milton, John. 2013. *Prose: Major writings on liberty, politics, religion, and education*. Ed. David Loewenstein. Chichester: Wiley-Blackwell.

Milton, John. 2019. *Visszanyert Paradicsom/Paradise Regained*. Trans. Miklós Péti. Budapest: Jelenkor.

Mohamed, Feisal. 2011. *Milton and the Post-Secular Present: Ethics, politics, terrorism*. Stanford, CA: Stanford University Press.

Molnár Gál, Péter. 1970. 'Kazimir Miltonja' [Kazimir's Milton]. *Népszabadság*, 15 July.

Monticelli, Daniele, and Anne Lange. 2014. 'Translation and totalitarianism: The case of Soviet Estonia'. *The Translator* 20.1: 95–111.

N. A. 1837. 'Milton'. *Honművész*, 23 March: 185–7.

Nagy, Emil. 1927. 'Az igazság' [Truth]. *Pesti Hirlap* 49.271: 1–2.

Nemes G., Zsuzsanna. 1970. 'Milton a körszínházban' [Milton in the Theatre-in-the-Round]. *Kritika* 10.8: 60–1.

Nemes Nagy, Ágnes. 1957. *Szárazvillám. Versek és műfordítások* [Dry Lightning: Poems and translations]. Budapest: Magvető.

Nemes Nagy, Ágnes. 1988. *Between: Selected poems of Ágnes Nemes Nagy*. Trans. Hugh Maxton. Budapest: Corvina.

Nemes Nagy, Ágnes. 2004. *The Night of Akhenaton*. Trans. and ed. George Szirtes. Tarset: Bloodaxe.

Nemes Nagy, Ágnes. 2007. *51 vers – 51 Poems*. Trans. P. Zollman. Budapest: Maecenas.

Nemes Nagy, Ágnes. 2008. 'Nemes Nagy Ágnes hagyatékából (II)' [From the heritage of Ágnes Nemes Nagy]. Ed. Győző Ferencz. *Holmi* 20.5: 592–607.

Nemes Nagy, Ágnes. 2016. *Nemes Nagy Ágnes összegyűjtött versei* [The collected poems of Ágnes Nemes Nagy]. Budapest: Jelenkor.

Németh, László. 1974. *Sajkódi esték* [Evenings at Sajkód]. Budapest: Magvető.

Neubauer, John. 2004. 'Introduction'. In Marcel Cornis-Pope and John Neubauer, eds, *History of the Literary Cultures of East-Central Europe: Junctures and Disjunctures in the 19th and 20th Centuries*, vol. 3. Amsterdam: John Benjamins.

Olgyay, Bertalan. 1936. 'Angol remekírók műveinek nevelő értéke' [The educative value of English classics]. In Ernő Fináncy, Gyula Kornis and Ferenc Kemény, eds. *Pedagógiai Lexikon* [Pedagogical lexicon], 2 vols, 1: 84–6. Budapest: Révai.

Pál, Zoltán. 2010. 'Lutter Tibor államvédelmi megfigyelése' [The surveillance of Tibor Lutter by Communist state security]. *Betekintő* 2010.3.

Pataky, Adrienn. 2016. *Szabad Kötöttség. Szonettekről és politikai líráról a '45 utáni Magyar irodalomban* [Free in Tethers: About sonnets and political literature in Hungarian after '45]. Budapest: Ráció.

Peacey, Jason. 2016. 'Miltonic texts and European politics, 1674–1682'. In Blair Hoxby and Ann Baynes Coiro, eds, *Milton in the Long Restoration*. Oxford: Oxford University Press.
Pearce, Brian. 1958. 'South Bank and Tolpuddle'. *The Newsletter* 2.81: 332.
Péter, Ágnes. 2011. 'The Romantic myth of Milton in Hungary: Mór Jókai's *Milton*'. In Bálint Gárdos et al., eds, *Confrontations and Interactions: Essays on cultural memory*. Budapest: L'Harmattan, 191–211.
Péter, Ágnes. 2012. 'Milton in the Hungarian cultural memory: Two case studies'. In Gábor Ittzés and Miklós Péti, eds, *Milton Through the Centuries*. Budapest: KGRE–L'Harmattan, 165–87.
Péteri, György. 2006. 'Introduction'. In *Nylon Curtain: Transnational and transsystemic tendencies in the cultural life of state-socialist Russia and East-Central Europe*. Trondheim: Trondheim Studies on East European Cultures and Societies.
Pető, Andrea. 2001. 'Hungarian women's writing 1945–95'. In C. Hawkesworth, ed., *A History of Central European Women's Writing*. London: Palgrave Macmillan, 2001, 240–55.
Péti, Miklós. 2014. 'A heap of broken images or, why Milton is an iconoclast?'. *Classical Receptions Journal* 6.2: 270–93.
Péti, Miklós. 2017. 'In Milton's prison: Milton in Hungarian translation'. In Angelica Duran, Islam Issa and Jonathan R. Olson, eds, *Milton in Translation*. Oxford: Oxford University Press, 329–48.
Péti, Miklós. 2018. '*Paradise Lost* on the Hungarian stage in 1970'. *Milton Quarterly* 52.3: 153–283.
Péti, Miklós. 2021a. 'Milton's new hero: Homeric revisions in *Paradise Regained*'. *Review of English Studies* 72.305: 459–80.
Péti, Miklós. 2021b. 'Samson: An unlikely hero of socialism'. In David Ainsworth and Thomas Festa, eds, *Locating Milton*. Clemson, SC: Clemson University Press, 185–205.
Péti, Miklós. 2021c. '"I am not 'masculine'. I am weak": Ágnes Nemes Nagy's translation of Sonnet 23'. In Mandy Green and Sharihan Al-Akhras, eds, *Women (Re)Writing Milton*. New York: Routledge, 106–20.
Petrochevich Horváth, Lázár. 1846. 'A Vesztett Paradicsom' [Paradise Lost]. *Honderű*, 10 February: 101–4.
Pomogáts, Béla. 2000. 'Egy prózai és egy verses vallomás: Szabó Lőrinc 1956-ban' [A confession in prose and one in verse: Lőrinc Szabó in 1956]. *Új holnap* 45: 70–3.
Pope, Alexander. 1969. 'Preface to the *Iliad*'. In Geoffrey Tillotson, Paul Fussell Jr and Marshall Waingrow, eds, *Eighteenth Century English Literature*. New York: Harcourt, Brace, and Jovanovich, 587–600.
Porter, William. 1993. *Reading the Classics and Paradise Lost*. Lincoln: University of Nebraska Press.
Prusinszky, Sándor. 2014. *Halhatatlan Cenzúra* [Immortal censorship]. Budapest: Médiatudományi Intézet.
Rába, György. 1969. *A szép hűtlenek (Babits, Kosztolányi, Tóth Árpád versfordításai* [Les Belles Infidèles (poem translations by Babits, Kosztolányi and Árpád Tóth)]. Budapest: Akadémiai Kiadó.
Radnóti, Sándor. 1974. 'Között. Nemes Nagy Ágnes lírája' [Between: the lyric of Ágnes Nemes Nagy]. *Kortárs* 19.7–12: 1298–1304.
Radzinowicz, Mary Ann. 1978. *Toward Samson Agonistes: The Growth of Milton's Mind*. Princeton, NJ: Princeton University Press.
Reményi, Ede. 1895. 'Leírások Milton eposzaiban' [Descriptions in Milton's epics]. *Egyetemes Filológiai Közlöny* 19.1: 213–23.
Reményi, Ede. 1898. 'Milton Krisztusa és Sátánja' [Milton's Christ and Satan]. *Egyetemes Filológia Közlöny* 22.1: 433–46.
Rév, István. 1994. 'The postmortem victory of communism'. *Daedalus* 123.3: 159–70.
Richmond, Hugh M. 1988. '*Paradise Lost*: Performance as criticism'. *Milton Quarterly* 22.1: 17–20.
Rickword, Edgell. 1949. 'Milton: The revolutionary intellectual'. In Christopher Hill, ed., *The English Revolution 1640: Three essays*. London: Lawrence and Wishart, 1949.
Rumrich, John P. 1996. *Milton Unbound: Controversy and reinterpretation*. Cambridge: Cambridge University Press.
Sauer, Elizabeth. 2001. 'The neo-Christian bias and its discontents: Milton studies and the case of *Samson Agonistes*'. *Renaissance and Reformation/Renaissance et Réforme* 25.4: 157–70.
Schandl, Veronika. 2008. *Socialist Shakespeare Productions in Kádár-Regime Hungary: Shakespeare behind the Iron Curtain*. Lewiston, NY: Edwin Mellen Press.
Schlueter, Kurt. 1995. 'Milton's heroical sonnets'. *Studies in English Literature, 1500–1900* 35.1: 123–36.

Sheen, Erica, and Isabel Karremann, eds. 2016. *Shakespeare in Cold War Europe: Conflict, commemoration, celebration*. London: Palgrave Macmillan.
Shore, Daniel. 2012. 'Why Milton is not an iconoclast'. *PMLA* 127.1: 22–37.
Shurbanov, Alexander, and Boika Sokolova. 2001. *Painting Shakespeare Red: An East-European appropriation*. London: Associated University Presses.
Sík, Csaba. 1958. *Nemes Nagy Ágnes: Szárazvillám*. Review. *Irodalomtörténet* 46: 305–7.
Smith, Nigel. 2021. 'Milton and radicalism'. In Emma Depledge, John S. Garrison and Marissa Nicosia, eds, *Making Milton: Print, authorship, afterlives*. Oxford: Oxford University Press, 198–215.
Sós, Endre. 1949. '"A regénypályázat eredménytelen . . ."' [The novel competition ends without results . . .]. *Magyar Nemzet* 5.255: 1–2.
Sőtér, István, ed. 1962. *Világirodalmi antológia. III. kötet. A XVII. és a XVIII. század irodalma* [Anthology of world literature, vol. 3. The literature of the 17th and 18th centuries]. Budapest: Tankönyvkiadó.
Stroup, Thomas B. 1960. 'Aeneas' vision of Creusa and Milton's twenty-third sonnet'. *Philological Quarterly* 39: 125–6.
Szabó, Lőrinc. 1993. *Harminchat év: Szabó Lőrinc és felesége levelezése. 2 (1945–1957); párhuzamosok* [Thirty-six years: The correspondence of Lőrinc Szabó and his wife. 2. (1945–1957); parallels]. Budapest: Magvető.
Szabó, Lőrinc. 2000. *Huszonöt év: Szabó Lőrinc és Vékesné Korzáti Erzsébet levelezése* [Twenty-five years: The correspondence of Lőrinc Szabó and Erzsébet Korzáti-Vékes]. Budapest: Magvető.
Szabó, Lőrinc. 2002. *Örök barátaink: a költő kisebb lírai versfordításai* [Our eternal friends: The poet's translations of shorter lyric poems], 2 vols. Budapest: Osiris.
Szabó, Lőrinc. 2003a. *Emlékezések és publicisztikák* [Reminiscences and journalism]. Budapest: Osiris.
Szabó, Lőrinc. 2003b. *Összes versei* [The complete poems], 2 vols. Budapest: Osiris.
Szabó, Lőrinc. 2008. *Vallomások: Naplók, beszélgetések, levelek* [Confessions: Diaries, conversations, letters]. Budapest: Osiris.
Szász, Károly. 1882. *A világirodalom nagy époszai* [Great epics of world literature], 2 vols. Budapest: A Magyar Tudományos Akadémia Könyvkiadó-Vállalata.
Szegedy-Maszák, Mihály. 1968. 'William Empson: Milton's God'. *Helikon* 14.1: 161.
Szenczi, Miklós. 1932. *Webster tragikus művészete* [The tragic art of Webster]. Budapest: A Kir. Magy. Pázmány Péter Tudományegyetem Angol Philológiai Intézetének Kiadványai IX.
Szenczi, Miklós [N. J. Szenczi]. 1937. 'East and West in Hungarian literature'. *Slavonic and East European Review* 16.46: 141–54.
Szenczi, Miklós [N. J. Szenczi]. 1939. 'Great Britain and the War of Hungarian Independence'. *Slavonic and East European Review* 17.51: 556–70.
Szenczi, Miklós [N. J. Szenczi]. 1946. 'British influences on Hungarian literature'. *Slavonic and East European Review* 24.63: 172–9.
Szenczi, Miklós. 1958. 'John Milton (Kálnoky László versfordításaival)' [John Milton (with translation of the poems by László Kálnoky)]. *Nagyvilág* 3.12: 1815–21.
Szenczi, Miklós. 1961. *Angol reneszánsz drámák* [English Renaissance plays], 2 vols. Budapest: Európa.
Szenczi, Miklós. 1965. 'A szovjet Shakespeare-kritika kialakulása és főbb eredményei' [The development and major results of Soviet Shakespeare criticism]. In Kéry László, Országh László and Szenczi Miklós, eds, *Shakespeare-tanulmányok*. Budapest: Akadémiai Kiadó, 173–216.
Szenczi, Miklós. 1967. 'Milton on Russia'. *New Hungarian Quarterly* 25.8: 177–82.
Szenczi, Miklós [N. J. Szenczi]. 1971. 'Milton's dialectic in *Paradise Lost*: Some patterns of interpretation'. In László Kéry and N. J. Szenczi, eds, *Studies in English and American Philology*. Budapest: English Department of Budapest University, 58–92.
Szenczi, Miklós, ed. 1975. *Milton, az angol forradalom tükre* [Milton, the mirror of the English Revolution]. Budapest: Gondolat.
Szenczi, Miklós, Tibor Szobotka and Anna Katona. 1972. *Az angol irodalom története* [The history of English literature]. Budapest: Gondolat.
Szenczi, Miklós. 1989. *Tanulmányok.* [Critical Works]. Selected and edited by István Géher. Budapest: Akadémiai Kiadó.
Szerb, Antal. 1957. *A világirodalom története* [History of world literature], 2 vols. Budapest: Bibliotheca.

Szigeti, Jenő. 1970. 'Milton Elveszett paradicsom-a Magyarországon' [Milton's *Paradise Lost* in Hungary]. *Irodalomtörténeti közlemények* 1970.2: 205–13.
Szilágyi, Ferenc. 1979. 'A "Milton" Elveszett paradicsomáról' (Csokonai Vitéz Mihály ismeretlen költeménye)' [On Milton's *Paradise Lost*: An unknown poem by Mihály Csokonai Vitéz]. *Magyar tudomány*. 24.4: 312–19.
Taine, Hippolyte Adolphe. 1882. *Az angol irodalom története* [The history of English literature], 2 vols. Trans. Gergely Csiky. Budapest: A Magyar Tudományos Akadémia Könyvkiadó-Vállalata.
Takács, Ferenc. 1975. 'Milton időszerűsége' [Milton's timeliness]. *Világosság* 16.7: 406–8.
Takács, Ferenc. 2002. 'The Unbought Grace – Literature and Publishing under Socialism'. *Hungarian Quarterly* 43 (2002): 75–8.
Tamás, Gáspár Miklós. 1991. 'A rendszerváltás zimankója' [The bitter cold of the change of system]. *Élet és irodalom*, 5 April 1991: 10.
Tarnai, Andor. 1965. 'The Hungarian Milton debate in the 18th century'. *New Hungarian Quarterly* 19.6: 167–70.
Taylor, Mary N. 2021. *Movement of the People: Hungarian folk dance, populism, and citizenship*. Bloomington: Indiana University Press.
Teskey, Gordon. 2015. *The Poetry of John Milton*. Cambridge, MA: Harvard University Press.
Thomas, Alfred. 2014. *Shakespeare, Dissent, and the Cold War*. London: Palgrave Macmillan.
Thomson, George. 1946. *Marxism and Poetry*. New York: International Publishers.
Ulreich, John C. 1974. 'Typological symbolism in Milton's Sonnet XXIII'. *Milton Quarterly* 8.1: 7–10.
Ungvári, Tamás. 1970. 'Az elveszett Paradicsom. Bemutató a Körszínházban' [*Paradise Lost*: First night in the Theater-in-the-Round]. *Magyar Nemzet*, 14 July: 4.
Uzakova, Oydin. 2014. 'The reception history of John Milton in Russia and the former Soviet Union'. PhD thesis, Oklahoma State University.
Várady, Szabolcs. 1975. 'Lektori Jelentés. John Milton: *A küzdő Sámson*' [Reader's report. John Milton, *Samson Agonistes*]. Unpublished reader's report for the Európa Publishing House, 25 April.
Vas, István, ed. and trans. 1946. *Angol barokk líra/Seventeenth Century Poets*. Budapest: Officina.
Veress, Dániel. 1958. 'A Lord Protektor titkára' [The secretary of the Lord Protector]. *Utunk* 26.2: 2.
Vesenyi, Paul E. 1972. 'Milton on stage behind the Iron Curtain'. *Milton Quarterly* 6.2: 16–17.
Viktor, János. 1955. 'Milton: Sámson'. *Magyar Nemzet*, 16 July: 5.
Visick, Mary. 1949. 'John Milton and the revolution'. *Modern Quarterly* n.s. 4.2: 189–90.
Voinovich, Géza. 1926. *Az angol irodalom története* [The history of English literature]. Budapest: Franklin.
Walker, William. 2014. *Antiformalist, Unrevolutionary, Illiberal Milton: Political prose, 1644–1660*. London: Ashgate.
Wéber, Antal. 1970. 'Milton eposza új fordításban' [Milton's epic in new translation]. *Nagyvilág* 15.11:1726–8.
Wesling, Donald. 1980. *The Chances of Rhyme: Device and modernity*. Oakland: University of California Press.
Williams, William Carlos. 2001. *The Collected Poems of William Carlos Williams*, vol. 2, 1939–1962. Edited by Christopher MacGowan. New York: New Directions.
Wittreich, Joseph Anthony Jr, ed. 1970. *The Romantics on Milton: Formal essays and critical asides*. Cleveland, OH: The Press of Case Western Reserve University.
Wittreich, Joseph. 'Speaking for Myself.' *Milton Quarterly* 45.4 (2011): 267–70.
Wlislocki, Henrik. 1884. 'Az *Elveszett Paradicsom* költője és a sajtószabadság' [The poet of *Paradise Lost* and the freedom of the press]. *Egyetemes Philologiai Közlöny* 1884.8: 109–12.
Wolfe, Don M. 1963. *Milton in the Puritan Revolution*. London: Cohen & West.
Worden, Blair. 1995. 'Milton, *Samson Agonistes*, and the Restoration'. In Gerald Maclean, ed., *Culture and Society in the Stuart Restoration: Literature, drama, history*. Cambridge: Cambridge University Press.
Yolland, Arthur. 1912. 'Milton János' [John Milton]. *Katholikus szemle* 1912.5: 503–16.
Yurchak, Alexei. 2005. *Everything Was Forever, Until It Was No More: The last Soviet generation*. Princeton, NJ: Princeton University Press.

Index

Achinstein, Sharon, 9, 12, 61, 66–7, 106
actually existing socialism, 2, 16
Aczél, György, 15. *See also* three Ts / three Ps
Ady, Endre, 111
aestheticism, 77
Apollo (periodical), 117
Aragon, Louis, 75
Arany, János, 88
armaments race, 46
atomic war, 46

Babits, Mihály, 73, 90, 125
barbed wire, 60–61
Baroque, 5, 113, 125–6, 128, 129
Bart, István, 15–6
Bartos, Tibor, 122
Beethoven, Ludwig van, 46, 125
Berlin Wall, 146
Bernát, István, 95
Bessenyei, Ferenc, 89
Bessenyei, Sándor, 20, 21–2, 127–8
blank verse, 23, 28, 47, 66
Blatchford, Joseph, 24
Boguszowicz, Szymon, 119
Brown, John, 88
Bunyan, John, 91
Bush, Douglas, 103

Caudwell, Christopher, 8, 25, 28, 69, 71, 85
Ceauşescu, Nicolae, 84
censorship, 14, 84, 95, 96, 107, 144
change of system, 4, 14, 21, 81, 86
Chapman, Alison, 35
Charles I, 93, 94
Chateaubriand, François-René de, 118
Chernaik, Warren, 105
Christian liberty, 101, 117
Cold War, 9, 12, 25, 88, 91, 106, 117, 146
Communist Manifesto, 98, 101
communist takeover, 4, 74, 91
compromises, 5, 12, 15, 16, 27, 44, 50, 87.
    See also consolidation and goulash
    communism
consolidation, 15, 44, 50, 61, 129. *See also*
    compromises and goulash communism
counter-revolution, 10, 28, 71, 88, 101, 123
counterculture, 15, 56, 64
Cromwell, Oliver, 11, 24, 66, 70, 91, 97, 112, 124, 125, 130, 142

Cs. Szabó, László, 1–4, 117
Csengeri, István, 93
Csokonai Vitéz, Mihály, 21–22
Csorba, Győző, 12
Czigány, Lóránt, 17, 38, 63
Czigányik, Zsolt, 18
Czuczor, Gergely, 1–3

Daily People (*The People*), 69
Damkó, József, 24
Danielik, János, 94
Dante, Alighieri, 29, 42, 101
    Divine Comedy (stage version), 52
Darbishire, Helen, 61, 121
Dávidházi, Péter, 47, 115
Defoe, Daniel, 91
DeLeon, Daniel, 69–70
democratic opposition, 16
Déry, Tibor, 64
Dickens, Charles, 75
dictatorship, 11, 12, 14, 15, 19, 33, 43, 70, 74, 91, 99, 130, 141
dictatorship of the proletariat, 31–2, 76
Doré, Gustave, 75
Douglass, Frederick, 88
Dryden, John, 43
    The State of Innocence and Fall of Man, 4, 52
Dugovics, Titusz, 88. *See also* heroic suicide
    and Wagner, Alexander von
Dunn, Kevin, 105
Dupré de Saint-Maur, Nicolas-François, 21, 127
Dybas, Tihamér (Ian MacLeod), 82, 83, 84
    translation of *Samson Agonistes*, 74–81
    as 'defector', 80, 122

Egri, Péter, 125–6
Élet és irodalom (literary weekly), 51
Eliot, T. S., 20, 46, 103
Empson, William, 85, 87
Engels, Friedrich, 7, 17, 45, 68, 97, 101, 113
English as an academic subject, 91
English Civil War, 3, 109, 119. *See also* English Revolution
English Revolution, 3, 8, 9, 18, 27, 71, 79, 97, 100, 107, 108, 116. *See also* English Civil War
Eörsi, István, 79
Eötvös József Collegium, 98, 107, 109

Eötvös Loránd University, 44, 101, 107.
    See also Pázmány Péter University
epic *Kunstsprache*, 48
Euripides, 135
Európa Publishing House, 14, 20, 74, 80, 84, 121–2
Evelyn, John, 91

Faithorne, William, 117
Faludy, György (George Faludy), 11–2
fascism, 2, 61. *See also* Nazism
Ferencz, Győző, 129–30, 136, 142
'fight for peace', 124
Fish, Stanley, 47
Fodor, József, 11–2
Foot, Paul, 71–2, 76
France, Anatole, 75, 101
Frank, Tibor, 119
Franklin Publishing House, 19, 32
freedom
    of conscience, 92, 96
    of speech, 105
    of the Church, 94
    of the press, 95, 104, 118
    of the will, 109
French Revolution, 66, 75, 118
Funeral Sermon and Prayer, 36

Gáborjáni, Klára, 89
Gál, István, 90–1, 117, 118
Géher, István, 115
Gibbons, Stella, 99
Gilgamesh (stage version), 52
Gömöri, George, 93
Gondolat Publishing House, 114
goulash communism, 12, 16, 87. *See also* compromises and consolidation
grand style, 51
Greenblatt, Stephen, 16
Gregerson, Linda, 89
Gyergyai, Albert, 116

Halász, Gábor, 91, 96–7, 117, 118
Hammond, Paul, 67
Heller, Ágnes, 81, 86
heroic suicide, 72. *See also* Dugovics, Titusz and Wagner, Alexander von
Hill, Christopher, 8, 9, 10, 44, 68, 70, 71, 87, 89, 103, 112–3
    'Milton the radical', 85
    The English Revolution 1640, 8, 17
    Milton and the English Revolution, 85, 86
hippies, 51, 53, 56, 57
Hitler, Adolf, 2, 30, 37, 39–40
Homer, 42, 135, 141, 145–6
Horváth, Viktor, 63, 148
Hungarian–English Association, 117
Hungarian Protestant Bible ('Károlyi' Bible, 1590), 47, 77, 83
Hungarian Radio, 74, 77, 80

Inber, Vera, 75
Internationale, 71
internationalism, 2, 3, 7, 67, 97

invocation, 31, 35–6, 47–8, 54, 136
Iron Curtain, 4, 5, 9, 13, 51, 61, 68, 117, 146–7
Irving, Washington, 99

James, C. L. R. (G. F. Eckstein), 9
Jameson, Frederic, 88
Jánosházy, György
    on *Paradise Regained*, 26–7
    translation of *Samson Agonistes*, 81–4
Jánosi, Gusztáv, 20, 23, 45, 47, 48, 62, 73, 94, 97, 122, 128
    translation of *Paradise Lost*, 28–9
Jánosy, István, 21, 57, 125, 128, 147
    translation of *Paradise Lost*, 4, 20, 43–51, 84, 85, 110, 146
    script of the stage version of *Paradise Lost*, 52–56, 146
Johnson, Samuel, 20, 47, 62
Jókai, Mór, 6
Jonson, Ben, 118

Kabdebó, Lóránt, 29
Kádár era, 15, 50, 114, 124
Kádár, János, 15, 123
Kalevala (stage version), 52
Kálnoky, László, 125
Kardos, László, 78, 99
Kaverin, Veniamin, 75
Kazimir, Károly, 45, 52–61, 146–7
Keats, John, 141
Keeble, N. H., 5
Kendrick, Christopher, 88
Képes, Géza, 125, 126
Kerényi, Károly (Carl Kerényi), 61
Kermode, Frank, 148
Kéry, László, 78, 80
Kettle, Arnold, 70
Khrushchev, Nikita Sergeyevich, 14
Kiséry, András, 147
Knight, G. Wilson, 10
Kogan, Pauline, 9
Komáromy, Zsolt, 147
Könczöl, Miklós, 147
Kontler, László, 18
Kossuth, Lajos, 90
Kossuth Prize, 32
Kriterion Publishing House, 81, 86
Kriza, János, 22–3
Kühnová, Šárka, 76
Kulcsár-Szabó, Zoltán, 30, 35

Labour Monthly, 70–1
Lange, Anne, 146
Lenin (Vladimir Ilyich Ulyanov), 14, 146.
    See also 'Marxist-Leninist' scholarship
Levellers, 70, 71–2, 101, 119
Lewis, C. S., 28
liberalism, 12, 15, 61
liberty, 70, 71, 76–7, 82, 92, 94, 95, 101, 104, 112
Lindsay, Jack, 103
Loewenstein, David, 98
Longfellow, Henry Wadsworth, 68

Lukács, György (Georg Lukács), 14–5, 126
Lutter, Tibor, 5, 44, 63, 80, 84, 92, 98–9, 103, 106, 107, 108, 109, 111, 114, 115, 116, 129, 130, 146
  ambivalence towards Anglo-American scholarship, 119
  course synopsis on Milton, 62, 101–2
  John Milton, the Poet of the English Bourgeois Revolution, 27, 103–5, 108
  on Milton's republicanism, 101
  preface to the 1958 *Poems*, 122–4, 126, 129
  reader's reports, 99, 118
  relationship with Miklós Szenczi, 119
  translating and/or editing excerpts from *Areopagitica*, 97, 107
  views on *Paradise Lost*, 27–9
  views on *Paradise Regained*, 25, 62
  views on *Samson Agonistes*, 79

Macaulay, Thomas Babington, 5, 72, 94, 95
Madách, Imre, 22, 24, 53, 57, 75
Mádi-Szabó, Gábor, 89
Madsen, William George, 121
Mann, Thomas, 2, 75
Mark, James, 16, 17
Marvell, Andrew, 19
Marx, Karl, 7–8, 45, 68, 71, 101
Marxism, 24, 61, 68, 70, 85, 88, 95, 98, 104, 109, 112–3, 116, 147
Marxist criticism, 8, 10, 14, 17, 25, 44, 69, 70, 83, 106, 112–3, 115
'Marxist fig leaf', 109
'Marxist-Leninist' scholarship, 10, 25, 28, 44, 72, 74, 84, 85, 87, 99, 100, 103, 107, 108, 111, 144, 146, 147
Masson, David, 28, 102
materialist dialectic, 44
McCarthyism, 66
McDowell, Nicholas, 10, 91
metaphysical poets, 102
Mihály, Árpád, 147
Milton, John
  as 'contemporary', 7, 27, 111
  as 'radical', 7, 9, 10, 66, 67, 72, 85–6, 104, 106
  as revolutionary, 7, 8, 9, 10, 13, 25, 26, 27, 44, 66, 68, 70, 72, 74, 96–7, 102, 104–6, 112, 114, 116–7, 123
  A Brief History of Moscovia, 110, 115
  An Apology against a Pamphlet, 111
  Areopagitica, 15, 68, 70, 91, 94, 95, 96, 97–8, 101, 104, 107, 109, 112, 113, 115, 147
  Comus, 67, 72, 122, 148
  De Doctrina Christiana, 105, 115
  Defensio pro Populo Anglicano, 93–95, 108
  Defensio Secunda, 108
  difficulties of his poetry, 19–21
  Eikonoklastes, 95
  his 'cult' in Hungary, 6
  his Puritan revolutionary ethics, 104
  his 'revolutionary classicism', 87
  'Il Penseroso', 96, 124, 125
  Italian poems, 122, 129
  'L'Allegro', 124, 125
  Latin poems, 72, 104, 148
  'Lycidas', 5, 124, 125
  Of Education, 91, 115
  Of Reformation, 112
  'On Shakespeare', 124, 125
  'On the new forcers of conscience', 11
  Paradise Lost, 4, 7, 8, 9, 10, 12, 13, 15, 17, 68, 72, 73, 74, 79, 80, 83, 84–6, 92, 93, 94, 96, 97, 100, 102, 104, 105, 106, 108, 110, 111, 113, 114, 122, 124, 127, 128, 134, 136, 145–6, 147. See also Chapter 1
  Paradise Lost (stage adaptation of), 4, 57–61, 146. See also Chapter 1, figures, 1.1–7
  Paradise Regained, 4, 21, 21–7, 61, 62, 67, 69, 72, 74, 87, 89, 111, 127, 128, 144, 147. See also Chapter 1
  Prolusions, 115
  Reason of Church Government, 92, 104
  regicide tracts, 93–4, 95
  revolutionary potential of his works: 27, 51–2, 71, 74, 75–6, 79–81, 83, 87, 146
  Samson Agonistes, 5, 7, 9, 25. 26. 27. 104. 106. 108. 111, 114, 126, 128, 136. See also Chapter 2, figure 2.1
  Sonnet 1 ('O Nightingale'), 124
  Sonnet 7 ('How soon hath time'), 142
  Sonnet 8 ('Captain, Colonel, or Knight in Arms'), 124
  Sonnet 15 ('Fairfax, whose name'), 124
  Sonnet 16 ('To Oliver Cromwell'), 124, 125, 130
  Sonnet 17 ('Vane, young in yeares'), 124
  Sonnet 18 ('On the late Massacher in Piemont'), 124, 125, 126, 129. See also Waldensians
  Sonnet 19 ('When I consider how my light is spent'), 123, 125, 126
  Sonnet 20 ('Lawrence of virtuous Father'), 124, 130
  Sonnet 22 ('Cyriack, this three years day'), 117, 124, 125, 130
  Sonnet 23 ('Methought I saw my late espoused Saint'), 6, Chapter 4
  The History of Britain, 115
  The Readie and Easie Way to Establish a Free Commonwealth, 109
  The Tenure of Kings and Magistrates, 105
Miltonic montage, 134, 143
Modern Quarterly (*Marxist Quarterly*), 8, 70
Mohamed, Feisal, 148
Mond, Sir Alfred, 24
Monticelli, Daniele, 146
Morris, William, 8
Munich Agreement, 70
Munkácsy, Mihály, 6

Nádasdy, Ádám, 119, 142
Nagyvilág (periodical), 14, 51, 103, 107, 121
National Széchényi Library, 99, 272
nationalisation, 14, 32, 33
nationalism, 2, 3, 41, 77, 96, 97, 112, 113
Nazism, 2, 10
Nemes G, Zsuzsanna, 60–1
Nemes Nagy, Ágnes, 6, 126–41
New Critics, 44, 103, 106
New International, 70
Nyugat (periodical), 16, 29, 45, 118, 125

Pázmány Péter University, 98, 101, 118. *See also* Eötvös Loránd University
Pearce, Brian, 70
people ('the people'), 8, 25, 36, 40, 42, 67, 68, 83, 87, 101, 105, 119
Pepys, Samuel, 91
Péter, Ágnes, 17
Péteri, György, 119
Petőfi Literary Museum, 118
Petőfi, Sándor, 42
Petrochevich Horváth, Lázár, 94
Pope, Alexander, 43
popular sovereignty, 92, 95
population explosion, 46
Powell, Mary, 128, 142
progression (political), 2
proletariat, 67, 68, 71, 72, 83. *See also* dictatorship of the proletariat
Prometheus, 83
Protestant colleges, 93
provocation in style, 58
'Puritan' as 'progressive', 28, 102
Puritan republicanism, 101, 105
Puritanism, 5, 9, 23, 66, 77, 94, 104, 126, 131

Rába, György, 125
Radnóti, Sándor, 134
Radzinowicz, Mary Ann, 89
Rákóczi, György, 91
Rákosi, Mátyás, 14, 15, 74, 91
Ramayana (stage version), 52
Ravasz, László, 20, 29, 73, 128
reader's reports, 6, 79, 80, 84, 89, 99, 121
recomposition-in-performance, 4, 61
Red Scare, 9, 65
redemptionist vs. revisionist schools of interpretation, 86–7
Reform Era, 93
Reformation, 96, 97, 101, 109, 112
regicide, 7, 11, 93, 94
Restoration, 31, 66
Révai, József, 14
revolution, 3, 5, 9, 10, 15, 25–7, 31, 43, 66, 69, 70, 71, 75, 80, 87, 92, 95, 100, 108, 113, 123, 126, 129
Réz, Ádám, 17
Richmond, Hugh, 52, 54
Rickword, Edgell, 8, 85
Rideg, Sándor, 88
rock and roll, 56
Ronsard, Pierre de, 130–1
Roosevelt, Theodore, 69–70
Rousseau, Jean-Jacques, 95
Rumrich, John P., 87
rural Protestant communities, 22
Ruttkay, Veronika, 62

Salmasius (Claude Saumaise), 93
Samarin, R. M., 87, 115
Sauer, Elizabeth, 71
School of Slavonic and East European Studies (SSEES), 109
Second Vienna Award, 96
sectarianism, 98
self-censorship, 84
self-fashioning, 8, 36, 117

Shakespeare, William, 6, 13, 42, 63, 99, 110
Shelley, Percy Bysshe, 8
Shore, Daniel, 145–6
Smith, Nigel, 7
socialist realism, 14
Socialist Review, 71
Stalin, Joseph Vissarionovich, 70, 103
Stalinism, 9, 44, 70, 74, 97, 103
sublime, 20, 33, 46, 48, 51, 73
Summer of Love, 56
systemic relativism, 119
Szabó, Lőrinc, 4, 19–21, 29, 44, 45, 73–4, 125
  Cricket Song, 30–1
  political views, 29–30, 32, 37
  translation of *Paradise Lost*, 27–43, 47–8, 49, 122
  views on translation, 29
Szacsvay, Sándor, 93
Szász, Károly, 23, 62
Szegedy-Maszák, Mihály, 85
Szenczi, Miklós, 5, 25, 44, 50, 80, 107–17, 121, 128, 147
  collaboration with Jánosy and Kazimir, 52, 147
  'Milton Agonistes', 51, 85, 86, 89, 98, 110–1
  Milton, the Mirror of the English Revolution, 92, 113–7
  on Milton's sonnets, 129
  on *Paradise Lost*, 44–45
  on *Paradise Regained*, 26
  on *Samson Agonistes*, 85, 111
  relationship with Lutter, 119
Szentkuthy, Miklós, 96–8, 118
Szepessy, Tibor, 115
Szerb, Antal, 10, 73
Szigeti, Jenő, 62
Szirtes, George, 138, 139, 272

Takács, Ferenc18, 85–6
Tamás, Gáspár Miklós, 30
Táncsics, Mihály, 95, 118
Tandori, Dezső, 125
Teleki-Bolyai Library, 93
Tellér, Gyula, 125
Teskey, Gordon, 134, 143
The Comrade: An illustrated socialist monthly, 68–9, 72
Theatre in the Round, 52, 272
Thomson, George, 8, 83, 103
three Ts (three Ps), 15, 18
Tillyard, E. M. W., 28, 103
Tompa, Mihály, 88
Tóth, Árpád, 5, 96–7, 122, 123–4, 125, 126, 142
Transylvania, 81, 91, 96, 97
Trevor-Roper, Hugh, 106
Trotsky, Leon, 70–1
Twelve Points, 95

Új Magyar Könyvkiadó (New Hungarian Publishing House), 14, 74, 79
Újhold (periodical), 45
Uzakova, Oydin, 87

Vámosi, Pál, 115
Váradi, Hédi, 89

Várady, Szabolcs, 84
Vas, István, 124, 125, 128, 129, 142
Verlaine, Paul-Marie, 125
Versailles Peace Treaty, 97
Vesenyi, Paul E., 60
Világosság (periodical), 85
Visiak, Edward Harold, 89
Visick, Mary, 70, 71
Voinovich, Géza, 23–4
Vörösmarty, Mihály, 1, 38

Wagner, Alexander von, 88. *See also* Dugovics, Titusz *and* heroic suicide
Western Marxism, 15
Waldensians, 91. *See also* Milton, Sonnet 18 ('On the late Massacher in Piemont')
Whiting, George, 121

Williams, William Carlos, 65–6, 67
Winstanley, Gerrard, 7, 9, 101
Wittreich, Joseph, 17, 86
Wlislocki, Henrik, 95
Wolfe, Don, 7, 9, 67, 106
Woodcock, Catherine, 142
Worden, Blair, 66
Wordsworth, William, 123, 129
World Peace Council, 25, 121
World War II, 2, 5, 8, 10, 29, 32, 36, 42, 43, 74, 96, 118

Yolland, Arthur, 23, 73, 95

Zádor, Anna, 32–3, 62
Zollman, Peter, 141

Lightning Source UK Ltd.
Milton Keynes UK
UKHW021300080822
407005UK00019B/242